LIVE THROUGH THE DREAM

Ian Waterson

authorHOUSE®

AuthorHouse™ UK Ltd.
500 Avebury Boulevard
Central Milton Keynes, MK9 2BE
www.authorhouse.co.uk
Phone: 08001974150

First published by AuthorHouse 12/7/2009

ISBN: 978-1-4490-2755-1 (sc)

Matthew Lewis/Getty Images
Phil Cole/Getty Images
Mike Hewitt/Getty Images
Jamie McDonald/Getty Images/AFP
Andrew Yates/Getty Images
John Peters/Getty Images
Glyn Kirk/Getty Images/AFP
Paul Ellis/Getty Images/AFP

This book is printed on acid-free paper.

For my wife Suzy and our children

Kelly, Lewis, Kieran and Hannah.

LIVE THROUGH THE DREAM - CONTENTS

FOREWORD BY MATCH OF THE DAY 2 REPORTER – KEVIN DAY

I am aware that there are people who don't love football. Strange people who don't know the shared joy, anger, excitement and despair that following a football team with thousands of like minded people brings. I'm not saying that people should only love football. I am second to none in my admiration of classical music and modern interpretative dance - I have no doubt they are marvellous ways to pass the time, but only while you are waiting for Saturday to roll round so you can really enjoy yourself.

People who don't love football miss out on so much. As a child I learnt about the history and culture of Britain through football - I found out why Luton were called The Hatters, that there was a crooked spire in Chesterfield and that Heart of Midlothian wasn't a place, it was a book. I would never have known any of that had I wasted my childhood birdwatching, and I wouldn't be half as useful in pub quizzes. As a young man I learnt about loyalty, humour, stoicism and the patience of girlfriends as I followed Crystal Palace up and down the country. I love the theatre but I can absolutely guarantee that I have never been as happy in a theatre as I was as one of seventy-nine Palace fans witnessing an unexpected win at Wrexham on a bone-cold Saturday afternoon.

As an older man, and as the fans' reporter on BBC2's Match of the Day 2 I have learnt that beneath the corporate veneer of top flight football in this country there are thousands of football fans like Ian Waterson. Proud of their football team, articulate and passionate in that pride, funny and philosophical in their passion. Ian has chronicled his beloved club Hull City's first ever season in the Premier League. Those of you who genuinely love football will thoroughly enjoy this fascinating insight into the very high highs and the very low lows. And if you're one of those unfortunate people who don't get football, read this book, find out what you're missing and come and join us anytime you like. Ian will even buy you a motorway service station pasty on that tricky midweek trip back from Wigan.

ABOUT THE AUTHOR – IAN WATERSON

I'm just like you. I love football and in particular Hull City. Born a Hull lad, bred a Hull lad and raised a Hull lad, its true what they say: **"You can take the boy out of Hull, but you can't take the Hull out of the boy."** Personally, I find that statement unerringly accurate. In many ways, it galvanised me into becoming the Hull City fan I am today. Let me explain...

At 9 years of age, I had to up sticks and move from Hull to the south bank of the Humber because of my Dad's job. Grimsby. It really is a grim as it sounds. Six years I was there. Six long years... This was the first time in my life I felt different. I distinctly noticed the awkward sense of not quite fitting in while here. I felt like the proverbial fish out of water – if you can allow me the obvious pun.

But why am I telling you this? Well, simply, it pinpoints the time in my life when I was truly aware and proud of my Hull roots. You see, I wasn't from Grimsby, god no! I was proudly from Hull actually. I don't support Grimsby. I'm a Hull City fan. The Tigers. That's me, they are my team.

Schoolyard fights weren't particularly frequent, but certainly, they did arise from such strong and passionate football beliefs at such a tender age. These minor school age skirmishes made me stronger and tightened the bind between myself and the club. And bizarrely, I'd only ever been to the odd game that my Dad had got tickets for. Yet here I was in my formative years defending the good name of Hull City in the junior school playgrounds on the south bank of the Humber – and yes – of course I was holding my own for our club.

So much so, I was motivated into earning a living with a paper round to get to see the mighty Tigers, even though I was now berthed on the opposite bank of the river. By sheer chance, the newsagent on our estate was from Hull and also a City fan to boot. So, getting trips over to see the team with my earnings on a Saturday was relatively easy as it happened – and with plenty of family to stay with – surprisingly I got see the Tigers more regularly than I perhaps otherwise would have done.

These were splendid times from my youth. A sense of growing up was occurring without me truly realising it at the time. Indeed, I was blissfully unaware of it. Sometimes I was travelling on my own from Great Coates train station to Barton-upon-Humber and then hopping onto a bus over the bridge to Hull. How my parents ever allowed it, I'll never know. I'm not sure I'd let my kids do it now. Still, this was the early 80s. You can tell as much by the 5p bus fare from Hull bus station to Bricknell Ave on a Friday night. Staying with family, these were weekends to treasure, weekends with my close relatives – and of course, weekends with Hull City. Happy days indeed...

I was hooked for sure, but then, it got really serious. My Dad got a transfer back to Hull when I was 15 years old. We were leaving the south bank and heading home. It meant just one thing. Well, for me it did. When I leave school and get a job, I'm earning for one thing and one thing only; a season ticket and getting to away games as often as my Youth Training Scheme wages would allow me. I was home. Life was good. And Hull City were now about to become very frequent and prominent in my life.

Back then, still a mid-teen, I was booking trips the length and breadth of the country on Eleanor's buses running out of the club from YEB on Ferensway and calling at Boothferry Park, Darley's and Goole. From Carlisle to Bournemouth, I was there. Me and my mates from school, plus a few more of the regular Tiger Travel coach go-ers, week in, week out. That was just the beginning...

Much has changed since then. My job, getting married and all the children my wife Suzy and I now share to name but a few, but the constant of Hull City has remained and spans over 30 years now. Sometimes, I really think it should've waned, this passion I have, but for some seemingly unfathomable reason, it hasn't. I am unashamedly and squarely hooked. Hull City have got me. When a rainy Tuesday evening in Hartlepool can still set the pulse racing for some meaningless trophy you've never heard of – and long since forgotten – you know you've been bitten badly. Those that don't me will probably find I'm looked upon as being in that niche bracket. Those that do know me, well... I'm sure they will testify my words.

You see, like you, I've fudged work patterns, bent holidays, even changed jobs all to persist in the call of Hull City duty. I've been doing this for three decades. It's like a gravitational pull, to the point of being unexplainable. I am conscious of what I'm doing but rendered powerless to occasionally irrational behaviour – and even worse than that – being looked at as plain weird and branded as mad all in the swish of the same conversation.

Still, the cheap jibes never bothered me. I was engrossed in the fortunes of my club. Indeed, I was fortunate because my two passions – writing and football – were soon to collide in the most unusual of manners. A Tuesday night game at home to Mansfield landed me a friend for life – not that I knew it at the time. He was selling fanzines in the rain – and I was berating him for not updating the Hull City fanzine teletext page on ITV. I read it avidly every Thursday. I'm not sure who was the maddest on reflection. It landed me a job, though. ***"You write the bloody thing then!"*** was the reply.

And so I did. Every week, without fail. And shortly after, I was scribbling away for the fanzine proper, too. Then, the website was taking off and more work came there. Before I knew it, I was asked to become co-editor of the magazine. And all these years on, I'm still doing that and more. Perhaps I have a lot to blame my fellow editor Ian Farrow for when looking back on the rainy night against Mansfield. That quid I handed over got me far more than I ever bargained for. No regrets though, I owe him for bringing me here today and giving me a platform to fulfil an ambition.

However, a pertinent fact of my Tiger supporting years had never come to fruition. Despite my 'obsession' with Hull City, the one thing I'd never done was go through a whole season completing a full set of Hull City matches. A lack of money, getting time off work and enduring the mother of all hangovers from a heavy night on the tiles being three good reasons. And yes, it is excruciating to confess, the latter really did prevent me from seeing City demolish Crewe Alexandra one Saturday at Boothferry Park. Just the 7 goals were needed to polish off the Railwaymen that particular weekend. Typical, eh? City win 7-1 and I'm lying in my pit addled with booze. Stupid boy!

But I'm digressing. The point of getting to every game in a season; it still had not been accomplished by me, despite three decades of watching the Tigers. Indeed, the thought of such – and subsequently achieving the goal – would be like embarking on a quest for the Holy Grail... and then ultimately finding it at the end of your travels. Probably in Blackpool or some other salubrious location, dependent on what mood the fixture computer was in of course.

Only now, as I find myself putting pen to paper (finger to keyboard actually) has it dawned on me why another of my lifetime ambitions has been left unfulfilled, namely to write a book. I often mulled the thought over, then parked it and ultimately allowed the prospect of penning my wares to gnaw away at me silently in the background. It would get done. One day. But the fact is; it wasn't getting done. Another time, another place maybe, it was always the same excuse. And anyway, despite my love for writing, I was getting my regular fix editing a website and scribing in the club's fanzine City Independent. The book can wait. Always waiting...

Fate was soon to change all that, though. Cue Saturday May 24th 2008 at Wembley. In a St Paul on the road to Damascus type of experience – on a more meaningful scale, of course – these two ambitions of mine that were prominent in my life right now cataclysmically came together. The opportunity to fulfil both dreams beckoned me. To resist this opportune moment would be folly on my part. Our first ever season in the Premier League...what better way to complete a lifetime's ambition? I have got to do this. I must do this. I'm going to do this.

So here I am, effectively killing two birds with one stone. I'm setting out on a mission to go to every game and finally complete a full compliment of fixtures, while also documenting the journey along the way to produce my very own book. Me, yes me, finally writing a book. This was perfect... Despite failing to grasp my English O level, I knew I could do this, I could do it. It sounds like a plan... indeed, it was a plan.

And so the journey begins...

ABOUT THE BOOK –
LIVE THROUGH THE DREAM

We're leaving the Championship terminus now, but I'll level with you; this is genuinely a journey into the unknown. Firstly, because I've never written on this type of scale in my entire life before – and secondly, I don't know how on earth this book will be greeted by the reader. Simply, because I just don't know what is going to happen! All I hope is that you enjoy the book as much as I did preparing it all for you. I do know that many, many years later – perhaps even beyond my remaining years – a void in Hull City's life as a football club will certainly need to be filled.

To this end, I hope what you are about to read contributes towards bridging any gap that appears and becomes one story of many that can be treasured by those that experienced the rich trappings of English top flight football for the first time ever in Hull City's life. I'd like this book to be one that can reflect on our inaugural achievement and provide just one insight to what it is like to support our great club among the cream of England's finest teams.

What you will read from now was a pleasure to scribe and comes complete with real life experiences and occurrences throughout the entirety of the book. From Saturday May 24th 2008 to the exact same point one year later, this is a 12 month voyage that will herald Hull City being in the Premier League for the first time ever.

Categorically, this will be – regardless of the outcome – Hull City's finest ever finish in the English game, period. You are about to step into the shoes of just one of thousands of Hull City fans that made this top flight pilgrimage. The season was chronologically depicted on your behalf, with due diligence given, as the season unfolds. To the writer and the reader, neither one of us are actually aware of where this embarkation is taking us. Every account scribed is monitored as and when it happens throughout the greatest 365 days in Hull City's history.

All that remains to be stated before commencing your journey through this book is; you can be one hundred percent assured – *"This is the best trip, we've ever been on."*

And that will be a fact, whatever happens.

LIVE THROUGH THE DREAM –
ACKNOWLEDGEMENTS

First and foremost, it is not written lightly what I am about to state next. This book truly wouldn't be in your hands right now without the love, patience and understanding of one person. I am unequivocally indebted to my wife Suzy. I could not have fulfilled this lifetime ambition without her belief and support throughout this venture. Suzy made this happen. Suzy helped me chase my dream and realise it. I love you so much. To my children, I am fully aware that *"Dad is away again this Saturday."* I am proud of your patience and understanding despite your tender years. Rest assured, the good times are now coming your way. My time is most definitely now yours.

Again, in no small part, I simply have to acknowledge my mother and father. Both have been a huge influence in bringing this book to your collection. At times of real need and hardship, for those snatched moments of peace and tranquillity in my old bedroom, I could not have pieced this work together without your commitment and guidance to help me complete one of my greatest ambitions ever and get this book written. I'm not sure how I can ever repay you, err... the cheque is in the post. Ahem...

It is by no coincidence that all the greatest journeys undertaken by man are done with companions. Well, in my opinion that's true. Life is for sharing. It's the same with Hull City. Who really goes to football on their own? I have been privileged to undertake Hull City's greatest journey with friends that have been plentiful, resilient and above all else as insane as me on the way to realising this Premier League dream. It would be no fun without you all, I promise. I thank you for sharing this experience with me. It was fun.

I firmly believe it's the people that make the Hull City football experience what it is. Genuinely, the result is secondary – indeed forgotten in a fug of alcohol if it's been a really bad weekend – but you simply cannot buy friendship like I have experienced through all the years travelling to City games. To those that have helped me on my way; that have driven to matches on my behalf – and sourced cheap travel to far flung places on trains – those that have encouraged me to keep scribbling away, I salute you one and all and thank you for the memories that will undoubtedly stay with us all forever. You all helped shape this book into what it is, please take a bow, you've earned it.

At the risk of getting sentimental, I do need to pay tribute to my working partner in all of this. I don't think either of us ever envisaged how far we could take the Hull City fanzine City Independent when I clambered aboard nearly a decade ago, but what I have learnt in the countless years myself and Ian Farrow have worked on the magazine and websites together is; anything is possible with dedication and a desire to succeed. It may run into the witching hours at times, we may need to resort to unhealthy doses of caffeine (and then, subsequently, alcohol), dawn may indeed break before we've finished our wares, but together, we have overcome any given barrier or obstacle. I appreciate the support afforded to me from a good friend that simply stated when embarking on this project – *"Go on just do the book, you've got to."* He was right. And neither did he waver from that stance either. Thank you, Ian.

I must also express my gratitude to Kevin Day of Match of the Day 2 fame – amongst other strings to his talented bow. I have been bowled over by the warmth of a complete stranger during our chance meeting before the Liverpool home game back in April 2009 and the impression left by Kevin since. It has been a real pleasure to meet a man of his word and discover what a thoroughly nice chap to boot he actually was. Let me assure you it is truly appreciated the time you have dedicated to share a few words about this incredible experience I immersed myself into. You sir, are a gentleman – and I genuinely hope we do meet up again to share a beer and some proper Hull fish and chips as we discussed.

But of course, none of this would ever have been possible at all without the man managing our team, the chairman running our club and his backers and the players that stared destiny in the face in the name of Hull City back in May 2008 at Wembley and fearlessly grasped the biggest prize in football when the opportunity presented itself. To Phil Brown and all his backroom and playing staff, to Paul Duffen and his consortium, many, many thanks for turning our club around from Football League also-rans into a fully-fledged top flight club. You realised the dreams of thousands upon thousands of Hull City fans, of which I am unashamedly one. I'm sure I speak for all when stating we are eternally grateful for the achievements you brought our way and wish you every success in keeping up the fine work.

With reference to the making of this book there are more acknowledgements that need to be made. Firstly, to Matt Rudd – a friend of mine who generously took time out from his own busy schedule to proof read my wares and check my spelling and grammar was up to scratch. It only cost a beer or two, so Matt comes highly recommended! But in all seriousness, this was a fantastically generous gesture on his part and comes warmly appreciated by myself. I will recompense you with more alcohol at the very least – the currency of friendship – if hard cash will not be accepted. I would like to thank Hannah Dibley at Authorhouse for the guidance and expertise afforded to help a complete novice like me turn a blank page into something you are now holding in your hand. Once again, thanks for your help allowing me to get my book out there for everyone else to enjoy. Plus, I must mention the kind service received from the staff at Getty Images for all the photographs used on the front and back cover design – even though they do drive a hard bargain. Thank you one and all.

Lastly, I want mention my sister Louise who has done absolutely sod all to warrant a mention in this book but has incessantly pestered me to see her name in print the second this germ of an idea saw the green shoots of growth. That means I must mention my other sister Liz, because if I don't there will probably be a riot, but at least she had the good sense to divert my nephew Luke into the black and amber fold with my subtle kit purchases at birthdays and Christmas time and Grandad's spare pass for Hull City games.

And I do want to mention my Nana for no other than reason she has always been proud of my Hull City roots and dedication. When the Tiger world was losing its head all around us, my Nana never questioned my commitment to the Hull City cause. Not once. I love you Nana.

I thank you all, each and every one of you. I hope you like what is before you. Above everything else, all I'm wishing for from this book is; nothing more than total enjoyment for the reader. Dive in...

LIVE THROUGH THE DREAM – PROLOGUE

Hull City stood on the threshold of greatness at the home of football at 3pm on Saturday 24th May. Cometh the hour, cometh the man – Hull's very own Dean Windass.

Ecstatic. Delighted. Overwhelmed. And well and truly hungover. After 104 years of being outcast in the football wilderness, finally – no incredibly – the holy grail of top flight football was found at 5.01pm on a gorgeous sunny Saturday in Wembley Stadium. The home of football.

One man, one strike, one amazing goal, all provided one winner. The man in question was Hull City's 39 year old Dean Windass. Shunned and ridiculed by so many, so often, the wily old pro is demonstrating precisely why he is the talismanic driving force behind this now legendary Hull City side and guiding the club into uncharted territory.

The strike was befitting to win any match – let alone one that decides who gets to play in the Premier League. It was a stunning, wondrous drive that was worthy of gracing the top flight of English football for sure. Well, effectively, it was our first Premier League goal. Now... WE ARE PREMIER LEAGUE!

And that moment, in the 39th minute of a pulsating match with Bristol City – the Robins valiant triers throughout – meant the Gipsyville-born boy had done what no other Hull City legend had done before. Dean Windass took Hull City to the pinnacle of the English game. 104 years of suffering, now unburdened in one instant.

For me, the build up had begun way back. Friday lunchtime I left Paragon station to arrive at Kings Cross, nervous, unexpectant and doing my level best to comprehend precisely why I was boarding a tube train to Wembley Park. Hull City don't do Wembley. Or winning trophies. Or even top flight football. This does not compute. I think I am suffering a footballing malfunction or a syntax error.

Stepping off the platform on the Friday late afternoon at Wembley Park, I was greeted by the enormous Wembley arc. A very slow stroll down Wembley Way. I was in awe. Err... what are Hull City doing here? Something is clearly awry...

On the approach, Wembley had been suitably decorated with play-off regalia. In the top left corner of Wembley's facia - in pride of place I thought - Hull City's Coca-Cola emblem clearly stood out proud amongst the six teams who would be participating for promotion this weekend in the divisional play-offs.

It wasn't sinking in. It really wasn't sinking in. A picture with the legendary Robert Moore OBE was duly taken and a leisurely stroll around the stadium produced the unbelievable chance meeting of all chance meetings. City fans, I give you Hull City Chairman – Paul Duffen. Yes, Paul Duffen.

"How are you Ian, excited?" says a confident Hull City chairman

"Nervous, but delighted to be here." I reply.

The next words that followed from the chairman will stay with me for as long as my days. Indeed, they became impressed on me from this very moment onwards. These words took centre stage for the entire weekend. The second any perceived doubts were cast on the weekend's lists of outcomes – let's face it ultimate glory or abject disappointment – this sentence was plucked from my memory to shield me from such evil thoughts like failure. The nerves disintegrated, the vibe was uplifting, the mood was now positive. I was ready and I now believed. Those words... our chairman's words... were like the antidote shot in arm that revives the recipient in a split-second as seen in all the typically trashy movies.

"Relax. Go out tonight and have a few beers. We will win the game – and one of the Hull lads will score the winner. We will win this match for certain – and we will do it the 90 minutes. So, enjoy it!"

Now, if I was a betting man, I'd be quids in. How unerringly accurate was that? It's almost chilling! But those words were all true, spoken within yards of Wembley one Friday tea time before the eve of our apparent destiny. Paul Duffen isn't quite god – but he is now a prophet for certain. I can testify to that. What a man.

So, that was it. With my official club statement locked in the memory bank, I did just that. We hit Camden on Friday night and stumbled in at daft o'clock. I never flinched once. Nerves of steel me. No doubting here. I believed. Hull City were going to emerge victorious. It was in the bag.

Wembley morning. Incredibly, I'm awake by 6.50am and showered and ready. Greasy spoon found, head intact, and waiting to be released from my straining leash. Um... what now? I take a meditational walk around Wembley as dawn is breaking, I check out of the hotel, drop my bags off back at Kings Cross and hit the pub. COME ON YOU 'ULL!

But, throughout all that, the best atmosphere was not in the pub. It was actually outside in the London streets. Thousands upon thousands of Hull citizens had descended on the capital; it was a truly spectacular site. The atmosphere was decent and the chat with Bristol City fans was similar. All of us happy to be here, but... got to win.

You see, that's the thing about Wembley. It really is not the place for losers. The whole world is watching. Failure means you're forgotten in an instant. That cannot happen. Not here, not now, not after 104 years of patiently waiting our turn. This was our time. Surely, this was our time... Paul Duffen had told me so and I believed. I clung to it like a child with a teddy bear at bedtime. His words were my mental staff for the weekend.

Walking up Wembley Way, circling the stadium the wrong way, I was amazed at the two atmosphere's developing at both ends of the stadium outside the turnstiles. The Bristol end was quiet, but confident. The Hull end was buoyant and expectant. This really was feeling like our time. This was shaping up to be Hull City's day. It had to be. And I had the official club statement to boot. Locked in the memory bank, safe...

Going through the mystic portal of the turnstile, Wembley's expanse was overwhelming. I felt consumed by greatness. It may be remodelled, redesigned and brand new, but Wembley had lost none of its standing – in the metaphorical sense at least. My timing was perfect. A couple of moments before the team ran out to train, I was taking it all in. Then the players emerged. Lump in throat, sharp intake of breath, something crystal welling up in my eyes.

But I'm not blubbing. Wembley is no place for the weak. No place for losers. I had to hold my nerves of steel, be strong and believe. That was in my job description today. And when the teams finally came out, didn't the lads look mean and sleek in black tracksuit tops? Yes, Hull City looked the part...

Anyone with an ounce of interest will have seen every morsel of the game. Savoured, devoured and scoffed the whole lot up. The salient points of the day have already been covered in glorious magnitude well before this prose every reaches you. The atmosphere was amazing, but bizarrely not the most enjoyable due to the rich rewards that are riding on the game. You can't really appreciate what is going on around you when in the midst of it all. I think that is what I'm trying to say.

Dele Adebola should've scored early on for Bristol City, but fluffed his shot with a weak effort. Bristol had settled better in the early exchanges, but the Tigers eventually started playing the more composed football when they came to terms with where they were and what they were attempting to achieve. Barmby almost got the opener to complete a record of a goal in each of the play-off games, but it wasn't to be. Yet... I still believed my chairman...

Trundle was constantly pushed onto his weaker right foot and Wayne Brown – after taking an early battering – got to grips with the powerful threat of Adebola. Sam Ricketts and Andy Dawson defended like Tigers – but Michael Turner showed why he is simply Premier League class with a man of the match performance.

Yet the moment that mattered was now upon us... Barmby fed Fraizer Campbell with a swift counter. Campbell frightened the Bristol City defence with some blistering pace and as the Robins continued to back off, the young Manchester United star danced his way to the byline.

With the presence to look up, he picked out Dean Windass outside of the box and the ball fell perfectly. Time stopped. Slow motion action arrived. This was Paul Duffen's vision... The old man of Hull volleyed... sweetly... It was the most precise and powerful shot I think I've ever seen. At Wembley. To take us to the Premier League...

For one tiny second the entire stadium hushed as Windass' boot connected with the ball *THUD* I heard it. I swear I heard it. Still muted Wembley watched agog. Piercing the silence a ripple of the net by the ball took place before, suddenly and without warning...

RRRRUUUUUUUSSSSHHHHHHHHHH! Searing, bursting, a cataclysmic explosion of joy now soared through my body. This was the 'Roy of the Rovers' script that the chairman had forewarned and meant; it really, truly, was written in the stars. It was happening before our very eyes – it was to be our day. Wasn't it?

The sell-out Hull City section went ballistic. Nigh on 40,000 occupants – the standard bearers for all our Tiger fore-fathers, all those that couldn't be with us and the dearly departed legions of black and amber, the die-hards who never got to realise their dream. The ones above us all in the heavens. That one, that goal, was especially for you... *Bristiol City 0-1 Hull City* read the scoreboard.

The half time whistle came. Dare to dream... Predictably, Bristol City came out like lions. I expected nothing less. And as the possession and territory became all over red like Bristol, it was only spiky interjections of sharp, pacy counter-attacking football by those in amber that kept our opponents on their toes.

Yet for all the Bristol dominance, Gary Johnson's side lacked a cutting edge. Hull City believed in its defence, happy to let Bristol have a go. But this black and amber brick wall would not budge. It would not relent – and goalkeeper Boaz Myhill was rarely troubled despite all the pressure. The clock counted down. Deano had long departed to the dugout now, his Hullensian ally Nick Barmby also. Sure, old father time was ticking, but not fast enough. Substitutes were thrown on by Gary Johnson. It was all hands to the Bristol pumps. 4-3-3 now, but no! The Tigers defence would not wilt. Injury time drifted into view. So close, so close...

Four minutes. Just hold on. Please, hold on. The 90 minutes were up. We should be Premier League now, please blow! Yet Alan Wiley, refereeing the match, was patently unaware Hull City had waited 104 years for his blasted whistle to peep, and now we were entering the 5th minute of injury time. The chairman's prophecy was on the brink of being fulfilled.

And when it came... when it came... *pause* well... you know the rest. You know what it meant. History at Hull City had finally arrived. A century-long stand was finally broken. A local lad, practically on his last legs, had given the city of Hull what it had craved all its life. What it deserved and duly earned.

At last - HULL CITY ARE PREMIER LEAGUE! Please forgive me, because it's still not sunk in...

PRE-SEASON PREMIER LEAGUE SEASON 2008-09

NORTH FERRIBY UNITED 0-4 HULL CITY

The Billy Bly Memorial Trophy remains in Hull City's possession after cruising to victory over their village rivals, but the evening – once again – was a huge success for all concerned.

It is without doubt the hidden jewel in City's pre-season crown. A short trip on cycle, train or car – and the perfect opportunity to catch up with old faces and City stalwarts from the terraces, as the pre-season gently gets underway at North Ferriby.

The tradition is now a strong one and the evening as a whole has become a fantastic event for all concerned. For Ferriby, having Premier League Hull City on their fixture list, for City it's an excellent piece of community PR, while for us fans... a few pints and pie, peas and chips never did us any harm, did it?

The game was a very easy paced affair that City strolled. As Phil Brown said to me afterwards, it's not about the result, it's about the occasion and tradition of the fixture with the club keen to help improve Ferriby and its facilities. And the City boss is spot on.

A packed crowd of 2,500 saw a glimpse of the Tigers' new Brazilian signing Geovanni who grabbed an assist for the opener scored by Dean Marney. Will Atkinson scored the second in a shortened 35 minute half that saw Matt Plummer taken off as a precaution to injury.

In the second half Brown changed the entire 11 and seemed content to play one up front with one behind the striker that produced two further goals for Michael Turner and Nick Barmby to seal a 0-4 victory.

It was a leisurely affair – quite rightly – but the promising signs were Craig Fagan looking razor sharp, Nicky Featherstone looking busy and creative in the hole and the players getting a game played at just the right tempo required. A success all round.

And to think, Peter Halmosi and two of his agents came all the way up from Devon to see this... Good on him. A medical today, a new signing tomorrow methinks. Onwards to Winterton...

WINTERTON RANGERS 0-4 HULL CITY

Another day, another 0-4 away win. Life as a Premier League club is a breeze by all accounts. A short trip over the bridge is undertaken and into the folds of the south bank of the Humber for City's second pre-season friendly.

The Tigers brushed aside their near village neighbours North Ferriby with a 0-4 away win to retain the Billy Bly Memorial Trophy at a canter – and the same occurred during this evening against Winterton Rangers.

The same score, the same performance, the same spread of goals from City across the park, but this time, Winterton proved to be much more stubborn by comparison, holding the Tigers to a 0-0 half time score line.

However, trialist Delron Buckley shone brightly in the second half to give Phil Brown food for thought in light of Henrik Pedersen's departure, with a pacy display and decent service into the strikers.

Geovanni opened the scoring with deflected strike shortly after the restart and put on a glittering array of passing skills to whet the appetite of the crowd. Then, Buckley capped a fine display latching onto one of the Brazilian's sublime passes to round the keeper for number two.

John Welsh smashed in a 20 yarder for the third of the evening before youngster Joe Lamplough nodded in a fourth at the back stick to round off an impressive performance from City. Another good night, another good win. Onwards to Belgium for Tiger world domination!

KV OOSTENDE 1-1 HULL CITY

I decided it was time to keep the Hull flag flying on foreign shores and team up with friends Andy, Matt and Steve for the overnight ferry to Zeebrugge and onto the Belgian seaside resort of Oostende. City in Europe! This was the Tigers third fixture of the pre-season campaign...

And did I have a good time? Is the pope Catholic? It was bloomin' marvellous. One day, after all the Wembley excitement becomes nothing more than a fantastic fireside tale from days of yore, Hull City may actually get to do these European jaunts properly.

From a supporter's point of view, it's all we've ever wanted. A chance to showcase what Hull City is all about to our continental neighbours and put the club and city firmly on the map. I would venture both were successfully achieved by the seaside in Belgium for this friendly fixture and we'd be more than welcome back.

From the moment City fans arrived, they were made to feel welcome. Our flags were a colourful addition the streets of Oostende and the beer flowed well among supporters. A resounding success.

The ground itself was a Belgian Second Division classic. Think Northampton Town – maybe Torquay United – and you won't be far off the mark. An away terrace like the latter was unerringly akin to the one housing us at Plainmoor not so many seasons ago. Weird.

The match itself was nothing to write home about – even if the trip as a whole was. Geovanni shone brightest for City, starting and finishing the best passing move of the match with a diving header after 15 minutes of Tiger dominance.

The gulf between the sides was pretty glaring. Craig Fagan and Nick Barmby hugged their touchlines tightly and stretched the hosts as a consequence. The 300 or so travelling from England made ample noise with chant of the day being *"We only hate Maradona"* for our Argentinian triallist keeper Sebastian Cejas.

At this juncture, I would've joined in heartily with the travelling Tigers. Yet, I was here representing local radio station KCFM. You see, I'd lugged a comrex machine across the North Sea for an outside live radio broadcast only to find the sodding phone line connection had been cut despite assurances from our Belgian hosts prior to setting sail everything was good to go.

What it meant was – aside from being cut off from my mates – I was reduced to phoning in from my own mobile phone from the open air press box along the touchline during the game. Yes, it was all very Barry Davies-esque if the truth be told. It brought back shades of those crackly telephone line commentaries we used to follow England with on the telly from my boyhood days of the 80s when we were playing some far Eastern European outpost. Indeed, it was a bit rubbish. Especially in comparison to the BBC Radio Humberside set up just yards away with their posh ISDN unit. Ho hum...

Anyway, back to Cejas our Argentinian keeper for the day. Frankly, we learned nothing as he had zilch to do. City ran the show. However, in the second half Oostende made hardly any substitutions due to their small squad, while Phil Brown hauled off 10 players only leaving Nathan Doyle on as left back this half, meaning there was no Dawson or Ricketts playing any of the game.

What it did mean was; George Boateng and Bernard Mendy received Tiger debuts – but both struggled to get into the game – pretty much like the second half side as a whole really. Wayne Brown and Matt Plummer got themselves into a tizz inside their own penalty box with a Chuckle Brothers 'to me, to you' routine that left Oostende the chance to snatch a very tame equaliser and City lost all fluency from then.

Indeed, the visitors looked laboured in the second half and only had substitute Will Atkinson's low drive as a genuine chance to regain the lead. All in though, a good workout and another great piece of PR – not only for the club – but the supporters as well, who did the England's city of Hull mighty proud.

Several memories will prevail, not least being the last man standing with 'drink like a fish Andy' on the ferry coming home. Another being Steve's ability to sneak off and find sleep in the most unusual of places. The third is poor Matt wilting in the early evening and retiring to his bed as the alcohol consumption had taken him over upon our return.

And, I won my bet of nailing six courses in one sitting on the ferry on the way home. Well, something had to soak up all the alcohol, right?

The pre-season however, is gathering pace...

CHESTERFIELD 0-3 HULL CITY

City cruise past the bent spire brigade with an easy 0-3 victory in Derbyshire, to maintain their unbeaten record in the pre-season friendly fixture schedule...

The big story of the evening was record £2m signing Peter Halmosi making his debut for City in the first half upon signing from Plymouth – and impressing – before being replaced by Bryan Hughes in the second period.

Goals from veteran striker Dean Windass, new signing Geovanni – yet again finding the score sheet for the Tigers – and Spireites old boy Caleb Folan, saw off Chesterfield's challenge.

Crewe Alexandra 4-0 Hull City

What the ...? And it was all going so well...Hopefully, Phil Brown will have seen his players get a good workout, because they've certainly been worked over by League One side Crewe Alexandra...

It could be simply written off as a bad day at the office. Or more likely – by the fans at least – who really cares? City took a thumping at Crewe Alexandra after finding themselves 4-0 to a Calvin Zola hat-trick and missing a Bernard Mendy penalty while 2-0 down.

Zola opened the scoring after just two minutes of the match tapping in from close in, but then smacked in a 20 yarder just a minute later to leave City looking stunned inside three minutes.

It got worse for the Tigers when Barmby was fouled in the box by Baudet, but Mendy saw his spot kick saved – and Crewe showed City how to do it when Maynard converted from their own attempt.

Zola signed off the half with a hat-trick prompting Phil Brown to change his entire starting XI for the second half, but City fared little better and a heavy defeat was the result – the first of the pre-season schedule.

OLDHAM ATHLETIC 1-1 HULL CITY

Hull City were pegged back to a 1-1 draw against Oldham with a better performance than Crewe at the weekend – but are still left with work to do before the season begins proper...

Caleb Folan headed the Tigers into a first half lead within a strong line up that saw Anthony Gardner make his debut. Oldham levelled affairs in the second half with a goal from Lewis Alessandra, but although the performance was far better than Saturday against Crewe, there is still work to do for Phil Brown and the players.

Afterwards, City boss Phil Brown stated - *"There was a positive mentality. The attitude was in question for the first time in the 16 months I've been here but that wasn't in question there. The quality was lacking in the final third which is something I've asked for over a long period of time but I'll continue to bang that drum."*

Adding - *"We were wasteful in the pass at times at times but when you get in the Premier League, the difference between the better teams and the teams that struggle will be putting away those half chances. We didn't capitalise. We've got to hit the ground running come the 16th of August."*

Before concluding - *"We've got to be fitter than any other team we come up against because we know we haven't quite got the quality of other teams. As far as I'm concerned, it's piecing together slowly but surely but there's still two and a half weeks to go and a lot of work to be done."*

HEARTS 1-0 HULL CITY

And another defeat is clocked up during City's pre-season campaign – this time up in Edinburgh, when taking on Heart of Midlothian of the Scottish Premier...

It appears the Tigers have lost their bite somewhat during the pre-season campaign from the momentum that brought Hull City into the Premier League, but results I keep telling myself results mean very little at this stage and fitness and preparation are the key ahead of the new season kicking off versus Fulham.

City lost at Tynecastle 1-0 with Audrius Ksanavicius heading in the only goal of the game (and try saying that after a few Scottish ales) in the first half. The Tigers enjoyed a better second half, but lacked a cutting edge to break the Hearts defence, even though Richard Garcia had a goal ruled out.

However, City can claim some small credit from their performance, despite the defeat. During his post match comments, Hearts manager Csaba Laszlo confessed the Tigers had not made it easy for his side, despite it being just a friendly.

The Tynecastle boss admitted Hull City had applied some pressure to his side when stating - *"I'm unhappy we lost the ball on the offence too early. We have some problem with ball control - we make everything too hurried."*

HULL CITY 0-1 OSASUNA

The last of the pre-season matches are completed – and with all of Hull City's defeats compiled in the build up to the new season – the Tigers are set to romp to Premier League glory. Ahem...

The stadium may well have looked Premier League and the pitch following suit in pristine fashion, but the crowd was nothing short of meagre for the Spanish La Liga side's visit and once again the match looked anything but top standard.

Osasuna looked neat and tidy on the ball and committed when not in possession. But neither side seemed to have the striking capability to break down the defences on show, except for one moment in the first half. The visitors took the lead with a neat passing move and a run that went on too long without a challenge to produce the one piece of good finishing in the match.

Brown was pursuing a 4-4-1-1 formation with Windass leading the line and Geovanni filling in the hole behind. The two wide players were Marney and Fagan – neither of whom could beat their respective fullbacks – a little worrying with the Premier League a week away.

The back four of Ricketts, Dawson, Turner and Gardner looked composed with Gardner looking like an excellent acquisition, assured on the ball and winning some good tackles on the ground while being commanding in the air, leaving Myhill with little to do.

Boateng and Ashbee in the midfield seem to have a good understanding, which is a plus point. The former holds a surprising knack of coming away with the ball among a sea of legs and this experienced Dutchman - a £1m signing from Middlesbrough - looks like another good acquisition.

But the lack of goals is a cause for concern and today did nothing to allay those fears, Geovanni apart. The early indications are that the new signings have improved the squad of players significantly, but only time will tell if the improvement is good enough for the Premier League.

The game ended in defeat meaning the sparring is now over and the serious stuff is about to commence. Undoubtedly though, the overwhelming feeling is that pre-season has finished on a whimper.

Of the positives to take from today, one thing does seem certain. This Saturday coming will surely see skipper Ian Ashbee create his own unique record by becoming the first player to captain a team through all four English divisions. Hopefully we will get to see the accolades Ashbee thoroughly deserves with a well earned starting place. How much he is worth on the transfer market, god only knows. But to Hull City; he is absolutely priceless.

The real thing is here. On Saturday August 16th, Hull City will go Premier League for the first time ever in the club's 105 year history. The assault course for our maiden Premier League voyage has been set. Our mission – despite how clichéd this probably sounds – is realistic and pertinent nonetheless... 'TARGET17th'

HULL CITY PREMIER LEAGUE FIXTURES	
AUGUST 2008	
Opening day Saturday 16th	FULHAM (h)
Saturday 23rd	Blackburn Rovers (a)
Saturday 30th	WIGAN ATHLETIC (h)
SEPTEMBER 2008	
Saturday 13th	Newcastle United (a)
Saturday 20th	EVERTON (h)
Saturday 27th	Arsenal (a)
OCTOBER 2008	
Sunday 5th	Tottenham Hotspur (a)
Sunday 18th	WEST HAM UNITED (h)
Saturday 25th	West Bromwich Albion (a)
Wednesday 29th	CHELSEA (h)
NOVEMBER 2008	
Saturday 1st	Manchester United (a)

Saturday 8th	BOLTON WANDERERS (h)
Sunday 16th	MANCHESTER CITY (h)
Saturday 22nd	Portsmouth (a)
Saturday 29th	Stoke City (a)
DECEMBER 2008	
Saturday 6th	MIDDLESBROUGH (h)
Saturday 13th	Liverpool (a)
Saturday 20th	SUNDERLAND (h)
Friday 26th	Manchester City (a)
Tuesday 30th	ASTON VILLA (h)
JANUARY 2009	
Saturday 10th	Everton (a)
Saturday 17th	ARSENAL (h)
Wednesday 28th	West Ham United (a)
Saturday 31st	WEST BROMWICH ALBION (h)
FEBRUARY 2009	
Saturday 7th	Chelsea (a)
Monday 22nd	TOTTENHAM HOTSPUR (h)
MARCH 2008	
Sunday 1st	BLACKBURN ROVERS (h)
Wednesday 4th	Fulham (a)
Saturday 14th	NEWCASTLE UNITED (h)
Sunday 22nd	Wigan Athletic (a)
APRIL2009	
Saturday 4th	PORTSMOUTH (h)
Saturday 11th	Middlesbrough (a)
Saturday 18th	Sunderland (a)
Saturday 25th	LIVERPOOL (h)
MAY 2009	
Monday 4th	Aston Villa (a)
Saturday 9th	STOKE CITY (h)
Saturday 16th	Bolton Wanderers (a)
Sunday 24th	MANCHESTER UNITED (h)

CHAPTER 1 – THE BIG BANG

WEDNESDAY 13TH AUGUST 2008 - LEAGUE CUP 2ND ROUND DRAW

The season hasn't even kicked off Yet but the rest of the clubs in the Football League were participating in their second competitive game inside four days. Ah yes, the good old League Cup First Round was here. At this juncture, teams from League One and League Two slug it out in the hope of landing a Premier League club in the draw for the next round. I remember it well.

Now, the League Cup has never really been a tournament that's captured my heart. And that's despite Wycombe Wanderers v Birmingham City desperately scrabbling around live in the living rooms of our fine nation. And mine too, but only because I'm testing if the satellite box still works after moving back into my house from the caravan in my garden thanks to the 2007 summer floods. And it does!

With just minutes remaining of this thrilling tie (0-4 to Birmingham by the way) our old boss Peter Taylor is about to bow out with Wycombe. But a graphic pops up on the screen telling me the second round draw is live and next. Go on then, you've suckered me. I'll stay and watch the excitement unfold.

Hull City are now seeded courtesy of going all Premier League. Which footballing minnow was about to receive a fair old Tiger lashing? That was the question. Bizarrely, the 'balls' were cubes, drawn from an 'ice bucket' huh? What's that all about then? Ah! Yes, of course... The CARLING Cup. Brilliant! Sheesh...

Strangely, after the adverts and post match guff - I was greeted with the news the non-seeded teams had already been drawn out. What? Are you having a laugh? Away from my - and everyone else's - prying eyes? What the ...? It's a fix!

So, 'the draw' would now see the seeded teams paired with teams already plucked out. Plus, what had already been pre-determined was whether the non-seeded team would be home or away. That's not a draw, it's a premeditated scam! Hardly, the FA Cup this, is it? A rigged draw springs to mind. Well, come on...?

Sky then showed another little graphic at the bottom of the screen that displayed the team already drawn with a gap either side signalling whether the seeded club would being playing their opponents home or away. So, when the image SWANSEA CITY v [BLANK] flashed up on screen, of course, the last thing anybody wanted to see was – 'No.9 Hull City'.

And as the cube was plucked from the ice bucket... the airwaves were broken with *"No.9... Hull City. Swansea City will play Hull City."* Bah! You have got to be joking! There's little wonder supporters hate the League Cup. Rank bad draws like this are a prime example. There's nothing attractive for Hull City, there's nothing attractive for Swansea. I'm not pleased. Indeed, I'm convinced. It's a stupid competition, anyway.

Then, the penny drops... Uh-oh... I've got to go to go to South Wales on a Tuesday night to probably watch our reserves turn out. What a grim prospect to fulfil an ambition... At this point, before a ball has even been kicked in anger, I realise the scale of the task and commitment I am about to undertake. What a stupid boy I am! Are my plans in danger of being derailed before they even started?

This ridiculous tie has left me with another conundrum now. I have to explain to my wife Suzy, precisely why her husband is trekking off to far flung foreign climes through the middle of a late summer's night. I know Suzy is an extremely understanding person but even so, this tie is stretching her good nature a more than a little.

I'd be a liar if I didn't admit to considering abandoning my project before it had even started...

THURSDAY 14TH AUGUST 2008

Premier League achieving Hull City manager Phil Brown is on the cusp of signing a brand new contract extension at the club, securing his long term future with Tigers ahead of the new season.

Brown, who became the first ever Hull City manager to guide the club into England's top flight with a play-off victory at Wembley, is set to sign an extended deal for three years keeping him at the Tigers until 2011.

The dotting of the 'i's and the crossing of the 't's have yet to be completed, with the contract on offer now with the manager's solicitors, but the City boss anticipates the deal could go through before the Tigers kick off their Premier League season against Fulham in two days time.

Speaking about the deal, Brown declared – *"I am very close to signing a new deal and it's in the hands of my solicitors at the moment. Fingers crossed, before Saturday's game I'll sign a new contract."*

FRIDAY 15TH AUGUST 2008 – HULL CITY V FULHAM PREVIEW

Bloomin' Carling Cup draw aside and firmly parked well in the back of my mind, here I am excited, apprehensive, but above all promising myself to enjoy this season come what may. I've decided. I'm going to Swansea. Well, deep down I suppose I always was. You can't let a midweek 18 hour round trip to South Wales come between yourself and your dreams and ambitions can you?

So, allow me to quote a short piece of text to sum up how I'm feeling - *"I have waited for this moment for 37 years. Saturday August 16th will finally see my club, our club, in the top flight of English football for the first time ever. It will be a historic day."* That's me, that is – and thousands of others like me, I guess. Brace yourself, we're going in – and we are going to enjoy it come what may...

This is it, the Premier League. Can anyone believe it's actually here? I'm not sure I ever thought this day would truly happen. But now, unequivocally, it has happened. Finishing third in the Championship, destroying Watford in the play-offs 6-1 on aggregate and then beating Bristol City 0-1 at Wembley... WOW! WE ARE PREMIER LEAGUE!

It's still not sunk in. It won't sink in for a good while yet. Like Wembley, tomorrow will be another jewel in our City supporting crown. When your football club waits 104 years for a seat at the top table, you simply have to savour the moment of being here. I most definitely will be, all season long in fact. I'm going to enjoy every moment like it's our last. Not that I want it to be, but I'm taking nothing for granted in the most ruthless league in world football.

How long it will last is irrelevant. You see, you have to expect nothing and perhaps gain everything in my opinion. I think that will be my motto this season. There will be no rash predictions from my quarters; how can you really accurately predict what's going to happen? Who actually knows? After 37 years I couldn't honestly tell you, that's why I will relish every Hull City game proudly. And then, diligently log it all as the journey begins to unfold. Where it goes, nobody knows. Exciting, isn't it?

Leading up to 3pm on Saturday, the fabled Premier League bell ringing ceremony that was bestowed upon our club when we moved to the Circle in 2002, amidst all the pre-match build up et al, I'll probably be having a private moment in my seat prior to kick off. Too many people for one reason or another will be missing this privileged moment I will witness - my thoughts will go with them. Tigers past and present, loyal fans of this club from days gone by, I salute you.

The match with Fulham itself becomes more intriguing as kick off approaches. Phil Brown will likely go with a 4-4-1-1 formation that pre-season has been screaming out at us. Myhill, Mendy, Turner, Gardner, Ricketts will make the back four I believe, with the latter on the left.

In the middle, the only real conundrum will be the form of Craig Fagan usurping the naturally right sided stalwart of last season, Richard Garcia. George Boateng and Ian Ashbee will combine centrally and Halmosi will pip Barmby for the left side berth, I guess.

Then, I would expect to see Geovanni play ahead of the Ashbee/Boateng axis and behind the lone central striker. Surely, that has to be Marlon King, after his arrival on loan from Wigan Athletic so late in the day before the season kicks off. But, is it good enough to win the match? Well, why the hell not?

Fulham will travel north without new striker Andy Johnson who has a thigh injury. Diomansy Kamara will be out with a long term knee problem, so summer signing Bobby Zamora will surely start. Zoltán Gera, Fredrik Stoor and Mark Schwarzer in goal will also be likely debut starters, after joining over the close season.

But enough about our visitors. Tomorrow will be all about Hull City taking centre stage in front of a sell-out crowd. Be loud, be proud, be a credit to Hull City. We are Premier League now, after all.

SATURDAY 16TH AUGUST 2008 – HULL CITY 2-1 FULHAM – REPORT

It feels like Christmas Day all over again. I probably should be ashamed to write those words – being 37 years old and all – but any true Hull City fan can surely relate to my inner feelings. For me personally, I've waited 30 years for this moment. Some have waited longer. Others, sadly, haven't even got to see this day such has been the scale of our underachievement. It has been 104-year torturous wait without any top flight football. But not any more!

I have promised myself to think of the legions of Tigers on this day that have trod this path before me. Those that made the exact same sacrifices and pilgrimages across the length and breadth of this country that I have – and like me – have absorbed the salubrious delights of English basement football and worse.

There are so many standard bearers of lower league mediocrity to (not exactly) savour. Try Macclesfield in the freezing wind, rain and hail on an open terrace in January. Take in the footballing giant that is Scarborough (now deceased) in a crunch end-of-season relegation encounter in the bowels of the Football League. Salivate at spending a Friday night in Southend watching Third Division football. Well, today, and for one full season at least, Hull City fans can banish all these haunting memories and countless others. At 3pm today we are officially a Premier League club. That feels mighty fine to pen.

There's little time for a pre-match bevvy. Anyone who knows me will know by now there are Premier League fanzines to sell. Hell! That sounds brilliant 'Premier League' fanzines! Thankfully, the sun is shining and the atmosphere is a vibrant, buoyant one ensuing outside the ground. A feeling of almost disbelief has descended upon the Circle, nobody can actually quite believe what type of journey we are about to embark on.

I can't recall feeling more excited about a game of football – and I include Wembley – that for me was riddled with tension and nerves as well as the excitement. It sounds almost childish to scribe, but we've never been 'top flight'.

Before the game, I like to think Hull City have been English football's sleeping beauty. Only the prince didn't arrive. And Yet when our royal charge did finally get round here – old and haggard as he was – all the charm of true love to break the curse was there.

Yes, another who mustn't be forgotten is our very own 'Prince Dean Windass' sat on our bench at 39 years of age today; the regal man who brought our rich Premier League trappings. Not the prettiest of men by his own admission, but this famous son of our fair city has been embedded into Hull City folklore for ever more, rest assured.

With selling done at 2.50pm, a skirt round the perimeter of the Circle to hand over my first ever Hull City top flight ticket is completed at the turnstile. History in motion, you call that. Along the concourse, through gate 17 – eyes scrunched in the bright Premier League sun – and it's an about turn up the steps and to the very back of the East Stand. This is it; our Premier League career is really all happening now...

As promised to myself, I watch the teams shake hands in scripted top flight style. I then melt into the background of the natural euphoria pouring out from all four stands, step back, bow my head and take a moment with closed eyes. A sharp intake of breath follows. Not for me and not because I'm overcome with emotion, but a small private non-vocal meditation takes place. Quietly, unassuming and unnoticed, my respects are paid to those not here at this precise moment in time.

I'm thinking of family in far flung places who can't be here to witness this history unfolding before my very eyes. I'm thinking of the exiled supporters – who again are missing this inaugural moment. I'm thinking of the many thousands and thousands of Tiger generations who sweated blood and tears for this day in the name of Hull City and are unfortunately no longer with us to relish every second. But I'm thinking; like at Wembley, they're all here today somewhere, they must be. Indeed, I'm certain they are...

One last roar of gusto breaks my train of thought. Referee Peter Walton blows his whistle. And now, unequivocally, Hull City are a fully fledged inaugurated English top flight side. OFFICIAL. A mad thought crosses my mind. If the world ended here and now, undisputedly – despite taking 105 years – Hull City would have been recorded as a Premier League club, right? But then... who would record it? And who would read it? Nobody would ever know! Does this self-imposed purgatory ever end? Aarrggh!

That silliness is shattered in the opening minute when Fulham midfielder Simon Davies thumps a volley into the ground and just off target within a minute of kick off. City respond immediately and Geovanni's far post header is miraculously clawed out low and at full stretch by Schwarzer. The big keeper is then assisted by a covering defender blocking the follow-up by Ashbee. Two minutes of Premier League life have passed and already it's helter-skelter stuff at breakneck speed.

Fulham come back again with some slick passing that is carving City open. Bullard is the architect in chief and with the freedom of the park at his disposal, the midfield playmaker is allowed to swing in a divine cross begging to be converted. Seol Ki-Hyeon duly obliges to nip between a static City centre back pairing of Gardner and Turner to divert his header beyond Myhill and into the bottom corner. 8 minutes had passed and were losing 0-1...

The visitors were now in apparent control. Fulham stroked the ball around with grace and aplomb, oozing confidence and leaving City chasing mere shadows. It looked very worrying to say the least. And remember, this was a team that survived on the frailty of goal difference with a late, late, final day win at Portsmouth last season. Worryingly, I'm ashamed to write we look out of our depth, as a precision training ground move from a Fulham corner sees Davies hammer another shot just over our bar. City are rocking...

The raucous atmosphere was sounding a little desperate, but the home fans knew this was always going to be a battle and backed their black and amber warriors to the hilt. Bullard again tore City open with an exquisite pass to Zoltán Gera who was clear in the box, but the winger made a hash of a simple volley when the goal gaped. My concerns about us were not being eased. If this is Fulham; what will Manchester United, Liverpool, Arsenal and Chelsea do to us? *gulp*

But fear not, after being second best for the opening quarter of the match, step forward our token Premier League Brazilian that all top flight clubs simply must have – namely Geovanni. This is why top flight clubs sign Brazilians; from a position just inside the Fulham half, City's no.10 jinked his way past three players, then unleashed a vicious, dipping drive that curled round Schwarzer and into the bottom corner.

The rush that coursed through me was immense. The stadium exploded with delight and Hull City's first ever Premier League goal was a corker and no mistake. In fairness it had come out of nothing – and very much against the run of play – but it provided the platform for City spring into action. With the crowd in full voice, a visible belief was restored to the home team, we are back in this match.

The crowd roared City on and the players responded. Fulham had their swagger knocked clean from their play and it was now a complete reversal of fortunes to what had gone on before. Indeed, as City pressed, a half time lead was almost garnered when Barmby powered a header wide, whilst cleverly making room in the box to get the opportunity.

At the break a 1-1 score line was more than satisfactory considering the start we had undergone. The mood to build on how we finished washed through the concourse and was carried into the stands to provide a buoyant atmosphere in the home quarters. However, with the sun blazing and heat taking its toll, mistakes began to creep into matters on the field in the second half.

City carried a little fragility at the back, especially when the impressive Bullard picked out Gera once again free in the box, but once again the winger wasted his golden chance with a poor effort. The Tigers were employing their height advantage to good effect and Turner powered over a header just the wrong side of the bar, before Geovanni squandered a close range chance when side-footing wide following Nick Barmby's precision cross. My hands cover my face, what a chance! Was that our moment gone?

But the hosts were in ascendancy and the febrile atmosphere encouraged the players to give it their all. Fulham were wilting and it was surprising to see City's superior fitness begin to tell, despite having less time to recover in the close season after our play-off exploits. Halmosi, Fagan and Folan all entered the arena and each was contributing to City's upper hand.

Peter Halmosi lashed in a fierce cross and Richard Garcia connected brilliantly to fire goal wards, but when it looked like being the goal to provide the lead, Schwarzer did magnificent to beat the ball out. The crowd roared City on; you could sense a win was not beyond the realms of possibility despite our dubious beginnings to Premier League life. Oh, how I would love to see us win this...

Right on cue an incredible sequence of events unfold. Fulham defender Konchesky dallied on the ball instead of clearing it into the stands when under pressure from the fresh legged Fagan. The winger pick-pocketed the ball (pun fully intended) and scampered in on goal leaving the beleaguered Fulham full back trailing. Schwarzer advances from goal, but Fagan has the presence of mind to spot Caleb Folan making a lung busting run towards the far post... what now...? Shoot? Or square it...?

Fagan unselfishly elects to square the ball. In doing so, Fagan undoubtedly passed all responsibility for Hull City's Premier League fortune and history in the same stroke. A brave and selfless move... Yet a decision that was proved to be the right one! Folan connects perfectly and calmly rolls the ball in beyond the last ditch defensive throes and the Circle overflows into a booming, euphoric mass of noise. Unbridled joy reins. A mesmeric turnaround of fortunes has occurred before our very eyes. Emotions are fit to bursting.

All around me, the stadium is celebrating. Nobody can believe the events – deserved it must be said – that Hull City are now leading this their first ever Premier League game. Fulham have had the stuffing knocked out of them and the Tigers are marching onwards to Premier League glory and history with a first win. Just eight minutes remain. Surely, Folan has produced the knockout blow in this contest amidst the sapping and ferocious heat?

Barring a couple of momentary half-baked frights, the goal from Folan was deemed enough to settle this contest. Fulham had been beaten fairly, squarely and with a performance of courage from the home team in difficult and trying circumstances, particularly after the early setback. It meant one thing; time to go out and celebrate!

With my mate Kev timing the Fulham game to coincide with his stag evening, we beat the sunbathed track back to the train station to head into Beverley. Fulham fans along the way were gracious in defeat, but gave cause for a trifle of concern by labelling the match 'Championship standard'. A tad harsh I thought.

Of course being out getting tanked up on a stag do meant missing our debut Premier League appearance on Match of the Day and (let's be frank) the chance of catching the early morning repeat were slim to none under the circumstances. Thankfully, good old Dad can Sky+ it all.

Hopefully, I should be recovered suitably to watch it all round about Thursday after all this celebrating. COME ON CITY! We're on the way...

MATCH STATS:
- Hull City: Myhill, Ricketts, Turner, Anthony Gardner, Dawson, Garcia (Fagan 74), Ashbee, Boateng, Barmby (Halmosi 62), Geovanni, King (Folan 70). Subs Not Used: Duke, Windass, Mendy, Marney.
- Booked: Ricketts, Dawson, Fagan.
- Goals: Geovanni 22, Folan 81.
- Fulham: Schwarzer, Pantsil, Hangeland, Hughes, Konchesky, Davies, Murphy (Andreasen 85), Ki-Hyeon (Nevland 85), Bullard, Gera, Zamora (Dempsey 81). Subs Not Used: Zuberbuhler, Teymourian, Stoor, Kallio.
- Goals: Ki-Hyeon 8.
- Att: 24,525
- Ref: Peter Walton (Northamptonshire)
- **Premier League position: 5th**

MONDAY 18TH AUGUST – MATCH OF THE DAY ON SKY+
Hull City are on Match of the Day! It seems... strange...

I'm suitably recovered from the weekend's heavy drinking exploits to pop round to my Dad's after work and watch the highlights of Hull City v Fulham. Interestingly, the opening credits see a little Hull City badge in the background. It's by no means prominent – probably with good reason – but it is most definitely there. Even two days after our first game, the opening credits have the power to make the hairs on the back of my neck stand on end. Weird!

City looked far better than I thought to be honest. The pundits all seemed in complimentary mood about us and Alan Hansen talked of how massive it was for a newly promoted club to gain some belief by claiming their first win so early in the season. I find myself agreeing. It may well have been Fulham and not Manchester United, but here is a team we are surely competing with - Fulham that is, not Manchester United. Well, probably not this season at least, anyway.

Mind you, we are fifth...

FRIDAY 22ND AUGUST – BLACKBURN ROVERS V HULL CITY PREVIEW

Can't the season end now? We're fifth in the table and European glory awaits us. The Premier League bandwagon sees us on the road for the first time with a trip over the Roses border to Lancashire. It's been a long time since I last came here to see an old Second Division league game.

This place has changed no end since I last visited. From a hazy recollection of some mid 80s time frame, I seem to remember the Tigers claiming a 2-2 draw at a pretty basic looking Ewood Park. Twenty odd years on - and a decade in the Premier League for the hosts - and all that's changed...

Ewood Park is massive by comparison now. This is just as well, as City intend to take a large following to Lancashire in an attempt to achieve a 100 per cent winning start to their maiden Premier League campaign. Wow! Did I just write that? Sounds good, eh? But more importantly, it's a massive monkey off our back. Now let's build on it.

So, perhaps the time to be starstruck and giddy in the Premier League tagged as the 'new boys' has already passed. It's down to serious business now. This game will be hard. Very hard. Blackburn are no longer that rag-bag Lancastrian outpost from the mid 80s, this team are established Premier League material now.

Indeed, failing to keep hold of Mark Hughes in the summer may have been a blow, but attracting arguably the hottest management property outside the Premier League - and English too - in Paul Ince, was a decent coup, if rather a gamble.

Ince has already sealed the deal with lethal striker Roque Santa Cruz - only today the South American forward has put pen to paper on a four year deal at Ewood - and that's a clear statement of intent by Rovers that they intend to be Premier League for a good while yet. Phil Brown's side will have to beware.

By contrast, City can't go into any game claiming to be favourites at this early stage of their Premier League campaign, but Saturday's deserved victory against Fulham certainly alerted the top flight to our arrival - and signalled our intentions that we're not here for the tour of duty, or to take the cash and run.

Any side approaching a game against us that thinks Hull City will be the whipping boys, underestimating our ability and our motives in this league, will get stung. What the Tigers lack in quality - which is not that far off the required - they more than make up in character, determination and a will to win.

Phil Brown appears to have bottled the spirit that got City into the top flight and by all accounts let the players have a few sips ahead of the Fulham game. In turn, backed by some brilliant home fans, the Tigers triumphed last Saturday - despite going a goal down - and the same mentality must be prevalent at Blackburn to achieve something on the road this week.

The City fans will be boisterous and determined and the players have already demonstrated they can deal with a setback in this league, so all the ingredients are there for a tasty looking Roses battle this weekend. Respect will be shown, but the Tigers will not be overawed.

Team news sees Phil Brown sweating on the fitness of George Boateng, impressive against Fulham, so Dean Marney and Peter Halmosi stand by.

The City boss declared getting a first win was vital for the up and coming Blackburn challenge ahead - *"It was a massive boost for us to beat Fulham but that's firmly behind us now - it's all about looking forward."*

Continuing with - *"We went into Saturday's game fully expecting to get something from Fulham and Blackburn is another opportunity to get something. We know what we are capable of and if we achieve that, we'll be okay this season."*

Paul Ince will welcome back Australian international Brett Emerton who has recovered from a pre-season foot injury to be considered for selection in his first competitive appearance in front of the home fans since leaving MK Dons in the summer.

The Blackburn boss stated ahead of Hull City's visit - *"You've seen it over the years, even with the biggest teams, that when players go away with their countries they struggle to perform on a Saturday. We've got to make sure that doesn't happen to us."*

I'm looking forward to this, I really am.

SATURDAY 23RD AUGUST 2008 - BLACKBURN ROVERS 1-1 HULL CITY - REPORT

My mates have all decided to hit the train tracks to Blackburn. I have to be back in Hull for a party in the evening so decline in favour of a lift there and back. Therefore, my Mum and Dad have kindly offered me a place in their car. It has now become apparent my daughter Kelly has got tickets with her friend Jules so a car originally containing two passengers has suddenly swelled to five. It's probably the Premier League factor.

But if this is the Premier League, give me more. I want more. Crossing the Pennines with me to Ewood Park were 5,000 City fans, and if the club can make the tickets more accessible in the future then maybe there could have been more joining us. Those that made it played their full part in the day's events. Superb support greeted the Tigers in Lancashire.

City boss Phil Brown made two changes to the line-up that faced Fulham. Huge responsibility was placed on Dean Marney to fill the enormous void left by George Boateng in the middle of the park. Craig Fagan also got a starting shirt, replacing Nick Barmby, but Richard Garcia was put on the left wing to accommodate the switch.

The away following was in fine fettle. Loud, proud and bouncing. Blackburn were playing at home for the first time this season - but you wouldn't know it. One of the quietest sets of home fans I can ever remember. Not the warmest welcome for Paul Ince then - or perhaps it's always like this. Who knows?

Thankfully, the noise from the away end was piercing the still Lancashire air around Ewood Park. Blackburn predictably started the brighter being the hosts. Jason Roberts was a lively character at the head of the field with his pace and movement. Newly-contracted Santa Cruz looked rather static and left me wondering what all the fuss was about to be frank. The South American was well shackled by City.

It was a snippet of encouragement for the visitors. Backed by the vociferous travelling fans, the Tigers grew into the game with Ashbee simply immense and Marney following his skipper's lead with an industrious display after a nervy opening spell. Garcia and Fagan provided suitable width - and you know what? City were starting to hold their own again in the Premier League.

Blackburn opened their tactical account with some fairly direct play. Rovers were looking for Santa Cruz's head and hoping to ruffle the Turner/Gardner partnership at the heart of the City defence. With the hosts getting little change there, that tactic was quickly shelved with the ball sprayed wide to attack the full backs. Blackburn's Morten Gamst Pedersen looked particularly menacing on the left flank, before fading badly in the second period. Yet Rovers seemed to get impatient rather quickly as City shut down the supply with the hardworking duo of Marney and Ashbee starving David Dunn of time on the ball. By contrast, the visitors' tactics allowed City to break at speed and Geovanni's clever movement brought the wide players into the game and it was Hull City fashioning the better chances, albeit sporadically.

But like the Fulham match seven days earlier, one ball caught the City defence flat and Jason Roberts hared onto the pass from Stephen Reid and coolly waited patiently for Myhill to commit himself before dinking the ball into a gaping net. THWACK! Here we go again, a right kick in the gonads...

The fans roared the Tigers on in the ensuing adversity. Immediately from the kick off Fagan and King interchanged well to leave the former putting in a hanging cross. Garcia drifting in from his wing was left completely unmarked to loop the ball back over Rovers keeper Robinson's head and into the net. Bloody hell! It's 1-1! What character shown by the visitors. It was a magnificently swift response to the setback. Brilliant stuff!

And the confidence factor was duly built upon. Blackburn looked frustrated. Ince was probably stewing on the management handbook rule book that read '1 - You are always at your most vulnerable defensively after scoring a goal.' Ah well, half time was here to put it all right again. City departed Ewood Park to thunderous cheers.

The second half started rather tepidly with neither wanting to take the game by the scruff of the neck. A little surprising considering Blackburn were the home side being held by 'a side we should be beating' - their words pre-match, not mine. But the credit for that goes to Hull City. The work ethic demonstrated by the Tigers was first class. Hustle, harry, chase. Blackburn did not get the time on the ball to settle.

Indeed, Rovers best (only?) attacking threat came from corners. But with Turner and Gardner in imperious form, little solace was being found there for the hosts. It was deathly silent in the home stands as a consequence. Brown was tactically outwitting Ince it seemed and Marlon King almost caught Blackburn napping with a clever ball from Marney needing Rovers keeper Robinson to smother the danger.

City then decided to go for broke with a more direct approach when the substitution of playmaker Geovanni - who had looked lively when on the ball - was made for Folan. Admittedly, it was a much more predictable attacking option by the visitors but it was reaping rewards. Blackburn were failing to create any clear cut chances by comparison, despite the heavier possession.

City fans roared the team on. Those on the terraces in the away end were appreciating the mighty effort the team were putting in to get something from the match. Substitutions by Rovers - including Brett Emerton and Tugay entering the battle - failed to ignite a creative spark and it was the visitors looking the more dangerous as the game came into the latter stages, as Caleb Folan's volley picked out Paul Robinson's midriff.

A last throw of the dice saw Phil Brown introduce the experience of Nick Barmby for the hard-working goalscorer Richard Garcia with the last few minutes of the match to play. It almost paid dividends with Sam Ricketts combining well with the former England man. The full back burst into the box and chose to shoot low himself with Barmby in space and arguably better placed. Robinson pouched the ball. Chance gone...

City had put in a humongous effort to get something from this game and although the win was probably a mite too far for the visitors, a point was the very least they deserved. The predictable groan from the home stands greeted the final whistle, undoubtedly peeved their side had not beaten 'a team like Hull City' blah, blah.

Rather funny, because nobody has been able to beat 'a team like Hull City' in the Premier League so far. Two games it may be, but long may this trait continue. And on this evidence, the same hard work and endeavour will mean Blackburn and Fulham won't be the only sides on the wrong end of underestimating a committed, driven and well drilled Phil Brown led side. Well done City, you were magnificent today.

MATCH STATS:

- Blackburn: Robinson, Ooijer, Samba, Nelsen, Warnock, Reid, Mokoena (Kerimoglu 67), Dunn (Emerton 46), Pedersen, Roque Santa Cruz, Roberts (McCarthy 81). Subs Not Used: Simpson, Treacy, Derbyshire, Brown.
- Goals: Roberts 38.
- Hull City: Myhill, Ricketts, Turner, Anthony Gardner, Dawson (Mendy 58), Garcia (Barmby 78), Ashbee, Marney, Fagan, Geovanni (Folan 65), King. Subs Not Used: Brown, Windass, Duke, Halmosi.
- Booked: Ashbee.
- Goals: Garcia 40.
- Att: 23,439
- Ref: Stuart Attwell (Warwickshire)
- **Premier League position: 3rd**

SUNDAY 24TH AUGUST 2008 –
BBC RADIO FIVE LIVE COMMENTING ON THE PREMIER LEAGUE

Hull City went to Blackburn yesterday with a massive 6,000 supporters. Already, the newly promoted club from East Yorkshire are proving to be a real credit to the Premier League.

MONDAY 25TH AUGUST 2008 –
SWANSEA CITY V HULL CITY – LEAGUE CUP ROUND 2 PREVIEW

Who the hell thought it was a good idea to enter the League Cup now we've gone Premier League? Bring me his head on a silver platter and let me curse thee til the end of time. Swansea away! Grrr...

What a rubbish competition anyway. Stupid midweek League Cup fixtures in far off countries indeed. What the hell is going on? Whose idea was this? You'd think now we are Premier League we'd be given several byes into the next few rounds or something, while the minnows knock themselves out.

I saw this harebrained buffoonery being drawn after the mighty Wycombe Wanderers v Birmingham City clash in round one, broadcast to the nation via Sky Sports. Or perhaps, more accurately, didn't see the draw at all because everyone at the Football League thought it much better to draw all the non-seeded teams out during the commercial break.

And there, with a cheesy Carling ice bucket - complete with cubes not balls I might add - a scrolling team at the bottom of the picture signified whether the non seeded team had been already been drawn home or away, while the big teams were plucked out.

So, seeing 'Swansea City v ' scroll up on the screen had me muttering "For god's sake not them…" You utter <insert your own expletive here> What a rubbish draw. Why isn't this thing regionalised or something? Like, north, south and Wales? Bah!

The League Cup has many critics, but it lends itself to ridicule by manufacturing idiotic midweek draws like this one - and this despite regionalising round 1 draws - so it's not like it can't be done in round 2.

Perhaps little Third and Fourth division clubs like Leeds United would welcome a Premier League club visiting them for a bit of glamour and a rare 'derby' in this competition, after fighting hard to get into the next round. But one from the other end of the country? One that will bring minimal support? Why bother?

The Football League gets this tournament seriously wrong. For all it's 'seeding' and 'regionalisation' and 'rule bending for big clubs', it still comes up with boneheaded Swansea City v Hull City and Queens Park Rangers v Carlisle United midweek ties. Who organises this claptrap?

It is little wonder why so many Premier League clubs treat the tournament with disdain. And this despite some top clubs being handed favourable third round entries. But you watch them play precisely no household names in round three versus Accrington Stanley or whoever. So what's the point?

And typically, what will City do ahead of their mouth watering clash with Swansea? You've guessed it, play a raft of fringe players - who let's face it - are not up to Premier League standard.

Those involved are likely to be players like Bryan Hughes in midfield and for all his heroics at this club, Dean Windass. Wayne Brown, possibly Ryan France and Nathan Doyle and others could well feature. Don't get me wrong, these are good players, but would struggle in the Premier League, surely?

Yet despite all this, I'm most angry with myself. Because – stupidly – I will be there. I can hide behind my work for being at the Liberty Stadium, but in truth, should a second rate cup competition be hosting ludicrous ties like this one at all? That's my big bone of contention. Let's hope the journey is worth it after all this… It's not looking good, is it?

Incredibly, I've just had a text to say this game is now all ticket. And it's not a joke. My mate Andy – a seasoned Amber Nectar fanzine follower – cycled round to the ticket office and did the honours for yours truly stuck at work.

The lunacy is complete. What a sham. Who in their right mind makes these crass decisions? What insane individual would deny anyone entry without a ticket and only stony, cold hard cash to show when they've travelled nigh on 300 miles to get here and there will be 10,000 plus empty seats inside? Madness, that's what it is, madness. Right, I'd best be off now. See you all at some ungodly hour…

TUESDAY 26TH AUGUST 2008 – SWANSEA CITY 2-1 HULL CITY (AET) LEAGUE CUP ROUND 2 – REPORT

One reserve side and one bloody long distance to travel sees one time hero Dean Windass bag us one goal. Yet the Tigers crash out of the League Cup after one game. Swansea away? Ace…

Oh well, that couldn't have gone any worse, eh? At least it's just a short jolly home starting from the Western tip of some foreign country. I'm typing this on the M4 – the far end of the M4 near Swansea – and City, that's Hull City by the way, are out of the Carling Cup after entering the tournament in round two.

It took extra time and penalties to resolve this tie, but at least the 150 hardy Hull City fans that made the ridiculous trip were spared the dreaded penalty shoot-out we'd undoubtedly lose. In truth, the second you walked into the pristine looking Liberty Stadium you feared the worst upon seeing the visiting starting XI.

Phil Brown clearly takes the Carling Cup about as seriously as me – as you've read in my preview. An entire team was fielded without a single starter from either of our two Premier League games so far this season. Those players have taken City to fourth in the top flight. Indeed, a team of reserves greeted us, with one or two shocks to boot.

16 year old Liam Cooper made his Hull City debut at centre back alongside Wayne Brown and the pair were flanked by Nathan Doyle and Bernard Mendy in the full back berths. It was also rather pleasing to record Matt Duke's first full return to the side after his cancer treatment at the turn of the year.

Meanwhile, the midfield was butchered from the one at Blackburn last Saturday with Ryan France and Bryan Hughes the axis of the side, leaving Peter Halmosi and Nick Barmby providing the width. Caleb Folan was joined at the top by Wembley hero Dean Windass, making his first appearance of the season for the club. Yet this was patently a reserve side. We're not 'going for it!' clearly.

The opening spell of the game saw the Tigers in complete control passing round a statuesque Swansea defence with apparent ease. The hosts were chasing and when getting the ball slamming it into each other. It was amusing for a few minutes before becoming tedious. No surprise then to see a neat move leaving Dean Windass free in the box to slide in the opening goal nice and early.

Swansea looked disorganised and a severely weakened Hull City side were enjoying the lion's share of possession and territory. But the Tigers fell foul of the offside flag continually and it disrupted some promising moves and prevented the visitors adding to their score. That ironically, always seemed a linesman's flag away.

The Tigers were needing to keep a watchful brief on Bouaza for the Swans, but other than that, the visitors were playing within themselves and coasted to a half time lead. Yet half two was entirely different. Like some transplant had taken place, the roles were completely reversed.

Swansea were now pressing, but lacked a cutting edge to seriously threaten. Any time they did, Duke was in fine form and probably took the man of the match performance for mere competence alone. Phil Brown made a substitution with Swansea waiting on a free kick - Windass replaced by Marlon King, who will miss Saturday's game v Wigan - and that rule about times and places to make a change resulted in the hosts scoring, as the ball was lofted into the box for a flicked header. Sigh...

The Tigers responded positively with King shooting low but wide and Ryan France having a decent pop. But gradually, as time ebbed away and I prayed for a winner to avoid the interminable extra time, it appeared one was likely. For Swansea that is. A post was struck by the hosts after a mazy run had gone way too long unchallenged and then a dumb tackle away from goal on the edge of the box provided Swansea a penalty to clinch it in the dying moments. But Duke saves! Yes! No! I have to stay here longer? Bah!

Incredibly, the visitors then fashioned two injury time chances with Bryan Hughes' diving header needing to be saved and then Ryan France nipping between the dozing Swansea defence, but scooping the ball over the bar from close range. Damn! Stuck in Swansea for even longer now...

So, wearily, extra time was here. The visitors started the brighter but the energy from the game was gone. Long gone. Indeed it was half way back to Hull for me. The match was a grey splurge of cack now and if the game was a lame dog, you'd have put it down ages ago. Boring, docile, benign football to watch. Let's short cut to penalties now. All in favour say 'AYE!'

And substitute Michael Turner obliged all when replacing flagging youngster Liam Cooper for extra time. A tangling of legs produced a pretty soft penalty right on the end of the first period - but this time Swansea converted the gift presented them to lead the match for the first time. What am I doing here?

There was nothing left in the tank. The second period saw nothing barring players dropping like flies with early season fitness cramps and the pattern was non-existent to the play. Frankly, I was actually dreading an equaliser that meant I was going to be delayed further with penalties. Quirkily, I was quite relieved to hear the final whistle. Right, let's get gone.

It is clear from tonight's evidence two salient points have emerged. Firstly, with an entire reserve team out on the pitch, Hull City had no intention of taking the League Cup seriously. If they had, there would have been eleven different names on the teamsheet. Secondly, City apparently do not have the strength in depth just yet to sustain Premier League status without incurring injuries. Thankfully, Phil Brown is working on that.

That aside, the Liberty looks half decent and massive improvement on the Vetch and surely Bernard Mendy is better than what I witnessed tonight. Someone mentioned 'Comedy Mendy' on the City Independent website recently. This is no laughing matter now. Woeful! Yet while still stuck in the eerie depths of deepest darkest South Wales, I wouldn't quite go with one comment bellowed out from the travelling City faithful as the game drew to a close...

"COME ON CITY! YOU'VE GOT 7 MINUTES TO SAVE YOUR SEASON!"

I like the touch of realism, but right now, like Phil Brown I guess, I'm happy Hull City are sitting in the Champions League places in the best league in the world rather than being in round three of the Carling Cup. Let's face it; we'd only field yet more reserves away at Southampton or wherever. Sincerely, well done Swansea, but here in Hull, we've got bigger fish to fry. That was patently obvious the second the team sheet was drafted. Only four hours until home zzzzzz...

MATCH STATS:

- Swansea: De Vries, Painter, Monk, Collins (Rangel 55), Serran, Orlandi, Gómez, Tudur-Jones, MacDonald, Allen (Pintado 54), Bauza (Brandy 81).
- Subs Not Used: O'Leary, Tate, Gower, Lawrence.
- Booked: Bauza.
- Goals: Pintado 63, Gómez 105 pen.
- Hull City: Duke, Brown, Mendy, Doyle, Cooper (Turner 91), Barmby (Featherstone 72), Hughes, France, Halmosi, Folan, Windass (King 62).
- Subs Not Used: Atkinson, Garcia, Welsh, Warner.
- Booked: Brown, Mendy, Halmosi.
- Goals: Windass 11.
- After Extra Time
- Att: 8,622.
- Ref: Mike Russell (Hertfordshire)

WEDNESDAY 27TH AUGUST 2008 – THE WITCHING HOURS...

The mind numbingly dour journey from deepest darkest South Wales took a new and unexpected twist. Allow me to put a little background into what happened next...

Our driver Steve has borrowed our mate Paul's seven-seater car for this journey to Swansea. Well, not exactly Paul's – he can't drive – more accurately so, his wife Ann-Marie's car. On the way down to Swansea it was clear Steve wasn't exactly relishing his marathon driving jaunt to South Wales and back. I had a plan to alleviate Steve's worries...

At Tamworth, I offered Steve the chance to let me drive us the rest of the way to Swansea and provide him with a decent break. My beers are left unattended in my bag. I suppose it's a small sacrifice, I thought, plenty of time later. Steve jumped at my offer. And then promptly fell asleep in the back. A trifle worrying, I must say. Yet we're here, Swansea has reeled us in.

After the combined marathon exploits of the match and the journey, I'm sitting in the front bashing my keys in the darkness of Swansea's outer perimeter, detailing the evening's events. Steve, now driving, is steadfast and quiet. The passengers in the back are subdued and occasionally breaking the tranquillity with the rip of a ring pull. Beer... it's the only way... Mine are still tucked in my bag, ready for emptying. Just a little more typing first...

The dirty South Wales drizzle has morphed into a late night rain lashing on the M4. Steve yawns. And then, yawns again. Rubs his eyes behind his glasses and I can tell, you're already thinking what I'm thinking... *"Are you all right Steve?"* A rather weary *"Yeah..."* returns.

Andy, the daddy of all drinkers in our clan, has astutely picked up on this rather concerning development despite his roundly intoxicated state. A knowing nod is exchanged between us. *"Let's stick the radio on"* I suggest. But deep down, I already know what's coming. We're barely off the M4 and we decide to pull in at some garage off the Welsh valleys in the dead of night. A wet, windy and chilly night, it must be said. After a slice of inquisition, a black coffee and some food intake, Steve is certain he's fine. I'm not convinced. Neither is Andy. We're not even over the border into England yet. Home feels a very long way, away.

It's evident to us all Steve is struggling shortly after his enforced break. This leaves us passengers with a major problem. Our driver clearly needs (more!) kip, some of us are working in the morning and we're still one country, several hours and many miles from home. And all of this coming on the back of an unwanted extra time League Cup second round defeat to Swansea. This is a nightmare.

Close study of Steve and it's abundantly clear as we cross the border, Steve is now a driving wreck and has absolutely no chance of steering us all back to Hull alive and well. With the windows open to keep Steve awake, I'm looking round the car. Wiseman, Cropper and Tony are all well and truly intoxicated. Andy is drunk but at least compos mentis. Indeed, Andy is the only person on the planet that still looks sober after 10 pints. No, I don't get it either – and I've known him for years and years. Whatever, I know, he's over the limit. As for Connor, well, he's Tony's son. And unfortunately, he's only 10 years old. So that's Connor out of the equation, which leaves... you've guessed it. Look who will be imminently getting the keys...

Part of me is cursing the fact I hadn't just drunk all my beer and drowned my sorrows in this forlorn and forgettable evening of League Cup football. However, the sensible head immediately kicks in as Steve veers waywardly across an empty (thank god!) lane of a motorway. *"Steve, pull over, we all need a pee."* Fortunately the services are near. We all pile out leaving me and Andy to discuss who is going to get the keys from Steve and take over. A pointless discussion at the urinals really, it could only be a sober me.

Rather than be mortally offended that we enquired after the keys to our chariot from Steve, our driver looked the most relieved man on earth. Willingly, Steve hurled the keys at us. It was now all down to me. Yeah, thanks... Everyone, to a man, has finished their beer within 20 minutes of me taking over driving duties, except Andy. Andy rarely sleeps, being a self-confessed alcoholic insomniac. Predictably, Steve was out for the count first and no messing. Cheers Steve!

For me at least, worse followed. To keep Andy awake, I had to relinquish my beer to keep him awake and company for the long road ahead. Well it was utterly redundant for me now, eh? The rain eased off, but the miles receded at a painfully slow rate. 1am, 2am, 3am... still on the M1 *groan* this is a torture I really hadn't bargained for. And remember, I out of all of us, had been working most of the day on my laptop unlike the rest of my beer swilling compatriots (Connor excepted, before social services ask). However, I will confess to having him pencilled in for reserve driving duties...

I was beginning to flag – but to Andy's credit he was hanging on grimly with me. It's 4.10am the M18 is rewarding me with double figure mileage signs to home and the bountiful boundaries of Hull are almost insight. We're going to make it. We're going to get home. We're close now, so close. I'm thinking 'warm bed, relaxation, sleep, precious sleep...' when suddenly *BANG!*

A horrible rumbling sound, the steering is out of control, the car is veering ferociously like an untamed Tiger on a leash. I'm wrestling with the steering wheel and in an instant the passengers lurch from the slumber. I yell out a quite a pitch *"I haven't fallen asleep! I haven't fallen asleep! It's not me, honest!"* Incredibly, in my sudden and enforced higher state of consciousness I tame the car and successfully find the relative safety of the hard shoulder. A second is taken to reflect on what has just happened. Is everyone is ok? Everyone is ok... *"What was that?"* someone blurted out. We all trooped out of the car. The back tyre was flat as a pancake. A blow out. Oh brilliant!

Now, this is not our car. Nobody in the car has ever seen the car before today. Nobody has ever owned a Nissan, whatever it was called, period. We can't find the spare. Thankfully, I'm in the AA. We call, they ask if we have the spare tyre, I lie and say 'Sure!' Truth is, it's not in the car, under the car, in the boot. Indeed, it's not anywhere. Where the hell is it? The AA will be here for 4.45am we are informed. We get looking...

For some reason – after our pitch black and unwanted 7 man tyre hunt around one average sized vehicle – we strike gold and find the spare behind the radiator and under the bonnet. What the ...? Anyway, we yank the thing out. Squinting in the darkness around a posse of mobile phone lights, we take the tyre from its housing. Only then, our misery gets worse. It's not flat, oh no, it's worse than that. It's bald as a coot and highly illegal. The AA are not going to fix this onto the car. It's 4.25am. We're drunk, tired, fed up, irritated and freezing cold. We now need to act like an F1 pit crew at the side of the M18 and get our bald saviour on the car and out of here sharp. It's not looking good.

Lorries thunder past in the nearside lane of the motorway at frightening speed. I'm scared, I'm wet, I'm tired and most of all I'm in a race against time to fix a flat tyre with a bald tyre before we get lynched and towed away for an extortionate amount of money we can ill afford. Dimly lit mobile phone lights are all the tools I get to help me in the cloak of absolute darkness. I've changed a tyre once in my entire life. This really is not my forte – or the rational time and place to be doing so.

But, success! The wheel comes off. The lads bowl it to the front and ram it back into the bonnet of the car. I'm frantically tightening up the spare and wasting no time with the jack. It is literally thrown in the back with the tools. Everyone piles back in the car. The dashboard blinks 4.41am. Go! Go! Go! The metal is pressed and we swerve off the hard shoulder, back onto the motorway and out of here.

Andy calls the AA – because we all know it's illegal to use your phone will driving so I couldn't – and cancels the rescue mission. Doncaster services are just 2 miles away, hurrah!

We pull into the services, properly pack the car up and contemplate how we are going to explain this entire sorry tale to the car's owner Ann-Marie. I'm not even supposed to be driving, remember? Steve is now surprisingly chirpy. That's good. Steve can have the keys, when I drop myself off first. Well, driver's privileges and all that, you have to rake 'em in. And as I am the enforced driver, what I say goes.

It's 5.30am when I roll into bed. I'd like to say it's all been worth it. Three games into this ambition of mine and it's already becoming crystal clear; this season-long journey isn't going to be a bed of roses. But I'm ready. I'm more determined than ever to achieve it. This will be the best trip you and I have ever been on. I'm certain. Although, I readily confess – this time at least – I really did want to go home after our midweek jaunt to Swansea.

FRIDAY 29TH AUGUST 2008

I might well still be recovering from the tiring midweek cup exploits in South Wales, but today I really do have reason to pick myself up off the floor. Hull City have tabled a club record £7m offer to Manchester United for striker Fraizer Campbell! That's (seven) million quid! For one player! To put this shattering news into perspective and to measure truly how far Hull City have come, our club has nearly gone bust for a mere fraction of that colossal figure less than a decade ago. Well, nobody can say we're not prepared to give the Premier League a real go now, can they?

All summer long, City fans have been eager to learn of one signing and one signing only. There isn't a City fan alive that wouldn't want Fraizer Campbell from Manchester United after last season's exploits with us. We've all been thinking and hoping; now we are Premier League, we surely have a chance to try and sign him? It seems we now are.

The transfer window shuts in three days time... but our long awaited bid is in. Hold the back page... But, just one thought prevails; why haven't we done this sooner? Anyway, enough of that, Wigan are in town tomorrow.

FRIDAY 29TH AUGUST 2008 – WIGAN ATHLETIC (H) PREVIEW

It's another critical fixture so early in the campaign facing Wigan Athletic this weekend. I'm still not sure I've recovered from my Carling Cup foray down in South Wales yet. A physically and emotionally draining experience down at Swansea's Liberty Stadium that saw me arriving back as day broke – again.

It can sometimes be a dangerous game resting players for cup matches in far away countries (get set for the UEFA Cup folks) particularly when it backfires as hideously as it did at Swansea when the match went into extra time, but Phil Brown has made that decision now and we have to go with it and take what came our way.

With two weeks off after the game with Wigan due to an international break, would it have been better to gather more momentum that was beginning to show in the team and continue with a morale boosting victory over Swansea's second string to back up a couple of fine results? It's always easier with hindsight. And in fairness, it is noticeable the step up in endeavour required to get anything in the Premier League.

Okay, I'm not the manager, but these are professional athletes and I doubt if an extra game would have killed the players. Sure, there's the old injury argument, but what game isn't a threat to the players? Surely winning is better than losing – as we unfortunately did at the Liberty.

I'll shut up. I'm probably sounding a little sore about our Carling Cup exploits. City are rested, fine tuned and ready to face Wigan this Saturday. This game is massive. This is a game I'm really looking forward to. If City can compete against Wigan – and win – this represents, in my opinion, a true barometer of if we will survive in the Premier League or not.

Perhaps it's a good thing we faced Fulham as early as we did. City were on a natural high and, with the crowd creating a fantastic atmosphere, even going behind didn't stop us claiming victory. The Blackburn draw at Ewood was of similar ilk and for me, the fans have been pivotal in both results.

This needs to be maintained against Wigan at home this Saturday. It's a vital fixture so early in the campaign. Yet with the right approach, same work ethic as Fulham and Blackburn, along with due respect but without being overawed by the Premier League, City can succeed for a second time at home.

Phil Brown has been boosted by some positive team news ahead of the game. Andy Dawson and Ian Ashbee will recover from knocks taken at Blackburn to take their places. The impressive Geovanni has also come through, but a cloud of doubt still hangs over George Boateng.

The main conundrum over team selection will be at the head of the field, though. Marlon King cannot play against his parent club and that could provide an opportunity for midweek goalscorer Dean Windass who has been chomping at the bit for a start. Something not lost on Phil Brown.

On that point, the City boss stated - *"Dean Windass just wants to play football. I gave him that opportunity at Swansea on Tuesday. He said to me he just wants to score goals and he has done that, so he is ticking all the boxes. Do I repay him with a start against Wigan? The answer to that will remain to be seen."*

Wigan will travel over the Pennines for the game with doubts over the influential Paul Scharner and one-time Tigers target Jason Koumas in the midfield, both having ankle injuries. Chris Kirkland's injury may not be as bad as first feared and he may well feature in Steve Bruce's team selection.

The Latics boss revealed - *"I think Chris Kirkland should be okay for the Hull game. He had a spasm while we were away in pre-season and it tightens up and stiffens up a bit, but we don't think it is anything too serious so with a bit of TLC he will be fine. He has been to see specialists and we're okay with him. He's comfortable with the whole situation at the moment so we don't think there is really anything to unduly worry us."*

I think I speak for more than a few when claiming Wigan are a team we have to respect, but also need to beat, and I'm hoping our unbeaten Premier League start remains intact come 5pm tomorrow.

SATURDAY 30TH AUGUST 2008 - HULL CITY 0-5 WIGAN ATHLETIC - REPORT

Welcome to the Premier League! Getting humped by the likes of Manchester United, Liverpool, Arsenal, Chelsea and... err...Wigan? Yep, you better sit down first. Read it and believe it and then probably run and hide behind the settee. Tell me it doesn't get worse than this!

One of those days... Are you kidding me? City were outclassed by a side who most certainly aren't relegation candidates from the Premier League. Wigan were as impressive as the scoreline suggests, while City will definitely need some strength in depth to have any hope of surviving. That is now a racing certainty.

Forgive me, but I think I whinged a little about this post-Swansea in the Carling Cup. I'd rather not say I told you so, but come on, it was there for all to see. City are miles off the eight ball and unless some quality comes in – and sharpish – we're not going to get by with battling qualities alone in this league.

Indeed, the tables were turned on City somewhat today, with Wigan's power-packed midfield crushing the hosts. The visitors simply outbattled the Tigers in every area of the park. Rarely have City been hounded out of a game under Phil Brown, but, credit to Steve Bruce and his team, they nailed us good and proper with a masterclass in finishing.

The predictable changes came in from the midweek Carling Cup side with Myhill recalled in goal, Ricketts and Dawson at full backs, while Wayne Brown kept his place after Anthony Gardner failed a fitness test to partner Michael Turner. Worried? Yes, and justifiably so, especially after Brown's inept performance at the Liberty Stadium.

The midfield had Marney in for Boateng, alongside Ashbee, Garcia and Fagan. Forgive me, but that looks way too light for my liking. We need more in the middle! At the head of the field Geovanni played behind Folan, who got the nod ahead of the evergreen Windass. So, essentially, the spine of our team had been ripped out because Marlon King couldn't play against his parent club.

Pre-match warnings traded between Wigan fans I knew (Jay, who runs the Wigan Athletic Rivals site, among others) left me feeling a little uneasy. If the aforementioned trio fails to appear, namely Boateng, Gardner and King, I fear the worst. Of course, King couldn't, but we looked so lightweight for a fight. Meanwhile, *"You're gonna get tonked when you see Zaki and co."* wasn't far off the mark as Jay commented upon our parting of the ways.

The scoreline looks terrible – and I am not going to make excuses. There isn't any. City weren't good enough, end of. Cattermole ran the show in midfield for Wigan, Heskey and Zaki tore into our weakened defence and were ruthless with the execution.

Ironically, the best chance City had arrived in the very first minute. Geovanni played in Craig Fagan who burst through the Wigan defence, but hurried his shot when he could've taken the ball on and picked his spot. The chance was passed up far too easily.

With just five minutes gone, a woefully mishit Wigan corner was scuffed to the near post and Ricketts somehow, managed to miskick the ball into his own net. A routine clearance fluffed. And all this from a botched corner too. Give me strength, not in this league, no, no, no!

City attempted to get back into the game but Wigan looked alert and dangerous, giving us absolutely no time on the ball. So, when a corner was won and only proved to be a catalyst for Wigan's second goal - as Valencia raced half the length of the field - you really did fear the worst. And just 13 minutes had passed at this point. As it turned out, I was right too, unfortunately.

To their credit, City didn't give up. But they were never in this game. Wigan seemed to attack when they felt like it and picked us off when convenient. Ian Ashbee spurned a knock down from a corner to inject some life into the game for City, but scuffing the shot wide horridly. It hardly had me thinking we'd be getting back in to the game anytime soon.

In the second half, Brown bowled his troops out early for the restart. A flirtatious attempt to get back into the match passed once again with Geovanni laying on a golden chance for Richard Garcia to bury the ball, but Kirkland in the Wigan goal snuffed the chance out all too easily.

As hard as City tried, Wigan powered forward when they wanted to, fully in control of the match. Shoddy defending with too much time given for Wigan to stroke the ball around our penalty box was duly punished and Zaki buried a low shot into the bottom corner for number three to effectively end the game as any sort of contest. More slapdash defending saw Emile Heskey allowed the freedom of the Hull City half and as Boaz Myhill hared out of goal to meet him, a deft touch wide of the Welsh international and time to steady himself sufficiently saw number four bulge the net - despite Turner's desperate lunge to prevent the ball crossing the line.

More salt was poured into the gaping wound when Zaki smashed the fifth goal of the game via the underside of the bar after the linesman signalled the ball had breached the whitewash. He was right. It was miles over the line. 5-0. Bloomin' 5-0! Wigan looked class, in truth, but hell. 0-5 at home! It was our record defeat at the KC Stadium.

In return, substitute Bernard Mendy had contrived to miss City's final chance when well placed in the box for a consolation, but blazed his rash shot over the bar. To their eternal credit – after an almighty stuffing – the City faithful kept churning out the chants. I think *"We're gonna win 6-5"* was pushing it a little, though. But it at least *"We've got more points than you"* was factually correct - for now...

I dread to think how a £7m bid tabled for Fraizer Campbell would have looked if it hadn't been made 24 hours earlier. Smacks of desperation? Perhaps, taking all things into context, we've learnt nothing we didn't already know about the Premier League today. It's going to be hard, you cannot make mistakes, but we sorely lack strength in depth.

Oh – and Wigan won't be in a relegation scrap this season. Did I just write that? Sure did. Something that perhaps I didn't know before the start of the day.

Forgive me for exiting stage left swiftly.

MATCH STATS:
- Hull City: Myhill, Ricketts, Brown, Turner, Dawson (Mendy 71), Fagan, Ashbee, Marney, Garcia (Barmby 60), Geovanni (Windass 56), Folan. Subs Not Used: Duke, Hughes,

Halmosi, Cooper.
- Booked: Ashbee.
- Wigan: Kirkland, Melchiot, Boyce, Bramble, Figueroa, Valencia, Palacios, Cattermole (Kapo 79), Kilbane (Brown 56), Heskey (Camara 85), Zaki. Subs Not Used: Pollitt, Koumas, De Ridder, Kupisz.
- Goals: Ricketts 5 og, Valencia 13, Zaki 63, Heskey 68, Zaki 81.
- Att: 24,282
- Ref: Michael Jones (Cheshire)
- **Premier League position: 10th**

CHAPTER 2 –
HELLO WORLD, WE'VE ARRIVED!

MONDAY 1ST SEPTEMBER 2008 – TRANSFER DEADLINE DAY

Transfer deadline day is here. I'm working from home today. In the background is Sky Sports News. An essential tool to watch the days events unfold.

At varying times throughout the summer, the rumours have been rife, ridiculous and rhetorical about Hull City. Sometimes all at the same time and occasionally all about the same player! This has not been assisted by Sky Sports News' dramatic entrance and exit music and a countdown clock throughout the month of August signifying the days, hours, minutes – yes, even the seconds – until the clock strikes 12 and all transfers must cease.

I have a sorry confession to make. This has been addictive. Compelling. I suppose it mixes the novelty factor of being Premier League and the enormous exposure Sky places on the English top flight anyway. Never before have City been a news story, featured item or have we seen the manager, players and chairman interviewed with so much regularity in my 30 plus years of watching us. I could run the risk of overdose here. Okay, maybe not...

So far since Wembley, Phil Brown has amassed a clutch of players for our maiden voyage into uncharted Premier League waters. Below is a full break down of all the club's transfer activity between the opening and closing of the last transfer window...

Players In: Peter Halmosi (Plymouth, £2m), George Boateng (Middlesbrough, £1m), Tony Warner (Fulham, free), Bernard Mendy (Paris St Germain, free), Geovanni (Manchester City, free), Craig Fagan (Derby, £750,000), Anthony Gardner (Tottenham, £2.5m), Marlon King (Wigan, loan), Paul McShane (Sunderland, loan), Kamil Zayatte (Young Boys, loan), Daniel Cousin (Rangers, undisclosed).

Players Out: Michael Bridges (Carlisle, loan), Henrik Pedersen (Silkeborg IF, free), David Livermore (Brighton, free).

Players speculated on over the summer but not signed: David Nugent, Colin Kazim-Richards, Antti Niemi, Darren Bent, David Healy, Marlon Harewood, Jason Koumas, Ivan

Campo, Christian Vieri, Roy Makaay, Giorgi Samaras, Seyi Olofinjana, Martin Rowlands, Noe Pamarot, Abdoulaye Méïté, Michael Chopra, Claudio Pizarro, Andre Bikey

However, above all this, one transfer story has absolutely dominated the thoughts of everyone at the club. And no, it was not the rumour about Christian Vieri (that was indeed true – City had tried) but the hopeful enticement of Fraizer Campbell from Manchester United. Our £7m bid had been lodged on Friday and now all City fans were glued to Sky Sports News waiting for developments. Okay, well I was at least.

Campbell, undoubtedly, was a revelation helping us gain promotion. 15 goals had catapulted us into the play-offs and then an exquisite run and piece of skill at Wembley in the play-off final had seen him tee up Dean Windass with the type of cross that was just begging to be belted in. Of course, our Deano obliged the 40,000 pilgrims and the rest has brought us to where we are today. Namely, sweating on £7m bids.

All summer long, it was now apparent that City may, just may, be able to capture the England U21 star from the Premier League champions. Everyone knew we were interested, but despite incessant media coverage nothing formal had actually landed on Manchester United's mat until the eve of the recent Wigan game. As deadline day was unfolding, I was watching more in hope than expectation that City were about to pull off what would most certainly be a major coup for a club of our standing. However, there was one minor factor clouding this, as yet untold.

Manchester United want Tottenham Hotspur striker Dimitar Berbatov. Campbell will not be leaving unless Sir Alex gets his man. That was becoming increasingly clear as the reports unfolded throughout the day. But for £30m, surely it was all going to happen? As the day unravels, it now transpires Wigan are interested in signing Campbell. Oh great... and then, as news reporters all around the country are checking in to Sky HQ, confusion descends.

The clock is ticking down, no word. Any mention from Brown or Duffen on the Campbell transfer is simply met with a quote along the lines 'the deal is not dead'. But time is now the enemy. The last hour, even my wife Suzy is entranced and watching. It really is compulsive viewing. I'm still not sure why Stoke fans are standing outside the Britannia Stadium as midnight approached, all giddy and delirious to learn their club have spent less than £5m on two average Championship players in Tom Soares and Michael Tonge, but hey, I'll go along with it.

We're into the last 10 minutes and up to this point none the wiser. Then, a twist to the Dimitar Berbatov transfer comes to fruition. At first the rumour circulating is now beginning to emerge as fact. Fraizer Campbell is going to Tottenham Hotspur. Not bought, probably not even wanted, just loaned out – for the entire season. I'm gutted.

Short of promising us Campbell, Sir Alex Ferguson was mightily impressed with the due diligence Phil Brown afforded his player while on loan with us. Indeed, weekly reports were filed to the Manchester United manager on his progress and that had taken Sir Alex aback on how thorough and respectful we were being towards their player. In not so many words, it had practically paved the way for us to try and sign Campbell. Ferguson had made all the right indications about us doing so. But now? News was breaking the thought of such had been vanquished.

In truth, I feel we may well have become the victim of a broken promise made by the Manchester United boss. The deadline passed. It was now clear Campbell was off on a season-long loan to North London – a fate none of us could really have seen coming – probably not even Sir Alex himself at the start of the day. I couldn't help feeling deflated, though.

The harsh realities of life in the Premier League have bitten hard for manager Phil Brown and chairman Paul Duffen for the second time in a matter of days and left me – the average fan – thinking we really have our work cut out to stay in this league. We've just been thumped 0-5 at home by Wigan and now this. What has been a remarkably dramatic day that has had me avidly watching transfer events unfold has ultimately left me feeling a little disappointed and a trifle raw.

I can't dwell on this any longer. Onwards...

THURSDAY 4TH SEPTEMBER 2008

It has become apparent even in the early days of our Premier League life that matters are done a little differently to elsewhere in the English Football League. Two factors are prevalent. The first is the phenomenal effort needed to gain even a point in the top flight. The second is the two week international break does not then trigger a series of squashed in midweek games like in the Championship and beyond.

However, there is a changing face of Hull City taking place. International breaks now mean international Tigers. Not all of Hull City's players will be getting a rest like we usually found in the Championship. Some of the squad will be participating in World Cup qualifiers for their respective countries over the next few days.

That certainly wasn't the case in the Championship. Yet here in the Premier League more and more of our players are participating in international fixtures. Look at this for an example...

Wales
Boaz Myhill and Sam Ricketts
Australia
Richard Garcia
Hungary
Peter Halmosi
Republic of Ireland
Paul McShane

Guinea
Kamil Zayatte
Gabon
Daniel Cousin

This is quite bizarre. Hull City are sending out seven players on international duty this week. Seriously, the closest we've ever really come to having international stars was Stuart Elliott for Northern Ireland, Ian Goodison and Theodore Whitmore for Jamaica and lets not forget naturalised Cayman Islander Jamie Wood. No laughing, its true. Yet here we are with seven proper, fully-fledged international players leaving the camp this week. Yes, the times really are changing.

MONDAY 8TH SEPTEMBER 2008

Adding insult to injury, it has now emerged Hull City manager Phil Brown is facing a misconduct charge from the Football Association following an incident during the Wigan Athletic 0-5 home defeat at the KC Stadium a week last Saturday...

Apparently the City boss has been cited for kicking a water bottle in anger during our home drubbing and unfortunately for Brown – intentional or not – the bottle in question hit the fourth official.

The FA being the FA, want to pursue the incident formally and has given Phil Brown until the 17th of September to respond to the charge. Sometimes, you really do have to wonder if this is really necessary at all. It's bordering pathetic. Under the circumstances of a 0-5 home loss you would think the FA would be grateful it was only a water bottle.

FRIDAY 12TH SEPTEMBER 2008 –
NEWCASTLE UNITED V HULL CITY PREVIEW

This past week has been quite amusing. All week on Sky Sports News we've watched Newcastle United rip their Premier League club to bits from all quarters. Basically, in a nutshell, Kevin Keegan has walked. No really! I can tell you're all shocked at this revelation but it is true. This is all to do with little Dennis Wise finding the players for the club and Keegan not having the final say. And on that bombshell, Keegan's gone.

What has now emerged is; Mike Ashley – Newcastle's owner – has become public enemy no.1 on Tyneside and the fans are pouring out to vent their anger at Keegan's departure. Sky Sports News is loving this. It is lapping up every second of this latest development. In fairness, so are we. Newcastle's next match is a home game to Hull City. It should be fun for us...

There are reports of mass protests, marches through the town and a "boycoutt" (sic) whatever the hell that is. Rarely has a club disintegrated as rapidly before our very eyes, but tomorrow we travel to Newcastle and I daresay the club can never have been in more turmoil in its history.

The good news for me and my mate is the fact we planned to get the train for this game weeks ago so we can all have a good drink. Now we can also watch the locals squirm in angst. Yet strangely, it's not difficult for us relate to a host of ill-fitting chairmen and owners ruining our club. We're the pastmasters at it.

Incredibly, though, Hull City are still seen as the little club that come up from the Championship. At least that's what all intelligible Geordies are claiming – *"Even so, we should be beating the likes of Hull tomorrow."* is the rough translation. Is that right, eh? Inside, I'm quietly confident. And I'm never usually so bold to state as such as anyone who knows me will testify. But strangely, I am.

Phil Brown is obviously going to make changes to his team from the Wigan debacle last time out in the Premier League and I wouldn't blame him. Marlon King coming back is one change that definitely needs to happen up front. But not many of the players can walk away from that particular match with a valid claim for a definite starting place.

It is going to be very interesting to see what type of atmosphere will develop tomorrow. Will it be a vehement outpouring of anger from the home fans? Will any of the home fans actually bother to attend, instead screaming and shouting obscenities from outside? Or will the sheer frustration of the current situation transmit to the players and ultimately the Geordies will choke, very much to our advantage?

One thing is for sure, I squarely believe there will never be a better time to play Newcastle United this season. I simply can't wait. We could be getting another Premier League win under our belts. And on our travels too.

SATURDAY 13TH SEPTEMBER 2008 – NEWCASTLE UNITED 1-2 HULL CITY – REPORT

I woke up this morning and I'm still feeling fine despite an early morning taxi to the train station. I've never really been a morning person. But with a full English breakfast on the inside and plenty of beer laden on the outside, its Newcastle here we come! Scared? Nah, the Toon are nailed on to bottle it today. Newcastle are traditional welshers whenever in crisis. And believe me, this is a club in crisis...

My Newcastle 'contact' (Ken, Newcastle Rivals editor) guided is safely into the pouch of the Sports Cafe Bar from the train station upon arrival. What an 'interesting' establishment that was. Liverpool v Manchester United was getting roundly cheered all across this tiered boozer and unwitting stags in Borat clad clothing were seduced into drinking competitions only to be bawled at by a Liverpool loving Geordie in a Toon shirt while scantily-clad ladies paraded around. And still they came, like lemmings...

It was a bizarre if somewhat lethal cocktail that somehow worked. Not as deadly as some of the cocktails those slaughtered lambs participating onstage were sampling I'm sure, but it was a good craic all the same and set us up nicely for the trip up the hill to 'SJP' as the locals refer to it. Up Sarah Jessica Parker? Yuk! No thanks.

Getting to the ground with minutes to spare before kick off, the mountaineering gear required to get to your seat really should be a pre-requisite with your ticket. Up in the clouds is almost not an exaggeration. For those interested, there didn't appear much of a boycott going on, but then, this was a 'boycoutt' (sic) after all. What did I know?

So, a red-hot atmosphere, spewing with noise. Hatred was about to pour out like molten lava on the Tigers, as the Toon fans have clearly chosen to get behind their team. Err... nope, actually. Those that had vowed to go to the game and back their side, plainly didn't. And the reason? Ickle Hull City were stroking the ball around the Toon manor liked they owned the place. Meh!

Indeed, in this next paragraph I'm going to detail an unmarked Danny Guthrie bobbling a shot wide from eight yards out and a Michael Owen header from a long punted free kick forcing Myhill to paw the ball from goal, is as good as it got for our hosts. That was Newcastle's sum total of attacking threat in the first half. Pathetic!

So in the interim, little Hull City looked like a team, played like a team and duly reaped rich rewards, like a team. Can you spot a theme here? Peter Halmosi's trickery foxed veteran Nicky Butt in the box to give Hull City a stonewall penalty and Marlon King hit the spot kick hard enough, low enough and accurately enough to beat Shay Given's despairing hand, pushing the ball onto the post's innards before rolling round the net.

Get in! Get in! As the travelling hordes in the gods pierced the Geordie air, the gloom in the home stands descended and set in. Newcastle had the pungent stench of a beaten team already. The penalty had seemingly sealed their fate. But wait! We've only played 35 minutes!

At half time, I was expecting the Newcastle express to railroad the Tigers in the second half. I think it got derailed somewhere near Gateshead. Whatever was said in the two respective dressing rooms, the team coming out fighting, with desire and a passion to win the match was Hull City. Newcastle couldn't even get out their half as the visitors dominated proceedings.

The home side's back four looked like a dog's hind leg and the impressive Peter Halmosi, prompted by the hardworking Marney and Ashbee, was causing serious problems down the left. On the right, it was even worse for Newcastle. Bernard Mendy was on fire! And with the presence of King and the irritating pace of Fagan, Newcastle were second best by some distance.

And City duly got their reward. Bizarrely, Newcastle bombed forward but abandoned defending while doing so. One at the back? Yeah, good tactic! King and Fagan made the hosts pay to scythe through the freedom of Newcastle and the former latched on to a pass in acres of space to turn and shoot into Given's bottom corner for a 0-2 Hull City lead.

I need oxygen. I'm in heaven. No, really I am. I'm so high up! It was completely in tandem with the play. Newcastle can have no complaints. And City pressed. And kept pressing. The home team were done for the day and then the Tigers swung in a corner for Michael Turner to score number three, but the header was ruled out. For what? It had been coming... "MAULED BY THE TIGERS!"

With that, a flurry of Newcastle shirts were thrown onto the pitch in disgust by the fans. It was a desperate gesture, by a troubled club in massive disarray. Newcastle were being pumped by the 'new Derby County of the Premier League' remember. "If we can't beat Hull..." I was hearing pre-match. *GUFFAW*

With City in complete control, mentions should go to Paul McShane for not proving to be the error strewn defender we first thought we'd signed on loan from Sunderland. The Mackem had a corking game on his debut. Anthony Gardner was a composed and reassuring figure at the back with Michael Turner - and Andy Dawson continued to defy all logic with another superb performance.

From one to 11 City were incredible to watch. And remember, this was without George Boateng and Geovanni! So it was somewhat disappointing to see a freak, lucky break allow Newcastle a possible lifeline in the game when Charles N'Zogbia's shot was palmed onto the post by Myhill, but fell kindly to Xisco for a debut goal with nine minutes left.

It would have been a travesty to throw this away now. God no! Newcastle do not deserve a bean out of this match after a truly shocking and, dare I say, gutless display. It should be 0-3, anyway! But alas, the Toon were to be given no reprieve despite an incredible five minutes of injury time added. With just two efforts on target in 90 minutes, what do they expect? The hosts were utterly abysmal.

And as a last act of damnation and frustration, a reckless Danny Guthrie put in an awful tackle on Craig Fagan. Guthrie just decided to kick the player for no apparent reason other than to say 'I am a thug and this is what I tried to do seconds ago, let me get it right this time'-type tackle. It sparked ugly scenes at the end that unsurprisingly, culminated in a red card. Idiot.

The result sparked mass protests outside the ground again with 'SACK THE BOARD' ringing all around. It was nice to be able to smugly collect all the points, grab a beer and safely retreat from a crisis that, for once, wasn't ours!

For those questioning if Newcastle are in turmoil off the pitch, let me tell you this; you're absolutely right – and in it deep too. Yet the fallout out of today has highlighted a bigger problem at the club that nobody had the foresight to accept until now. Newcastle ON the pitch are in dire straits. Do not be deceived by what appears to be a narrow 1-2 home defeat. Frankly, it flattered Newcastle. The gulf between the two sides was yawning.

Newcastle should be thankful for the footballing lesson and defeat little Hull City handed them today. I hope all those Geordies are grateful that ickle old Hull City have ruthlessly exposed a crisis torn club for what they are; namely a club that is rotten to the core. Well, we wouldn't one of the BIG FIVE * wallpapering over the cracks AGAIN would we? Cheers for the points!

* Only applicable in Newcastle

MATCH STATS:
- Newcastle: Given, Edgar (Bassong 68), Taylor, Coloccini, N'Zogbia, Geremi, Butt, Guthrie, Xisco, Owen, Ameobi (Gonzalez 61). Subs Not Used: Harper, Cacapa, Danquah, Doninger, Donaldson.
- Sent Off: Guthrie (90).
- Goals: Xisco 82.
- Hull: Myhill, McShane, Turner, Gardner, Dawson, Mendy (Folan 73), Marney (Hughes 78), Ashbee, Halmosi, King (Zayatte 83), Fagan. Subs Not Used: Duke, Windass, Geovanni, Ricketts.
- Booked: Folan, Halmosi.
- Goals: King 34 pen, 55.
- Att: 50,242.
- Ref: Andre Marriner (W Midlands)
- **Premier League position: 4th**

SUNDAY 14TH SEPTEMBER 2008

I've just watched Match of the Day. Yesterday's tackle on Craig Fagan by Danny Guthrie that resulted in a red card was truly horrific. And it was all so needless too. Not that you could properly see it from our vantage point yesterday. The players looked like pixels.

TUESDAY 16TH SEPTEMBER 2008

Hull City manager Phil Brown has responded to his 'water bottle gate' FA misconduct charge. It is clear though that Brown is seething about matters elsewhere, namely following the Newcastle game.

Brown has publicly slammed Danny Guthrie for a tackle on Craig Fagan that has broken the City's striker leg. Brown has described the incident as 'intolerable'.

Meanwhile it now being reported in the press that Guthrie himself has stated his intention to apologise to the player personally, but the mood surrounding the club, the manager and Fagan himself suggests such a move wouldn't wash well.

On the subject, Brown blasted - *"It cannot be tolerated. **When you see that the end product is him putting a fellow pro in a cast, it's just not right. That's the horrible side of the game.**"*

SATURDAY 20TH SEPTEMBER 2008 - HULL CITY V EVERTON

A Sunday afternoon kick off at 3pm - we really must be Premier League now. I think it is fair to state this is our first BIG test of Hull City's top flight campaign... wait, that was last week against Newcastle, wasn't it?

It might just be me, but Everton at home signals our first 'proper misters' Premier League clash of the season. This is a thoroughbred Premier League side, so reading the jip they've given us on the internet has brought a wry smile to my face. Er, why?

Here we have Everton, needing to take the mick out of ickle old Hull City? Yep, you'd better believe it. I genuinely thought that wouldn't happen. We must be BIG time on Merseyside, eh? I had mistakenly thought, they wouldn't be bothered about us. Perhaps Everton are worried about their trip to the Circle? Nice... nice...

More than anything, or anyone at the club this season, I've been impressed with Phil Brown. The guy is simply inspiring and infectious in his nature. You do 'believe' in the man whatever he conjures up, for any given scenario.

I doubt anyone else would have picked the team the City boss did up at Newcastle. More than a few eyebrows would have been raised if we weren't all dealing with the palpitations of getting to our seats after scaling the St James Park mountain. But Browny was right. City won the match.

Of course, the game was overshadowed by 'that' challenge on Craig Fagan. I'm going to state something we're probably all a little cautious to state so openly, but Fagan will be a huge loss to Hull City while recovering from a broken leg. I don't think anyone could believe the form he was in.

The natural replacement will be Hull City's debutant-in-waiting and deadline day signing from Rangers, Daniel Cousin, who was suspended for the Newcastle game after being sent off in the Old Firm clash. A pacy, niggly, get up the nose of a defender type attacker. And he can score, too.

Now, the obvious choice would be to keep a winning side and make a straight swap for the injured Fagan with Cousin. But while I wouldn't like to hazard a guess at the team and that happening, I bet Browny doesn't do anything like that.

With the creative Geovanni waiting in the wings - a surprise omission from Newcastle - George Boateng back from injury, Richard Garcia fit after a virus and the scourge of Everton, Nick Barmby 'threatening' to beat his calf injury, changes are a sure-fire guarantee. You would think...

Everton will be tired, leggy, jaded, unable to play full strength and have a fully stacked deck of excuses should they lose this match - probably. Me? I think - I hope - Moyes will come across better than that and we see a genuine contest without all this Europe bull cropping up. It was a home game anyway!

In fairness, Victor Anichebe faces a fitness test on the shin injury from the UEFA Cup match with Standard Liege and will be a doubt. Tim Howard should overcome a virus to feature in goal. Plus, midfielder Marouane Fellaini should return for the trip to the Circle - another boost for David Moyes.

I have a lot of respect for Everton. They truly are a proper Premier League club that one day I hope my club, our club, can emulate. Fine standing, fine tradition and a set of supporters who will give as good as they're going to get this Sunday. It's the way football should be. Come on City, let's av it!

SUNDAY 21ST SEPTEMBER 2008 - HULL CITY 2-2 EVERTON - REPORT

Two contrasting halves of football saw the Tigers capitalising on a low-key Everton's first 45 minutes - but thankfully City had enough in the bank to share the spoils - as NATIONAL TIGER reports for City Independent...

In the grand scheme of events, Hull City fans will look back on this result and realise this was a good point earned. Let's not kid ourselves here, Everton are one of the better Premier League sides - and we took a point off them.

The rancour will be prevalent in the short term, because throwing away a two goal lead may well be frowned upon, but we've more than earned Everton's respect during this 90 minutes - and Everton will leave East Yorkshire knowing they have been in a game and needed to be at their best to glean a point.

As ever, Phil Brown kept everyone guessing with his side. Anthony Gardner was an injury kept on the quiet, meaning Kamil Zayatte - an Everton target - gained his Hull City debut as a replacement. And it proved to be an impressive one, with the loan star from Young Boys dominating the aerial battle.

The second change was also enforced with Daniel Cousin also getting his first start, replacing broken leg victim Craig Fagan. So the team lined up with no Geovanni, no Boateng and no Garcia, despite all being fit. Interesting... Oh and for Everton's benefit, of course local lads Nick Barmby and Dean Windass were never going to play, either.

City started the brighter of the two teams with some crisp passing carving the Everton defence open and Peter Halmosi's wide play inducing a series of free kicks down the left channel. The visiting back four looked decidedly dodgy and with 'Bostick' King holding up everything, City had a sniff of something here...

Indeed, Bernard Mendy (can we call him Bendy please?) had a glorious chance to open the scoring with a free header, but planted it straight at Tim Howard in the Everton goal when well placed. Howard looked a bit dodgy actually and with a shaky back four in front... COME ON CITY!

Everton wasted two chances at the other end with Leon Osman side footing wide when free in the box and Mikela Arteta also spurning a good chance. But Mendy's pace got him behind the visiting defence again, only to shoot wide from close range. The Circle cranked up the noise...

A corner to City saw a distinct tactic of nailing the keeper and left Michael Turner criminally unmarked at the back stick to power in a header into the roof of the net from six yards. Who are Premier League now, Everton? The City fans taunted their guests in celebration. 1-0 City and deservedly so.

City kept the pressure up and Cousin and King were providing all manner of problems for the Everton back four. Bendy was exploiting space out wide and the Tigers were urged on by a febrile home crowd leaving the visitors stunned.

Yet nothing could be added before the break and that prompted David Moyes to have a major rethink and induce some serious pack shuffling and a double substitution, with the big guns of Saha and Lescott wheeled out for the second half.

But it didn't pay off in the first instance, with City incredibly doubling their advantage within minutes of the restart from a corner. Marney planted it on Howard once more and with King lurking, Phil Neville unwittingly bundled the ball over his own line to send City 2-0 up.

Now debate ranged in the pub afterwards that hereonin, City bottled it. But for me, that would be a gross underestimation of the effort Everton displayed to get themselves back into the game, rehashing their tactics following a wretched first half.

Everton poured forward and genuinely pushed City back, rather than us just sitting back and choosing to weather the storm. Castillo started dictating the play, finally surpassing the monumental efforts of Dean Marney and Ian Ashbee for us in the middle of the park - but at a valuation worth more than our entire team put together, so he should.

It was desperate from City but for all Everton's new found possession, nothing was coming creativity wise to genuinely threaten Myhill's goal. But all that changed when Tim Cahill slipped his marker and rifled onto the underside of the bar from eight yards. The goal was given by the linesman, but for me, I'll be amazed if the MOTD cameras don't uphold that opinion.

So, at 2-1 Everton were back in it and the muted away following were now roused into getting behind their side. City had their work cut out and the quality laden visitors ripped into City looking for the second.

It duly arrived - and deservedly so - when another foray down City's left allowed a whipped cross to be hooked in by Leon Osman - and from 2-0 down five minutes previously, it was 2-2 and the Tigers were rocking.

Phil Brown made substitutions to steady the ship and arrest the Everton onslaught, as the game then began to peter out. Both teams were probably delighted with their lot for entirely different reasons, like two boxers who had given their all.

When the game ended, a 2-2 draw was about right and for City; they became the first of the newly promoted teams to take a point off the Toffees on their own pitch. Considering Stoke and West Brom will be teams we are undoubtedly in competition with further into this season, perhaps this point earned is bigger than we all realise today. A good point, a fair point and decent game to boot.

MATCH STATS:
- Hull City: Myhill, McShane, Turner, Zayatte, Dawson, Mendy (Garcia 77), Ashbee, Marney, Halmosi, Cousin (Folan 69), King (Boateng 81).
- Subs Not Used: Duke, Geovanni, Hughes, Ricketts.
- Goals: Turner 18, Neville 50 og.
- Everton: Howard, Neville, Jagielka, Yobo, Baines (Lescott 46), Osman, Fellaini, Arteta, Castillo (Saha 46), Cahill, Yakubu (Vaughan 87).
- Subs Not Used: Nash, Nuno Valente, Rodwell, Baxter.
- Booked: Fellaini.
- Goals: Cahill 73, Osman 78.
- Att: 24,845
- Ref: Lee Mason (Lancashire)
- **Premier League position: 7th**

MONDAY 22ND SEPTEMBER 2008

The transfer window may have closed, but Hull City have pulled off a quite a scoop by revealing that Greek wide man Stelios Giannakopoulos has been in negotiations with the club and was present to witness the Tigers claim a 2-2 draw with Everton.

Apparently, manager Phil Brown has come one step closer to signing Stelios after the former Bolton Wanderers star was a guest at the Circle following talks with the City boss. But because Stelios is a free agent the signing would not contravene transfer window regulations which is a real bonus.

Speaking on the proposed move Brown confirmed - *"We're currently talking to Stelios. That's with regards to maybe a contract until the end of the season or possibly until the January transfer window. He has an ambition to play in the World Cup for Greece and he's without a club at the moment."*

Adding on the long term target - *"If we can convince him to sign for us, it will be a no-lose situation for us. He has been a right-sided player and I know him very well. I don't know how long Craig Fagan will take to come back, so to add another player at this stage when the transfer window is closed is a bonus."*

TUESDAY 23RD SEPTEMBER 2008

Stelios signs! And neither have the Tigers flouted the Premier League transfer window rules to capture the Greek star, because the winger was a free agent after being released by Bolton Wanderers at the end of the 2007-08 campaign.

The 34 year old is said to be keen on keeping his international playing career alive with Greece and being attached to a Premier League club getting games, will surely help reignite his international ambitions of reaching another World Cup in 2010.

A good deal all round it seems.

FRIDAY 26TH SEPTEMBER 2008

One man not too happy with how the Premier League campaign is panning out is veteran striker Dean Windass.

Indeed, there has been more than one or two mutterings of discontent from the ageing forward that has led to all sorts of rumours including walk-outs, bust-ups and transfers away from the Tigers. Yet all the talk about Dean Windass leaving Hull City appears wide of the mark according to club chairman Paul Duffen and manager Phil Brown, as the latest reports coming out of the club appear to indicate Deano is in fact staying. This has got to be good news. But he does need to learn to keep his mouth shut.

Answering the speculation Brown claimed - *"I know exactly how Dean Windass thinks and how he feels. Rightly so, he's not happy. In terms of commitment, every time he goes out on the training ground he's a million per cent. If I threw him in tomorrow, he'd be a million per cent."*

The City boss added - *"He has a part to play off the park and that's a leadership quality you only get in certain players. He has to understand that he still has a role to play. If Dean Windass wanted to leave this football club, it would be his decision not mine."*

And chairman Paul Duffen echoed those sentiments to state - *"Where Dean goes in terms of his career from here is no different to any other player. However, from my personal point of view, I really do hope Dean finds a way to be content to stay."*

FRIDAY 26TH SEPTEMBER 2008 - ARSENAL V HULL CITY PREVIEW

Expect nothing. Absolutely nothing. The media, the bookies and the dreaded Setanta cameras all suggest a right royal pasting. Yet I can't help believing anything other than a trouncing, will be a welcome bonus to us...

Let's not kid ourselves here, this is Arsenal. Bloody Arsenal! On their day, the Gunners can tear you a new Ars... ahem. This is a team who fielded a bunch of schoolkids and ripped asunder a full strength Sheffield United side 6-0 in the Carling Cup in midweek. And who's next up? Hull City.

But for crying out loud, this is what the Premier League is all about, isn't it? A huge sell-out travelling band of Tigers, full houses witnessing the best teams in the world and all this in the finest stadia. This is what we all craved, wasn't it? Well I did.

I'm genuinely looking forward to the trip. Yes, yes, we all know what the script says. And yes, the form book points to national humiliation live on the telly - thank god it's only Setanta - but in football you just never, ever know. It's why I/we all love it.

I'm not kidding anyone here when I say this; barring one notable exception that was mitigated by a pretty lengthy sick list, Hull City have performed extremely well in the Premier League, without shame and full of courage.

What will be required at the Emirates is an attitude and mentality that lets Arsenal know that Hull City are not scared. Phil Brown needs a team on the pitch to be committed, full of belief and aggressive - yet fair with it. I can guarantee the fans will be - and any stray Arsenal fans reading this, you will hear us.

Be brave, be bold, stand up to the challenge. Nothing is impossible. Not in football circles. The Tigers can - albeit stacked against very lengthy odds - produce a performance that could glean something from Arsenal. We've all seen that this season, City have stepped up to the plate in the Premier League.

Phil Brown is set to name an experienced group of players for the challenge that seems destined to include Dean Windass after the midweek rumpus over his involvement in first team affairs. Geovanni is another who will be pushing for a starting place also.

However, Anthony Gardner will not be included after failing to overcome his thigh injury. That means Kamil Zayatte will undoubtedly keep his place alongside Michael Turner in the centre of defence. Stelios Giannakopoulos has failed to make the fitness grade after joining the club in midweek and, disappointingly, will have to wait a little longer for his debut.

Phil Brown speaking ahead of the fixture stated he intends to adopt a physical approach – *"Last week Arsenal were unhappy with a tackle from Kevin Davies but there was nothing wrong with it. If you allow Arsenal to dictate that tackle goes out of the game, then we are finished."*

And then warned – *"We have got that tackle on our side - they have got the technical side of the game on their side. If they are allowed to express that technical side without tackling, without physical contact, we might as well not turn up."*

Well, for me, Phil Brown is absolutely spot on. You have to play to your strengths. Our greatest weapons are hard work, closing down and being strong in the tackle. Therefore, we bring these traits to Arsenal. We know what the Gunners can do, but are they prepared for us?

Arsenal manager Arsène Wenger will welcome back Gaël Clichy after a bruised shin sustained in 'that' tackle to which Phil Brown referred. Alex Song will recover from his hip injury and Mikele Silvestre is in line for his debut after signing from Manchester United. That said, one piece of bad news sees midfielder Samir Nasri ruled out with a knee injury.

Surprisingly, Arsène Wenger was very gracious towards the Tigers with his pre match comments – *"In every single game I believe the first importance is to focus on us being at our best and to cope with any difficulty which the opponents give us."*

He complimented the visitors with – *"You can take your hat off to Hull, because what they have done up to now is fantastic. They are the surprise package. It is a warning to us because we want an Arsenal side to be at our best to beat them."*

Yep, I nearly fell off my chair too. Arsenal (a) - bring it on!

SATURDAY 27TH SEPTEMBER 2008 - ARSENAL 1-2 HULL CITY - REPORT

No, your eyes are not deceiving you. Neither have I had one too many sherbets. This really is an accurate scoreline. Hull City have won at the Emirates and beaten Arsenal. You can pick yourself up off the floor now...

Vindicated. Read the match preview for the Arsenal game again. What did I tell you? What did I tell you all? Commitment, courage, desire and passion. Put them all together and you will always have a chance, no matter who you play. This Saturday, Hull City stitched the full kit and caboodle together and reaped the richest of Premier League rewards.

Phil Brown talked a courageous game ahead of squaring up to counterpart Arsène Wenger, bold play, brave tactics and a football philosophy that would be geared up to take on Arsenal. At the Emirates. That's the Premier League leaders, folks. Has Browny gone mad? The sellout travelling contingent made the journey south in hope rather than expectation. The pre-match chatter in the Twelve Pins opposite Finsbury Park tube station was all about respect. Playing for pride and honour and keeping the score down to an acceptable level. Arsenal should be grateful we did that for them. *ruddy barefaced cheek alert*

But back to the gaffer. Phil Brown must have balls of steel - and an unshakeable belief in his squad. I have nothing other than admiration for him. Get this; City played 4-3-3 at Arsenal. I'm not kidding, 4-3-3! At Arsenal! As Everton fans would say... 'You whoppers'

Myhill was in goal. The back four was Dawson left, McShane right, Turner and Zayatte at the back. To a man, each was superb. In the middle, it was a tough tackling trio of George Boateng, Ian Ashbee and Dean Marney. This particular threesome bust lungs for the cause. You know, a few detractors used to mock the prospect of Ashbee up against Fàbregas. Could you imagine that? Not any more. Not on this performance. Our inspirational leader was simply magnificent.

At the head of the field, the three pronged attack saw a brave move of playing Geovanni just behind a front two of Marlon King and Daniel Cousin. If that's not gutsy, then show me what is. These three had a duty to defend from the front. With this brassy formation, there would be no hiding place for any shirkers - and to their credit, there weren't any. But this was still a huge gamble, needing exceptional courage to pull it all off. This could end in tears, or...

A boisterous Hull City contingent made themselves heard. Thank god we were at the Emirates because the place would be like a morgue without us. Hopefully, you could all hear us back in the homeland too, with Setanta screening the game. Arsenal predictably started on the front foot. Nice passing, pretty football but unquestionably under pressure from the busy visitors. Browny had asked his troops to get in the faces of Arsenal - and to a man they all did.

But let's set the record straight here. City did not pack ten men in the box. Nor were they here for the point. The Tigers were having a genuine go. Talk about playing with fire! Yet Browny had ingrained into his players to match Arsenal and play without fear. And here we are at the Emirates, squaring up to bleeding Arsenal! Ballsy is the word. Come on City, come on!

And while it remained 0-0 the City contingent got louder. Turner and Zayatte cut out all inroads into the box, Dawson amazingly clung to the coat tails of the frighteningly quick Walcott and McShane's commitment to win every ball shone through.

Meanwhile, Dean Marney got forward, got back, got everywhere. The lad must have lungs the size of hot air balloons. My man of the match, I think. But hey, there were 14 heroes out on the pristine pitch including the subs. When Myhill was called into action, he was there. Decisive, bold and brave. Ah, those words again. Yes, a bit of theme was developing here. Did I tell you it is still 0-0?

Arsenal grew frustrated. City were forcing the odd corner to frustrate the hosts ever more and Geovanni was justifying his selection by making the ball stick - like King and Cousin to be fair - all holding the ball up to allow others into play. This is at Arsenal by the way. Still 0-0 here, remember... 3 minutes, 7 minutes, 12 minutes, 19 minutes, 26 minutes... yep, still 0-0.

Adebayor had an effort ruled out well before the ball hit the net for a foul - rightly given. We're not playing rugby here, fellow. But the Gunners were guilty yet again of that age old criticism levelled at them; namely, trying to walk the ball in the net. Why? Just bleeding shoot! Eboué was majorly guilty of this before the break when truly opening City up for the first time, but astoundingly he left 60,000 fans inside the Emirates aghast when electing to square it to Van Persie with the goal at his mercy. Huh? Snuffed out, chance gone... Well, cheers all the same!

Referee Alan Wiley peeped his whistle, half time was here. And neither was it the huge sigh of relief to hear it that you would think. Arsenal had been fading gradually as the half had worn on. City's 'in your face' tactics had reaped some reward. 0-0 at the Emirates? Surely, some mistake? Two things were joked about over the half time pint. At least the action will be up this end second half *blatant lie alert* and Arsenal were going to bring on Wednesday's junior side for the second half that had walloped Sheffield United 6-0 in the Carling Cup to remedy the 'faulty' score line. *big fat porky alert*

Well, in all honesty, I expected the onslaught to arrive in the second half. Arsenal to be the rabid dogs tearing the visitors to shreds. Who wouldn't? And sure enough a goal arrived for the hosts. It was a horribly scrappy, bundled affair that was so uncharacteristically not Arsenal. So we are led to believe... Fàbregas drilled it, ricochet, ping, pong - hooked away! ...But alas it was already in - I think it was own goal in the end. Arsenal took it, though. They knew they were in a real game here. Oh well, it had been fun while it lasted at 0-0. Let's keep it respectable, eh?

Arsenal were suddenly fluent. Crisp in the pass, sharp at the top. Uh-oh, there could be trouble ahead... City had to endure a some creaky moments at the back while Arsenal went hunting for the second. But the spirit in the visitors was something to behold. It was testament to what Phil Brown is trying to achieve here.

And after weathering the storm for the next ten minutes or so, the response by Hull City was gigantic. King, Cousin and Geovanni cranked up their game and assisted by a willing midfield trio the Tigers hit back - hard. As Arsenal stood off their guests, Hull City were about to make them pay. And dearly.

Geovanni was given time to receive a ball on the City left. Incredibly, like most of the game he remained unchecked. The Brazilian ran at Arsenal - and kept running. "SHOOT!" screamed the away end. So he did. PICK - THAT - OUT! What a goal! It was a wonder strike into the far top right corner. Ladies and gentleman, I give you September's goal of the month. Cue madness. Cue delirium. Cue unexpected territory. BUZZING!

But hold the back page. The Tigers were not done here, oh no. Phil Brown's men kept coming. Sure Arsenal looked great, always a threat, breaking at lightning speed, but City stood tall. And they were about to stand even taller. I know, I'm still 200 miles from home and I can't believe I'm about to write this next bit... but it's not a dream, it's all fact. It really, really did happen...

Daniel Cousin wriggled free of the fabled Arsenal back four and bore down on goal unleashing a shot that deflected wide. As the corner was whipped in devilishly towards Almunia's grasp, Cousin nipped in first and flicked it beyond the Arsenal custodian and into the far corner of the net. WHAT - THE! 1-2 City! At Arsenal! The league leaders at the start of the day! From 1-0 down! I'm bouncing. High on football adrenaline. WELCOME TO THE PREMIER LEAGUE! WE ARE 'ULL!

Now, rather unsporting timing, there was still bloody half an hour to go. That's not on. The pressure was truly now on. Brown and Wenger were feverishly changing tactics and a flurry of tit-for-tat substitutions did more for City than Arsenal thank god, proving to be a disruption than assist fluency. Time ticked on... and err... we're winning this? Un-be-live-able!

But the clock wasn't ticking quick enough. It never does when you're winning away from home, miles from the land of our fathers. It was going backwards at Arsenal. Amidst the senility of it all, I had to spare a thought for the immense Andy Dawson at left back. He waves off Walcott, only to see Vela, the hat-trick whizkid from midweek, come on. Poor lad. But Dawson didn't shirk the challenge. Indeed, nobody flinched in black and amber. Van Persie though... jeez NO... NO! Incredibly put wide from just yards, how?

Time kept ticking. Wenger was getting agitated on the Gunners bench. Grrr! Losing to Hull City! Gnash those teeth some more Arsène. Arsenal rounded on City once more, the Tigers repelled everything that the might of the Gunners could chuck at them. It was getting tantalisingly close now, so, so near. Please, please hang on City. COME ON! Another corner, Gallas header... hits the bar, the rebound... hacked clear! Phew...

Four minutes of injury time on the board... A precious free kick is won - more time killed by City. Myhill plucks another dangerous cross out the air - massive cheers in the away end. It is so damn near now... Fàbregas picks it up, piles in on goal, pulls the trigger 20 odd yards out... BADOOM... BADOOM... that's my heart... shattered...? It's arrowing in... but NO! Myhill leaps at full tilt and paws the ball over! WOW! Corner comes in... away! And then, and then... the whistle.

Hull City had done it. The result of the day - the season in fact. I can't believe I'm scribing this. But read it, cherish it, savour it. Our team - Hull City - beat Arsenal fair and square. Arsenal 1-2 Hull City. Dare to dream? You'd better believe it. But above all it was earned, it was deserved and crucially it was no fluke.

Hull City wanted it more. But then, you know that because fortunately, this match was broadcast to the entire nation. An audience left agog at this astonishing Hull City performance. How proud are we?

MATCH STATS:
- Arsenal: Almunia, Sagna, Touré, Gallas, Clichy, Eboué (Bendtner 69), Fàbregas, Denilson, Walcott (Vela 77), Adebayor, Van Persie. Subs Not Used: Fabiański, Ramsey, Song Billong, Silvestre, Djourou.
- Booked: Sagna, Gallas.
- Goals: McShane 51 og.
- Hull City: Myhill, McShane, Zayatte, Turner, Dawson, Marney, Boateng (Garcia 76), Geovanni (Hughes 72), Ashbee, Cousin (Mendy 80), King. Subs Not Used: Duke, Halmosi, Folan, Ricketts.
- Booked: Ashbee.
- Goals: Geovanni 62, Cousin 66.
- Att: 60,037
- **Premier League position: 6th**

SUNDAY 28TH SEPTEMBER 2008

This is the day after the night before. I am numb. I am in shock. The Sundays, the radio, Setanta, Sky, the internet, the whole bloody world (and I do mean the whole bloody world) have heard the name of Hull City now.

It's not sinking in. Like Wembley back in May, my head is a bit woozy, and not just because of the copious quantity of beer nailed all the way back home. I feel ten feet tall to be honest. I've spent the day watching Geovanni's stunning goal and admiring the accuracy of Daniel Cousin's winning header four minutes later over and over again.

The press and pundits are tripping over themselves to compliment us. Match of the Day are truly speechless at our incredible feat. I am trying to think of a time when I have been more proud of my team. I am struggling, Wembley included.

On the internet, from Afghanistan to Zimbabwe, they have all got something to say on the magnificent **Arsenal 1-2 Hull City** scoreline. I'll say it again, if only because I can **Arsenal 1-2 Hull City**. You know what? I'll let you into a little secret; I can't get bored of this. Indeed, let's say it again! **Arsenal 1-2 Hull City**. How can you ever get bored of that?

Yet of all the articles written on a truly historic day, the one that never fails to put a beaming smile upon my face is the story about Arsène Wenger post-match. The poor Frenchman felt more than a little queasy. What a shame!

The realisation the Hull City have turned up on his manor, outbattled his troops and trundled off with all the points by being more committed than his own side has left the Gunners boss feeling physically sick... Unbelievable! But true! Wenger was simply unable to stomach the result post match, after watching his glittering array of stars washed up by the Tigers.

Aside from counting the cost of defeat, Wenger was forced to accept the ramifications of losing to Hull City has cast serious doubts on their title chances - *"I don't know if we can afford to lose again. We don't know how costly it could be but they were committed and it was a good lesson for us. We now know that if our attitude isn't right, we can lose games."*

Wenger added - *"What we delivered against Hull was not good enough - we know that - so the important thing now is not how many games we can lose this season but preparing well for Tuesday night."*

Before dejectedly continuing - *"You can never afford defeats. We had a good chance to go top of the league but at the end of the day, if we had had the same level of concentration as Hull we would have won the game."*

And the Gunners boss was left bitterly recalling an unpleasant experience after a French League game earlier in his career with - *"There's nothing to celebrate, even if we had won. There were certainly enough ingredients in the game to make me physically sick again!"* Excuse me for a moment but... *"Ppppppprrrrrrrrfffffffffffftttttt!"*

CHAPTER 3 – LONDON 0 HULL 4

SATURDAY 4TH OCTOBER 2008 – TOTTENHAM HOTSPUR V HULL CITY PREVIEW

When I started writing this book, I'll confess it would have been beyond my wildest dreams that I ever thought I would be writing; 'Can City make it a north London double inside eight days?' When the fixtures first came out, everyone just looked at the Arsenal (a) and Tottenham (a) games as 'nil pointers'. Yet here we are genuinely contemplating the prospect of Hull City conquering Tottenham Hotspur, following our magnificent victory at Arsenal just over a week ago.

The real irony is; nothing pleases a Spurs fan more than seeing Arsenal get done over on their own patch – aside from a Tottenham win of course. Yet maybe, in the back of these Spurs fans' minds, there is a little alarm bell ringing and it's warning that the Tigers are coming next. Incredibly, the team at the bottom of the Premier League is not us. It's Spurs.

Now, for me, this is almost unfathomable. Something truly remarkable would have to happen for any Spurs fan to have the merest hint of worry at the prospect of Hull City arriving. Well, as all can now see, the Tigers are indeed the Premier League's surprise package, after a blistering start to their first ever season in the top flight.

Incredibly – and I cannot believe I am writing this – Hull City are unbeaten away from home in the Premier League. Ever. This is after coming from behind to draw at Blackburn, sweeping troubled Newcastle aside and then, then... hell... then beating Arsenal at the Emirates. Take a moment to digest all that. Mad, eh?

Now seeing Spurs prop up the table, yet to win a match this season, believe me, I've been watching City long enough to know this has got warning lights and everything leaping out at me. City are notoriously poor against lower opposition (Spurs = lower opposition!) and good at handing out gifts.

What City need is a spirit and resolve to take each game as it comes. A mentality that forgets the Arsenal match – that's been and gone. Instead, all efforts are now focussed on beating Spurs. Nothing else. Tactics will change, the formation will too and so will the team. Quite right in my opinion. I am convinced Phil Brown has been ensuring the players keep their feet firmly grounded.

The main concern for the City boss is whether striker Marlon King can overcome the back spasms that have prevented him from training this week. Former Spurs star Nick Barmby is reportedly in contention for a place on the bench after overcoming injury, but another former favourite Anthony Gardner is not expected to be risked. Dean Marney – yet another ex player – should start, though.

Manager Phil Brown stated ahead of the fixture – *"It's not going to be easy but the key to any success is that first goal. Just because we've beaten a team like Arsenal doesn't mean to say anybody's going to take their foot off the gas."*

Meanwhile, Tottenham pose a genuine interest for the club, as it is widely regarded as chairman Paul Duffen's team before he became involved with Hull City. Plus, to add to the numerous other connections, the Dawson brothers could come face to face if Juande Ramos selects Andy's brother Michael.

The Spurs boss is likely to make changes that will see Roman Pavyluchenko and Vedran Ćorluka recalled after Thursday's trip to Poland in the UEFA Cup. That could mean former Tigers loanee Fraizer Campbell dropping back to the bench. Ledley King could well be rested after the punishing European trip and Alan Hutton will definitely be out with a foot injury.

But, there is one point that is nagging away at me, aside from the Dawson brothers, ex-players, former Tigers stars playing for the home team, plus Spurs yet to win and Hull City yet to lose on the road in the Premier League – and it is this...

In the bible, when Delilah shaved off Samson's hair, he lost all his strength. Phil Brown and the players have bravely gone through September's 'tashback' campaign for the Everyman charity ... but all the facial hair has now gone. Um... what now for City on the field of play? Surely, we should have carried on! Jeez, what am I talking about? Shave off...

SUNDAY 5TH OCTOBER –
TOTTENHAM HOTSPUR 0-1 HULL CITY – REPORT

Ok, I'm shocked. Phil Brown – for the first time this season – picked the exact same starting XI that were victorious at Arsenal. I expected a slight tinkering of the team and tactics that triumphed over the Gunners at the Emirates eight days ago, at the very least. I still can't believe I can write that and now it's a fact! Hell...

Yet the manager didn't want to disturb a winning line-up. With Marlon King being declared fit enough to play, the eleven that caught the world's attention last weekend were thrust into the volatile climate hovering over the white side of north London. Surely, not more points in the offing? At White Hart Lane?

The hosts are having a miserable time and still seek their first Premier League victory. It's now October. And the meagre two points Tottenham do hold are keeping them firmly rooted to the foot of the table. Is there some mistake? Have the roles been reversed? Writing this about Spurs and not City is... strange.

Arsenal and Spurs may only be a few tube stops apart, but there was a wholly different atmosphere upon our return from eight days previous. Back then it was a gorgeous, sunny Saturday. The beer flowed, the fans were politely curious about our great start and some decent banter was to be had.

Now, the tube to this game was low key and progressive and didn't take us to the ground due to engineering works. The rain was pouring outside. It was dull, grey and depressing. A good 30 minute walk ended with a swift beer in the Antwerp Arms in sodden clothes and the mood was distinctly sombre and much less friendly. Indeed, there was an edge. Spurs fans were deeply troubled by their plight and you got the impression that losing to Hull City could well be the tipping point. A far cry from a week ago.

No point in hanging around, our beer was downed and it was on to the game. The Tigers have played some good football, stuck to their strategic game plan and defended with discipline. These have been the secrets of our early season success and perhaps, one day soon, an opponent might just twig. I had nagging doubts it would be Tottenham – particularly with the team's desperation for a win.

The rain continued to lash down on a grim day in north London. The visitors were prepared to go toe-to-toe with their illustrious guests – like last week – and attempt to play football in abysmal conditions. The manager wanted to attack a winless Spurs side who were desperate to turn over *"Mighty Hull – These bastards beat Arsenal last week"* as one Londoner bizarrely put it.

The first real chance fell to Hull City in the opening minutes when Geovanni wriggled between a dallying Spurs defence and lifted the ball up and over the advancing Gomes, but unfortunately for the Tigers over the bar. It was an early warning sign.

Spurs hit back with Gareth Bale barrelling forward down the left and Aaron Lennon likewise on the right. A sodden game slipped from one end of the pitch to the other with both teams up for the fight, but the Tigers were comfortably winning the terrace banter.

A foul on Marlon King produced a free kick for City 30 yards out. Geovanni hovered over the ball. I'm thinking; 'surely he's not going to shoot!' From there? But that Spurs wall looks a) in the wrong position. b) not very well constructed. And c) what postal district is keeper Gomes standing in? What are Spurs doing? This could end in tears... The brilliant Brazilian Geovanni steps up... SMACK! Pace, bend, precision... GOAL! Top corner screamer! YEEESSSSSS! It just had to happen!

I'm not sure what my team have done to be lavished by the footballing gods, but I'm not stopping to think about that at this precise juncture because Geovanni has just submitted his monthly subscription for goal of the month – again – and October is only five days old. Plus, I'm going mental and in grave danger of tumbling down the steps, never to be seen again.

Spurs roared back as you would expect with lots to prove – and at home. It was surreal watching Fraizer Campbell in a white Tottenham shirt. It didn't seem right. He doesn't look as happy in London as he did in Hull. *"SIGNED FOR A BIG CLUB! YOU SHOULD'VE SIGNED FOR A BIG CLUB!"* the City fans taunt Spurs with. Of course, he had little choice in the matter.

But with City lauding it with these new Premier League super-powers bestowed on us that sees us humbling some of the greatest clubs in the world in their own back yard, the funniest chant while leading 0-1 at Spurs was – *"ARE YOU ARSENAL IN DISGUISE?"* Even the Spurs fans had to concede that was funny and greeted the chant with a polite round of applause and a chuckle, despite their own desperate predicament.

Tottenham rained balls into the City box but Lennon and Bale lacked the sort of genuine accuracy that would trouble the visiting defence. Modrić looks talented but lacks a real penetrative trait to his game. Meanwhile the home strikers are shorn of some proper service it seems. It all begins to piece together quite why Spurs are rooted to the bottom of the league.

Gareth Bale stands over a disputed free kick from 30 yards out. Ashbee has received his customary yellow card. Rubbish decision, he's slain men for less. Tottenham's Welsh youngster lashes the ball towards goal in the squally wind and rain... Myhill gets fingertips onto it and helps the rasping drive onto the bar and over for a corner. Phew!

Tottenham's delivery into the box is continually poor and the threat is coming to nothing as City form a seemingly impregnable wall around the goal and Myhill. The Tigers break away and the best passing move of the game so far sees Marney swivelling to shoot from the edge of the box and crashing the inside of the post. So damn near! Lucky, lucky, Spurs. At the other end, the home side pile in once more and a shot is spearing goalwards but incredibly, Michael Turner - England's next centre back - gets his body in the way and deflects the pacy drive onto the post and the ball is hacked clear. Outstanding defending, nothing we aren't accustomed to these days where Turner is concerned, though.

At half time, the Tigers lead 0-1 and if this is a dream don't wake me up. Later on the tube home, a kindly Chelsea fan - who saw his team beat Aston Villa 2-0 - commented that the announcer at the Bridge bellowed the half time score out from the Lane FOUR times it was that good. Each time to rapturous cheers, I might add. Nice one!

The second half was a different story altogether. Spurs had to chuck everything at City - and without Pavlyuchenko who had retired midway through the first half injured. Darren

Bent came on, David Bentley too and even some other nondescript Geovanni (though spelled differently, and of the Dos Santos variety)...

Yet it was all to no avail. Despite manfully forcing City onto the back foot and clearly looking like they want to play for Juande Ramos, the home team couldn't get a ball into the box to truly threaten the visitors. And when they did - Modrić squaring to Bent being one chance - Turner was there to snuff it out with a courageous block.

The golden chance for Spurs to level arrived when Darren Bent finally evaded the offside flag and bearing down on goal should've buried his one-on-one chance. Look away now... Bent missed the target and in that hapless moment, you could sense it just wasn't meant to be Spurs' day.

Indeed, as the hosts pressed, Marlon King had a great chance to kill the game with a similar chance after substitute Peter Halmosi's neat pass cut the Tottenham back four in two but Gomes thwarted the goalbound effort and Spurs were relieved and reprieved.

But for all Spurs' dominance, territory and possession in the second half it smacked of desperation. Frustration set in and when Fraizer Campbell feebly attempted to win a penalty from the man in the penalty spotlight Rob Styles, you knew Tottenham had cashed in their lot and were going to be leaving a rain-soaked Lane pointless.

Right at the very death the fine Hull City defensive work was almost unpicked when a needless free kick was given away 30 yards out. Gareth Bale once more stood over the ball. Surely not? No! The shot sailed wide and the whistle blew. What an amazing result 0-1 at White Hart Lane. This is bordering silly now. Hull City are third! WOW!

The City fans rejoiced and cheekily unfurled a banner that had Alan Sugar's famous words emblazoned across it. 'JUANDE RAMOS - YOU'RE FIRED!' Whether that comes true or not only time will tell. But one thing does need to be said, Spurs did want to play for him today. If they could find a better ball in - and perhaps finish... Ssshh! It's not for me to say, or my problem. Thankfully...

Meanwhile, I'm back on the M1 again, basking in the glory of another three points taken from capital opposition. Six points from Arsenal (a) and Tottenham Hotspur (a) in a week. Nobody, but nobody, could have predicted that when the fixtures came out. Come on, hands up all those who said no points? I'm guiltily raising my hand...

What more adulation can I heap on the team? Phil Brown, you sir, are a genius. And incredibly, I told him so in person at the service station outside Cockfosters tube station. I know, I know, don't ask! Brilliant City, brilliant! You're doing the Premier League and Hull City proud. Keep up the excellent work. And now we can stay in third for two whole weeks thanks to the international break. Get in! And savour it!

MATCH STATS:
- Tottenham: Gomes, Gunter (Bentley 55), Ćorluka, Woodgate, Bale, Lennon (Giovani 74), Jenas, Zokora, Modrić, Pavlyuchenko (Bent 35), Campbell.
- Subs Not Used: Cesar, Dawson, O'Hara, Assou-Ekotto.
- Booked: Jenas, Lennon, Bent, Campbell.
- Hull City: Myhill, McShane, Turner, Zayatte, Dawson, Marney, Ashbee, Boateng, Geovanni (Halmosi 71), King (Folan 81), Cousin (Mendy 60).
- Subs Not Used: Hughes, Duke, Garcia, Ricketts.
- Booked: Ashbee, Boateng.
- Goals: Geovanni 9.
- Att: 36,062
- Ref: Rob Styles (Hampshire)
- **Premier League position: 3rd**

MONDAY 10TH OCTOBER 2008

A proud moment is realised. Hull City manager Phil Brown has been named as the Barclays Premier League 'Manager of the Month' for September, after a string of stunning results in the top flight saw City remain unbeaten throughout the month.

It's an astonishing achievement when you consider it was built on the platform of a 0-5 home drubbing to Wigan at the end of August. But shooting down the crisis-torn Magpies up at St James Park saw the Tigers capture a creditable 1-2 away win. Then followed a home game with Everton that saw City race into a 2-0 lead, before the Toffees rescued a deserved point with two late goals.

To round off the month just a week later, the Tigers travelled to London to square up to their first fixture against one of the alleged 'big four' and Brown's bold tactics of attacking at the Emirates with a 4-3-3 formation paid enormous dividends that saw the Tigers shock the football world to come from 1-0 down to triumph 1-2 over Arsenal.

It is only Phil Brown's second ever month in the Premier League – indeed the club's also – but undoubtedly, few could argue that this month's winner has not deserved the accolade. Very well done Phil Brown!

MONDAY 13TH OCTOBER 2008

We're really going big time. It's been announced those Hull City fans that will miss out on tickets for the Manchester United away fixture on Saturday 1st November will perhaps be pleased to learn the club have successfully negotiated a beam back of the game to take place.

Countless fans are desperate to the see the game at Old Trafford and share our notable Premier League success – and now chairman Paul Duffen has responded to the demand. All fans will at least get the opportunity to see the match, even if they are unsuccessful in gaining a ticket.

Duffen has confirmed the club will have permission from both Manchester United and the Premier League to host a live beam back of the game at the KC Stadium, in line with the 3pm kick off at Old Trafford.

Of course, the allocation for the fixture has seen the Tigers receive just 3,000 tickets – all fully subscribed before a single ticket has even been issued. So far, the club have been using a controversial ballot system to distribute Premier League away tickets – an argument that appears to be gathering speed the closer time gets to issue the Manchester United allocation. The main argument being, the system is far from transparent.

However, the beam back is a small piece of good news for those wanting to see the game. Fans have been told they can pay cash on the turnstiles priced at £10 per adult and £5 concessions for the DeVries Honda West Stand upper and lower, with the game being shown on the North Stand television screen. Despite myself being in the 'Away Direct' scheme (an automatic ticket distribution facility) this is good news.

But beam backs? We must be Premier League, we must be.

SATURDAY 18TH OCTOBER – HULL CITY V WEST HAM UNITED PREVIEW

It's been a month since we've last played at home. And since then, City appear to have set the Premier League tongues wagging with two astonishing away victories against a couple of London's finest. Bring on the Hammers…

Since the 2-2 home draw with Everton – that if we're honest we should've won – a month has passed that really has made the Premier League sit up and take notice of the 'upstarts' from the Championship who sneaked in via the play-offs.

With good reason mind, tomorrow's opponents aside, Hull City are the only team to win at the Emirates in the Premier League. And certainly the only team I can remember in the modern day to come from behind and beat the mighty Arsenal on their own muck.

Indeed, following that up with a fine 0-1 away victory at hapless Tottenham Hotspur, suddenly the eyes of the sporting world it seems are scrutinising the team that are lodged in third spot in the Premier League. 'Hull City? Who are they?'

I've said this before and I'll repeat it for the umpteenth time; should any stray Irons be reading this; we're not getting giddy here in Hull with our league position. We've not gone all 'big time Charlie', neither are we under any illusions how hard this league is. We got that message nice and early.

Victorious at Newcastle, Arsenal and Spurs we may be, and it is the Premier League's manager of the month will be on your opposing bench this Sunday, but that's all been and gone to us, West Ham fans. Welcome to a focussed, organised, well-drilled unit that the sum of the parts make a difficult team to beat. There's no hidden facade with our team. What you see, is what you get. Traditional qualities I like to call them. Old fashioned values.

Hull City's penchant to pass and move and instigate attacks will be backed by a febrile crowd. A sell-out gathering ready to salute their heroes after some dazzling away form. The roar from the Circle faithful will make the hairs stand up on the back of your neck. Well, it's been a month since our charges left these City walls and pillaged our supposed betters in the capital. They will be heralded.

And our battle hardened heroes need to be ready, because City boss Phil Brown has blown away the stereotypical image of West Ham to state the following ahead of the match. *"We have got a very difficult game on Sunday against a team that is underestimated. They are a very physical team."*

Adding – *"A lot of people think West Ham are a ball-playing team, a passing team – that is what they are renowned and famed for. I have statistics that point towards a very physical encounter. I am expecting one hell of a battle, not a pretty game of football. I hope we do get an opportunity to play some football but I am expecting probably one of the biggest battles of the season."*

All rather curious, eh? Or is it a testament to a Premier League manager who is not assuming anything? Phil Brown leaves no stone unturned and appears to be paying an incredible amount of attention to detail to ensure Hull City not only survive, but compete in the top flight. Marvellous, eh?

News on the injury front suggests striker Marlon King is winning his battle to be fit to face the Hammers. Nick Barmby appears ready to return to action, while Anthony Gardner is also back in contention after recent injury. However, Stelios Giannakopoulos will not feature for a debut, as the Greek international continues to build up his match fitness having only recently signed.

Our guests are in a similar position with their own 'out of window' signing Diego Tristan not quite ready to feature. Also, it will be too early for Lee Bowyer and James Collins to enter the fray for the Hammers while both regain full fitness from injury.

New West Ham United boss Gianfranco Zola had this to say ahead of the trip north – *"At this moment they are certainly a team to respect and to appreciate. They have had some very good results and got them by playing very well."*

Before adding – *"Obviously we want to break their dream and we will be trying our best to do that but we know we are going to be facing a team that is in good shape. But after the defeat we have just had [1-3 at home to Bolton] I know we will come back strongly."*

It's all shaping up for a rather tasty clash by the looks of things. I can't wait for my Sunday lunch. And hopefully, but not expectantly, embracing more points for the Hull City cause.

SUNDAY 19TH OCTOBER –
HULL CITY 1-0 WEST HAM UNITED – REPORT

At the beginning of the day – honestly – I would've settled for a point. Just don't lose. But once again, Hull City's meteoric leap of faith from the Championship into the Premier League has left everyone aghast. Today's visitors were West Ham United. London clubs, eh? Don't you just love 'em? Hull City's mesmeric record against the capital's finest is nothing short of jaw dropping. Fulham, Arsenal and Tottenham Hotspur. All beaten – now you can add West Ham United to the set for a maximum twelve points from twelve against London opposition. Did the Housemartins, the iconic Hull band, know something we didn't?

But let's not kid ourselves, or get ahead of the grand scheme of things here. This was an industrious performance - as Phil Brown rightly predicted pre-game. City had to work overtime for their victory, yet had the presence of mind and commitment needed to see a tough job through.

Brown kept the same side in place for the third game in succession, something of a luxury - or maybe a rarity in the Premier League. And the troops were warmly received after their capital double header had yielded a full and welcome six points while on the road.

City fizzed on a natural high to begin with. Yet the visitors were certainly not here for the jolly and gradually wrestled control of the match from the Tigers with a five man midfield swamping Hull City's three of Ashbee, Boateng and Marney. The trio worked hard – and needed to – but simply couldn't compete.

Had City been rumbled? The 4-3-3 formation that served the Tigers so well previously; was it about to fall apart? Well actually, no. Ashbee, Marney and Boateng rolled up their collective sleeves and battled manfully against a possession-dominant, if somewhat blunt, West Ham attack.

At the other end, when the three spearheading City got a sniff, King and Cousin won enough ball to suggest they would be a threat, Geovanni had the visiting back four on the turn around when holding court, but the chances were at a premium. So, stalemate ensued in the main.

For City, a sharp volley from Daniel Cousin flashed wide, while Carlton Cole could only find keeper Boaz Myhill when well placed. Marney was inspirational in the middle and had two efforts from distance to let West Ham know they were in a game, but neither seriously troubled Robert Green.

With the game nearing the break – and City somewhat flagging with the monumental effort put in attempting to contain West Ham in the middle – Bellamy missed the best chance of the game, firing high and wide from close range after Carlton Cole's knock down. In truth, I was pretty glad it was 0-0 at the break.

Yet the second half was a different story. City found renewed energy and a sharpness to their football. West Ham became more laboured and lacked their first half swagger. Maybe fatigue, maybe frustration at not finding a way through, but the break had certainly hampered the visitors and helped the hosts.

With King smashing a volley just wide, that served as a signal of what was to come. City tore into their guests with Phil Brown's words clearly ringing in their ears and a Dawson corner was expertly swung in for Michael Turner to power a header into the back of the net. GET IN! 1-0 City and the stadium exploded.

The mouthy Hammers fans had been taunting us with *"YOU'RE GOING DOWN WITH THE TOTTENHAM!"* yet strangely, they had gone silent now. City fans reminded our guests of that chant - and then some. West Ham were rocked. However, the best chance to level followed within moments of Turner's header. A neat move cut City open and Cole burst into the box and swivelled brilliantly to shoot from the edge of the six yard box, yet could only smack the underside of the bar. The ball was hacked clear by a desperate City defence. It was too close for comfort.

Daniel Cousin then had an effort ruled out for offside when firing in at the far post, a contentious decision but probably right. West Ham will also point to their own disallowed 'goal', which had been ruled out for cheekily swiping the ball from Myhill's grasp in the first half.

It is true, referee Chris Foy may not have been popular in the middle, but was just about right in all his decision-making during the afternoon.

The Tigers pressed again through an unlikely source, when centre back Kamil Zayatte rampaged through a West Ham United side that was guilty of standing off. Fortunately for the Hammers, the Guinea international fired over from the edge of the box.

West Ham rallied, but appeared devoid of posing a real threat. Matthew Etherington saw his free kick on the edge of the box charged down and then following good work from Cole, crashed the side netting. And that was about that from Zola's side.

Phil Brown's team was by no means at its best today – but fair play, West Ham gave it a real go. Yet the tenacity, the fitness and the work rate of this side nestled in East Yorkshire, is turning it into one that is proving an extremely tough nut to crack in the top flight.

I can do no more that take my hat off to them. Well done all - yet again.

MATCH STATS:
- Hull City: Myhill, McShane, Zayatte, Turner, Dawson, Marney, Ashbee, Boateng (Hughes 72), Geovanni (Halmosi 73), Cousin (Garcia 82), King. Subs Not Used: Duke, Mendy, Folan, Ricketts.
- Booked: Zayatte, Dawson.
- Goals: Turner 51.
- West Ham: Green, Faubert (Di Michele 73), Neill, Upson, Ilunga, Behrami, Parker, Noble, Etherington (Sears 83), Bellamy, Cole. Subs Not Used: Lastuvka, Lopez, Boa Morte, Mullins, Davenport.
- Booked: Ilunga.
- Att: 24,896.
- Ref: Chris Foy (Merseyside)
- **Premier League position: 3rd**

MONDAY 20TH OCTOBER 2008

Sensational news? Sensational news! Hull City centre back Michael Turner is playing with such panache at the minute, fans have been claiming *"Turner for England!"* during our Premier League matches to hail solid centre back Michael Turner. Yet that school of thought appears a closer realisation than first thought...

Turner is apparently making all the right moves to become an England international – and that's not just euphoric terrace talk – the manager himself at Hull City, has thrown weight behind the popular terrace belief.

Phil Brown has now jumped onto the fans' bandwagon and has nothing but praise for the way his centre back has performed in the Premier League – who rightly has been collecting plaudits from far and wide for some composed defending in the top flight.

Brown revealed - *"Where Michael is concerned he'll keep his feet on the ground because he's got good staff around him, and if he does get called up he'll get all the support he needs."*

Of course, we're all still savouring Turner scoring a magnificent towering header yesterday, to clinch all the points in our home game versus West Ham – his second goal in as many home games – and duly winning a deserved man of the match award in the process.

Intriguingly, it appears the performance of the talented defender may not have been lost on England officials. An unmarked, blacked out, executive car was seen pulling up the stadium pre-game with official FA branding clearly visible. Hmmm... we await with interest...

TUESDAY 21ST OCTOBER 2008

Even more 'Turner for England!' stuff! After yesterday's revelation that Michael Turner may be courting England interest, City fans are now hearing that midfield dynamo Dean Marney and former manager Phil Parkinson have both thrown their weight behind such a suggestion...

Marney stated - *"In the last two games he's played against players who are in front of him in Jonathan Woodgate and Matthew Upson, and he's looked head and shoulders above them."*

Adding - *"I'm sure if he keeps going the way he is then there's going to be a lot of people taking a lot of notice of him. It's unbelievable. He just keeps getting better and better with every game."*

Meanwhile, former Tigers manager Phil Parkinson has been keeping a brief on Hull City's centre back, whom he brought to the club during his short tenure in charge at the Circle for £350,000 from Brentford.

Parkinson declared - *"He has been a credit to himself and I'm personally delighted for him. He's shown real determination to prove he's a Premier League player. It's that hard work that's paid off and he's still improving."*

FRIDAY 24TH OCTOBER 2008 –
WEST BROMWICH ALBION V HULL CITY PREVIEW

When the fixtures were announced back in June, undoubtedly most fans of both the Tigers and Baggies would have circled this particular match in big red pen with 'must win' scribbled alongside it. And for my money, that's not changed. Hull City's trip to The Hawthorns must still be held in the exact same reverence. At the beginning of the season, all clubs will have looked to highlight the potential matches from which they could accrue the necessary points for survival - and this fixture will have been key.

That's no slight on West Bromwich Albion. Or their fans, who I'm sure, like us, have already earmarked Hull City (h) as a 'must win' game when totting up the required number of points needed for survival, too. Yet with eight games gone, I wonder if anyone had factored in Hull City would be third? I know... third!

I'd like to think Phil Brown will have continued his diligent approach to attacking the opposition. Indeed, in the alleged 'War Room' at the Mill House Woods Lane training complex, this particular fixture surely is seen as critical to the masterplan of Premier League survival.

Therefore, it is absolutely imperative that our third placed status does not allow Hull City to lose focus or cloud judgement as to the significance of this match. What's been has gone and Saturday is starting from a blank canvas for me. Nothing has changed. We are still aiming for Premier League survival.

Being grounded to that mentality among fans, players and the manager breeds a togetherness that has been pretty evident from the outset of this season. With a sell out 3,000 set to descend on the Hawthorns, our role is crucial tomorrow – just like it was last season beating the best team in the Championship on their own pitch.

And it seems the manager agrees with me, with Phil Brown stating ahead of the clash – *"They've definitely improved and they were undoubtedly the best team in the Championship last season. I know a lot of our fans are looking at Chelsea and Manchester United but we're looking at West Brom and that's all we're concerned about."* Good, we all seem to be firing from the same gun. Chelsea and Manchester United can wait.

Quite what the team will be for the game comes into question for the first time in four matches and after three successive victories. Phil Brown has hinted at changes to give players a rest and Anthony Gardner is now fit to feature in defence. Nick Barmby and Stelios Giannakopoulos are close also.

Tony Mowbray may well be hoping to see some changes from a successful Hull City side, after some extremely complimentary words pre-game. But let's not be fooled here, it's thinly-veiled over a very real threat that West Bromwich Albion aim to win the game.

Mowbray admitted – *"There may have been a danger if Hull had been struggling that there would have been an expectation on us to win this one. But Hull have shown, on the road in particular, that they are very strong. It will be a high-energy, high-octane game which drives our team on."*

Adding – *"Defensively, Hull are very hard to break down. They get lots of men behind the ball, they play a certain formation that is difficult to break down, as some good teams have found out, and we will be the next one to have a crack at it."*

The Baggies boss has one time Tiger target Abdoulaye Méïté ruled out with injury. Also, the news Felipe Teixeira has suffered another injury setback with a calf problem means the midfielder will once again be kept waiting for his first start since March. This has the makings of a genuinely tough contest – and unsurprisingly I can't wait. This match is more important than the up and coming glamour games of Chelsea and Manchester United, this is the Premier League and where it is at for Hull City. And the curry in The Vine is worth the drive alone. Bring it on!

SATURDAY 25TH OCTOBER 2008 –
WEST BROMWICH ALBION 0-3 HULL CITY – REPORT

Joint top of the league! Let's just end the season now. Hull City continue their unbelievable form in the top flight and remain undefeated away from home at the pinnacle of English football, ever! This is my team! My bloody team!

Okay, I admit it. I'm running out of excitable expressions to describe Hull City in the Premier League. Every week there's a new test, yet incredibly, our club exceeds all expectations and produces the truly remarkable performance and result. I am gobsmacked. Is the top flight always this easy?

Well, you wouldn't have guessed it from the first half of this game. Phil Brown, despite hinting at changes, stuck to his tried and tested formula of 4-3-3 with the same personnel that have despatched Arsenal, Tottenham and West Ham United. Squad rotation? Pah! We'll leave to the flamboyant foreigners.

A good old-fashioned, defensively tough, but exceptionally quick counter-attacking style was the order of the day, but like West Ham the week before, City had to weather a pretty robust challenge from the Baggies, still smarting from a 4-0 thumping at Old Trafford.

Pre-game talk with the very likeable home fans in the 'finely cuisined' Vine public house had set us up for an intriguing encounter between the two sides. The reality was a great advert for the Premier League from two of the clubs the Championship offered this season's league, although the Baggies will rightly be displeased with the final scoreline.

Here we had two teams who were prepared to go toe-to-toe and attack. The onus was on West Brom to come at us and they enjoyed the lion's share of the ball and the territory. Olsson crashing the bar with a header being one great chance, Bednář and Miller both spurning theirs. Although City failed to truly trouble Carson at the other end in the first half, every so often, the speed of our attacking breaks nudged the Baggies in the kidneys to remind them that we're still in this. A Zayatte header and a King shot being two such chances.

Yet the reason why City remained in the game was because West Brom missed some good opportunities in front of goal, with Ishmael Miller the culprit-in-chief. The five strung across the middle caused City problems, but the one up front had forgotten his shooting boots with Bednář not at his best today.

At half time, I was a touch coy about the outcome of this match. I'd take a point here and now, that'll do nicely, just don't lose. It was true, admit it, you thought it too. Well, any thoughts of losing quickly disintegrated upon the restart. Phil Brown had shoved a rocket up City for the second half and the Tigers were on the offensive.

Daniel Cousin fired in a shot that took a huge deflection and Carson did brilliantly after being wrong footed to shovel the ball out and it bobbled for a corner. Yet the pre-game warnings that West Brom were susceptible to set-pieces really came home to roost. City are not bad at them. From the corner Kamil Zayatte powered his volley home to send the 3,000 barmy army wild to put City into a 0-1 lead. BANG! Here we go again! This is truly astonishing away form, is this really my team? I'm not used to this new found triumphalism about us. Mowbray's side hit back hard - as expected - and Myhill had to produce two magnificent low saves down to his right as the Baggies poured forward in numbers desperate to restore parity. Forgive me, but I thought we'd buckle. I really should know better these days... I can't get used to us being ace! Old habits die hard...

While the hosts pressed vehemently determined to draw level, gaps appeared at the back for the Baggies. City broke swiftly and sharply. King collected a ball - looking suspiciously offside - but no! No flag. A check back, a dink over the defender and Geovanni scores with a diving header for 0-2! Talk about a sucker punch. The away section is going berserk and I can barely draw breath, West Brom stagger around like a punch drunk boxer and City aren't hanging around offering sympathy. Within four minutes, the complexion of the entire match rapidly changed for the definitive.

Marlon King again collected a through ball - this time definitely onside - and curled a precise shot beyond Carson for 0-3. This was last season's Championship champions, as they had reminded us in the first half. Who was laughing now, though? Thousands then swarmed out of the ground from the home stands. Where were they all going? There's some fantastic football being played, why leave early? Hell, one footballing masterclass and they all bugger off sulking! Loyal supporters? Okay, I'm having a tiny pop while I can. Simply put, City's finishing was superior. That was the only real difference. But you have to take your chances at this level.

In truth, this is just another three points towards safety. Hull City fans realise the true expectations of this team, and as good as we are playing, anything above 18th will be considered a huge success and the rest will be classed as bonus territory. That's of course, if anything more happens. If West Brom fans are rubbing their eyes wondering how the hell they've been thumped 0-3 at home this Saturday, rest assured here in Hull, we're all thinking the same. But this is the Premier League, we're having a laugh - and determined to enjoy every last bit of it, come what may.

MATCH STATS:

- West Brom: Carson, Zuiverloon, Donk, Olsson, Robinson, Morrison (Moore 80), Greening, Koren (Brunt 80), Borja Valero, Miller (MacDonald 80), Bednář.
- Subs Not Used: Kiely, Hoefkens, Čech, Barnett.
- Booked: Miller.
- Hull City: Myhill, McShane, Zayatte, Turner, Dawson (Ricketts 10), Marney, Ashbee (Hughes 75), Boateng, Cousin, King, Geovanni (Garcia 78). Subs Not Used: Duke, Mendy, Halmosi, Folan.
- Booked: Ricketts, Ashbee.
- Goals: Zayatte 47, Geovanni 62, King 66.
- Att: 26,323.
- Ref: Lee Probert (Wiltshire)
- **Premier League position: 3rd**

TUESDAY 28TH OCTOBER 2008 – HULL CITY V CHELSEA PREVIEW

The old cup cliché of 'Chelsea won't fancy a wet and cold Wednesday night up in Hull' provides a wry smile. I wonder what Chelsea will make of that now? It's third hosting second in the Premier League, with the teams on 20 points apiece.

I haven't started drinking yet. Honestly. Hull City have been the sensation of the English game this season and sit proudly behind Chelsea on goal difference at the head of the Premier League, with a home match against the Blues that could see City move three points ahead of the Londoners.

Barking? No, it's Chelsea tonight, like I've already stated. Hull City are not only box office, they're realistically and creditably BIG FOUR, or BIG FIVE if you can't stand the very thought of it. Mark Lawrenson please take note, if you will.

The rest of the nation are agog at what Hull City Football Club is achieving. That's my team they're talking about, my team! Phil Brown has ripped up the Premier League guide for newbies and set his own fearless agenda. Everyone keeps asking how long it will last, or in Lawrenson's case, it's this week the bubble will surely burst.

Me? Well, the only point I'm fearful of making is stating that a point would be a good one tonight. I'm patently aware that is almost disrespectful to what this team is achieving and certainly dumbing down our efforts. Although, it does feel like a malfunction – a syntax error if you will – to state Hull City can defeat Chelsea on Wednesday night. That's what 30 odd years of abjectness does for you.

But we fans have to believe City can win. Not dream it, believe it. What more does the team have to do to prove they can do it? Hull City are third in the Premier League on merit. Not through luck, not by fluke, but on merit. Phil Brown has instilled this belief into his players, so the fans have to follow suit on the terraces. And we will.

Chelsea supporters will travel to this freezing cold northern outpost in their free buses to be met by a fierce, intense home crowd that will back their team vociferously. The home fans will be equally as hungry as the players, but above all, in unison. We all believe we can turn these southern jessies over.

But so what if we don't? Who actually cares? We've been stuffed 0-5 at home by Wigan already this season. That's ignominy, not when it happens at home to multi-millionaire Chelsea with their world class stars from one to 11. Yet I doubt that's going to happen. Indeed, I'm sure it won't.

The reason for this appears clear in the manager's thoughts. Here are Phil Brown's comments ahead of lavish Chelsea's visit to the Circle – *"It is a massive game for us because, one, it is the next one and, two, we have won four on the bounce."*

Adding – *"Confidence levels are sky high but what that manifests itself in is us looking forward to the game rather than being frightened. At the start of the season people would have been fearing this fixture but now all of a sudden we're not, we're looking forward to it."*

Transmit those sentiments to the players and it could yet be 'London 0 Hull 5' after marvellous victories against Fulham, West Ham, Tottenham and Arsenal. Cuh! How short-sighted were the Housemartins? Incredibly, the team that has been cranking out these splendid results is unchanged. Andy Dawson's dead leg suffered in the 0-3 away win at West Bromwich Albion jeopardised that, but the news is apparently positive leading up to kick off. Dawson may actually make it. Who needs squad rotation?

Chelsea, by contrast, have just ended an 86-game unbeaten home run in losing to fellow title contenders Liverpool. Losing to fellow title contenders Hull City – hey, who's laughing, we're bleedin' third – will be a severe and damaging blow to the Blues. But in all honesty, it could happen. What then? Last time we met in the league, City stuffed Chelsea 3-0 at Boothferry Park, remember?

Assistant manager Ray Wilkins stated (probably because Scolari has no idea who the hell we are) – *"It is great to see the work they have done there at Hull, their work ethic is fantastic so we know we are in for one hell of a game there."*

Adding rather complimentarily – *"They have done exceptionally well, wins at Arsenal, wins at Tottenham. It is up to us to go and put ourselves upon Hull and make it a very interesting night for them."*

Before warning the rest of the Premier League – *"I don't think a defeat tomorrow will burst their bubble because they have demonstrated they can play. One defeat is not going to upset them too much - but it is our aim to inflict that defeat on them."*

Be loud, be proud, be Hull City. Believe in what Phil Brown is trying to achieve and make yourselves heard this Wednesday evening. You can rest assured the players believe they can triumph tonight, with a sell-out Circle feeling likewise, who would want to be in Chelsea's boots? Let's av it!

WEDNESDAY 29 TH OCTOBER 2008 – HULL CITY 0-3 CHELSEA – REPORT

Bubble's burst! Sack Brown! The season is over! Stop the Premier League rollercoaster; we want to get off! Hull City have lost 0-3 at home to Chelsea. But you know what? So what?

ITV rang me this afternoon. Can you come and tell us how great Hull City are ahead of this top of the table clash with Chelsea? I'm thinking 'to say what? I've run out of praise to heap on them!' Oh well, a good chance to get fish and chips from Londesborough Street chippy I suppose, before the beer-fest.

I told them we've earned our place, we've been competitive and we're third on merit. Um, what more can you say? But, this is Chelsea. A wounded Chelsea. A Chelsea side desperate for revenge after relinquishing an 86-match unbeaten home run to Liverpool - who now head the Premier League by three points.

Phil Brown had little choice other than to opt for the 4-3-3 and unchanged side with City topping the Premier League form guide and all. Yeah, I know, Hull City with the best record in the last six matches, who would have thought that? Certainly not the Chelsea fans who were on the telly with me earlier.

Yet within moments of the game kicking off, Hull City's challenge appeared to fall at the first. Chelsea were busy, hungry, lively. No resting players here for the match against the Championship play-off winners. The Blues had even patched up Joe Cole for the game such was the seriousness of this encounter for them.

But as City failed to get a challenge and a clearance out of their own box, the ball was pushed back to Frank Lampard - and City paid. Now Lawrenson will tell you it was England class, I'll tell you he was trying to float one in at the far post. Between those two extreme view points Lampard found the back of the net as the ball foxed all.

Bugger. Barely a minute or two on the bloody watch. The fans kept at it though, that was good to see. Chelsea are fluent, fast, precise. For a billion pounds they should be, but tonight Chelsea truly were head and shoulders above what has turned out to be a pretty reasonable Premier League side for a newbie.

City predictably struggled to match Chelsea in the middle with Marney, Ashbee and Boateng close to burnout. The ball always breaks to Chelsea, the bobble always goes their way, the referee's decision is always theirs too. I guess that is the difference. That is what billions of pounds buys you. You make your own luck. And you get it.

I can't get bitter about it. With more of the ball, territory and possession in key places, the law of averages will tell you it's bound to happen. Of course it's all going Chelsea's way, we can't get the sodding ball! But I couldn't fault City for their effort. Here's a side that will never give up while Phil Brown leads the way.

Indeed, City had to resort to long range free kicks from Geovanni such was Chelsea's strength. Even 45 yards out the little Brazilian still had Petr Čech troubled and spilling the ball. But the best effort was a brilliant mazy run and shot from Daniel Cousin that beat Čech all ends up and crashed the base of the post. Damn! Cousin was excellent and man of the match for me.

Chelsea were far superior though, no question. The money bags didn't appear to be weighing them down or hindering their performance. The only criticism I would level is Chelsea looking a little too casual trying to finish the game off at 0-1. And that left you with hope, as the teams trooped off at the break.

Yet it was soon over as contest upon the restart. The half had barely found rhythm when a shocking defensive error cost City the game. Turner and Zayatte both stopped - presumably because Myhill called - but the ball never reached the goalkeeper and Anelka nipped between all three and stroked home the second. Schoolboy error. Disastrous.

That knocked the stuffing out of City and Chelsea cruised around the pitch. It was only a matter of time before the third was arriving, but a glut of chances were spurned first. Shoddy finishing – some I would've been embarrassed about while playing on FIFA 09 when playing it with the kids to be honest.

City still put the miles in, kept at the task in hand, but a low cross caught the home defence flat footed and Malouda could barely miss from three yards to poke home and make it 0-3. Harsh, but fair. But so what? It's not like we're really competing with Chelsea, is it?

All we need is a Russian oligarch, a world class manager and a liberal sprinkling of international stars from the four corners of the globe and we'll be about ready to compete with Chelsea. I can wait another season or two for that. Right, the champions away next. Welcome to the Premier League! And I love it.

MATCH STATS:
- Hull City: Myhill, McShane, Turner, Zayatte, Dawson, Marney (Garcia 71), Ashbee, Boateng (Halmosi 62), Geovanni, King (Windass 84), Cousin. Subs Not Used: Duke, Hughes, Mendy, Ricketts.
- Chelsea: Čech, Bosingwa (Ivanovic 86), Carvalho, Terry, Ashley Cole, Deco (Kalou 78), Mikel, Lampard, Joe Cole (Belletti 54), Anelka, Malouda. Subs Not Used: Cudicini, Di Santo, Bridge, Alex.
- Booked: Joe Cole, Deco.
- Goals: Lampard 3, Anelka 50, Malouda 75.

- Att: 24,906
- Ref: Andre Marriner (W Midlands)
- **Premier League position: 5th**

THURSDAY 30TH OCTOBER 2008

In a recent interview, Hull City skipper Ian Ashbee confessed he has been there, seen it, but not quite done it all. The City captain appears to have one more amazing conquest left in his box of ambitions. Well, he can dream about it, anyway...

Ashbee is in a buoyant mood – and after experiencing the delights of Rochdale and Lincoln in his fledgling Tiger years, perhaps it's now time to 'think big' and dream of conquering Europe. Well, while we can, at least...

Ashbee began the interview by unfolding the realms of fantasy and to dream of advancing his Hull City captaincy even further – *"I watched bits and bobs from Europe last week – mainly from the Chelsea game. Wouldn't it be great? Leading Hull out at Roma?"*

Adding – *"It would not be so much the icing on the cake as the hundreds and thousands on top of that. We know what we are trying to achieve, but if we keep winning football matches... I know there are going to be losses along the way but you never know."*

Going back through the mists of time, Ashbee recalled – *"I remember we played Rochdale away when there were about 2,200 fans there on a wet Tuesday night. There had been a pile-up on the motorway and we got there ten minutes before kick-off. It was even silly things like we had to buy our own drinks to have on the coach. I have seen the other side."*

But back to the present, the legend concluded the vision with – *"If you had asked me five years ago when I was leading the side out against Lincoln if we would be playing against Manchester United and Chelsea, I would have said no. So Europe is something I would never say no to."*

CHAPTER 4 – FROM CHAMPIONS TO CHAMPIONSHIP COMPATRIOTS

SATURDAY 1ST NOVEMBER 2008 – MANCHESTER UNITED V HULL CITY PREVIEW

This is arguably the signature fixture of gaining promotion to the top table. Although for me, in terms of atmosphere at least, it probably is not. Fifth-placed Hull City, travel to sixth-placed Manchester United in the Premier League. One day, I'm certain, people will look back on that last sentence and wonder if I have been taking illicit substances.

So this is it then. This is probably the most high profile fixture in the Premier League calendar for Hull City and their followers. As far as the 'fans' go, it's probably at the big expense of the ardent 'supporters'. What a pity. And in turn, these new 'fans' will contribute what towards the atmosphere? Yep, this does need saying, I'm fearing the worst...

Last weekend, a sell-out contingent roared Hull City on in a critical fixture in our first ever Premier League campaign. It was a fixture ten times more important than this up and coming glamour trip to Manchester United – not that certain 'fans' will realise. I'm talking about West Bromwich Albion away, of course. Some there tomorrow will have been completely oblivious to the fine 0-3 win recorded at The Hawthorns seven days earlier, you watch.

The 3,000 supporters who were there - and there most weeks through the years - were a significant factor driving the team onwards and forwards, fully playing their part in helping our side garner a massive three points against a club we really are realistically competing with this season. These games – the 'lesser' fixtures in the Premier League – are the hidden gems for us 'proper' supporters.

I was mightily proud of our collective effort of support at the Hawthorns last weekend. Together we are strong, concentrated and committed. This reflects on the team and undoubtedly spurs the players on to greater achievements. We're a close-knit bunch with the players. Indeed, I'd be as bold to state the supporters are the very secret of our success this season. Unity, strength, passion. Players on the field, fans in the stands, together as one. It's how it should be.

Interestingly, it was a somewhat diluted atmosphere against a rampaging Chelsea on Wednesday evening. This is Chelsea, a team definitely not taking us lightly and determined to go to any lengths for their trip to Hull City, such as patching up a suspect Joe Cole. The Blues were worried about us and no mistake. Yet in adversity during midweek, the home fans faltered. Why was that? Hmmm...

Okay, nobody is saying Chelsea didn't deserve it. Or the team can't function without the crowd. Chelsea were at their scintillating best, City were by no means disgraced, but in the stands, there was definite room for improvement. The team needs us, like we need them. It's a two-way operation.

At the point of the Manchester United away fixture being imminent, the rumour, counter-rumour and down right skullduggery that has done the rounds has been and gone regarding ticket allocation. Those lucky lotto winners in the ballot will be few - as I suspect - the corporates, sponsors and hangers-on pilfer 'our' tickets. You know, the supporters' tickets. Bitter? Just a trifle...

Countless fans who stood alongside me on the terraces of Macclesfield, Rochdale and Mansfield will be missing tomorrow. Elbowed out for the new breed of fan that craves what we built, have now earned, without contributing a jot towards the success we helped construct. They are a scourge on our support. I make no bones about it.

These fans want to sample being a supporter in the best stadia, against the best teams, with all the Premier League trimmings. Yet back in the days when tickets were plentiful and Southend and Bournemouth beckoned, these fans were distinctly AWOL. I wasn't. And many hundreds and sometimes thousands like me weren't, either.

Yet come tomorrow, a mere fraction of that loyal support will be trying to uphold the 'old-school', the hardcore, the proper mister's Hull City experience. How very sad. These suited and booted buffoons with little Timmy and Angelica tagging along will be occupying your seat. It's outrageous. And why have they come? To taste the atmosphere we built. What atmosphere is this, then? There won't be one, you've stripped it with your presence, fools.

But enough of the politics. This is the next game in a long series of matches that Hull City need points from for Premier League survival. Manchester United, champions et al, but still another place to perhaps get points on the road to survival and beyond. And why not? We've bagged 20 so far and sit proudly above Manchester United in the table. Say it while we can. Don't scoff at the thought, we've earned our place. And it's November now, not August. No flash in the pan here, thank you very much.

We've earned some respect. In many ways it could be our downfall from now, but we'd rather attack with a bold 4-3-3 formation than meekly buckle at the knees and roll over. Yes, we have been spanked - and heavily at times this season - but only twice and those losses are dwarfed by victories at Arsenal, Newcastle, Tottenham and West Brom.

These ingredients set us up for an 'unbeaten on the road' away trip to last season's champions. Hull City have absolutely nothing to lose. We'll go to Old Trafford, we'll burst lungs for the cause, hustle, harry and make ourselves a nuisance and hopefully pounce with one of our swift counter attacks. In between the Alamo of course.

Phil Brown has set the agenda firmly – *"There are a lot of teams out there who would like to have 20 points from 10 games, excluding the top four. We've got to learn from the Chelsea defeat on Wednesday night and go to Old Trafford. I've said to the players that if anybody doesn't fancy getting something on Saturday, don't bother coming."*

You know, in many ways, those words apply to the supporters. They should listen to our manager and his wise words. But certain fans won't. Some won't even know who Phil Brown is, or what he does. And I swear, if I hear anything like *"Who is number..."* I'll swing for 'em. I mean it, I will.

Unfortunately, City will have to take on Manchester United in their own backyard without captain Ian Ashbee. The skipper serves his one match ban for five yellow cards. Harsh on the man who has led us from Division Four to Old Trafford, but I'm surprised he's got to November in truth before a suspension. Ashbee has improved immeasurably. Here is a true great in the English game.

His place is likely to go to Bryan Hughes or Bernard Mendy, depending how the City boss intends to play the fixture. Anthony Gardner is once again sidelined after his troubling thigh injury flared up, one wonders if we'll ever see the bloke again...

Meanwhile, Manchester United have to square up to the Tigers without Wes Brown who collected an ankle injury versus West Ham in midweek. Gary Neville will return to the side and may feature alongside two more recalled players in Edwin van der Sar and Michael Carrick. The real headache will be who to select up front, although Berbatov appears to be winning the race.

Ferguson revealed on the Bulgarian – *"On Wednesday I wanted to see how the combination of Berbatov and Tévez was together. Carlos was so wound up to do well himself that they became two different parts."*

Before adding decisively – *"I think it will be far better tomorrow, if I pick him. Carlos has been out for a few games and he was so keen to do well he used up so much energy trying to do well - that's not a bad thing to try too hard."*

So, we're all set then. Champions v Upstarts. Unlike the rest of the Premier League at least we only have to play Manchester United once this season, whatever happens. Surely, it will be mission accomplished before 24th May 2009? Surely...?

SATURDAY 1ST NOVEMBER 2008 –
MANCHESTER UNITED 4-3 HULL CITY – REPORT

Get this; Hull City frighten the living daylights out of Manchester United at Old Trafford, as the new boys have the audacity to roar back from 4-1 down to leave multi-million pound talent hoofing for safety and 70,000 plus begging for the final whistle...

You come to Old Trafford and you expect nothing. The danger here is that teams can beat themselves before crossing the white line to play. Hull City? Cuh! I don't think so. Phil Brown's team never know when they are beaten. Ask Manchester United how 'comfortable' yesterday was.

Fifth-placed Hull City gave sixth-placed Manchester United a worthy test for our respective positions. The match was an outstanding advert for the Premier League – and once again proved with the right attitude, anything is possible if you believe and are prepared to work hard.

Of course, the last time I was here watching Hull City was in the 80s when wincing at the Tigers getting a tonking 5-0 in the League Cup. I genuinely thought we'd fare far better today – and I was right. Interestingly, Old Trafford hasn't changed that much in truth over a couple of decades passing, barring a few spikes and crash barriers being ripped out, mind.

After Wednesday's game against the other Champions League finalists - this is the level we are at now - the last thing Hull City could afford was conceding an early goal like in the Chelsea match. Third minute in, it was Ronaldo in acres of space with a low strike kissing the near post for the opener. Not again City!

Manchester United then stood off us, almost content to let us have the ball. We're not finely tuned, a bit rough and ready, but we will have a go if given the chance. And we did. The Reds didn't get forward a great deal, but when they did, they looked ruthless and capable of extending their lead.

But it was City who struck next when Marlon King was fouled by Vidić. The resultant free-kick was whipped in and Daniel Cousin ghosted in front of his marker to glance in the leveller. Old Trafford was stunned while a little corner in the East Stand went berserk. Manchester United got angry with this outrageous attempt from the upstarts looking to upset the applecart. Carrick was unchecked surging forward and you knew there was a strong chance of punishment. Thwack! Just like Ronaldo, a low drive across Myhill steered in off the same upright and City were behind again. It was our own fault.

To compound the misery, although City played well, ruthless finishing scuppered the Tigers once more. This time from a set-piece, when Ronaldo's header was turned in off the underside of the bar despite Myhill's best efforts. For all the millions and billions separating the sides, one quality what you really get for your money is precision. The Reds have it in spades.

Hull City matched Manchester United for effort, endeavour and, hell, even belief, but the home side were sharp in front of goal when getting there. That's the primary difference. The second half team talk appeared lost in a sea of red shortly after the restart, when Vidić converted a Rooney corner. It's 4-1, and a little harsh.

But that's what Manchester United do. There is no mercy in these surroundings - and nor should you expect any. Hull City have attempted to apply the same in their own battles this season, with eyecatching success. See Sir Alex devoting half his programme notes to us for proof. We're making strides in the Premier League - let's not forget that.

What followed next, justified the reason why. The fifth placed team on merit showed why they are fifth. Hull City never know when they are beaten and will never, ever, give up. City went hunting for goals at Old Trafford. We have the balls to do so.

Bernard Mendy's introduction to the fray was decisive and pivotal. The Frenchman was the outlet providing width and pace. It worked and then some. Shamefully left untracked, a dink over the defender's head gave Mendy room to scoot the ball over the advancing Van der Sar, putting enough on the lob before Vidić hooked it away. City fans were dancing with delight when the linesman gave it.

Manchester United spurned some good chances and even Carlos Tévez was wheeled out in attempt to get a game clinching fifth goal for the hosts but it wasn't forthcoming thanks to fine goalkeeping, last ditch defending and surprisingly, the lack of cool finishing – the trademark of Manchester United's first half.

Then Mendy went on a burst deep into the Manchester United half. And into the box... and over in the penalty area... but this the Stretford End, Manchester. But no, Mike Dean points to the spot! Wow! When did that last happen? Geovanni stepped up... GOAL! 4-3! Game on! Wow! Three goals at Old Trafford? When did that last happen, as well?

Sir Alex Ferguson's side were rocked. Sure they pressed, but the fragility of a one goal advantage was uncomfortable from a position of dominance. Instead, with the injury board showing three minutes remaining, multi-million pound talent belted the ball 50 yards upfield while 70 odd thousand begged for the final whistle. Some turnaround against Hull City!

There can be no denial Manchester United deserved the points when the much begged-for whistle finally arrived, but City had preserved their credibility and then some. What character to come back from a position of helplessness. It meant my team will continue to make Premier League headlines for all the right reasons at Old Trafford. A seven goal 'shared' thriller.

It's some journey Hull City supporters are on. Today proved that ideas of Manchester United coming over to Hull on the final day to collect their Championship trophy won't be the formality many from Old Trafford first thought. Indeed, take it from me, on the evidence of the last four days, it's all eyes on Chelsea for my money. That's not sour grapes, either.

No disgrace. No humiliation. No regrets. Hull City, on this evidence, merit their place in the top six. Staying there will take some doing, but what is clear, this team clearly has the fight to carry it on for some considerable time yet. Keep it up Hull City, keep it up. And if you're going to lose your unbeaten away record in the Premier League, ever, do it at the Champions, do it at Old Trafford – and make it a 4-3 thriller. Hull City will be back. I hope.

MATCH STATS:
- Man Utd: Van der Sar, Neville, Ferdinand, Vidić, Evra, Ronaldo, Carrick (Giggs 72), Anderson (O'Shea 88), Nani (Tévez 64), Berbatov, Rooney. Subs Not Used: Foster, Park, Rafael Da Silva, Fletcher.
- Booked: Rooney, Tévez.
- Goals: Ronaldo 3, Carrick 29, Ronaldo 44, Vidić 57.
- Hull City: Myhill, McShane, Turner, Zayatte, Dawson, Marney, Hughes (Mendy 59), Boateng (Folan 86), Geovanni, King (Halmosi 63), Cousin. Subs Not Used: Duke, Barmby, Garcia, Ricketts.
- Booked: Turner, Mendy.
- Goals: Cousin 23, Mendy 69, Geovanni 82 pen.
- Att: 75,398
- Ref: Mike Dean (Wirral)
- **Premier League position: 6th**

SUNDAY 2ND NOVEMBER 2008

Somebody left a program behind as we filed out of Old Trafford, ah what the hell, it's mine now. I don't do match day programmes as a rule but one piece really did catch my attention.

Sir Alex Ferguson's pre-match notes make sizeable and interesting reading. Concerning Hull City, here is what the legendary manager had to say before the match commenced...

"Hull City could win the league. The table doesn't lie, and even after losing to Chelsea in midweek they are still level on points with Arsenal and Villa in third and fourth. Vitally, from our point of view the Tigers are two points in front of us. Need I say more about the importance of this match? They have certainly have been living up to their nickname; despite playing in the top league for the first time in their 104 year history – and being widely tipped for a swift return to the Championship, Hull have taken their place among the pacesetters.

Who in their right mind, would have predicted such an amazing impact after winning promotion via the play-offs? Look what happened to Derby County last season's play-off promoted team. They had a torrid time on their way back down but already Hull have picked up almost double the points Derby managed all season. So far, they are the success story of the decade, and while they may find it difficult to maintain their present level of giant-killing form, the fact remains that they are buzzing at the moment and represent a tremendous challenge as we welcome them to Old Trafford.

Hull are in good shape with a new stadium, a chairman who has kept them out of debt and a management team who know what they are doing. Phil Brown learned his trade under Sam Allardyce and like his old manager is well versed in the sports science part of the modern game. Phil is backed up by the experience of staff like Brian Horton, himself a former manager at Hull and Steve Parkin who was in charge at Rochdale among other clubs. They have clearly bonded into an efficient and knowledgeable team. And when Phil was at the Football Writers Association Awards dinner in Manchester at the weekend, to collect his promotion prize, all three of them were there and Phil made a point of stressing the important contribution made by his staff.

Hull have a common sense approach with the emphasis on basics and the team working their socks off, plus playing positive football. They have made some shrewd signings too such as Geovanni from Manchester City and on loan Guinean defender Kamil Zayatte. Veteran Dean Windass played a crucial role on the promotion trail, as did our Fraizer Campbell who was on loan with them last season to emerge as their top scorer. Hull made a £6 million offer for Fraizer during the summer but we had to steer him to Spurs as part of our agreement to take Dimitar Berbatov to Old Trafford.

Typical of their thoroughness Hull sent reports every week on our man, which I thought was very professional and respectful to the player and his parent club."

Sir Alex Ferguson – Manchester United manager

MONDAY 3RD NOVEMBER 2008

It is now starting to dawn on me how much City have achieved in such a short space of time. Take Hull City striker Daniel Cousin as a case in point. Cousin has urged the team to continue their fine start to the Premier League and push themselves all the way for UEFA Cup place

Here's a player that believes a European dream can be realised after securing 20 points from their first 11 games. Well, 9 games if you ignore our last two fixtures agains the Champions League finalists.

Cousin stated post match after scoring against Manchester United – *"I think we should target a UEFA Cup spot. Why not? That was a great moment in a great stadium against a great club. But in football, it is important to turn the page quickly and perform again and again."*

WEDNESDAY 5TH NOVEMBER 2008

More evidence of our astonishing campaign has been unearthed with the Barclays Premier League Player of the Month for October being named as Hull City attacker Geovanni after a series of stunning displays.

Geovanni has been a sensation this season it has to be said and the award comes hot on the heels of Phil Brown claiming the Manager of the Month award for September – as well as Geovanni claiming Goal of the Month during the same period for his belter at Arsenal. * dreamily recalls wonder goal *

However, such has been Geovanni's impact at Hull City, the club have already been moved to slap an £8m price tag on the Brazil international – and Chelsea manager Luis Felipe Scolari has hinted the 28 year old would be a player he'd perhaps like at Stamford Bridge. Get your mitts off!

FRIDAY 8TH NOVEMBER 2008 – HULL CITY V BOLTON WANDERERS PREVIEW

Make no bones about it. The match with Bolton Wanderers on Saturday will be as tough as they come. Once again, expect nothing else. Do not be fooled. Do not be deceived. Bolton Wanderers are as hardworking, disciplined and resolute as they come. This is nothing new to the Premier League, or Gary Megson's style of management. Taking anything for granted will no doubt end in failure. City must be on their guard.

Incredible though, eh? Here we are pontificating about taking Bolton for granted. Surely, that should've been the other way round at the start of the season? But in all honesty, the aforementioned traits are just some of the key ingredients Phil Brown has blended into a steely looking Hull City side full of belief. Perhaps, that is the only key difference between the teams - belief.

I haven't seen much of Bolton this season to start assessing or criticising the reason why our visitors languish in the relegation zone. I do know that Phil Brown from the outset has drilled into his players the belief that they are good enough for the Premier League and should play with passion and determination and never, ever quit. It has paid handsomely. The spirit in the camp is soaring.

Yes, setbacks have come along in the Premier League – as you would expect – with a home hammering to Wigan. More recently back-to-back defeats to the European champions and the European runners-up inside four days have now added more recent obstacles. Interestingly, the Wigan fiasco produced a five match unbeaten run, including four victories. Good teams do tend to bounce back rather quickly.

Phil Brown needs to show the same meticulous approach to tackling Bolton, like he has the previous 11 matches. You've got to feel City have the tools in the box for success, if they do. And there is no reason to suggest the manager won't have done his homework. Indeed, Phil Brown has probably pored over the Bolton fixture more than any other, after spending much of his career there.

But Brown has been quick to dispel any divided loyalties ahead of the game, stating – *"It holds a special place in my heart, Bolton Wanderers, but that's in the past. The only club that I have a special anything for is Hull City and the future of Hull City, more to the point."*

Before confirming adamantly – *"There will be no divided loyalties on Saturday. We have had back-to-back defeats for the first time in 11 months after our losses against Chelsea and Manchester United and we're looking to put that right."*

It's true the Tigers have suffered back-to-back defeats for the first time since the Preston/ Southampton debacle in the Championship at the back end of 2007. Those heavy defeats sparked an incredible surge to Wembley and a play-off triumph. Defeats to Chelsea and Manchester United need to be treated in the exact same manner.

Two additions have been added to the City squad for the Bolton test. Inspirational leader Ian Ashbee returns following his one match ban, while free agent Stelios Giannakopoulos has forced his way into contention after building up his fitness and scoring for the reserves in midweek. Oh the irony, should the Greek star make his debut against his former club Bolton. What price a winner there, eh?

As Hull City welcome back their own skipper, Gary Megson is without his. Kevin Nolan is suspended for the trip to East Yorkshire but £10m summer buy Johan Elmander could recover from a groin strain to head up the visiting attack. Also in contention is midfielder Mustapha Riga in midfield.

Bolton boss Gary Megson is wary of the tough trip along the M62 – *"Hull have had a really good start and got some fantastic results away from home. At home they have had a couple of good results as well, so it's a credit to everybody involved."*

Before adding – *"It will be a big test because they have lost their last two games, so they will want to get back on track, but we are well capable of going anywhere and putting in performances and getting results. Kevin Nolan is suspended for us and it's not ideal playing without your captain after just 11 games."*

As quoted at the head of this preview, do not underestimate Bolton Wanderers this Saturday. Like last season, Bolton have been slow starters, yet came good when it really mattered. Beating Manchester City last time out will fill the visitors with confidence, but Phil Brown will surely have noted that.

Same effort, same application, same belief and you have to back the home side. Yet if just one of those ingredients is absent, expect nothing other than a thorough examination of City's credentials and the possibility of an unwelcome result. Third beckons with victory. Surely, that's all the motivation you will ever need?

SATURDAY 8TH NOVEMBER 2008 – HULL CITY 0-1 BOLTON WANDERERS – REPORT

Kind of predictable, huh? More than a hint of what was to come was weaved into the preview of this game I wrote yesterday and unfortunately, it came to pass. What a truly forgettable encounter at the Circle.

I doubt this game will remain long in the memory of City fans. And if it does, it will be for all the wrong reasons. What a shocking advert for Premier League football. It wasn't pretty and Hull City were out Hull City-ed by a team clearly here for a point and incredibly waltzing off with all three.

Before the game, Phil Brown promised one or two surprises for the Bolton game. The kidology there was outlandish to say the least, as Ian Ashbee coming in for Bryan Hughes was the only change. And that fooled nobody. Not even Gary Megson.

As expected, the City boss who never was - courtesy of Phil Brown ransacking Cardiff City 4-1 many moons ago on the day Megson allegedly signed a contract - predictably set out a defensive stall to get a point. No surprise there. Hull City failed to live up to the challenge, perhaps for the first time this season, facing a team who didn't intend to attack us. A Premier League first for us?

With the boot on the other foot, City struggled. Bolton had more play, but zero shots on target that would merit Myhill's intervention, while Brown's team slowly sucked themselves into Bolton clutches and inexplicably began launching everything. What happened to passing the ball around?

The best chance of the half saw Marlon King outrageously flicking the ball onto a post with Jussi Jääskeläinen rooted to the spot. Take note, it was the only time of the afternoon you could say that. Bolton had a fair amount of the ball but never looked capable of scoring in a month of Sundays. City, by contrast, looked sharper up top but lacked the composure that has been a fine trait.

It was excruciating on the eye. City tangled themselves up in Bolton's defensive web. The visitors broke on the counter - like we have been doing all season - but clearly the Bolton finishing is some way behind City's, hence sitting in 18th place. Yet despite the obvious indicators, the initiative failed to be seized and City would pay very heavily indeed.

Second half - yeah let's forget the first, so abysmal was it - and the sucker punch arrived five minutes in. Ta-da! A tame Matty Taylor shot through a forest of legs squirmed its way past an unsighted Myhill and nestled into the bottom corner. Talk about soft, it crawled in. We're in trouble here...

Clunk. The shutters slammed down in front of the Bolton goal. Brown changed things immediately. Bernard Mendy, the former Bolton star, came on to good effect and sparked City into a bit more life. Predictably it was 11 men behind the ball from the visitors. Something only to be expected.

What followed was the Jussi Jääskeläinen show. A good keeper, make no mistake, but embraced by luck today. Bolton kept a clean sheet because of him and earned their three points with a series of logic-defying saves. You can't get bitter about it, plain pointless. Every dog has its day and today was Bolton's.

Two City free kicks saw the Finnish keeper pouch the first from Dawson, then, incredibly, fly across his goal to keep out Geovanni's second effort. Another double save followed as the Brazilian's goalbound headed effort was desperately beaten away and the follow-up was blocked when it looked for all the world to be in.

Next was Marlon King's turn to be thwarted before Geovanni was yet again denied by an inspired performance between the sticks from Jääskeläinen. Ian Ashbee blazed the last chance over the bar and it left the overwhelming majority miffed at the whistle, brooding about a game that should never really have been lost.

But let's round on those fans. By some distance this was the worst atmosphere at the Circle this season - arguably ever. It was a below par performance from those on the pitch for certain, but in the stands it was far worse than on the field. This is the Premier League, not a bleeding charity outing. Poor effort.

The bigger picture states this defeat is far, far more damaging than we perhaps realise. A team who undoubtedly will be fighting relegation employing such negative tactics has claimed all the points off us on home turf. Better teams than us will sweep Bolton aside. Luckier teams will, also. This could well be a team we are squaring up to at the business end of the season if we don't buck our ideas up. Chance lost...

I'm taking nothing for granted. The last thing we need is complacency setting in the camp. There is much work to do and we've achieved absolutely nothing to date. Amid the dire spectacle on show today, perhaps that school of thought got trampled underfoot. It cannot happen again. We didn't get 20 points with performances like this, just as I'm pretty certain Bolton won't get three points every week if they play like they did today.

It is little wonder Bolton fans want Browny back - although the chanting was truly embarrassing and cringeworthy from the visitors. Still, could you imagine having to watch that every week? City fans got a lucky escape. If this is what is required to stay in the Premier League, I'd rather not bother watching it. Back to attacking, back to what we know best. Thankfully, we've only got Gary Megson's Bolton once more. That's if he keeps his job mind... Browny won't want it, that's a racing certainty.

MATCH STATS:
- Hull City: Myhill, McShane, Turner, Zayatte, Dawson (Ricketts 64), Boateng (Folan 73), Ashbee, Marney, Geovanni, King, Cousin (Mendy 54).
- Subs Not Used: Duke, Barmby, Garcia, Halmosi.
- Booked: Dawson.
- Bolton: Jääskeläinen, Steinsson, Cahill, Andrew O'Brien, Samuel, Muamba, Gardner, McCann, Taylor, Elmander (Smolarek 77), Davies.
- Subs Not Used: Al Habsi, Helguson, Shittu, Basham, Sissons, Obadeyi.
- Booked: Muamba, Gardner.
- Goals: Taylor 50.
- Att: 24,903
- Ref: Alan Wiley (Staffordshire)
- **Premier League position: 6th**

THURSDAY 13TH OCTOBER 2008

You know you've made it to the Premier League when...

...Tabloids scream out headlines about your football club on the front page of their respective publications. Woo-hoo! Hull City have landed in the Premier League! We must be top six or something...

'KING BUTTS WINDASS!'

No really! And there was a bloody nose and everything. A fracas for a whole two minutes in Scarborough's high rolling casino The Open House! It's true! I read it in the paper...

YAWN... what a non-story. Basically, team goes on bonding session, hit the bright lights of Scarborough, King takes Windass to the cleaners on the chip table and it came to blows. Allegedly.

You can read this in the Daily Mail and The Sun if you like. Riveting read. Oh the shame of it. Where will it all end? How come when this all went on before in the lower leagues, it never made the front page?

So, the evidence is clear cut. Hull City must be 'Billy big time' now, commanding high profile splashes in trashy tabloid publications. We're honoured - indeed, we truly are Premier League. It said so in the papers.

SATURDAY 15TH NOVEMBER 2008 – HULL CITY V MANCHESTER CITY PREVIEW

After three straight defeats, two at home and one against lowly Bolton, the doom and gloom merchants tracking us will be revelling in the 'Welcome to the Premier League' derogatory mindset for our live Sky TV game. Well, I'm not joining in...

Let me assure anyone who takes a few moments out of their time to read this – before you get stuck in – this will not be a fretful, wobbling preview form days of yore at this club, that certain sections of our support quickly become accustomed to at the merest hint of a crisis.

Nobody is denying the club have failed to take any points from nine. I'm not ducking the fact Hull City have lost three games and neither am I turning a blind eye to the situation and burying my head in the sand. Please, allow me to put some it into perspective.

Losing to the European and Premier League champions 4-3 at their own gaff is no disgrace. Losing to Roman Abramovich's billionaire plaything - European losing finalists I might add - isn't either. Indeed, both were games that weren't really a 'level' contest. Yes, yes, I know this is what the Premier League is all about, but hell, give us a break to find our feet. We're only 12 games in after 104 years of waiting.

No, we've all got to start somewhere. Last week's home loss to Bolton was hard to stomach for a multitude of reasons, but none more so than seeing Megson's side come here for a point and then galling us all by outrageously waltzing off with all three. Typically, Jääskeläinen chose to have the game of his life.

But for me, that's a positive. Brown's side created a plethora of chances - most would have gone in on any other day - but it was just one of those days with some undiscovered superhero performing the absurd in goal. Absorbing a defeat when you've battered the door down to get something out of the game can be tolerated in such circumstances. The effort was still there, the chances came...

However, there's no time to dwell on that now. Onwards and upwards. Hull City have been exceptional this season. Committed, passionate and working with belief. Phil Brown's 'drip, drip' approach to team mentality and getting the players to believe they are good enough to be here on merit, is working. And he's absolutely right. We deserve to be top six right now. We really do.

The same diligent approach to the Manchester City match must be instilled. A similar work ethic to what we've all seen so far this season and a genuine belief that Hull City can win the game, will give the Tigers an excellent opportunity to show the nation precisely why we've been the talk of England when the Sky cameras visit.

How team manager Phil Brown intends to tackle the game will genuinely enter the debate this weekend, after a series of sticking with the tried and trusted. Ditch 4-3-3 for 4-4-2? Makes some changes? Not least because left back Andy Dawson has sustained a knock against Bolton that saw him substituted and missing some training this week. Welsh international Sam Ricketts stands by.

Then there is 'casino-gate'. Marlon King apparently sticking the nut on Dean Windass in a Scarborough gaming venue during a team bonding session is almost laughable - but seriously, how will that affect team morale? Hopefully, we are all big lads about it and as Brian Horton has assured everyone - as we discussed here on CI - it was something and nothing.

Of course, Sunday will be a special day for Horton himself, the one time Sky Blues boss is still fondly thought of at Manchester City. Ahead of the game, the assistant manager to Phil Brown stated – *"When we played Chelsea, even Luis Felipe Scolari said that it's sometimes harder to play at home."*

Adding – *"At home is where you need your top players to perform and to get on the ball. It's about bravery and by that we don't just mean winning tackles and headers. It's about getting on the ball. People want you to take the game to the opposition when you're at home. We have to give the crowd something to shout about."*

Yet Horton's one time side will be making several changes for their trip along the M62 leaving manager Mark Hughes with a selection headache. Gelson Fernandes and Richard Dunne are both suspended after getting red cards last time out versus Spurs, while Dean Sturridge is a doubt with an ankle problem. Vincent Kompany should return to boost the visiting ranks, though.

Whatever happens this Sunday, we cannot afford a repeat of the Bolton game. And I'm not just talking about the result, I'm talking about you, that's you reading this. The fans failed the team last Saturday with a low key performance. It's time to put that right this Sunday. Let's not lose it... Anyway, Brian said so.

SUNDAY 16TH NOVEMBER 2008 –
HULL CITY 2-2 MANCHESTER CITY – REPORT

A see-saw televised encounter with the blue half of Manchester produces an entertaining game – if not necessarily for all the right reasons. All I wanted was not be embarrassed on national television. After such a brilliant start to life in the Premier League, the last thing we needed was a public humiliation in front of a watching nation, particularly after three straight defeats.

I was hoping we'd put on a show. Demonstrate to interested onlookers precisely why we are a top six side in England. After being perched at lofty heights in the Premier League for so long, it was time to come out from behind the curtain and burst onto the stage.

Browny made just the one change. Ricketts for Dawson - who clearly had failed to recover from the knock sustained against Bolton eight days ago. The 4-3-3 formation remained intact and few would now argue that this particular strategy is going to be our 'standard' tactic for most Premier League encounters.

The good thing from a watching perspective is that this formation more often than not produces a game that's pretty on the eye. Manchester City thought likewise and opted to come at the hosts with an attacking 4-4-2 formation including Robinho, signed for a cool £30m (give or take a mill or two).

The home side started much the brighter in the contest and pushed Manchester City onto the back foot. Indeed, the visitors looked far from comfortable in the Circle's surroundings and the home supporters improved tenfold on the dismal noise output from the Bolton game.

The opener came after a horrific error from Ben-Haim presented the Tigers with a gift. An abysmal back pass, weak and off-target, was gobbled up by Daniel Cousin who rolled the ball past flailing keeper Joe Hart to put the hosts 1-0 up. Hart needed treatment and was subbed shortly after. It was a true howler.

Manchester City were rocked and the Tigers weren't offering sympathy as they continued to press for more. Geovanni was the main thrust and caused the Sky Blues problems upon facing his old club, after receiving a generous welcome from the visiting contingent at the head of the game.

Marney was particularly impressive in the midfield and once again Boateng and Ashbee proved to be able foils. But the real highlight of the game was the work ethic of the spearhead provided by King and Cousin, who were relentless in their quest to ruffle the back four; the former having one of his best games for City.

So, it was something of a shock to see the North Stand celebrate a goal that came literally out of the blue. A threaded ball should have been Myhill's but Zayatte choose to steer it away from danger and play it out to safety, but instead ran it straight into the path of Stephen Ireland, who had a gaping goal bfore him. The first goal was bad, this was even worse.

As much as you wanted to exact your anger at the centre back, how could you? Zayatte has been a towering, imposing figure at the back and won countless points for City's cause. How on earth could this have happened? Worse still, Manchester City now had their spirits resurrected and wanted some.

It was now Mark Hughes' side who sprung up from nowhere and were the life and soul of this party. The hosts looked like they'd had the wind taken out of their sails after cruising and looking for number two, now it was 1-1 and pretty scruffy.

Then a real kick in the nuts arrived. Daniel Cousin tried an impossible ball from one wing to the other that was easily intercepted and the visitors broke at lightening speed. Garrido cut the ball back to the mightily impressive Stephen Ireland who curled a sweet shot beyond Myhill from inside the box and speared a knife through the heart of the hosts.

From 1-0 up and bossing the game, Brown's team had been rocked, with stuffing knocked out of them and losing 1-2 to a team who had threatened nothing until being gifted a leveller. The second half was to be just as exciting, but we didn't know that at the time.

Out came the Tigers looking to restore parity with far more gumption. Geovanni was revelling playing against his former employers and acrobatically almost tied affairs with a stunning scissor kick. The home side continued to press.

Then, a free kick 20 yards out. Of course it had to be Geo. Stepping up, the kick takes a diversion off the wall and wrong foots the substitute goalkeeper Kasper Schmeichel and the teams are level at 2-2. The game then really opened up in a classic end to end affair.

Within seconds of the equaliser, Cousin flashed a header across goal attempting to put the hosts ahead once more. Darius Vassell then hit fresh air rather than the ball into the net with the visitors' next chance. There then followed a Geovanni free kick that was taken three times for persistent Manchester City encroaching.

But the game remained 2-2. With injury time and both teams striving for a winner, the last real chance fell to Manchester City that prompted a magnificent save from Myhill from Vassell's close range volley. Phew! It had been breathtaking stuff…

All in, it was great to stop a run of three defeats. The game will be remembered for two defensive mishaps for sure, but it was attacking fare that was appealing to the eye from both sides. And City defended Robinho brilliantly to keep the Brazilian relatively quiet. But then, the 25,000 inside had come to see the other one in black and amber, surely?

A great game. A positive result and no disgrace or embarrassment with this performance. On to Portsmouth, keep up the good work Browny. On this evidence we could well be giving the south coast side a game.

MATCH STATS:
- Hull City: Myhill, McShane, Turner, Zayatte, Ricketts, Boateng (Halmosi 85), Ashbee, Marney, Geovanni, Cousin (Barmby 76), King. Subs Not Used: Duke, Doyle, Garcia, Folan, Giannakopoulos.
- Booked: McShane, Marney.
- Goals: Cousin 14, Geovanni 60.
- Man City: Hart (Schmeichel 19), Zabaleta, Richards, Ben-Haim, Garrido, Wright-Phillips, Kompany, Ireland, Mwaruwari (Jô 76), Robinho, Vassell. Subs Not Used: Onuoha, Michael Ball, Hamann, Elano, Evans.
- Booked: Ben-Haim, Wright-Phillips, Ireland.
- Goals: Ireland 37, 45.
- Att: 24,902
- Ref: Phil Dowd (Staffordshire)
- **Premier League position: 6th**

MONDAY 17TH NOVEMBER 2008

Hull City chairman Paul Duffen has revealed the forthcoming plans geared towards expansion, with a team of experts already in position to assist the growth of the Premier League's newest club... The City chief believes the Premier League financial clout that has come to Hull City should be invested back into club for the long term future – and that means rather than expanding the stadium capacity, ploughing resources into a multi-million pound football academy on a brand new site will take precedence.

Duffen revealed – *"Right now, my absolute burning ambition is to prioritise creating a unified training ground and academy on a 25 to 30-acre site. It will be a platform to properly invest in a structure that will feed this football club in many ways in the future."*

Continuing with – *"We've got an active brief with a team of professionals who are identifying sites and looking at planning issues at the moment. A best of class training ground and academy is a much bigger priority than touching the capacity of the KC Stadium."*

And then confirmed – *"It would be an enormous distraction if you start fiddling with the stadium. We need to focus all our energies on Premier League football. We need to make sure that any of those infrastructure changes take place away from the stadium at this moment in time. That's why I believe investing in the training ground and an academy are the priority."*

TUESDAY 18TH NOVEMBER 2008

Now I didn't realise this, but that pre-season tournament in the Far East that the Premier League undergo every year - The Asia Cup - could well see Hull City destined for a tour of the continent as part of the Premier League's global exposure.

Because of our amazing start, Premier League shareholders have handed a provisional invitation to Hull City that would allow the club to take part in the top flight's Asia Cup tournament - a competition that has now become established on the pre-season Premier League calendar. China, Hong Kong and South Korea have all expressed an interest in hosting the 2009 tournament, with Shanghai and Beijing being two places mooted as favourites to host the pre-season round of matches.

Chairman Paul Duffen confirmed - *"It would be a massive thing for the exposure of this football club. There will be three Premier League sides and a local club - hopefully one of those will be us. It's yet to be confirmed but that would be magnificent. For this club to play in Asia for a week would be a wonderful thing."*

Duffen continued - *"It's a tournament that's been going on for a while now. There are three Premier League teams that go out and they play against a local Asian team for a week in July. It would effectively take up some of our pre-season. But what an opportunity for some people in this city to go to Asia and support their football team in a tournament, it would be fantastic."*

Portsmouth won the tournament in 2007, beating fellow Premier League sides Bolton Wanderers and Liverpool to the £100,000 prize money that included several lucrative spin-offs in the Asian business market for winning the cup. After discussions with all the clubs approached, Premier League chief Richard Scudamore is expected to firm up the clubs taking part next month. This is quite surreal. Hull City playing in China? Not exactly Macclesfield, eh?

WEDNESDAY 19TH NOVEMBER 2008

You nasty little man, you! Kicking a water bottle in frustration, tut, tut! Hull City manager Phil Brown has been slapped with a fine for his actions from the do-gooders at English FA Headquarters. And do you know? Had I not been documenting this season, I would've forgotten about this ages ago. It was back in August for crying out loud!

Still, a £1,000 fine has been slapped on Hull City manager Phil Brown during the home defeat to Wigan Athletic when the teams met at the Circle on August 30th. The 'incident' occurred when Wigan scored their second goal of the afternoon and Brown turned in frustration to kick a water bottle in anger. Allegedly, the bottle hit the fourth official at the time and the City boss immediately apologised.

Indeed, I hadn't realised, but Brown chose to impose his own touchline ban by resorting to the directors' seats in the lower West Stand and watched the second half alongside club chairman Paul Duffen.

Now, after being found guilty, the FA have charged the City boss with improper conduct and hit the boss with a four figure fine. Admittedly, one of the less crazy punishments meted out by the governing body, but a bloody sad state of affairs nonetheless.

THURSDAY 20TH NOVEMBER 2008

Last night, I represented City Independent for the last time at the Fans Liaison Committee meeting. For the few who actually did make the gathering, it felt more like a wake. Allow me to explain...

This is how it shall end. Not with a bang... but a whimper. The agenda was set. The question asked at the last meeting – 'What is the point of the Fans Liaison Committee?' It was difficult to argue in the positive given that only five members out of the sixteen named representatives turned up for the meeting.

In many ways after seven – or whatever years – it was sad. Adam Pearson set up the Committee as a conduit between himself as the chairman of the football club and the fans. In the first years, as we moved upwards and onwards there was a lot to sort out at the club. A lot to debate and argue over, plus with the move to the KC Stadium, there was plenty of positive input. The FLC did play a crucial part in all those things.

When the FLC began in a small fusty old cupboard at Boothferry Park there was not a Hull City supporter network as such. Adam Pearson needed the FLC. There is a big supporters club now - and Mr Duffen feels that with the amount of time he and Mr Pratt spend visiting supporter groups these days, that he is now answering the same questions that the FLC pose anyway.

Supporters in his view can still have their say. They still have access to the Fans Liaison Officer (or whatever Dan calls himself these days) and the fanzines will still have access to the chairman. Obviously, Paul Duffen and commercial director Andy Dawson are often seen on the concourses at away grounds, so anyone can pass on their views and questions.

Whether this will be the case if, God forbid, things start to turn sour is another matter. But, let's hope there will never be a need for a FLC in the future.

The club is a very different position to when the FLC was first formed. Mr Pearson as mentioned needed access to fans views. He was able to assess the mood, feelings and opinions and make decisions. We are now, however, not just a one man operation. Mr Duffen now has a board. The FLC – it could be said – didn't only act as Pearson's sounding board but his board of directors. Paul Duffen does have a board of directors that he has to consult. Hull City is a different club now.

As a final note it was agreed that the FLC will not be fully defunct. There was mention of 'special' meetings with such as the police (this is a must as they won't go to supporters meetings), John Cooper and the catering people.

But, compared to what has gone before... this is the end.

FRIDAY 21ST OCTOBER 2008 - PORTSMOUTH V HULL CITY PREVIEW

As the country braces itself for an icy blast from the north, Hull City will be escaping to the sunny south coast and the delights of one of the proper 'old skool' Premier League grounds on the circuit.

Welcome to Portsmouth. And for me, this will be a first time visit to Fratton Park. I'm mightily glad they've decided to stick a roof on the old gal for the visiting supporters these days, as the weather threatens to take a cold and wet turn for the worst. Well come on, it's a bloody long way to go to get saturated.

At Arsenal's Emirates Stadium - the jewel in the Premier League crown for stadia we are led to believe - the atmosphere was bland without our presence. Fortunately, things really did spice up when we had the audacity to equalise - and then go on to win the game. Post-match, we were dubbed 'the Portsmouth of the north' by Gooners. Is that a compliment?

Well, if you like your football to be passionate and noisy, enjoy a bit of the old terrace banter, plus be prepared to yell your head off for 90 minutes, then Portsmouth away is the one for you. It's why I wouldn't miss it for the world, back end of November or whenever. It'll be grand old terrace war, make no mistake.

You have to pay a lot of respect to what Portsmouth have achieved in the Premier League. Indeed, the south coast club wouldn't be a bad role model to follow in our fledgling top flight career. The club has not changed. Nor have my goals, in fact. It's still all about survival this year, sixth place or not. Portsmouth did this and then kicked on, so you can bet Saturday is going to be a mighty tough game.

Perhaps, though, City can draw some confidence from the home side's recent managerial shuffle. Tony Adams is still finding his feet as the number one at Fratton Park and our away form is brilliant this season. Five victories, one draw and a solitary loss last time out provides much confidence to draw upon. Only Manchester United - the champions - have beaten us on the road. And that was 4-3.

But Phil Brown is facing some disruption to his team selection at the head of the field if Daniel Cousin fails to overcome his knee problem. Caleb Folan and veteran striker Dean

Windass stand by should they be needed. Better news sees Andy Dawson come back into contention at left back, while all our international stars will be monitored this week before being considered for selection.

Manager Phil Brown stated on the matter – *"Our training ahead of Saturday is certainly as important, if not more, than at any other time this season. Some of the players will have had 11 or 12 hours on a flight and maybe just five or six hours sleep before being back on the training ground. It's going to be about their mental state and their physical state more than ability and I think that will play a part in team selection."*

Adding – *"I'll have a look at the whites of their eyes and decide. Confidence levels will play a big part. Some players are coming back, like Marlon King with Jamaica, having won 3-0 and scored, and others will be coming back having played a full game which they expected to win having not scored and been on the end of a defeat."*

Portsmouth have several injuries ahead of City's visit. Captain Sol Campbell has a toe injury, while the influential duo of Nico Kranjčar and Lassana Diarra have ankle injuries and will also be missing from action. England striker Jermain Defoe faces a late test after hobbling off at half time following the midweek win over Germany.

New Portsmouth manager Tony Adams has been more than respectful with his pre-game comments towards Hull City declaring – *"They've done fantastically well and Geovanni's obviously a quality player who needed time to settle into the game here. Hull have worked extremely hard and deserve the points they've got."*

Before concluding – *"They've spent some money and their position in the table doesn't lie. They are showing that clubs who use the little cash-injection they get when they come up can stay up."*

This match seems set be a cracker. Both teams will be setting out to win the match and play the game in the correct manner with some pacy attacking football. Frankly, I can't wait for it. 540 mile round trip and everything included.

SATURDAY 22ND NOVEMBER 2008 – PORTSMOUTH 2-2 HULL CITY – REPORT

An early start - a mite too early in fact - but here we go. Leaving the cold climate of Hull bracing itself for snow, the carriage to take me to the tropical southern destination of Portsmouth had now arrived. South of England here we come!

Ahead of the game, the old fashioned, traditional settings of Fratton Park were deemed appealing. The atmosphere was expected to be reasonably tasty, but in truth neither matched up to the billing. Fortunately, the game itself was better fare and the result turned out to be a hugely satisfactory one in the context and pattern of the match.

En route to the ground, a couple of hostelries were sampled with each providing friendly locals with whom to have a pre-match natter. Plenty of 'old-school' City faces were present for this one and the atmosphere had a decent buzz about it.

Yet upon entering Fratton Park that quickly evaporated. Firstly, the stewarding is ridiculously over-zealous and the freak sideshow to our left had the annoyingly dull thumping of a bass drum and ruddy cowbell all game. An open question to Portsmouth fans; is that what you want for all your home games? That wouldn't last two minutes in Hull, I tell you.

But City creating an atmosphere was suitably stifled by the overreacting stewards that didn't tolerate standing, shouting, moving, farting and breathing. I kid you not. Yet elsewhere in the surrounding stands, this was perfectly acceptable. That whopping great stand opposite us gleefully gloated all game they were standing, with several chants about the fact. Bah! Early on, Portsmouth thought they'd opened the scoring to put the woollies up us. City watched anxiously as Bouba Diop's header hit the bar and cries yelped from the home stands that the ball had crashed down over the line. From our end, you had no chance of telling. Controversial 'ghost goal' referee Stuart Attwell deemed it was no goal, so it's highly probable Portsmouth have a case.

The home side were on the offensive from the outset, as City struggled to keep pace. The opening goal came their way from Peter Crouch powering in a close range header, as Myhill's best attempts to keep the ball out failed. We were 1-0 down and the atmosphere was pants with City fans spending most of the game battling with the stewards just to be permitted to support the side.

But City responded admirably and fought back well from their one-goal deficit. The visitors took hold of the match and pressed Portsmouth back. Large chunks of possession came our way and Marlon King missed two great chances when firing each wide from either side of the goal.

The best effort of the half came out of nothing when the inspirational Geovanni collected the ball from 30 yards out and left England goalkeeper David James rooted to the spot, watching helplessly as the ball smacked the angle of post and bar. Damn! City deserved to be level.

Half time came and City had enjoyed the lion's share but were lacking in the crucial goals column. After the break, the Tigers picked up from the same place and pushed Portsmouth back desperate for the equaliser. It came from a set-piece - just seconds after reminding my travel companions this was our best route to goal. Marney swung it in, Turner powered the header home. Yes! 1-1!

City continued to press and looked the most likely to win the game. Marney had forced James into a smart save and Cousin was a real thorn in Portsmouth's side all afternoon. So it was something of a kick in the gonads when Fratton Park exploded in delight once more.

In truth, it was a peach and a certain candidate for goal of the month – even if it had come from an unlikely source. Defender Glen Johnson capitalised on City not clearing their lines correctly when unleashing a vicious volley from 25 yards out that beat Myhill all ends up. Some goal, even if it had come against the run of play a little.

Browny made changes to get back into the game, bringing on Halmosi, Giannakopoulos for a debut and local hero Dean Windass. But Portsmouth had renewed vigour now and Utaka missed two glorious chances when drilling across the face of goal and then spooning a close range effort from a corner over the bar, as the game flew from end to end.

City had far from given up the ghost. The Tigers were behind to an amazing strike, but even the most ardent Portsmouth fan couldn't deny Hull City were simply not giving up. The new width provided by City's substitutions stretched the home side and the effort put in really did merit some reward from the match if only for sheer bloody-mindedness.

And it came. There was a touch of fortune about it but who cares? Another corner caused Portsmouth panic and with the ball pinging around the box, Dean Windass – amid home fans' taunts of **"YOU FAT BASTARD!"** – glanced a header goalwards that deflected off Noe Pamarot and into the net with two minutes to spare. Cue pandemonium. And a raucous chorus of **"YOU FAT BASTARD!"** from us! Despite a frantic bout of injury time with both sides pressing, the game rightly concluded at 2-2 and City had worked mightily hard for their point. The ground and the atmosphere may not have quite met pre-game expectations but the open, attacking football more than warmed the cockles on the long journey back. Apparently, there's snow waiting for us back in Hull...

Good point, decent match and an impressive performance from Daniel Cousin and my own man of the match Paul McShane. You would never have believed he had completed a huge stint for Ireland four days prior. Top performance, arguably his best ever in a City shirt. Brilliant stuff.

MATCH STATS:
- Portsmouth: James, Johnson, Kaboul, Distin, Pamarot, Diop, Davis, Hughes (Nugent 58), Belhadj (Armand Traore 58), Crouch, Utaka (Kanu 74) Subs Not Used:Ashdown, Hreidarsson, Mvuemba, Little.
- Booked: Diop, Davis.
- Goals: Crouch 20, Johnson 63.
- Hull: Myhill, McShane, Turner, Zayatte, Ricketts, Marney (Giannakopoulos 82), Ashbee, Boateng (Halmosi 72), Geovanni, King (Windass 72), Cousin. Subs Not Used:Duke, Doyle, Barmby, Garcia.
- Booked: Windass.
- Goals: Turner 54, Windass 89.
- Att: 20,240
- Ref: Stuart Attwell (Warwickshire)
- **Premier League position: 6th**

FRIDAY 28TH NOVEMBER 2008 - STOKE CITY V HULL CITY PREVIEW

Stoke City away on a freezing cold November day is hardly the most dazzling of Premier League fixtures, but this supposedly charmless affair has a certain spice to it the media have seemingly missed.

It's been billed as the battle of the promoted Championship sides, that perhaps may be true, but to quote as such is probably doing a disservice to both teams. Firstly, Hull City for their incredible start to life as a Premier League club and secondly, Stoke for some resurgent form that sees the Potters in mid-table.

When the fixtures came out and you totted up where you were going to get the points from to succeed in the Premier League, most people would've scribbled down 'Stoke City (a) - 3 points'. The way the season started for the Potters, you'd be right, but now? After four straight home wins, can you be so sure? Well for me, I still think so.

Stoke fans this week have been typically bullish ahead of the meet. It's a little disconcerting that some of their fans seem oblivious to what Hull City have achieved and are content to hide behind 'You're rubbish, you haven't won in five games'. Hey, they're right, but do any Hull City fans think we've played badly in that run? Not created chances? Failed to score? Built up sustained pressure against good teams? Nah, I didn't think so. Two in two unbeaten we are.

It may stick in the throat of Stoke fans that we took the glamour route to the Premier League via Wembley. And then upon arriving here have gone on to pull off some magnificent results with fast, aggressive, attacking football - played without fear and rightly receiving plaudits from far and wide. That's happening because Hull City to date have been roundly excellent. It's why we are sixth in the table today.

Sure, we're not going to win every game. There will be many trials and tribulations along the Premier League road - Wigan and Bolton at home are prime examples - but the Tigers have each time, so far, bounced back this season. And they never know when they are beaten. Stoke are wary of this, they know we have been on the front foot all season. It worries them although they won't admit it.

Then, compare that to Stoke. Here's a team that has conceded the first goal seven times and lost all seven. That smacks of brittle confidence to me. Sure, their home form might be good now - but we all know form is temporary. Stoke are hardly prolific scorers, unlike ourselves, particularly away from home. Stoke have reasons to be worried, but they'd rather not think about it.

Remember, the Tigers have lost just once on the Premier League road this season and that was to champions Manchester United in an amazing game that ended 4-3. Stoke by contrast - and just two weeks later - were hammered 5-0 by the same side at the same venue. But that doesn't mean anything, probably. Pulis' side will be given a game, I'm sure. Stoke will have to come to terms with that at some point.

However, City will have to set about their task without Andy Dawson who remains troubled with an Achilles injury. Caleb Folan is battling to beat his knee injury, but old man Windass will want to keep his shirt after a 'goalscoring' appearance from the bench at Portsmouth that earned a 2-2 draw.

Bernard Mendy is said to be making a speedy recovery from a minor operation and has an outside chance of featuring, but Anthony Gardner will be kept wating another week at least. With Phil Brown stating he'll chose his 'best' team over his 'big' team for the visit to Stoke, I think it's safe to say it will be 4-3-3 with the same personnel as last week. We'll go for it like we have all season long.

Phil Brown knows the first goal is all-important at the Britannia. This is particularly with Stoke not winning by more than a single goal in 29 attempts. Brown states – *"They've conceded the first goal on seven occasions and lost all seven. When they've scored first on five occasions they've won, so it's the first goal that matters."* Hey, it appears we've both spotted a Stoke weakness...

Stoke themselves will be boosted by the return of striker Ricardo Fuller. Manager Tony Pulis refuses to rule out Ryan Shawcross with fractured bones in his back and £5.5m misfit Dave Kitson. Both saw specialists this week. Who is he kidding? Meanwhile, it seems almost desperate, but skipper Andy Griffin will play with a broken hand. What happens if he goes over? Barking...

Pulis stated ahead of the game – *"They are very competitive, a strong team. They have lots of things going for them and the main thing is confidence. Results breed confidence, and they are full of it."* Yep, he's got that right.

Before adding – *"They don't give up and they are playing with a togetherness that pushes teams forward. But we are confident too. We are very pleased with the way our players have performed."*

I'll leave you with this. If Hull City win we could be top four and put Stoke back in the drop zone. If Hull City lose, we'll still be better than Stoke by two points and get to play them at home at the business end of the season. Sure, this game is massive, but at the end of the day, it's just Stoke. It's not that big a deal, is it?

SATURDAY 29TH NOVEMBER 2008 – STOKE CITY 1-1 HULL CITY – REPORT

Foggy, cold and dull. And the weather wasn't up to much either. A stalemate ensues at the Britannia Stadium, as two of last season's promoted clubs play out a draw that very few could argue against.

The rumours beforehand in the Harvester pub was that the game was subject to a 1pm inspection. A look out the window confirmed it was still foggy, but how can you definitively call a game off two hours in advance due to fog? Maybe the referee had a crystal ball.

On to the match and allow me to be frank here. It was an eyesore for the football purist. The game lacked any fluency, chances were at a premium and the shots on target were distinctly absent from both sides. For me it was somewhat disappointing that the Tigers had chosen an unorthodox 4-5-1 formation for the first time on the road this season. Barmby had replaced Cousin up front in the only change.

Still, Browny knows best. Stoke came out of the blocks quickest, but their whole game is geared towards getting the ball into the box as quickly as possible from any area of the park. We know this - we've seen this for the fourth season running now - but you still can't help commenting on such primitive football. I mean, the whole crowd gets excited about a bleedin' throw in. Yuk. It's horrid to watch.

The Tigers had no real outlet with Marlon King the sole contender to take on 'big bloke Stoke's' back four. But, the visitors were rigid. A sturdy formation ensured Stoke's attacking threat was neutralised and the atmosphere waned pretty quickly as the match progressed. Not surprising in truth, the football was rubbish and a poor advert for the Premier League.

The fleeting glimpses of passing football were all by Phil Brown's side, but Geovanni had three men on him at all times and the formation being employed hadn't provided the necessary width to seriously threaten Stoke. It was like a stand-off. The visitors playing it cautious, Stoke lacking ability or the armoury to seriously threaten. The hosts struggled to find a shot on target with the onus on them to attack and it was clear pretty quickly that this was always going to be last game on Match of the Day tonight.

Highlights so far included the visitors enclosure baiting the Stoke fans with mock throwing gestures and Tigers boss Phil Brown getting naughty with the gamesmanship tactics that Stoke exploit to maximum advantage, by getting Dean Windass to warm up when Delap was about to hurl another one in from a throw. Windass predictably got booked, but he'd been a good nuisance for few minutes.

However, the sterile fare on the field was painful. Fortunately, it was brightened up by a splendid goal from Marlon King right on half time. A free kick midway inside the Stoke half was sent to the back post and Michael Turner headed back across the box to an unmarked King who hooked brilliantly into the top corner. It was a cracking goal and rocked the hosts. Big game, big tactics, you have to take your chances. So much for cursing 4-5-1.

What the goal did was provide a shot in the arm for the second half. It could scarcely be any worse than the first. Stoke pressed to get on level terms, but for a home side, the chances were pretty much non-existent. Indeed, I recall just three attempts as a lasting impression. And none were particularly threatening, although Michael Tonge's low drive across the six yard box could've been dangerous if followed in.

Brown's side played a lovely one touch move that cut Stoke apart with Ricketts, Geovanni, Barmby and King setting up Marney's fierce drive that Sørensen did well to get down to and hold. But it was a largely fruitless task at the front of the field for the visitors, who had set their stall out with a less than ambitious philosophy of not getting beaten. It was a first for us this season on the Premier League road. The downside to this was too few numbers to build up a head of steam in the killer third of the pitch, but hey, these were the chosen tactics.

With Stoke running out of ideas - or, more accurately, their throws being ineffective - a gift was presented to them. Fuller burst the visiting back line and Myhill charged out to meet him and as the striker attempted to round him, the Welshman felled the Jamaican. You would argue a case at the other end I suppose, no complaints here. Fuller's weak penalty didn't send Myhill the wrong way and the big keeper should've kept it out as he got his body down to the ball, but it squirmed under him and into the net much to Myhill's disgust. Lucky old Stoke, eh?

Despite Phil Brown changing matters and bringing on Halmosi and Cousin - who had made way for Barmby - a chance to win the game never really materialised. But then, nor did it for Stoke. Instead, it was left to the visitors to antagonise the hosts with the point they probably would have settled for by imitating Rory Delap's towel and throw routine. Take a bow Ricketts and McShane, they don't like it up 'em.

Still, as the whistle came, fortress Britannia had been breached if not overthrown with this 1-1 draw. The visitors for the first time this season had chosen not to attack their hosts due to the bigger picture in mind; Stoke not getting maximum points at home to Hull City is surely going to hurt come the business end of the season. Perhaps Browny has been cannier than we all maybe realise tonight.

No doubt we could've won this, but the safety and survival first approach is rightly and sensibly taking precedence after a blistering start that has accumulated a raft of points. Today, you couldn't really argue. It was a good point gained from a team who had won their last four at home, yet worryingly for them, a team in that sort of form couldn't beat a side who have now gone six games without a win. Well, I suppose we are sixth, we must be reasonably decent, I guess.

But, more importantly than that, we are three games unbeaten now. Only Manchester United - the champions - have beaten us on their home turf this season. Stoke, at no point, threatened to do likewise, despite a boasting a recent magnificent home record. No prizes for guessing who is the happier tonight? That point won at the Britannia will do nicely thank you very much - and will be added to the stockpile already safely stored in the bank. Onwards...

MATCH STATS:
- Stoke: Sørensen, Griffin, Abdoulaye Faye, Cort, Higginbotham, Soares (Tonge 62), Amdy Faye, Diao, Delap, Sidibe. Subs Not Used: Simonsen, Olofinjana, Whelan, Cresswell,

Dickinson, Sonko.
- Booked: Griffin, Diao.
- Goals: Fuller 73 pen.
- Hull: Myhill, McShane, Turner, Zayatte, Ricketts, Marney, Boateng (Cousin 78), Ashbee, Barmby (Halmosi 69), Geovanni (Garcia 90), King. Subs Not Used: Duke, Windass, Mendy, Giannakopoulos.
- Booked: Windass, Myhill, Zayatte.
- Goals: King 45.
- Att: 27,500
- Ref: Keith Stroud (Hampshire)
- **Premier League position: 6th**

SUNDAY 30TH NOVEMBER 2008

The draw for the third round of the FA Cup has been made today. I managed to see this live. For the first time ever, I was sitting there thinking; 'I hope we don't get one of the big clubs'. In fact, I hope we don't get any Premier League club.

"Hull City will play... Newcastle United"

Great. Cheers for that.

CHAPTER 5 – OUT IN THE COLD

MONDAY 1ST DECEMBER 2008

Hull City manager Phil Brown has given his reaction to the Third Round FA Cup draw that has seen the Tigers paired with Newcastle United at the Circle when the teams meet in January. He sounds mildly more excited about the prospect than me, it must be said.

Brown began his comments with - *"The league is more and more of a priority for every club these days. The financial differences between being in the Championship and being in the Premier League are huge, but we have the beauty of a strong squad."*

Before adding - *"Even if we did make six or seven changes, we would still have a very strong team. You look at our team-sheet last week and the bench was full of quality. You had a Greek international [Stelios Giannakopoulos], you had a 39-year-old experienced goalscorer [Dean Windass] and an ex-England international [Nick Barmby]."*

Continuing with - *"On top of that, you had a Hungarian international [Peter Halmosi], an Australian international [Richard Garcia], a former England youth international [Nathan Doyle] and a very capable goalkeeper in Matt Duke. That to me shows what quality we can call on."*

Concluding - *"It's winnable and it's a route into Europe. I am looking forward to it. We are one of the big guns now which is great news for us and being a top-six side going into the draw gives us a lot of satisfaction."*

THURSDAY 4TH DECEMBER 2008

Roy Keane has walked away from the Sunderland manager's job, stating that he has taken the Black Cats as far as he can. For the time being, coach Ricky Sbragia has taken over the role. However, as expected, it didn't take long for the media to put two and two together and link hometown boy Phil Brown with the club he supported in his youth – Sunderland.

Yet before Sunderland fans could get too excited about snatching 'manager of the season' Phil Brown away from the Tigers, the City boss appears to have ruled himself out of contention for the post.

Despite speculation very quickly linking Brown with the Stadium of Light (already a 9-1 second favourite with some bookmakers) it appears rather ironic that an old chum from Brown's Bolton Wanderers days – Sam Allardyce – is favourite.

When quizzed on Roy Keane's resignation from Sunderland Brown claimed - *"All I can say is that it's a tough job in the Premier League full stop. What has gone on at Sunderland is Sunderland's business and nothing to do with me."*

And then enhanced the belief he would be going nowhere by confirming - *"I've got to make sure that the next couple of years in Hull City's history are proud moments for everybody in the area and that's going to be my intention starting from Saturday."*

FRIDAY 5TH DECEMBER 2008 – HULL CITY V MIDDLESBROUGH PREVIEW

This is a proper 'old-school' fixture from days gone by. The Yorkshire traditionalists will still claim this as one of 'God's own county' derbies. What can't be denied is the certain spice of a Hull City v Middlesbrough fixture...

To this day, after 30 odd years of supporting Hull City, I've never quite fathomed out why Hull City v Middlesbrough brings out the best (and worst?) of supporters from each side. What I do know is; this is a fixture I genuinely looked forward to when the Premier League fixtures were announced.

There's something about Middlesbrough. Maybe it's because both are Yorkshire outposts, often cut from the heart of the county - rightly or wrongly - with both settlements coming from a very working class, hard-nosed, industrial setting. Proper northern conurbations, hard, fair and proud.

And when the two respective sides meet, there is always a certain needle, a cracking atmosphere that sits awkwardly between the two respective camps. It's not a derby by any stretch, but then strangely it is. The Middlesbrough fixture is a genuinely unique encounter for the experienced and discerning Hull City supporter. You wouldn't want to miss it.

Battles on the pitch are notoriously close. Away from the pitch, there's a distinct 'one-upmanship' between the rivals that occasionally can spill over on to the mean streets of either location. I've never really understood why. I don't really care. I just know I love the tinder box atmosphere this fixture always creates.

Thankfully, due to the FA Cup, two fixtures arrived two seasons ago. It rekindled the same old burning desires inside from past encounters from yesteryear and two cracking fixtures demonstrated exactly why the magic of the cup reigns supreme, when the Championship Tigers roared into Premier League Middlesbrough.

After a replay, Middlesbrough inched past City with a nervy 4-3 victory, but those that witnessed the two games had certainly had their fill and had duly quelled the 'Middlesbrough fix' that had been abandoned for far too long. City's promotion to the top table may well just revive what is still regarded as a much revered fixture among both tribes.

Excellent news all round, I'd say. These up and coming two league meetings are two you do not want to miss. Particularly, for the first time in a long time, City are handily placed and marginal favourites to win the game. And it's about time too.

The hosts are sixth in the Premier League and due a victory - one at home at that - here's hoping the triumph will be over Middlesbrough. Phil Brown certainly seems to think so judging by his pre-game comments, when stating – *"It's now three undefeated, three good draws, two on our journeys. We're back at the KC Stadium, hopefully to bring back that winning mentality."*

To carve out the much craved win, Brown has received a double injury boost. Full back Andy Dawson could return following Achilles trouble which is nice - remember that goal in the replay against Boro two seasons ago? Also fit is Dean Marney who has struggled in the early part of the week with a knock. Caleb Folan is out with a knee injury, so your friend and mine, ex-Boro boy Dean Windass will be on the bench. It couldn't be scripted any better... Middlesbrough, meanwhile, have been blowing hot and cold. On their day, it could be a fierce test of City's top six credentials. If, however, Boro let their guard slip, you can bet the Tigers will tear their guests for the day to shreds. In not one game this season have City sat back. Against Middlesbrough it will surely be no different.

Gareth Southgate is hoping to have Gary O'Neil and Emmanuel Pogatetz declared fit for the clash after recent injuries. Long term injury victim Robert Huth is also in line to come back into contention and may well start if cleared to play.

Saturday's game should – if previous meetings act as a barometer to go by – prove to be an absolute cracker on the pitch and in the stands. A corking atmosphere awaits, it's going to be tough, not one for the faint-hearted - and hell, I've even shaved my head for it. Bring it on!

SATURDAY 6TH DECEMBER 2008 – HULL CITY 2-1 MIDDLESBROUGH - REPORT

This was a big, big game and I could think in the pub beforehand was 'please, just don't lose!' With Liverpool coming up next week, it was critical not to suffer defeat at home to

Middlesbrough today. A draw is acceptable given the points tally we've accrued, but a win? Well, that would be very welcome indeed.

You see, City may not have won for six games before taking on Middlesbrough, but Browny's side have been playing well. And in any case, the latter three of that half dozen games have been draws. All points in the bag and very welcome towards the target of survival.

Phil Brown elected to keep the same side that entered the battle at Stoke and earned a point. It was a line-up that included two former Middlesbrough players in George Boateng and Nick Barmby. The former received a warm welcome from the travelling fans, the latter was subjected to abuse practically all game.

The opening exchanges were dominated by the visitors and Middlesbrough boss Gareth Southgate had pressed four players high up the field and sat them squarely on City's back four. A melee in the box could just have easily been turned in, before it was hacked away within the opening minutes.

Indeed, the hosts struggled to find any sort of foothold in the game and were subjected to some pretty fierce attacking play from Middlesbrough, intent on getting an early goal as quickly as possible. City offered token gestures going forward but couldn't produce a save from Ross Turnbull in the visiting goal. Yet a bit like a boxer going banzai in the opening rounds, Middlesbrough quickly ran out steam. City grew into the game and Geovanni was becoming more and more influential. However, two clear headers from close range - one with the freedom of the box at the Brazilian's disposal - were woefully wide.

It had been a half of half chances, some ropey defending to add into the mix and some pretty wretched finishing that really should have produced a goal for someone - anyone - but incredibly, it was scoreless at the interval. Don't mistake this 0-0 for dull and boring, though. It was anything but. Ineptitude on both sides made this game intriguing.

The second half saw the balance of play edge much more into the hosts' favour. City had been sent out a minute or two earlier than Southgate's men and had the more urgency to get forward. Middlesbrough remained dangerous on the break and Digard was having a fine game centrally for the visitors, overshadowing the usually pivotal Arca. King was doing a good job holding the ball up for City and Ricketts and McShane provided ample width to join in the forays forward, but again - pretty much like Middlesbrough in fact - the most dangerous Brown's side looked was when taking a set-piece.

The City boss decided to change matters an hour in and on trotted the double substitution of Bernard Mendy and Daniel Cousin for Dean Marney and Nick Barmby. Immediately, the Tigers had more impetus and with Geovanni in a wider role, problems emerged for Middlesbrough when City broke at pace.

So, it came as a rare old shock to watch Middlesbrough seemingly clinch the game with ten minutes left on the watch. Justin Hoyte scampered down the wing unchecked and ran and ran and ran until he was looking at the whites of Myhill's eyes on the corner of the six yard box, before pulling back for Tuncay to turn in.

Damn, my heart sank. That's surely the winner, gutted. But no. As Alan Hansen keeps reminding us all on Match of the Day, this team never know when they are beaten, somewhat bucking the Premier League trend. And Middlesbrough are becoming another team that still haven't learnt that taking the lead against us, ten minutes left or not, means you still have to stay focussed. In fairness, even I forget sometimes. These Tigers are dangerous when behind.

Middlesbrough switched off the second they had taken the lead. Immediately from the kick off, Bernard Mendy did what Hoyte had done seconds before, but this time shot at the near post. It smacked the base of the upright but rebounded off the flailing Ross Turnbull and crept over the line off the back of the keeper to squeeze in. Incredible! It was 1-1. Middlesbrough's joy was gone in a flash.

The game became massively stretched and gaps appeared all over the park. Hell, someone's gonna win it here. And they did. Geovanni popped up in acres of spaces to run directly at the heart of the Middlesbrough defence, which backed off. Geovanni kept running, and then as the Brazilian reached the box, Wheater hit him and over goes the City number ten. Penalty!

Wheater protested, but his second yellow of the game meant he had to walk. After an age, Marlon King stepped up for the spot kick. Decisively, the ball was hit hard and low into the bottom corner, with Turnbull guessing right but helpless due to the precision, and City were incredibly 2-1 up from being 1-0 down just four minutes earlier.

The stadium erupted and City fans took great delight in advising the visitors housed in the North Stand exactly how and where they had screwed up a winning advantage with 10 minutes to go. Middlesbrough naturally pressed for something despite depleted numbers, but City held station and took a massive three points.

By no means was this a classic. I doubt Match of the Day will be pushing this game to the front of the highlights queue, but it was a pulsating, tension-filled match with both teams at least having a go to win. Today, it was City's day. On another day, it may well not have been.

Regardless, the underlying lesson from Phil Brown's side is this: Hull City never, ever know when they are beaten. Unfortunately for Middlesbrough, they hadn't heeded the many warnings beforehand in the Premier League.

Phil Brown's side may lack all-round quality, but City are fifth on merit. Spirit, resolve, commitment and a desire to never, ever quit have got us there. And still no team has sussed that yet. Long may it continue! With such tenacity consistently being shown, Hull City fully deserve their present rewards. Another three points closer to survival...

MATCH STATS:

- Hull City: Myhill, McShane, Turner, Zayatte, Ricketts, Boateng, Ashbee, Marney (Cousin 61), Barmby (Mendy 61), Geovanni (Halmosi 86), King. Subs Not Used: Duke, Windass, Garcia, Giannakopoulos.
- Booked: Ashbee.
- Goals: Turnbull 82 og, King 85 pen.
- Middlesbrough: Turnbull, Hoyte, Wheater, Pogatetz, Taylor, Aliadiere, Arca, Digard (Hines 87), Downing, Sanli, Alves. Subs Not Used: Jones, Emnes, Johnson, McMahon, Grounds, Walker.
- Sent Off: Wheater 84.
- Booked: Sanli.
- Goals: Sanli 79.
- Att: 24,912
- Ref: Steve Tanner (Somerset)
- **Premier League position: 5th**

WEDNESDAY 10TH DECEMBER 2008

Such has been Hull City's start to the season we're currently the 5th best side in the country. I know, I can't believe it either. Indeed, club chairman Paul Duffen has revealed the club are no longer looking over their shoulder at the relegation picture, instead focus has remained on a trying to stabilise a position in the top six of the Premier League. Are you sure we're talking about my club here?

Duffen believes we are no longer looking backwards at the troubles of a relegation scrap, instead the club is now turning its attentions to cementing a place in the upper echelons of the Premier League.

The City chairman claimed - *"Obviously, retaining our place in the Premier League is still the focus for this season. Saturday's result was a big one for the club as it cemented our place in the top six."*

Adding confidently - *"At this moment in time, as we look at the league ladder, we are only focusing on the teams that are around us, and how we can move up."*

Duffen, clearly bristling concluded - *"When we are watching results from elsewhere in the Premier League, we are no longer watching for the results of the clubs at the bottom of the table, we are looking at the teams between fifth and tenth, as that is the area we see ourselves in at the moment. If a side at the top is playing a side lower in the league, we want the team lower down to win as it helps us at the top."*

FRIDAY 12TH DECEMBER 2008 - LIVERPOOL V HULL CITY PREVIEW

Hull City are about to embark on a trip to the most successful club in the country. And it's not for a cup match either. The top six Tigers are coming to Anfield. Not for a jolly, but to actually attack...

Okay, confession time for me. After decades of support for Hull City, trawling all over the country to a plethora of nondescript Football League backwaters, I never thought I would see this day with my club. Well, League Cup and FA Cup ties apart. Not for a moment did I ever think Hull City, my team, would be walking out at Anfield for a league game in the top flight. We've arrived...

And let's be right here, not just turning up for the fans to have a beano and enjoy the thrill of a day out at one of the big four in the spotlight, oh no. Hull City arrive at Anfield, deservedly sixth in the Premier League, beaten just once on the road all season and with one of the best goalscoring and away records in the division. Making up the numbers we aint.

I, like everybody (including the whole country I would imagine) have marvelled at the way Phil Brown and his team have ripped up the Premier League newcomers' handbook to shreds and really torn into teams. Hull City, my team, your team, our team, have been a breath of fresh air this season. Indeed, I'd be as bold as to say we are precisely what the Premier League has needed for some time.

The alleged 'big four' have felt our presence this season. Just ask Arsenal fans after our exceptional performance brought about a 1-2 win at the Emirates. Remember those Manchester United fans hollering for the final whistle, clinging on to a slender 4-3 lead in the dying minutes? Yep, Hull City have arrived all right. Only the truly ignorant could have failed to notice us. Yet that in some ways, contributes to the mystery of Hull City. Who are they? Who plays for them? How are they getting these results? How is Phil Brown doing it? It's true; there is no stockpile of funds. Indeed, at times, ageing local veterans are occasionally trundled out. And the stadium capacity is modest by Premier League standards. Just what is the secret to Hull City's success?

Well, for me, the secret is; there is no secret. Phil Brown has stuck to some old fashioned - perhaps forgotten - Premier League principles of hard work, a binding, close-knit squad, plus an installation of incredible belief into his players. With a fearless approach to every opponent that says we're here on merit and we are going to play to win, hell, you have to concede its working!

Yet now, that image at the head of this piece slides into view. It was - maybe still is - the most harrowing sight in football for a visiting team. 'This is Anfield' above the tunnel reminded you of where you are, who you are facing and exactly what this club has achieved. You already knew you were in for a game when visiting Liverpool, then you were intimidated by 'the sign' before being ferociously greeted by the Kop for good measure.

You can hold nothing but respect for Liverpool. Love them or hate them, you have to acknowledge what Liverpool have achieved down the years. In a small way, I'm actually quite pleased Hull City are visiting Anfield with the Reds top of the table, looking to move four points clear and seeking a first win at home in the league for three games. We should be facing a Liverpool side at their best in the league for some years. It adds to the occasion, it gives the fixture genuine depth and a certain spice.

During the 1980s - my era for growing up and watching football - Liverpool dominated pretty much everything, like the kids of today watch Manchester United do now. Liverpool were always the team to beat back in those days. For me, to see my team come up against the mighty Reds on equal (ish) terms – by league standings – and possibly beat them for the first time ever... Ah, those were dreams...

Snap back to reality and I can hardly believe I am writing this but, why not? Why can't we fulfil a dream and beat Liverpool for the first time ever? Will we ever get a better chance? Phil Brown will go for it, the players have proved time and again they're bang up for every game and there is no need to motivate the chosen few fans lucky enough to get a ticket for this one. If Liverpool have an off day and Hull City piece together their magnificent away form once again, who knows?

The team will almost pick itself with news that left back Andy Dawson and striker Caleb Folan are still injured. Daniel Cousin may well be recalled to make up our now famous 4-3-3 attacking formation that has gleaned a magnificent 15 goals – second only to Chelsea this season, and they've won all of their away games – and 15 points on the Premier League road.

Despite being arrested in midweek for a much-publicised nightclub spat down in London, on loan Marlon King will definitely start up front for City. King is a strange one to say the least. Off the field, clearly not the most likeable, but on it - under Phil Brown's watchful presence - the striker has been first rate this season.

Speaking on the up and coming Anfield test Brown warned – *"It is a million miles an hour and a great platform to play on, and that brings its problems. But where the players are concerned at this football club, their feet are still on the ground and we are going to go to Liverpool with that kind of mentality and attitude to hopefully get something from the game."*

The hosts for the game may well get to see one of their old boys – if not the other. Hull-born Nick Barmby will surely make the bench for City if not the starting XI, while Liverpool lad Tony Warner will have to watch the game from the stands while he remains third choice keeper at the Tigers, behind first choice Boaz Myhill and understudy Matt Duke.

On to Liverpool, and the Reds have been buoyed by winning their Champions League group with a 1-3 away win at PSV Eindhoven in midweek – and resting a clutch of first team stars to achieve such. Rafa Benitez will recall a host of household names to his side – including captain Steven Gerrard - but Fernando Torres misses out through injury as the Reds look to extend their top of the table position against... yes, my team, our team, Hull City.

On Hull City, Liverpool boss Rafa Benitez was extremely complimentary – *"We have great respect for Hull and what they have achieved. Geovanni is scoring goals and Marlon King is doing a good job up front, but the team has a good mentality and that's the key."*

Adding – *"Hull have a very good offensive mentality, they're scoring goals. They have won against Arsenal and Tottenham. We know it will be tough, but that's the Premier League. From watching their games, I can understand why they're doing well, so we have to be careful."*

SATURDAY 13TH DECEMBER 2008 – LIVERPOOL 2-2 HULL CITY REPORT

Working late, it's the early hours, tired... Alarm goes off for the train... zzzz... A missed text message. Then a phone call - eh? What time is it? Hell, I'm late. Quick shower, shave and out. Grabbed a breakfast sandwich and caught a timely passing bus to station – only just mind. I'm minutes from missing the train, but I arrive. That was all too close for comfort.

Which is just as well as it turns out. This sleepyhead did not want to be missing this. Liverpool away. A top six fixture in the country – and my team are participating in it. Wake up son! Even more so as the result turned out. Imagine missing this? It turned out be another Premier League classic involving Hull City.

We duly gatecrashed Liverpool – and with a tiny snippet of inside knowledge - found this quirky drinking establishment on Anfield Road called Epstein's – of The Beatles' manager Brian Epstein fame. It looked like some bloke's house to be honest and walking through the door, yep, I was in the guy's living room. A man made bar at the back of this 'house' was selling cans of various descriptions. Some cheap ones too, being out of date. All very strange...

The environment had a look of being suspiciously illegal but with the away turnstiles literally 30 seconds away, who cares? Perfect. The guy running the gaff was mad as a box of frogs and the atmosphere quickly livened up with a few away fan songs.

Um... Not the done thing apparently...

Eccentric bloke running affairs came round with free nibbles and chocolates and a friendly *"Eh lads, don't come back in after the game, ta."* We took the hint. Onwards to Anfield. Hidden behind a veil of terraced housing, it was eerily quiet on the outside. On the inside? Don't be silly! "This is the best trip, I've ever been on!"

At the risk of sounding blasé – particularly as we're at Anfield against the leaders and the most successful club in the country – but we had set ourselves out to attack again. Nice one. Why not? Browny has balls of steel. The players are bristling with confidence and Mendy - finally - had done enough to warrant a start after some highly effective substitute appearances. Dean Marney was a touch unfortunate to be missing out.

3pm. City clearly won the toss turning Liverpool round away from the Kop for the second half, cute City, cute. Then... WALLOP! The visitors screamed out of the blocks. Liverpool were at sixes and sevens - arguably surprised to see at first hand just how gutsy this Hull City side are this season.

An early foray had Liverpool's defence all at sea and when the ball was fizzed in from the City left, Mascherano clearly handled the ball in the box, but referee Alan Wiley was unmoved, pointing for a corner. On the right, Mendy was ripping Dossena to shreds - really having a fine game, the Frenchman - and squared a menacing ball across the six yard box shortly after, but Liverpool hacked clear.

A free-kick out wide provided the visitors another opportunity to launch a ball into the Liverpool penalty area. The cross cleared all, but Marlon King was at the back stick to gather, turn and curl it to the far post. McShane came from nowhere, somewhere, header... goal! Bloody hell! We're 0-1 up at Anfield after 12 minutes. Rushing.

Sit back and defend? Are you kidding? Keep bloomin' going! This is Premier League Hull City. This is what we do. Sure, 'This is Anfield' but better to try than die wondering. Mendy, Barmby, King and Geovanni. They all wanted the ball. Hunting for it, getting it and turning Liverpool around. City wanted it more. Mendy was simply blistering to watch with pace to burn. Liverpool in general were not exactly comfortable with City's in your face, bolshy tactics.

And it got worse for the league leaders. A flustered Carragher committed a foul on half way. With the Liverpool defender still protesting, Geovanni took it quickly, found King, back to Geovanni, pass wide to Mendy... we're in... Mendy powered past Dossena and a searing ball scooted across the Liverpool six yard box. City swarmed in and the belatedly-retreating Carragher - who had been caught by the swift free kick - sliced the ball into his own net while attempting to recover.

What the...? Is he having a laugh? Hull City are 0-2 up at Liverpool! Yes, Liverpool! 22 minutes gone and incredibly the Hull City success story trundles ever onwards. I'm absolutely buzzing. This shouldn't be happening to my club, I mean, who the hell are we? I'm loving it! But... let's put rationale to one side for a moment and savour this scoreline. Let's not think about making Liverpool really, really angry now. A chorus of 'Mauled by the Tigers' while we can should do the trick.

Predictably, the penance then came. This is Anfield after all. We're not reliving our Macclesfield Town days now. The Kop - visibly stunned - realised they had to lift their team, like it or not. After hearing the stories, raising eyebrows at our some of our past results this season, watching us do to them what we've already done to others meant the rallying cries were sounded at Anfield.

With the Kop's alarm now raised, Liverpool's crisp, clean, first-touch passing was breathtaking to watch. City couldn't match that, but they had a damn good go trying to snuff it out. Commitment and effort were there in spades. But quickly after Carragher's howler, Liverpool had halved the deficit - and from who else in a time of crisis? Steven Gerrard. A calm finish from six yards was converted, but Michael Turner looked to be interfered with in the build-up by Kuyt.

It was all Liverpool now. Wave after wave poured forward. City were still smarting from the first goal - and Alan Wiley's reluctance to see any Red fouls put City in a minor flap. Then, the salient moment of the game. McShane had to leave the field concussed, Marney came on and the menacing Mendy was retreated to the right back berth. The outlet was gone... damn!

Liverpool were desperate to draw level. City battled manfully, but that sickening feeling of a Liverpool equaliser was nearing. When it came, again Turner appeared impeded by Kuyt - a clear instruction from Benitez it seemed. Alan Wiley let it go and Benayoun hooked the ball over Zayatte and Gerrard rifled into the roof of the net to tie up the scores. City's players protested vehemently but to no avail.

And the crusade to City's goal continued. Alonso drilled wide and Boateng was clearing another goal bound effort off the line to keep the visitors on terms. The half time whistle was welcome respite in truth. Time to draw breath. Do we go for it, or cash our chips in? Nah, there's still goals in this, let's keep at it. And we did, but missing Mendy from the midfield hurt City, unquestionably.

In the second half, though, City's readjusted back four was much more disciplined and settled. Ricketts and Mendy cut the crosses out. Any that did stray into the box Turner and Zayatte comfortably mopped up. Liverpool pressured, but the shots on goal were sparse. Indeed, with a £20m striker on the bench in Keane - and apparently none on the pitch - it was difficult to work out what Liverpool were actually trying to achieve. Liverpool were summed up with three second half incidents, for all their expected pressure. Centre back Sami Hyypia hitting the post with a header was the Reds' most potent threat. That surely can't be right? Kuyt skied a great chance when given some rare time in the box and winger Riera drilled a decent shot in that Myhill beat away. Surely though, a cross to a striker would be better? But, I'll shut up, nothing to do with me...

City - albeit sporadically - continued to keep the Liverpool back four on their toes. Let's face it, no team is realistically going to lord it at Anfield, least of all us. But Geovanni was the new outlet and the Brazilian did enough to warn Liverpool that Hull City were still firmly in this contest. Desperation came into it and with subs tripping off the home bench and the scores locked at 2-2, Liverpool began snatching chances. The comeback kings had everybody in the away section nervous, but come on, Hull City had earned a brave point at the very least, surely? I admit without shame - Mr Wiley, blow up! Four minutes added time, no, no, no...

Huff, puff, but the blow when it came brought the house down in the away end. It was Hull City celebrating a magnificent away point. Richly deserved, having a decent go and earning a ripple of grudging applause from the Kop and surroundings. My team, yes my team got that! An away point at the Premier League leaders, incredible. I have nothing but admiration for my team and the management.

Afterwards, as we'd been barred from old Epstein's drinking den of iniquity, King Harry's provided the celebratory pint. The plaudits continued from the locals, gutted Liverpool had not beaten us, sure, but sporting enough to accept we'd had a go. *"You lot are safe for another season, see you next year, well played."* Wow! That was music to my ears.

And on this evidence, getting this type of result at one of the Premier League's greatest clubs, it really is hard to disagree. I can't quite take it in what Hull City are achieving this season, but if Carlsberg did Premier League dreams for unfashionable clubs, then ours would surely be the dream everybody would want. Long may it continue.

MATCH STATS:
- Liverpool: Reina, Arbeloa, Hyypia, Carragher, Dossena, Mascherano (Leiva Lucas 87), Alonso, Benayoun (El Zhar 74), Gerrard, Riera (Babel 82), Kuyt.
- Subs Not Used: Cavalieri, Agger, Keane, Ngog.
- Booked: El Zhar, Hyypia, Alonso.
- Goals: Gerrard 24, 32.
- Hull City: Myhill, McShane (Marney 27), Zayatte, Turner, Ricketts, Mendy, Ashbee, Boateng (Halmosi 66), Geovanni, Barmby (Windass 77), King. Subs Not Used: Warner, Garcia, Cousin, Giannakopoulos.
- Booked: McShane, Boateng, Marney.
- Goals: McShane 12, Carragher 22 og.
- Att: 43,835
- Ref: Alan Wiley (Staffordshire)
- **Premier League position: 6th**

THURSDAY 18TH DECEMBER 2008

It was after the West Ham United home game that chatter amongst City fans would hope Michael Turner was going to play for England. Okay, this was mentioned more than a little light-heartedly I accept, but not anymore. News is breaking that Hull City can expect a visit from England manager Fabio Capello shortly.

It['s true Turner has been in stunning form for the Tigers and has taken to the top flight with aplomb, with some standout performances that have helped Hull City establish the club in the top six of the Premier League for the entire season. Could you really believe that would be the case, when we beat Bristol City at Wembley?

But with Fabio Capello reportedly taking in more than 90 matches in the Premier League to date, the England manager is set to see the Tigers first hand – and more importantly Michael Turner – with an imminent visit to the city.

An FA spokesperson confirmed the news in a short statement released by the game's governing body - *"He [Fabio Capello] assures Hull City fans that he plans to watch Phil Brown's team in person very soon."*

Meanwhile, Hull City chairman Paul Duffen welcomed the news and promises to make the national team manager most welcome when Capello arrives to state - *"We'd be happy to accommodate England manager Fabio Capello if he wanted to watch us at the KC."*

FRIDAY 19TH DECEMBER 2008 – HULL CITY V SUNDERLAND PREVIEW

Hull City take on their second opponents from the north east in successive home games. Another victory would be the perfect festive tonic against Sunderland and guarantee the Tigers a top six spot on Christmas Day.

And yet again, a real theme to this book, I can't believe I've just written that. Own up, who honestly thought in their wildest possible dreams, that Hull City would be playing to preserve their top six status over Christmas? I love football! This is precisely the reason why I do. The unpredictability, the amazing feats that can be achieved, the never truly knowing. And they have all been there in our season so far.

Last week, fans filtered out of Anfield with paralysed emotions, unsure whether to laugh or cry. On the one hand City were 0-2 up and screwed it up, but... whoa! Hang on... 0-2 up at Anfield! The Premier League leaders! And not even Liverpool could beat us. Proud? You bloody well should be. All in, 2-2 at the country's most successful club should not be sniffed at.

And so Phil Brown continues to weave his magic at the Tigers. Here is a manager who is not only England's most successful this season, but building a credible case and portfolio to step into the top management job in football at the current rate of progression. And that statement is not made lightly. England? Why not?

Somewhat predictably, one of the first names to be linked with the now vacant Sunderland management job upon Roy Keane's resignation two games ago, was local boy Phil Brown. But immediately, yet respectfully, the City boss distanced himself from the position, recognising the unfinished business of two and half years left at Hull City. 'To build a big club' as chairman Paul Duffen keeps reminding us all.

Undoubtedly, Phil Brown is enjoying the good times at the club. But the man deserves to. Brown has earned the rich rewards coming his way. Team spirit, bonding, a desire and belief that the club can succeed are clearly evident. Yet it all takes time. Realistically, why would Phil Brown want to go to Sunderland? Everything required is here and in place - built by the man himself, of course.

Selecting a side to face Sunderland will need some consideration following the 2-2 draw at Anfield. On loan Black Cats defender Paul McShane was ineligible anyway to face his parent club but nevertheless suffered concussion during the Liverpool draw.

Craig Fagan and Anthony Gardner are now both back in training with the first team but neither will be considered for this game at least, as the pair build up fitness. Of course, veteran Dean Windass is once again knocking on the door for a start, but Brown will surely keep him on the bench.

Speaking about the visitors, the 39 year old striker recalled time spent with Sunderland's caretaker boss Ricky Sbragia in the past and is wary enough of the Black Cats' current state of flux to claim – *"I would rather be playing Sunderland with Roy Keane in charge than Ricky Sbragia."*

Before remembering – *"I know Ricky from when I was at York years ago on trial and he is a good coach. He's been around the block as well. I think under a caretaker the shackles come off a bit and the players play with more freedom and a smile on their face. It will be a very tough game."*

The caretaker boss has no fresh injury concerns ahead of the trip to East Yorkshire. After a last gasp 1-0 defeat at Manchester United, Sbragia followed that up by thumping beleaguered West Bromwich Albion 4-0 at home. Sunderland will not be short of confidence, despite being short of a manager.

Sbragia stated ahead of the game – *"It's hard not to be surprised by how well Hull have done but good on them. Their manager Phil Brown has done a great job. He has invested well and he has them organised. I took over at Bolton when he left and I met him a few times. He's very thoughtful about the game and has some great ideas which he is putting into practice at Hull."*

SATURDAY 20TH DECEMBER - HULL CITY 1-4 SUNDERLAND - REPORT

An extraordinary game and extremely difficult to sum up in many respects. The scoreline does nothing to tell the story of the match – yet bizarrely will be the hallmark of the fixture. There will be no complaints from me about where the points went in this game. Yet if a scoreline was ever to mask a match story then surely this one would be the perfect camouflage. It may have been 1-4, but it certainly never looked like a game that would eventually end up that way.

Numerous factors contributed to the closing finale - the period that won the game - and I'm not about to turn this text into a sour-graped rant, because in truth, City never did enough to win the match. But, to be perfectly honest, up until 12 minutes to go, neither did Sunderland. We'll come back to that later.

Brown made changes to accommodate Paul McShane's absence against his parent club. Richard Garcia was handed a rare start in midfield and the attack minded Bernard Mendy was reared to the right back berth. Garcia missed his chance for me and showed how much we miss Dean Marney in midfield. It also cast skipper Ian Ashbee in a poor light with far too much work to do. To be fair, Brown wasn't to know that until he tried it.

Overall, Sunderland look a renewed team without Keane in charge. His leaving is evidently a good thing with a last-gasp defeat at Manchester United and two hammerings by four goals now handed out to promoted sides since the Irishman's departure, suggesting the time to leave was indeed correct.

City didn't get off to a particularly bright start. There is something acutely wrong with the team on home turf. The weight of expectation perhaps? But while Brown's team continues to perform heroics away from the Circle, then the expectation is not misplaced. The secret to our lofty position is not down to our home form, though. Sunderland are yet another team to profit on our apparent weakness here in Hull.

The visitors got the early breakthrough ten minutes in with a fine goal. Danny Collins was given too much room to pick out Steed Malbranque lurking outside the box and a well placed, precise strike opened the scoring. Confidence soared at that point for the visitors and City knew they were in a game.

But absolute credit to Brown's side. With the Sunderland bubble blowing big, the spirit and resolve demonstrated by his team should not be underestimated. And within ten minutes of a buoyant Sunderland taking the lead, gritty City, unbowed, scored. After an almighty scramble in the visitors' box, Turner poked the ball into Barmby's path and the local lad drilled the ball home to level.

Suddenly, the complexion of the match changed. Sunderland had lost their swagger and were not so self-assured as they once were. A brittleness was now evident and passes went astray as City began to seize control. A spell of the game emerged that saw the hosts trying to grasp the lead but Sunderland held on and the pressure began to peter out with the half drawing in.

The visitors survived. Sunderland came out fighting for the second half on parity. City by contrast were lacking the same first half fluency. Now the last thing I want to do is start criticising a team who have been sixth for weeks, but we looked a mite predictable and a little one-dimensional.

City were at their best running at Sunderland who did not enjoy the probing play of Geovanni at all. But the underused Brazilian was sacrificed to some extent with a swift counter-attacking long ball and the visitors learned what was coming and managed the threat too easily.

It was turning into a frustrating affair with relatively few clear chances for either side. Sunderland had the ball, but struggled to fashion chances, City's counter attack was second guessed with regularity. Neither side looked like winning matters on the evidence before us. Substitute Daniel Cousin rounded off a brilliant – if somewhat rare passing move – but was rightly flagged offside.

So what would change? With 12 minutes left, a stalemate ensuing and honours even, nothing was suggesting three goals and a red card, put it that way. And really, despite Sunderland enjoying more of the ball, the visitors were lacking clear cut chances to win the game and City couldn't find the spark of creation needed enough. Until...

Yes. A mad two minutes was needed. First, Kieran Richardson - a frustrated chap it has to be said - tried a pot shot from distance. It spooned wickedly off Kamil Zayatte and left Boaz Myhill outrageously wrong-footed, watching the ball nestle into the net. It was an inordinate stroke of luck. Arguably, the only way this match could have been settled.

What followed compounded City's misery. Within two minutes of that, any chance the home team had of getting back into the game was quickly vanquished. Referee Mike Riley produced a second yellow card for Sam Ricketts and that should've been that with a depleted City - already reeling - now shorthanded.

Gaps appeared all over as Brown urged his Tigers on from the sidelines. But with attacker Peter Halmosi now the adopted left back, it was too easy for Sunderland to exploit the vastly weakened defence and two more goals followed from the left.

The first was a near post cross headed in by Kenwyne Jones, the second was Djibril Cissé with the freedom of the park, left to curl in beyond Myhill and put the result beyond doubt. It was a scoreline vastly out of kilter with a relatively chanceless game.

Oh well. I'm not bitter. Hull City have been ace this season - and will be again. Plus, we had a similar stroke of luck last time here against Middlesbrough with Bernard Mendy's strike off the keeper and a 50-50 penalty going our way. Luck was in Sunderland's corner to break the deadlock late in the game, ours was the previous game against Middlesbrough.

This result is not a reflection of our season, or indeed how City have played to currently sit sixth in the table. It was just one of those days. It's Manchester City next - and if there are two traits the Tigers have done well at this season, they are to bounce back immediately from disappointment and play exceptionally well on the road. Bring on Eastlands...

MATCH STATS:
- Hull City: Myhill, Mendy, Turner, Zayatte, Ricketts, Garcia (Cousin 57), Ashbee, Boateng (Halmosi 81), Geovanni, Barmby (Giannakopoulos 68), King. Subs Not Used: Duke, Doyle, Windass, Marney.
- Sent Off: Ricketts (81).

- Booked: Boateng, Ricketts, King.
- Goals: Barmby 19.
- Sunderland: Fülöp , Bardsley, Nosworthy, Ferdinand, Collins, Malbranque, Tainio (Leadbitter 79), Richardson (Edwards 89), Reid (Whitehead 74), Jones, Cissé. Subs Not Used: Colgan, Murphy, Yorke, Healy.
- Booked: Richardson.
- Goals: Malbranque 10, Zayatte 78 og, Jones 84, Cissé 90.
- Att: 24,917.
- Ref: Mike Riley (Yorkshire)
- **Premier League position: 6th**

THURSDAY 25TH DECMEBER 2008 – MANCHESTER CITY V HULL CITY PREVIEW

The short fixture in the Premier League is against Manchester City. Hull City's Boxing Day fixture away at Eastlands is a match coming just over a month after the televised draw at the Circle.

In some small way, of all the teams to play in quick succession in the Premier League, Manchester City is probably the one this season. Well, certainly completing our duo of fixtures before the transfer window re-opens at the very least now seems helpful to our cause.

When Manchester City came here in November, new owners had recently bought the club and seemingly had a bottomless pit of money to invest. Robinho arrived in the nick of time for £30 odd million before the transfer window shut in September - and you can bet your boots that is only the beginning.

By the end of January 2009, it is quite feasible Manchester City will be the most expensive Premier League side ever assembled. Some teams could be in for right royal hiding. These hidings may come around on almost weekly occurrences. Thankfully, we'll have completed our tour of duty against the blue half of Manchester. Odds must be short for Hughes' side to start surging up the league come January.

For now – and somewhat surprisingly – the home boss is under enormous pressure with his side in the bottom three. And on closer inspection, home form at Eastlands is sketchy at best with four wins and five defeats so far. Not as strong as first thought, if confessions are on the table.

Even more bizarre, reports in Manchester have Mark Hughes claiming this match is a 'must win'. A little self-induced pressure is usually a bad sign. And Hull City have been outstanding on the road this season. Ironically, our only defeat on the Premier League was at city neighbours Manchester United - a 4-3 loss. Hopefully losing in Manchester will not become a habit.

Yet Hull City need to recover from a 1-4 home loss. The Tigers have bounced back from adversity so far in the Premier League and hopefully that trait will continue on Boxing Day. There is relatively little pressure on the visitors after such a meteoric start, but a chance to make hay against a team that has only won once in seven games should not be passed up lightly.

Phil Brown will have to make changes for the Eastlands trip. Sam Ricketts was sent off in the Sunderland debacle last time out, so will definitely miss the game with a ban. As for the match with the Black Cats, Manchester City would be wise to read into the events of the game rather than take it as read it was a regulation 1-4 home loss. It never really told the true story, did it? But let's not rake over old coals.

Paul McShane can be recalled to plug the gap left by Ricketts and Andy Dawson has a chance of featuring for the first time since Bolton back in November. Craig Fagan and Anthony Gardner grow ever closer to selection. Dean Marney will be pushing for a central midfield berth once again, while it would be a luxury to push Bernard Mendy further up the field.

In truth, the tried and trusted 4-3-3 away formation is surely perfect for this game. Manchester City have to go for it and counter attacking has become a bit of a forte for the Tigers so it should suit both sides. Like last time, there could well be goals. Let's hope so, because it has the ingredients to be a cracker over Christmas. Bring it on!

FRIDAY 26TH DECEMBER –
MANCHESTER CITY 5-1 HULL CITY – REPORT

A Christmas turkey and stuffing this Boxing Day. If this is the season of goodwill, Hull City will win top Premier League honours this year and no mistake. But there can be no getting away from the fact this was truly a nightmare after Christmas at Eastlands…

Oh dear. I reckon that will be the last time Phil Brown gives his players the day off at Christmas. The players took the generous gesture of a day's rest 24 hours too far, by turning up around about half time at Eastlands. Phil Brown was livid with events before him – and rightly. It was a performance that smacked of embarrassment and followed a hiding from Sunderland six days before.

Brown made changes by dropping last week's - and in form man of the match - Nick Barmby for Dean Marney. Dean Windass came in up front to partner Marlon King, while the defensive crisis was going to be solved by shifting Paul McShane to left back and putting Bernard Mendy at right back. Many changes…

And the disjointed looking line-up was pulled apart - particularly down both flanks - with the hosts getting the ball forward, wide and quickly during the first half. It's a tactic we've used to good effect, indeed, the trademark of our season. But the proud record of being beaten once on the Premier League road counted for nothing at Eastlands with a dreadful first half performance, roundly punished.

This is the Premier League, so very unforgiving. The slightest whiff of weakness is found out, exploited and taken full advantage of. Manchester City gorged on a hatful of anomalies in the Tigers side and it really pains me to criticise the team after the season we've all thoroughly enjoyed so far, but this was not the Hull City I have been watching in the top flight.

The opening few minutes didn't really suggest what was going to be served up. Indeed Phil Brown's side had a glorious chance to open the scoring when King drove a fierce shot goalwards but Hart spooned the ball over for a corner. There endeth the resistance, though. What followed is painful.

A serious theme to Manchester City's play was piling the ball onto the full backs and exposing them. Today we found out that although McShane is a 100 per cent trier, a left back he is not. Another raking ball carved the Tigers wide open and the rampant Stephen Ireland maximised the yawning space, pulled the ball back from the byline and it was an easy tap in for Caicedo.

Even at 1-0 the Tigers looked beat. Yes, I know, it's sad to write that. Where has our team gone? The second quickly followed - cue an exact carbon copy of the first. Same wing, same move, same players, same result. If the visitors hadn't learned from the stunning two goal away performance by Stephen Ireland at our place, it was criminal not to learn the same lesson just minutes later with the second goal. Before we could come to terms with the mountain we had to climb, Robinho left Mendy flapping on the opposite wing and the Brazilian stepped inside the covering defence and coolly slotted the ball into the bottom corner for the third. Disaster! What a shambles all over the park.

And the misery continued. For a third time Manchester City waltzed down the left, Ireland yet again centred from, the only difference was Robinho shovelled the ball in from two yards. I'd seen all this before. Sucker punch, hit me, sucker punch, hit me, sucker punch, hit me. When are we going to learn? It was a nightmare before my very eyes.

I wanted to get angry, but how can I? This club has been outstanding this season. However much the angst welled up inside, putting the ire into physical emotion was a distinct no-no. I couldn't just turn on them now, even though inside I wanted to. But it was abysmal to watch. How can professionals not learn from their errors. Nnrnrrnrrrgggg!

At half time, Phil Brown strode onto the pitch and turned his players around, frog marched them all into the corner in view of the glaring public. A semi-circle of doom was formed and a public flogging was meted out right in front of the away fans. It was excruciating to watch. If anything, it showed Phil Brown cared but, ouch...

The second half was vastly improved, understandably, but Manchester City needed to do nothing. The Tigers had much of the ball but failed to create any clear cut chances and no pressure on the home defence was troubling the hosts.

Craig Fagan had come on at the break for the first time since suffering a broken leg. So had Nathan Doyle, with Mendy pushed further forward. Yet despite the extra zip, the going was still tough.

Brown's side fashioned a goal late in the half by following the Manchester City lead of hitting the byline and Fagan bundled in a consolation. But even that was messed up within a minute as the mightily impressive Stephen Ireland stroked home the last goal of the game after a fine move to make it 5-1.

I want to be upset, I want to be vexed, I want to scream until I'm hoarse at the abject display before me, but I can't. Indeed, I won't, whatever happens this season. Hull City have had a go in the Premier League - a real go. Yet today, sadly - and for the first time - Hull City did not have a go. They didn't have the decency to turn up.

Of course, now I expect a rousing response against Aston Villa on Tuesday evening. I'd be so bold to state we'll get it too. As wretched as today has been, it can't be allowed to ruin our Christmas.

'Tis the season of goodwill, after all, as Manchester City found out today with our overt generosity. But lessons simply have to be learned and learnt I'm sure they will be. Bah humbug!

MATCH STATS:
- Man City: Hart, Zabaleta, Dunne, Richards (Onuoha 46), Ball, Wright-Phillips, Ireland (Fernandes 85), Kompany, Elano, Robinho, Caicedo (Jô 46). Subs Not Used: Schmeichel, Vassell, Garrido, Sturridge.
- Goals: Caicedo 15, 27, Robinho 28, 36, Ireland 82.
- Hull City: Myhill, Mendy, Zayatte, Turner, McShane, Boateng (Doyle 34), Geovanni (Cousin 70), Ashbee, Marney, Windass (Fagan 46), King. Subs Not Used: Duke, Barmby, Hughes, Halmosi.
- Booked: Geovanni, Zayatte, Fagan, Mendy.
- Goals: Fagan 80.
- Att: 45,196
- Ref: Andre Marriner (W Midlands)
- **Premier League position: 7th**

SUNDAY 28TH DECEMBER 2008

For the past couple of weeks, many of the users on the City Independent website have been canvassing support on behalf of Ian Ashbee, the man who has skippered Hull City to promotion from the bottom division to the top flight. Ashbee was one of the unfashionable nominees amongst a clutch of the Premier League's glitterati for the 'Morgan on Sport British Football Personality of the Year award' Well, the results are in and look who has won the award... Ian Ashbee.

The following text below is a column written by Piers Morgan of the Daily Mail who has been campaigning for the 'Morgan on Sport British Football Personality of the Year award'. The Hull City captain won the poll with 44 per cent of the vote, which is incredible when you look at some of the household names included. Allow Piers Morgan himself to talk about his winner, Ian Ashbee...

"This is a tale of two footballers. One is the most famous modern player on the planet. The other is not even the most famous player in Hull. One has 14 million hits on Google, the other just 51,000. David Beckham was born on May 2, 1975, in Leytonstone, Essex. He has played 426 games for Manchester United, Real Madrid, and LA Galaxy, scoring 80 goals. And 107 games for England, scoring 17 goals. Oh, and he is currently on loan to AC Milan.

Ian Ashbee was born on September 6, 1976, in Birmingham. He has played 458 games for Derby, Cambridge United and Hull City, scoring 40 goals. Oh, and he once went on loan to Icelandic team IR Knattsprynudeild.

Both have suffered bad injuries. Beckham's broken metatarsal made front page news around the world for weeks, and even had the Queen concerned (I know, because she told me herself at a Windsor Castle party). Ashbee's degenerative problem with his femur barely made the back page of the Hull Daily Mail, and did not, as far as I'm aware, penetrate the consciousness of the Royal Family.

Beckham signed for LA Galaxy in a deal worth $250million. Ashbee signed for Hull on a free transfer, and currently stars in a Hull City Monopoly board game, valued at a price of £400. Beckham sold his wedding, to long-time girlfriend Victoria, to OK! magazine for £1million.

Ashbee did not sell his wedding to long-time girlfriend Anna. Beckham's best friend is Tom Cruise. Ashbee's mates are not believed to include any $30m-a-flick movie stars. Beckham has spent the past 10 years flogging sunglasses, hair products, mobile phones, underpants, video games, cola and razor blades. Ashbee has just played football. This week, both men appeared in front of the public, and the result of these two totally different career paths was laid bare for all to see.

Beckham walked out to resounding apathy at the San Siro, from an AC Milan crowd that just didn't give a monkey's cuss about him. This was the moment of great awakening for dear old Becks. The moment when his peculiarly self-regarding game was well and truly up.

It takes a supreme kind of arrogance to march out in front of some of the most passionate, well-informed football fans in the world and expect them to cheer a player whose sole contribution to the game in the past year is to help his American pub team come bottom of their league. And who is only at Milan for two months of shameless, bench-sitting, shirtsalesmanship.

With their silence, the Milan fans showed that they know when they're being conned, and that they have correctly identified Beckham as a 33-year-old fading has-been on the make. Ashbee, by contrast, last weekend walked out at Hull City's ground, the Kingston Communications Stadium, to a deafening ovation from fans who absolutely love him.

They love the fact that he has captained Hull throughout their rise from the bottom of the league to the top. They love the fact that he fought back from career threatening injury. They love the fact that he is their longest-serving and most loyal player. They love the fact that he is totally dedicated to one thing - kicking a football. I have nothing personal against Beckham. In fact, as with Ashbee, I've never even met the man. But I suspect we'll both get over it.

Beckham has been a good player, but nothing special as far as I'm concerned. I don't think he'd get into my all-time Top 100 footballers list. Take his free-kicks out of the equation and he's just a workmanlike, increasingly slow, midfielder."

HOW THE PUBLIC VOTED
Ian Ashbee - 44% - WINNER!
Ryan Giggs - 29%
Steven Gerrard - 9%
Paul Scoles - 5%
Jimmy Bullard - 4%
Theo Walcott - 3%
Emile Heskey - 2%
John Terry - 2%
David James - 1%
Michael Owen - 1%

The art in which he has been an absolute world-beater is self-exploitation. His career has been the most shameless prostitution of one torso in the history of mankind. Well, after Abi Titmuss, anyway." - Piers Morgan

MONDAY 29TH DECEMBER 2008 – HULL CITY V ASTON VILLA PREVIEW

The next test on the Premier League journey is, by hook or by crook, the sternest Hull City will face to date. After two poor results, unaccustomed half time surroundings and a team squarely hurting, it's top four chasing Aston Villa next.

And for the first time this season, Hull City manager Phil Brown is probably feeling the pinch in the Premier League. Still, if you're going to start feeling the pressure cooker trappings of the top flight, better to cope with them while you're eighth in the table at the end of the year rather than 20th, as every man and his dog took great delight predicting we would be before a ball was kicked.

Yes, amid the madness of a successive 1-4 home defeat to Sunderland and the Boxing Day 5-1 massacre at Manchester City, perhaps it has been trampled underfoot all too quickly what has gone on before. Phil Brown's team has slid down the table from sixth to eighth in a month. It's difficult to know how us Hull City fans will cope with such travesty. Especially, with it all being so new to us. Travesty, that is.

A bit of perspective is needed by some when looking into our club. Hull City are not a bad Premier League side. Results on the pitch more often than not have caused more headlines for the right reasons, rather than the opposite. And upon closer inspection, the last results against both Sunderland and Manchester City are arguably exaggerated and need putting into context.

For Sunderland, there was nothing in it at 1-1 with 12 minutes to go. A wicked deflection turned that game, compounded by Sam Ricketts receiving a red card just moments later. Predictably, an average Sunderland side plundered goals three and four for a fairly deceiving 1-4 away win. Interestingly, new manager and then caretaker boss Ricky Sbragia has not won since.

As for Manchester City, with no recognised full backs playing and 39 year old Dean Windass up front, problems were afoot from the off. Not repaying the manager's confidence with a sluggish performance all round in the first half was a slap in the face, particularly after being treated to Christmas Day off. A reward fairly deserved for me, after a brilliant Premier League campaign to date.

But 4-0 down after 38 minutes? Yep, Phil Brown snapped. Marching onto the pitch and leading his players to the away fans for a public flogging was a measure of how little nonsense the man is going to stand for. Rumours of possibly losing the dressing room following such actions are surely well wide of the mark after all the confidence building within the players that Brown has put in before, but footballers these days are a funny breed.

It would be remiss of the players to forget the faith Phil Brown has shown them, and in among the insanity of ludicrous wages and showbiz lifestyles, I believe the City boss still holds court amongst his squad. The players owe him that much. Common decency should win the day. I'm typing, hopefully, not blinded by the dazzling Premier League gold.

Hull City all season long have been nothing short of honest. That trait has produced 27 points when coupled with a strong work ethic and the manager's belief. Phil Brown, rightly, will be looking for a reaction from his players. Tonight, against Aston Villa, I guess the proof of the pudding will be there for all, including the watching nation courtesy of Sky, to see. We'll perform. No, that's it, Hull City WILL perform.

The official line on team selection suggests full back Sam Ricketts will return from his one game ban, Paul McShane will revert to his more familiar right back berth and Bernard Mendy will pushed further up the field. Yet rumours of sweeping changes are being predicted for the clash with speculation suggesting that Marlon King, George Boateng and Geovanni will be some of the high profile casualties to pay for the abject first 45 minutes at Manchester City.

For me, I'd like to send the bulk of the players who were party to the last two results out onto to the pitch and restore some pride in the Hull City shirt in front of a packed home crowd. Prove they are worthy of the belief Phil Brown has placed in them and demonstrate the character that has produced many of the biggest shocks in the Premier League this season.

Phil Brown has no qualms about his alfresco half time team talk at Eastlands in hindsight. Here are some comments since – *"I have got no regrets about it whatsoever. If it bruised one or two egos then so be it, although it wasn't intended to be that way. We were embarrassed, but that wasn't to do with the half-time dressing-down, it was the first-half performance."*

Adding – *"We didn't bring our best game to the table and we got our comeuppance. We can't allow that to happen ever again. Hopefully the mentality of the group will be stronger for the experience. We probably need five wins to stay up, but to turn this kind of form around it needs to be done as soon as possible."*

Meanwhile, a defensively makeshift Aston Villa side roll into the Circle with Martin Laursen out with a knee injury and Carlos Cuellar suffering with a knock. Zat Knight will step in once again and Nigel Reo-Coker will undertake an unfamiliar defensive role at right back. Up front John Carew remains out with a back injury.

No excuses, no faint hearts, no backward steps. The players need to repay some of the manager's faith and that time is right now. The supporters need to do likewise and support the side tonight. A nation watches – and will again – because the Hull City Premier League story has been one worth watching. Do not fail your club. That goes for us all. But we won't, right?

TUESDAY 30TH DECEMBER - HULL CITY 0-1 ASTON VILLA - REPORT

Lucky, lucky, lucky Aston Villa. But you don't need me to tell you that, you saw it all for yourselves on Sky TV. A thriller with the Villa produces an astonishing amount of talking points for many days to come. And defeat again *wince*

Permission is granted to feel like you've just been kicked in the nuts. Because frankly, you have. Rarely will a team get as lucky as Aston Villa - a top four side who could manage all of no shots on target in the entire game - and yet still waltz off with all the points. With fortune like this, they'll definitely be top four.

But where to start on this match? Phil Brown's team selection left everyone aghast at kick off. After the 5-1 drubbing at Eastlands, the ultimate punishment was meted out. Practically - and I kid you not - most of last season's Championship side greeted Aston Villa with Garcia in central midfield, Halmosi out wide and a lone striker in Cousin up front setting alarm bells ringing before a ball was kicked.

The madness of King Brown? Only time would tell... You could be forgiven for looking at the bench wistfully and wondering if Geovanni, King et al would really make this team so much better. But, 5-1 was 5-1 and Browny was laying down the new law. Perform, or you're out. I was scared, I admit it.

If the half time team talk in front of the travelling masses wasn't enough to talk of Brown losing the dressing room, tonight's team and performance was surely going to make or break it. Yet the City boss is an infectious character. He genuinely believes the chosen XI would not let him down - or, more accurately, dare not let him down. The guy has balls of steel.

And despite the grave reservations, blow me, Brown was right. Villa predictably looked to get on the front foot and batter a team supposedly low on confidence and morale, but unfortunately for them, City were having none of that. Ferocious tackling, positive play, first to every 50-50, this really mattered to City.

The home fans roared on Phil's brave team selection with every passing moment. Villa fans - a little motormouthish to begin with - expected the plucky first 10 minutes from the hosts before we should predictably crumble and allow them serenely on their way to top four stardom. But that wasn't happening tonight. *"You've only come to see the Villa?"* they sang. Err, the best team Villa saw tonight was us. Thanks for coming.

City should have had an early lead when the mightily impressive Nick Barmby pounced on Brad Friedel's failure to gather in a high ball. Breaking loose in the six yard box, the local lad bundled the ball goalwards and Zat Knight could only help it in. Yet Steve Bennett refereeing, saw fit to chalk the goal off for a foul. Rubbish! Not one Villa player even appealed!

That decision would haunt City much later, but for the time being it spurred the hosts on to even greater play. Villa looked a little rattled and although trying to pass the ball around, had absolutely no cutting edge. Young and Milner were well marshalled by a team shipping goals and Agbonlahor didn't get a sniff of the ball. Brilliant riposte by the scratch XI.

Indeed, the entire back four shone brightly and shut Villa's pacy attack out with relative ease. Meanwhile, City's own speedy play through Mendy had the visitors worried and the Frenchman fizzed in a superb ball that Halmosi was inches from converting for a deserved lead.

As the half drew in, the Tigers grew in stature and the away fans grew quiet all of a sudden. *"Down with the Baggies!"* Not so cocksure now as they watched the game unfold before them, it would seem. We're eighth for a reason – and it had bugger all to do with the last two games, as well.

At half time, I had nothing but admiration for Phil Brown picking the – and let's be clear here – second string XI. Moreover, the players on the pitch were proving they wanted to show they are more than peripheral team members. It could have horribly backfired. Those supposedly being punished, needing to show a reaction, were on the bench, some even dropped. No chance of a reaction from there... but Brown had called it spot on – again. The second half saw City wrestle control of the game. Okay, I'll be the first to admit the chances created were at an absolute premium, but the visitors had yet to record a meaningful opening of any description. Villa weren't bad, but City just wouldn't give them an inch, end of. From corners, Michael Turner continues to be a Premier League menace. City's best chance of the half to fell to Barmby when Mendy's cross saw the former England man head straight at Nigel Reo-Coker. But with Marlon King on for Daniel Cousin, City always looked the more likely to add to their goalscoring tally. Oh, wait... Steve Bennett had chalked our legitimate effort off. Damn, how remiss of me...

Then, the mother of all boots to the nuts arrived. Ashley Young finally got away down the wing, substitute Bryan Hughes - still not up to speed with the game - failed to track his runner and the City defence was under pressure. Cross comes in... Zayatte's covering... Nooooooooooooo! Incredibly, unluckily, the ball is steered into his own net! No, no, no, no! In 100 attempts he couldn't have beaten Myhill...

Villa fans suddenly find their voice after being clammed shut for about the last hour and they laud it. Just when you think they can't get any luckier too. No shots on target but unbelievably leading 0-1 with two minutes to go – Steve Bennett awards us a penalty for handball in the dying seconds. But the linesman – begrudgingly right – scrubs that decision after mass consultation. Bah! It should be 1-1 anyway!

At the whistle, the predictable and fully audible boos ring round the stadium. The City players had given 100 per cent. Brown had surely proved he has not lost the dressing room. The team deserved something, anything out of the game. Hull City got nothing. Not a jot. Just a right royal kicking when we're down.

Thankfully, the game was on telly. It was there for all to see. Three straight losses it might well be for Hull City, but we're eighth. And for a reason. Tonight, proudly, we showed the rest of the Premier League why we will not be going back from whence we came. Pride and reputation, plus worth in league standing, is suitably restored – even without the rewards we deserved. Congratulations Phil Brown, the players and to you supporting. City will definitely be back.

MATCH STATS:
- Hull City: Myhill, McShane, Turner, Zayatte, Ricketts, Mendy, Garcia (Fagan 89), Ashbee, Halmosi, Barmby (Hughes 85), Cousin (King 69). Subs Not Used: Duke, Doyle, Geovanni, Giannakopoulos.
- Booked: Zayatte.
- Aston Villa: Friedel, Reo-Coker, Knight, Davies, Luke Young, Milner, Sidwell (Gardner 86), Petrov, Barry, Ashley Young, Agbonlahor. Subs Not Used: Guzan, Harewood, Delfouneso, Salifou, Shorey, Osbourne.
- Booked: Barry, Petrov.
- Goals: Zayatte 88 og.
- Att: 24,727
- Ref: Steve Bennett (Kent)
- **Premier League position: 8th**

CHAPTER 6 – NEW YEAR AND A NEW ERA DAWNS

FRIDAY 2ND JANUARY 2009 –
HULL CITY V NEWCASTLE UNITED FA CUP ROUND 3 PREVIEW

The new year is here and the prestigious FA Cup third round traditionally heralds the beginning of the sporting calendar. This year, Hull City have drawn fellow Premier League opposition Newcastle United at home. Hmmm...

Just a few short weeks ago, this all Premier League affair (one of three) sparked contrasting opinions from the respective managers of Hull City and Newcastle United. Hull City? Brown was a little reserved by suggesting everyone may get a chance to shine. In other words, rest the first XI. Newcastle? Kinnear cried *"We're going for it!"*

Since then, despite a 2-2 at Liverpool and beating Middlesbrough, City have stumbled spectacularly. Sunderland... bleurggh! Manchester City... ouch! And the controversy surrounding Aston Villa, overshadowed a fine performance from the heavily changed supposed first XI lucking out to a late own goal and ultimate defeat.

But such was the creditable performance from our second string Premier League side against a top four team, what now is our strongest side? Will it be the same again? Will those benched for the horror show at Eastlands return to show their worth? Will the kids be blooded including Nicky Featherstone and fringe players like Ryan France? Who the hell knows now?

Meanwhile, Newcastle boss Joe Kinnear appeared desperate for the FA Cup to swing round and relieve him and the team from the rigours of the Premier League. A chance to get the pressure off the first XI, relax and play football. But now, with injuries wrecking his side, training has reportedly been abandoned for much of the week.

Indeed, the hapless Magpies have other worries too. The transfer window is open and goalkeeper Shay Given is courting unwanted attention, while star striker Michael Owen has not penned a new contract yet. More worries for the already bowing Joe Kinnear who deserves massive credit for trying to sponge up all the pressure on himself, rather than his players.

But cracks are undeniably now appearing on Tyneside. The 1-5 home mauling by Liverpool over Christmas has done little to buoy the Magpies. Already missing are Mark Viduka, Obafemi Martins, Joey Barton and Claudio Cacapa. Plus, needing late fitness tests are Nicky Butt, Jose Enrique and Shola Ameobi. Not surprisingly, Joe Kinnear is left with whoever is fit, will play.

By contrast, Hull City are somewhat spoilt for choice now long term leg break victim Craig Fagan has featured twice as a substitute. Only centre back Anthony Gardner and left back Andy Dawson remain sidelined. But what an irony if Fagan gets a start. Against Newcastle, against Danny Guthrie, the man who broke his leg in the 1-2 away win at St James Park in the league. We haven't forgotten...

Fagan on the prospect of facing Danny Guthrie revealed – *"It happened, there is nothing I can do about it now. There is no point me going out there to do the same, it is not going to benefit me in any way. I just want to get back to the form of before I was injured. I know our fans won't give him the best of times but I just want to concentrate on my game."*

Adding - *"It's great to be back, I feel good, sharper than I thought I would. I managed to get on at half-time against Manchester City, which was unexpected, and nick a goal. It was was great for myself but obviously it was a disappointing day for the team."*

With results showing three straight losses, Phil Brown surely cannot afford to take chances with younger and outer perimeter players. And anyway, what message does that send to those who fought admirably doing the filling in against Aston Villa on Tuesday? Surely, a full strength side will greet Newcastle? And those worthy enough from Tuesday, of course.

This time last year, no such thoughts of a weakened team would've entered anyone's head for the third round. Hopefully, this year, the cup will not attract a glib approach by the club. The FA Cup is important. This is the sixth time the sides have faced each other in the competition. Newcastle have won four of the five ties. That statistic alone needs addressing, as does our current form. Let's have it, City! Let's have it. And rubbish this 'weaker team' suggestion while we're at it.

SATURDAY 3RD JANUARY 2009 – HULL CITY 0-0 NEWCASTLE UNITED – FA CUP 3RD REPORT

A blank drawn at the Circle between the Tigers and the Toon will see both sides unwillingly having to go through it all again at St James Park, after the pairing almost predictably ended up with a replay.

I'll confess I was quite looking forward to this cup tie. A break from the Premier League, a chance to experiment a little and a freedom to play without the pressure of being under the microscope of the top flight. Whatever happens, it won't be a cup shock, will it?

In many ways, that's a true measure of how far our football club has come. Only last year, a Premier League side at home would've been big news, a sell-out and eagerly anticipated. Somewhat disappointingly, this was not a maximum capacity gate and neither was the team at full strength. Maybe the two clubs hadn't quite pitched the pricing right? What a shame.

Team wise, Newcastle had practically no choice anyway, who was fit was in. But City? Well, they had some selections to make. Phil Brown chose to play 4-5-1, shore up the defence and midfield, then hammer into his players that we will not concede. Not conceding means, not losing. This time it worked unlike - rather harshly - the Aston Villa game four days earlier.

The penance for such play was watching a rather mediocre Newcastle - yes, I know they have injuries – attempt to attack us. If Newcastle could finish... It would be no joke to write the Magpies could - perhaps should - have been 0-3 or 0-4 up after half an hour. Chances galore of all varieties all going begging. Now if only Joe can point them in the direction of that big white netty thing... True, City had ridden their luck. But while Newcastle continued to demonstrate their ineptitude in front of goal, including Michael Owen missing a one-on-one when blazing high and wide, there seemed little to concern ourselves with. Indeed, it was the hosts who had two fine chances on target and drawing saves from the impressive Shay Given. Ricketts had one, Cousin the other.

As the two sets of fans traded some hearty put-downs, there was a chilling realisation that Shay Given was proving to be the only difference between the two teams. I'd be as bold to say, without the Irishman, Newcastle are screwed, although Bassong also impressed at the back too. *"Sold in the morning!"* The East Stand cried once more. The North Stand will cry if he is...

Yes, Newcastle had roundly enjoyed the lion's share of the half, but were horribly wasteful with some good chances carved out and failed to test City reserve keeper Matt Duke at all. But in the second half, all that shifted handsomely in City's favour. Similar to the Villa game in fact, the visitors ran out of steam and ideas, and it was Brown's team now beginning to take over.

Barring a couple of corners – taken by Guthrie, who got rabid abuse all game – plus a superb last ditch tackle by Michael Turner to snuff out a searing run, Newcastle struggled to match their first half performance. Giannakopoulos, in his first start for the Tigers, should've scored when free to shoot from eight yards, but Given snuffed out the chance.

Geovanni probed away at the Newcastle defence and had the visitors on the turnaround, helping set up Cousin who had a similar chance to the Greek winger, but again was thwarted by action man Given. Geovanni belted in a free-kick from the side of the box, but incredibly the keeper palmed it away from the top corner when it looked for all the world in.

But the best chance came from a corner when Michael Turner clattered the underside of the bar with a header and as the ball bounced down, Given pounced and smothered it amid claims it had crossed the line. Unlikely from my vantage point high in the East Stand, but we've seen worse decisions this season...

In truth, the game was scoreless because Given kept goal brilliantly and Newcastle couldn't have hit a barn door even if they'd had until midnight to do it. It was two out of form sides, praying for a mistake to arrive that would present them with a chance to win the game – though both would've probably fluffed it anyway, had it come.

But 0-0 after the results we've had recently can only help build confidence. Our defence had worked hard and earned their clean sheet. We're still in the FA Cup – just – but probably on our way to a predictable hiding to nothing at St James Park now. However, with a bit of luck, Shay Given might have been sold by then and we'll cruise through. Well, the cup is all about dreaming, isn't it?

MATCH STATS:
- Hull City: Duke, Doyle, Turner, McShane, Ricketts, Fagan (Halmosi 73), Giannakopoulos, Boateng, Marney, Geovanni, Cousin (King 73). Subs Not Used: Ashbee, France, Zayatte, Warner, Featherstone.
- Booked: Giannakopoulos, McShane, Fagan, Geovanni.
- Newcastle: Given, Coloccini, Bassong, Taylor, José Enrique, Duff, Guthrie, Butt, N'Zogbia (Gutiérrez 36), Owen, Carroll. Subs Not Used: Harper, Xisco, Geremi, Kadar, Edgar, LuaLua.
- Booked: Butt, Gutiérrez .
- Att: 20,557
- Ref: Chris Foy (Merseyside)

TUESDAY 6TH JANUARY 2009

This is the news none of us wanted to read, but probably always knew was coming. Such is the nature of the man; Dean Windass – at nearly 40 – desperately still wants to play. Now the realisation is it's unlikely to be any longer here with Hull City.

Indeed, Windass has revealed his days at Hull City appear to be over, following a meeting with assistant manager Brian Horton earlier this week, that confirmed the veteran striker is out of the picture where first team affairs are concerned.

Of course, Windass returned to the club in January 2007 as one of Phil Brown's first signings upon taking over the reins and scored eight goals, including the crucial and only goal of the game at Cardiff City that preserved Hull City's Championship status and relegated Leeds United to the Third Division.

From there, veteran Windass formed a deadly partnership with rookie Fraizer Campbell he following season and the pair scored 15 goals apiece to fire Hull City into the Premier League via the Wembley play-off final with a 0-1 victory over Bristol City. A game the latter set up the former for the only goal of the match in front of more than 86,000 fans at the home of football.

But, with just six appearances this season – of which Swansea in the League Cup and Manchester City on Boxing Day were his only starts – time appears to have been called on a frustrating final period of the forward's Hull City's career that has yielded two goals.

Windass has made no secret of his frustration at the lack of starts and landed himself in hot water with City manager Phil Brown after a series of comments on internet blogs and in newspaper columns alluded to criticism of the current selection policy at the club.

The news that Windass' name has been circulated amongst football circles and the player will now be made available, has predictably attracted the attentions of other clubs within hours.

Windass revealed - *"It's not true I've been released but assistant manager Brian Horton called me and told me the club were accepting offers to take me on loan. That tells you all you need to know about my future here."*

And first to show appear to be Hartlepool United when striker also confirmed - *"So far one club, Hartlepool, has come in for me and I'm waiting to see how things develop. I'm going to talk over the move with my family over the next couple of days and take it from there."*

Although this has been realistically coming for a long time now, it's still pretty sad for all concerned with Hull City.

THURSDAY 8TH JANUARY 2009

The winter transfer window has now been open for a week and it is the season for all kinds of rumours, but one man not enamoured with the system is Hull City manager Phil Brown, who claims it is nothing short of a 'farce'.

The City boss has been left miffed with the latest transfer window opening in January, claiming trading is heavily weighted towards the selling club and therefore making the system a 'cornered market'.

Brown has been left disappointed with some of the valuations he has come across when eyeing up proposed targets and claims the system has become nothing more than a 'false market' – echoing the comments of club chairman Paul Duffen who called for abolition of the current structure in the summer.

Brown blasted - *"It is an opportunity, of course it is, but also it's a cornered market that's in favour of the seller. We have valuations of players and are then valued out of the market by the player's demands or fee. I'm not in favour of these transfer windows at all. The agents and sellers have created a really false market."*

Before continuing his tirade with - *"We'll be looking to tweak the team with getting in one or two in the window this time but we plan long-term and it seems to me that the window is all about short-term fixes. And the fact there is a countdown to it all, day by day, makes it a complete farce; the game suffers because of the excitement of it all."*

FRIDAY 9TH JANUARY 2009 – EVERTON V HULL CITY PREVIEW

Everton. The visit to this ground is probably the missing link within the coveted '92' for a very large batch of Hull City supporters. For me, Goodison Park marks the last northern outpost to be filled in on the road to such feats. It's been 45 years since we were last here you know...

Yes, 45 years. That was the last time Hull City played Everton at Goodison Park. It was an FA Cup match - a replay in fact. The two sides had managed a 1-1 draw at Boothferry Park in early January, three days later, Everton won the replay 2-1. 1964...

Nearly half a century has passed since. Now, Hull City travel to Goodison as equals with just five points separating the clubs with Everton in sixth and ourselves in eighth. With perseverance, the snail eventually reaches the ark. But hell fire, January is here already and the Tigers are still eighth. Either Phil Brown and his players have been brilliant, or the Premier League is actually just rubbish. I think we all know the answer...

Yet being fair, the gloss has come off a little in recent weeks. The brightest, prettiest club in the Premier League we are no longer. One win in 11 games tells its own story and Phil Brown has called for the club to 'get ugly' once more. The guy speaks a lot of sense. Slowly but surely, the Premier League has realised Hull City are not going to accept relegation lightly, but in accordance with that, the tests are much tougher now.

Saturday at Goodison, though, is intriguing to say the least. Bluntly, Everton have been shocking at home this season with just two wins on home turf. Yet on the road, seven victories have taken the Toffees to their lofty perch. The only draw for Moyes' men was the 2-2 at the Circle back in September with us. Not a bad result on reflection.

Like Everton, Hull City have not been shy on the Premier League road, with just two defeats all season. Reminder to us; we must stay out of Manchester. Liverpool is a much better place, anyway. And like against the Toffees, when visiting Anfield last month, the Tigers raced into a 2-0 lead but ended up pegged back both times against Mersey opposition. Tomorrow, will we see such a goalfest?

Everton have been employing a 4-5-1 system recently, mainly due to an over-burdening injury crisis up front, but it does make for a testing challenge. With Phil Brown doing likewise in recent weeks to shore up the leaking defence, will the 'get ugly' strategy mean 4-5-1 for us? Or, will the City boss revert to the tried and trusted 4-3-3 formation on the road that has served us admirably for much of the season? Well, recalls are expected in the side after more than a few first teamers were rested for the 0-0 draw with Newcastle in the FA Cup. Skipper Ian Ashbee will return, Boaz Myhill will be back between the sticks and Kamil Zayatte will return to the defence. Bernard Mendy and Dean Marney will also be pushing for a starting shirt too.

But the name that attracts the biggest interest is Nick Barmby. The Hull lad has been in sensational form before his rest in the FA Cup and there will be no doubt the former England man will be right up for a visit to his old club. And if selected, Goodison will be lying in wait to unleash their wrath. Guilty as charged for leaving Everton to further his career at one of the big four, Liverpool. As we all know, Barmby loves these situations...

But getting the balance right - and more importantly - steeling up a wobbling defence, is far more important than a potential sideshow in the Goodison stalls. Hull City need four, maybe five more victories for Premier League survival, so let's not lose sight of the bigger picture. Progress is being made, one goal conceded in two games.

On the match - and that point in particular - City boss Phil Brown warned - *"Maybe realism went out of people's expectations. To be a realist sometimes is seen to be negative. 'Dare to Dream' has been our common statement and we're still dreaming about our Premier League status."*

Adding - *"But the bottom line is that we've won once in 11 league games now. If you look at those games, though, there was only Manchester City where we didn't have the chance to get our noses in front."*

And summed up with - *"You can look back and the reality check is that we have to keep believing we can win games at this level. I've never looked over my shoulder in my life. We're looking up still and we're looking to maintain that all season, but the only way to stay there is by winning games, starting with a tough one at Everton."*

Whatever critics Phil Brown has - and there are now many - the guy speaks a lot of sense. There's nobody getting giddy in the Hull City camp, manager, players and fans alike. The task in hand has not changed - and now January is here - and we sit deservedly eighth, the season objective remains the same. Keep trying to win games.

Attempting to stop that from happening is Everton manager David Moyes. Pushing for a starting shirt will be promising young striker Dan Gosling. That chance could be improved by the midfield quandary posed with Belgian midfielder Marouane Fellaini. The Belgian stands on nine bookings and if he receives a card against us, it will trigger an automatic two game ban and miss both derbies with Liverpool in the league and cup. Unlucky...

Moyes himself commenting on the clash is wary of the threat Hull City will serve up to state – *"For a lot of people they have been a surprise package. Phil has done a really good job. He got them up through the play-offs and he has kept the momentum going. At the start of the season it was a surprise, but now it is not. People are looking at Hull and expecting good results from them now."*

Concluding – *"Their away form is something we have got to be wary about. They won at Arsenal and have had some other really good results away from home. So you cannot take anything for granted."*

So, after a 45 year wait, we're all set. There is the bizarre ritual of playing the theme from Z-Cars as the teams run out at Goodison. Why? The tune was based on a folk song called 'Johnny Todd'; also a rhyme, and a game played by the children of Liverpool in days gone by. The song itself tells a tale of a sailor betrayed by his lover while at sea.

The sea-faring link comes from many of the Irish dock workers who settled in Liverpool, but favoured the blue half. Toffee is slang for Irish, hence the nickname. Although, the famous local toffee shop at Goodison lays fair claims to the mantle also. So now you know, history lesson over. Or the Evertonians will put us right on their internet messageboard.

What you probably didn't know was the record that Hull City hold over Everton. Get this; of the 13 competitive matches played between the two sides the statistics show Everton 4 wins, 4 draws and Hull City edging matters with 5 wins. Hell, we must be favourites, then? Who would've thought that? *whopper alert*

SATURDAY 10TH JANUARY 2009 – EVERTON 2-0 HULL CITY – REPORT

Hull City go down 2-0 at Goodison Park in a poor game with Everton settled in controversial circumstances. At least City can concentrate on the cup now, rather than trouble ourselves with top half misdemeanours...

You know, I'm not really sure what the point of Everton's preview was, but I expected a bit more than the swipe at our manager who has done a decent job in his - and our - first Premier League campaign. Ripping Hull City can only be for two reasons; because Everton are scared we're eighth (unlikely) or to be puerile. It must be the latter. Well done, objective achieved. Big scalp there. *sigh*

Arriving at Goodison - the self-appointed 'People's club' emblazoned across the face of the stadium with an oversized table tennis net - the ground looked every bit as traditional as I imagined it to be. I've only waited 37 years to get here. The anticipation welled inside. However, not for long, as the innards of the stadium were a massive disappointment. And the view was dire in the lower tier.

Everton reminds us of tradition, the place reeks of it with Z-Cars at the start of the game and the 'Grand old team' blaring at the start of the second half. Goodison doesn't do executive boxes, it doesn't do modern facilities - see plastic for those that dared to move with the times – this is a proper 'old-school' ground, no frills, no fancy adornments here.

But in fairness, we're here to see football regardless. This is sixth versus eighth in the best league in the world. Indeed, this is a match that in all honesty is a proper 'top four' clash, as neither side realistically are going to ever break the dominance of the big four – particularly based on this evidence. Moyes was bemoaning only pre-game he wouldn't be participating in the transfer merry-go-round much. So, little sign of busting the 'big four' by Everton's own admission, then.

Sadly, the match was a shocker. From the outset we had three sides competing for honours. Everton, Hull City and the match officials. Three 'teams' produced 'two' winners and left 'one' big disappointment as a consequence. Granted, Everton won't care now the game is over, because they won. But they won it in suspicious circumstances.

The match was devoid of any real goalscoring chances. Everton enjoyed the possession in great swathes, but never really got in behind the City defence to trouble Myhill for all the ball they received. Curiously, City ditched their 4-3-3 formation on the road for a 4-5-1 effort used only one other time at the brickyard that is Stoke City. And that, unfortunately, proved to be our downfall here.

King against four defenders was pointless and the ball was too quickly aimed forward to be effective. The tactic is fair enough when there are three to compete for the ball, but when there's only one, predictably Everton were soon on the attack again. Yet the Toffees were wasteful with possession; City's defence was stretched, but rarely looked like being breached.

What couldn't be denied was the risk Everton took playing Fellaini. On the one hand, he ran the show. But Browny knew the influential Belgian was walking a tightrope. Twice the fuzzy-maned one amazingly escaped the petty wrath of referee Martin Atkinson, but when the booking did come shortly after the break, the foul looked debatable. Influence over in instant.

That booking summed the Wezzie officiating this affair up. Ridiculous decisions, woeful bookings and a performance that screamed 'look at me!'. I rather doubt either side was happy with those responsible for decision-making today - but unfortunately those charged with doing so significantly contributed to the way this game swayed.

The opener arrived with a Fellaini free header six yards out after 18 minutes. It was a free header because he was yards offside. The bungling officials missed it, so the game moves to 1-0 to Everton. I've not seen the replay, not seen Match of the Day, indeed it won't be until Match of the Day 2 comes on. But I bet I'm right.

That said, it couldn't hide City's fruitless, monotone football. It was far too predictable and played straight into the hosts' hands. There was no doubt about the endeavour on show, but the output was far from efficient. Everton simply weren't threatened.

The second goal killed matters on the stroke of half time. Another poor decision gifted Everton a free kick. Mikel Arteta hit through a crumbling City wall and into the top corner to put referee Mart... sorry Everton 2-0 up and into an unassailable position.

Brown rallied the troops at the interval and sure enough, City came out fighting and wrestling far more possession from the hosts, but it was all in vain. It simply wasn't penetrating enough and Tim Howard was more a relieved spectator than a goalkeeper.

That left the fans to make something of the game and some terrace banter unfurled as the football wasn't spectacular to watch. However, *"Die, die, Nicky, Nicky, die"* was a pathetic chant that smacked of poor taste. Barmby did magnificently for Everton, earned the club £6m, so why begrudge the player wanting to further his career at a top four club and win something? He left years ago; it really is time to get over it.

With referee Martin Atkinson continuing to dominate proceedings and City's tactical substitutions failing to spark any serious attacking threat, the game petered out into a forgettable affair that both teams will want to put further from their mind.

So, the quest for four more wins move on. On reflection, visiting Goodison could and probably should've been tackled far better than this. Browny may have got this fixture wrong, but he has got the Premier League season pretty much right.

A bit more luck coming our way and there will be no need to worry. Like the football, City were devoid of that trait in the blue half of Liverpool this Saturday. So, it's on to Arsenal at home. At least we've beaten them at the Emirates already. Hey, not even Everton can say that.

MATCH STATS:
- Everton: Howard, Hibbert, Jagielka, Lescott, Baines, Osman, Arteta (Rodwell 90), Neville, Pienaar, Fellaini, Cahill (Anichebe 73). Subs Not Used: Nash, Van der Meyde, Castillo, Jutkiewicz, Gosling.
- Booked: Fellaini, Cahill.
- Goals: Fellaini 18, Arteta 45.
- Hull City: Myhill, McShane (Halmosi 79), Zayatte, Turner, Ricketts, Mendy, Ashbee, Marney (Fagan 54), Geovanni (Cousin 66), Barmby, King. Subs Not Used: Duke, Doyle, France, Boateng.

- Booked: Mendy, Zayatte, Ricketts, Cousin, Fagan.
- Att: 37,527
- Ref: Martin Atkinson (W Yorkshire)
- **Premier League position: 8th**

TUESDAY 13TH JANUARY 2009

As City continue to struggle to find a win a bullish Hull City chairman Paul Duffen has stated in no uncertain terms that the Tigers will be staying for a second season in the Premier League and Phil Brown will be leading the charge next summer...

On Setanta Sports' television show 'Football Matters' the chairman claimed the Tigers will survive any supposed relegation scrap heading the club's way – and Phil Brown will be leading the club for a second successive season in the Premier League.

Asked about the future of boss Phil Brown, the City chairman brushed off suggestions his manager could leave the club amidst some poor form to categorically state - *"If he took a step up now and didn't succeed, never having completed one campaign in the Premier League successfully, it would be an enormous thing for his career."*

Duffen then added realistically - *"I think, just from a logical perspective, there'd be no reason for Phil to leave or look at anything else other than continue at Hull City for the foreseeable future."*

When quizzed about the prospect of the club entering a relegation battle in the Premier League this season, Duffen claimed confidently - *"I don't believe that, at any time in your life, you should look anywhere other than where you want to arrive. There's absolutely nothing to be gained by considering relegation."*

Concluding - *"It's a massive thing - however, you cannot go through life peering over your shoulder. You have to be bloody bold and resolute. I'm absolutely confident that we will be playing our second Premier League campaign next season. I know we have the talent and the application."*

TUESDAY 13TH JANUARY 2009 – NEWCASTLE UNITED V HULL CITY FA CUP 3RD ROUND REPLAY PREVIEW

This is going to be an unforgettable Wednesday evening whatever happens. We've got a carful, enough booze to sink a battleship and we're all off north to drink in the magic of the FA Cup with this third round replay at Newcastle United...

Ding ding! Round two! Well, it's round three actually, but with Hull City and Newcastle United fashioning a 0-0 draw at the Circle a week last Saturday, it's all hands on deck for the replay up at St James Park.

Well, probably not all hands on deck looking at some of the other attendances in the FA Cup for the replays - possibly lower than 20,000 I hasten to add - but off to Newcastle we shall go with spirit in our bottles at the very least.

It's not really captured the imagination. Can't you tell we've gone all 'Premier League' these days? It was less than a decade ago that a Wednesday night in Newcastle prompted a mass exodus from the City and saw Mark Hateley's troops backed by more than 5,000 fans while in Division Four. How times change.

But Newcastle fans will be loath to put extra money into the beleaguered Mike Ashley's pocket. An uneasy peace reigns over the Magpies at the present; the owner having failed to find a buyer and thus withdrawn the club from the market. It's left Newcastle in limbo.

Neither is this tie helped by the respective teams rumoured to be on show, never mind the stupid price of £20 a ticket. City intend to play a string of fringe players again including John Welsh, Ryan France, Tony Warner and Nicky Featherstone - of which none have played a game this season.

Added to that are Caleb Folan, Nathan Doyle and possibly Anthony Gardner whose collective appearances don't amass double figures. It's the most expensive reserve team game I'll ever pay to witness, I guarantee it.

Phil Brown explains the reasoning with – *"We've got a fair sized squad so we will be making changes. We'll be going there with the mentality that we can win the game and take that confidence into our league game with Arsenal."*

By contrast, Newcastle are bereft of a first team of choice, with 11 players injured and Joe Kinnear warning up to six academy players will be included in the team and/or the bench. You can't beat a bit of reserve team action between fixtures against Everton last weekend and Arsenal this.

Joe Kinnear warned he's more concerned with survival than the FA Cup when stating – *"We are just in a position where we have got 11 key players missing, so it is impossible for me to even think about selling anybody else. We would only weaken our team and weaken our opportunities of survival."*

So, it sounds like it's going to be cracker. Even the television cameras managed to swerve this one such was the intensity of two Premier League clubs slugging it out with their scratch teams. The magic of the FA Cup; you just can't beat it. And at least you can drink yourself to oblivion while getting there.

WEDNESDAY 14TH JANUARY 2009 – NEWCASTLE UNITED 0-1 HULL CITY – FA CUP 3RD ROUND REPLAY REPORT

Hull City came through this all Premier League replay at St James Park, beating an injury ravaged Newcastle United with a scratch side of their own, tantamount to reserves.

And so it will be on to a fourth round tie with Millwall, then. Don't you just love coming to Newcastle? So charitable with the results, they are. After taking the league spoils with our first team back in September, this time it was the reserves' turn to have a go at beating the Geordies at St James Park. And once again the Tigers triumphed, even with their second string. Indeed, Newcastle truly are in the mire.

I'll cut to the chase. The FA Cup has lost its magic. Thousands upon thousands of empty seats adorned the home stands and the away following probably only just breached four figures. As a consequence the atmosphere was mint. Well in the away end at least. No corporates, no free loaders, no bandwagon jumpers. Just proper 'old-school' City support.

Brown chose to select a 4-5-1 formation with Cousin up top and continue the 'not concede' philosophy that reigns within the club at the present. France got a cup start like he had at Swansea in the Carling Cup, while Doyle, Garcia and Halmosi earned first team places also, with Boateng the lynchpin in midfield. Duke got the gloves again.

As for the match – played in a distinctly subdued environment except in the gods that housed the away fans – it was two sides trading tentative jabs to see who really wanted it the most. The prize of hosting Millwall was hardly setting the pulses racing, but City slowly looked like they had more purpose about them, despite lacking in the territory and possession departments a little.

But, with the onus on Newcastle to attack, just getting the ball to Michael Owen at all was proving an arduous task, with City showing decent resilience to any home threats. Injuries there may have been in the home camp, but on paper even this Newcastle side should have at least had enough about it to trouble City's reserves.

Chances were non-existent though. Only a thunderous tackle briefly disturbed the nodding crowd and comically had both managers squaring up to each other before being sent to the stands like naughty school boys by referee Phil Dowd. Eee, it wasn't the greatest spectacle on earth, trust me.

Effort wise, Newcastle kissed the bar while City had Fagan's low strike scrubbed out for offside. And that was about it for the entire first half. City failed to truly penetrate while Newcastle lacked any attacking threat to trouble Matt Duke. From an away team perspective though, you always felt more confident. Sporadic as chances had been, at least City looked like they might actually score.

So onto half two and the urgency increased marginally. Woo-hoo! Yet it was still far from exhilarating, considering this was the magic of the cup. It was a good job I was slated thanks to the booze, as the football was far from inspiring. Then, Michael Owen broke the City back line with the best chance of the game bursting clear into the box. Yet Duke was first rate, alert and closed in quickly to divert the ball wide for a corner. Excellent save. That pepped City up and from then, the ball was pushed wider. It was a clear instruction from the half time team talk. Halmosi and Fagan were stretching Newcastle's back line, but chances were still at a premium. Worryingly, Boateng was then carried off after a clash in the Newcastle box and Ashbee took to the field to compensate the loss.

But with the game still locked at 0-0 after nearly three hours of trying, Brown decided now was the time to go for broke and produced the pacy Mendy to step up matters. The substitution edged things in City's favour and more and more the visitors got in behind the home defence. Newcastle were beginning to wilt and it was now clear the Tigers wanted to face the Lions in the next round. Mendy skipped past his marker and homed in on goal with less than 10 minutes of the tie remaining. Beating one, then another, the Frenchman drilled a shot at Given. It was too hot to handle and was beaten away but straight into Garcia's path. Coolly, the Aussie composed himself, neatly squared the ball across the box to cut out Given and Cousin had the freedom of the park to steer the ball into the bottom corner of an open net. YES!

The celebrations up in the cold Newcastle sky were delightful and would mean the booze would taste that little bit sweeter if we could hang on. '1-0 to the Hull reserves!' was the bizarre chant of choice by the pilgrims. Before the more traditional 'Que sera, sera' that would rightly follow. From here, there was little evidence Newcastle would muster much of a fight as seen over the two games played so far and so it proved. Not a single save was needed from the Duke and City coasted into round four to face Millwall. It's a round City have not entered since 1989. Now if that doesn't warrant more booze on the way home, I don't know what will.

Interestingly, man of the match tonight was probably Paul McShane, even though Matt Duke inspired supreme confidence between the sticks. Make no mistake, for all the flak the Sunderland lad sometimes gets, for effort, commitment and sheer bloody-mindedness you cannot fault him. And on this showing, he loves playing the Mags, just like he did when he first arrived on his City debut at St James Park. I for one, hope he sticks around.

Bring on the 'wall! I love the FA Cup.

MATCH STATS:
- Newcastle: Given, Edgar, Bassong, Coloccini, N'Zogbia, Gutiérrez (LuaLua 82), Butt, Guthrie, Duff, Owen, Xisco (Carroll 76). Subs Not Used: Harper, Taylor, Kadar, Donaldson, Ranger.
- Booked: Coloccini.
- Hull City: Duke, Doyle, McShane, Zayatte, Ricketts, Fagan (Mendy 74), Halmosi, Boateng (Ashbee 67), France, Garcia, Cousin (Folan 86). Subs Not Used: Warner, Featherstone, Giannakopoulos, Atkinson.

- Booked: Ricketts, Fagan.
- Goals: Cousin 81.
- Att: 31,380
- Ref: Phil Dowd (Staffordshire)

THURSDAY 15TH JANUARY 2009

The games are coming thick and fast, but its transfer window time and the latest rumour circulating is Hull City have moved to bring Spanish La Liga star, Steve Finnan, back to the Premier League, after the full back was sold by Liverpool last September.

Phil Brown has responded swiftly because Sunderland have chosen to recall defender Paul McShane. This is a real blow, as the Irish defender has been a full-blooded servant for us during our first Premier League season.

The move for Finnan is a logical one. He has bags of Premier League experience with more than 300 appearances – primarily Liverpool and latterly for Fulham – in a top flight career that has stretched back eight years, before leaving to join Espanyol in September.

But the word in Spain is City have tabled a bid believed to be in the region of £1.5m – a fee that if correct would recoup precisely what the La Liga side paid Liverpool.

City had been expecting competition for Finnan's signature from Tottenham Hotspur, but Espanyol have refused to accept Harry Redknapp's offer of a loan spell at White Hart Lane since the Tigers tabled their cash bid. Finnan is expected at the club later today to discuss terms and undergo a medical.

But the speculation isn't ending with Finnan. More news breaking suggests Hull City are closing in on their first signings of the January transfer window. Talks are due to begin with both Wigan Athletic's Kevin Kilbane and West Ham United's Luis Boa Morte.

With the club hoping to complete both transfers before the televised teatime clash with Arsenal this weekend on home turf, assistant manager Brian Horton confirmed that preliminary discussions with Kilbane at least have taken place.

Meanwhile, the fee has been agreed with West Ham United for Portuguese star Boa Morte and Horton confirmed the player has passed a medical, but so far personal terms have yet to be finalised with the player.

This means potentially, the Tigers could have four new signings in place for the visit of Arsenal with Finnan flying in from Spain to hopefully complete a £1.5m switch. There is a rumour of a tabled bid for Sunderland midfielder Dean Whitehead, but Black Cats boss Ricky Sbragia is denying the offer has reached them at all.

Friday 16th January 2009

It's busy, busy, busy during the transfer window, but Phil Brown has caught us all out and continued to make additions to his squad with a name that has slipped by everyone, namely by taking another of Manchester United's strikers in Manucho.

Brown has turned to Sir Alex Ferguson once again this season to capture the Angolan international forward – a 25 year old front man who has bagged 6 goals in 11 matches for his national side.

Manucho has only made three substitute appearances so far and City will need a work permit granting before he can be included in the squad for Arsenal, but Brown is optimistic the paperwork will be completed in time for the game with the Gunners.

On Manucho signing, Brown claimed - *"The lad is a proven goalscorer at certain levels, though not yet at Premier League level. He is 6ft 3in, 6ft 4in, great stature, he has a good eye for goal, and is certainly good aerially."*

FRIDAY 16TH JANUARY 2009 – HULL CITY V ARSENAL PREVIEW

Somebody is gunning for revenge. A tasty encounter eagerly awaits the teatime television audience for Hull City's clash with Champions League chasing Arsenal – the corresponding fixture producing the unthinkable. A City win at the Emirates!

Here's a thing. Hull City completed a real first when visiting the Emirates for the first time ever in their history, in their first ever 'big four' clash, in their first ever Premier League season. Victory at the Emirates! Sweet, so sweet...

Manchester United, Liverpool, Chelsea – in fact, barring West Ham with a dodgy penalty, the entire Premier League – join a clutch of glamorous European super clubs who have all tried and failed to win at the Emirates. The shock of the season? Oh aye! And then some!

Incredibly, Hull City are now in the enviable position of recording a Premier League first against the Gunners since the move to their brand spanking new 'fortress'. The Tigers could be the first team ever – yes ever – to record a top flight 'double' over Arsenal since the move. Not even Manchester United – World, European and English champions have achieved that. And how many goes have they had? City are on the brink of history...

Yet here comes the payback for such a stunning 1-2 victory in North London one late summer's eve. Arsenal will be hell bent on revenge. A result that left Gunners boss Arsène Wenger physically sick will not be allowed to pass unchallenged, unchecked and without a ferocious battle at the Circle this Saturday teatime.

Arsenal were hurt, embarrassed and humiliated by some Championship play-off winning ragbag, newbie upstarts, fresh into the Premier League. The 'new Derby' as we were commonly written off as. Such nonchalance uttered by all and sundry - and I don't mean Arsenal specifically - we are talking generically here. Boy, did the final result come back to haunt more than few that night in September.

It was supposed to be Hull City hurt, embarrassed and humiliated in front of the Setanta tea-time cameras in North London. Instead, the annoying tick [Setanta] attempting to halt the mammoth that is Sky, witnessed the greatest shock arguably in Premier League history. Some coup for them, eh? Not even Hull City fans expected it, it just... sort of... happened. But not by accident, it was fully deserved. Ask any rational Arsenal fans.

But, it wasn't scripted to be like that. The Tigers have since proved their victory was no flash in the pan with outstanding wins at Tottenham Hotspur, West Bromwich Albion and Newcastle United backing up this incredible, profound, landmark result against Arsenal on the road. Even today, City sit eighth in the Premier League, just three places below Arsenal. Come on, we would all have settled for that upon leaving the Emirates that glorious summer's night? Hull City are top eight on merit.

Admittedly, form has taken somewhat of a downturn recently in the league, but some valuable confidence was restored against Newcastle in the FA Cup with two clean sheets and another fine away victory.

But the time is now to arrest our home form. It pales into insignificance compared to our excellent away record. The quest for survival - and that's still the season objective - will surely need some positive home form soon to help it, and to allow us to realise our ultimate goal of being here next season. To face the likes of Arsenal again.

Thanks to the FA Cup, belief is back in the squad, morale has been lifted and two new faces have arrived in the transfer window to strengthen the team. Experienced left sided Irish international Kevin Kilbane from Wigan Athletic and striker Manucho from Manchester United will both go into the reckoning - after the latter received his work permit in time. Two decent acquisitions so far.

Of course, Phil Brown has to fill the voids in defence left by Kamil Zayatte who is suspended and the obvious replacement Paul McShane being recalled from his season long loan by Sunderland. Both Andy Dawson and Anthony Gardner have been declared fit with impeccable timing, but word is Sam Ricketts could be favourite to partner Michael Turner in the centre of defence.

On the match ahead, the City boss claimed – *"We got a performance, an attitude, a mentality, a clean sheet and a win away from home. [versus Newcastle on Wednesday] People had questioned whether we could do that again and now we have to carry that confidence into the Arsenal game. It is a big game for us - the KC Stadium will be packed to the rafters and the atmosphere will be tremendous."*

Itching to set the record straight though, will be Arsenal boss Arsène Wenger. Like the Tigers, the Gunners have defensive worries with William Gallas and Mikaël Silvestre ruled out with injury. Alex Song also requires a late fitness test. Theo Walcott, Cesc Fàbregas and Thomas Rosicky remain on the long term sick list and will not feature for the Gunners.

Wenger, bringing his side to Hull City for the first time ever, attempted to hide the pain and to camouflage any thoughts of revenge with his pre-game comments – *"We want to continue our progress - it is not about revenge. We feel we are on a good run and want to focus. I am confident that we look solid and have a team who can make results away from home."*

We all know by now that Arsène Wenger is too cute with the mind games to be drawn into an all-out raging war. Particularly with clubs of the ilk of Hull City. But the very nature of his character cannot hide the theory that privately, the Frenchman is seething about the result at the Emirates and will be looking to 'restore order' with a cricket score at the Circle.

It has all the makings of an absolute classic. Could Setanta be on the end of another historic night of broadcasting once again? All those connected with Hull City will be hoping so.

Those with colours nailed to an Arsenal mast will be shuddering at the very prospect of such preposterous nonsense. Brilliant, isn't it?

SATURDAY 17TH DECEMBER - HULL CITY 1-3 ARSENAL - REPORT

History almost repeated itself. Yet two late strikes by the Gunners put a fairly ill-fitting reflection on this game and left the Tigers without a Premier League point in five attempts now. Time to get worried? Nah, not on this evidence... So near and yet so far. Hull City turned in a spirited performance against Arsenal at the Circle, full of endeavour and commitment, but almost cruelly coming up short in the last eight minutes to unstitch a good evening's work against such high calibre opposition.

Arsenal, on many counts are not even in our league. But, with a second half performance of some merit, you'd be hard pushed to distinguish which side has splashed millions on players and which had sneaked into the Premier League via the Championship play-offs.

Right from the beginning of the game, the scene was set for another mind blowing performance that could potentially produce the unthinkable. You know; another Hull City victory over Arsenal. Setanta couldn't resist and were back in Hull for the return fixture, Alan Wiley was officiating once again like at the Emirates, even the kick off time was synchronised. Surely not?

Brown choose to cover the yawning gap at centre back due to Kamil Zayatte's ban with Sam Ricketts partnering Michael Turner, and the Welshman had a fine game covering. Kevin Kilbane earned a debut at left back and again looked solid enough considering he's only been at the club 48 hours. Nathan Doyle was handed a start at right back and Peter Halmosi took the left midfield berth. The boys from the Toon had earned their shirts.

But the real shock of the evening was Ryan France making it into the elitist 'Fantastic Four' at the club by getting his first ever Premier League start in the middle of the park. Along with Boaz Myhill, Andy Dawson and skipper Ian Ashbee, Ryan France has now played in all four divisions for the club. A splendid moment for the lad signed from non-league Alfreton for just £15,000.

And City got off to an absolute flier in the match. Cousin was pretty much on his own, but Geovanni was a willing foil from midfield when appropriate and proved to be a constant thorn in Arsenal's side - just like at the Emirates. Two corners in the opening minute pegged Wenger's side back.

Nathan Doyle also capitalised on some rare Arsenal dropping off to rifle a shot in, but Almunia had the ball covered. Slowly, the visitors started to get a grip of the game and Diaby in particular dominated the midfield battle. The guy was everywhere. But City stood up to the growing threat and considering it was an untried back four, the defence looked remarkably composed and disciplined.

Indeed, Arsenal's best chances all came from set-pieces. Van Persie had seen one deflected effort pushed round the post by Myhill, before another fizzed off the bar after Myhill got the merest touch. The rebound was bundled just past the post to relative safety by the impressive Bernard Mendy. Yet the reprieve was to be short lived. Within a minute, another Arsenal corner produced the first goal. Flighted into the back post, Adebayor rose highest and headed back across goal, off the post and in. Gutted. Phil Brown will be too, as it came from a set-piece. Not to worry, we've been in this exact situation before, haven't we?

The response from City took a little time to emerge and Eboué steered a woeful effort well wide when excellently placed to add to Arsenal's lead. But as the half came to a close, the home support rallied and when more good work from Cousin and Geovanni fashioned a free kick outside the box, it was disappointingly smashed into the wall.

Phil Brown didn't waste much time after the break before changing matters. Manchester United loanee Manucho was wheeled into the attack for Peter Halmosi and City had more cut and thrust about them. With Adebayor forcing a smart, close range save from Myhill, the home team then took control of the game desperate to get on terms.

The new Angolan forward made an immediate impact. Getting between the Arsenal defence, the striker lofted the ball over Djourou into Cousin's path and was clattered after the ball had left. Alan Wiley was unmoved, but the striker was stricken and left needing treatment. A big decision; going against us. Again! That just inspired the Tigers to bigger and bolder endeavours.

Mendy was tying Clichy up in knots and the Frenchman's pace was causing real problems. It was no surprise that City's equaliser deservedly came precisely from the same side. Mendy skinned his fullback and whipped in a devilish centre. Cousin slipped his marker, made for the near post and with a bullet header got the Tigers back on level terms. The Circle erupted!

The home fans roared on the side desperately willing for a second and a repeat of the delights sampled in North London. There would be no backward steps from the hosts now. Arsenal fans resembled that mural they used to have at Highbury. The silence in the away end spoke volumes - so to speak. Come on City! Come on! Painful memories of what happened at the Emirates were surely evoked for the London visitors.

Arsenal were not enjoying their time in Hull as the wind and rain lashed across the match. Wenger brought on Bendtner, desperate to avoid a repeat of events at the Emirates - and credit where credit is due - it worked. Within minutes a fine save was drawn from Myhill by the rangey striker.

As City looked to have given it absolutely everything, Arsenal got a sniff of a winner. Nasri made space in the box and the Van Persie found him. It was trouble time... Unerringly, a precise, low drive nestled in the corner and the game was up with just eight minutes left on the watch. The stuffing had firmly been knocked from City.

Worse still, a shocking decision to allow Bendtner play on when clearly offside was punished with an Arsenal third goal and the substitute even had time to crash a post as the giant forward had sensationally wrestled the game away from Hull City and ensured Arsenal would avenge their shock loss to the Tigers at the Emirates.

At the whistle, you couldn't help but stand and applaud the magnificent effort the hosts had put in to giving Arsenal a game. The scoreline flattered the Gunners, but you cannot argue about the clinical finishing on show from them. It's five games without a point now and you have to wonder where the next one is coming from. But surely - and I'm sure Arsenal fans would concede - if we carry on playing like this, we will survive. It will come, keep the faith.

We'll just have to take out all our frustrations on Millwall in the FA Cup fourth round next Saturday. It should be fun.

MATCH STATS:
- Hull City: Myhill, Doyle, Turner, Ricketts, Kilbane, Mendy, France (Fagan 83), Ashbee, Halmosi (Manucho 53), Geovanni (Garcia 87), Cousin. Subs Not Used: Duke, Dawson, Folan, Giannakopoulos.

- Booked: Ashbee.
- Goals: Cousin 65.
- Arsenal: Almunia, Sagna, Touré, Djourou, Clichy, Eboué (Bendtner 69), Diaby, Denilson, Nasri, Adebayor (Song Billong 87), Van Persie. Subs Not Used: Fabiański, Vela, Ramsey, Gibbs, Merida.
- Booked: Clichy.
- Goals: Adebayor 30, Nasri 82, Bendtner 86.
- Att: 24,924
- Ref: Alan Wiley (Staffordshire)
- **Premier League position: 8th**

TUESDAY 20TH JANUARY 2009

The fall out from the FA Cup replay has landed on the club. Hull City manager Phil Brown and Newcastle United manager Joe Kinnear will be facing FA charges for the brief touchline dust up in the FA Cup third round replay at St James Park.

The argument was sparked when City boss Brown was incensed with a challenge on Daniel Cousin by Fabrizio Coloccini.

Referee for the evening, Phil Dowd, subsequently sent both managers to the stands following the bust up, but both men in their post-match press conferences played down the incident as nothing other than a few heated words.

The Tigers went on to win the game 0-1 thanks to Cousin's well taken goal with ten minutes remaining to set up a fourth round home tie with Millwall. Both managers have until 3rd February to respond to the charge of improper conduct.

THURSDAY 22ND JANUARY 2009

Nobody, but nobody, saw this coming. Hull City manager Phil Brown has swooped for talismanic Fulham central midfielder Jimmy Bullard – and Cottagers boss Roy Hodgson has accepted the offer tabled by the Tigers. This is major transfer news.

Brown has made no secret of his wish to bolster Hull City's midfield, but by launching a sensational bid for Fulham midfielder Jimmy Bullard? Well, that was surely beyond anyone's realistic comprehension. The club record £5m fee offered to the London based club has been accepted and the deal looks certain to be completed.

The Tigers are looking to beef up the midfield after losing George Boateng through injury during the FA Cup Third replay at Newcastle United for a period likely to be around three months. But to go for England squad member Jimmy Bullard? Wow!

The experienced 30 year old midfielder – who has recently begun to emerge as a regular in the England set up under Fabio Capello's stewardship – would be the biggest signing in the club's history if it comes off. Bullard joined Fulham from Wigan Athletic for a fee of £2.5m in the summer of 2006 and his since gone on to make more than 40 appearances for the Craven Cottage outfit, scoring six times. Prior to that, Bullard made more than 150 appearances for Wigan and will arrive at the peak of his Premier League career – if personal terms can be agreed.

Excited? It feels like Christmas has had a second coming!

FRIDAY 23RD JANUARY 2009

It's really happening! Jimmy Bullard has completed a medical, agreed personal terms and the fee with Fulham was struck. The paperwork to complete the deal has been lodged with the FA and is due to be processed. Jimmy Bullard will be a Hull City player. An England player!

A noon press conference this Saturday will formally herald the signing of Bullard from Fulham, meaning the England squad player will not debut for the club against Millwall in the FA Cup fourth round – even though he is not cup-tied.

Speaking on his switch to the Tigers from Fulham, Bullard divulged the move is ideal to advance his career and he is looking forward to personal and club success with City, that Bullard believes could see both parties playing in Europe.

Bullard began his first Hull City words with – *"Hull are the biggest club I've played for. I know all about their fanbase and great ambition. I felt at home here as soon as I arrived. It took me ten minutes to decide to sign for them."*

Adding – *"The league table doesn't lie and Hull have done fantastic so far this season. My next step is to play regularly for Hull and hopefully get back into the England squad, Hull can help me do this."*

Concluding – *"If we can just kick on now and get a few points, then who knows? It was refreshing to hear the manager talk about playing attacking football, enjoy it and play it as the game should be played. I want to see us become a good established side in the Premier League. After that, who knows, we can push for Europe definitely."*

Now for me, if ever Hull City wanted to make a statement of intent about how serious they take the Premier League, then the record transfer signing of Jimmy Bullard from Fulham is surely that solemn pledge.

At a whopping £5m – that's double the previous record paid to Tottenham Hotspur for Anthony Gardner – Jimmy Bullard has become the 900th Tiger in Hull City's history and will make his debut for the club in the televised game with West Ham United on January 28th 2009. Ironically, this is the club Bullard supported as a boy and where he was an academy player.

These are uncharted waters for Hull City. Never, ever in your wildest dreams would you even contemplate the Tigers making a back page tabloid splash with a £5m signing who is currently around the England squad. That's simply not Hull City.

Yet Paul Duffen and Phil Brown's serious promise of making the club – and I quote our chairman here – *"A permanent constituent of the Premier League"* has been more than backed up by the signing of a player with the class of Jimmy Bullard. Bullard is an East End boy who plays the game with a smile on his face and exudes a passion that sits a little out of kilter of the very serious business of the Premier League. Don't get me wrong, Bullard is as focussed as they come on the pitch, but has an almost boyish outlook on the game that makes him such a pleasure to watch. Including the fact he holds an armoury of dazzling football talents, of course.

For £5m, City have certainly bought a skilful footballer. Bullard comes with masses of Premier League experience at both Wigan Athletic and Fulham. The 30 year old is a hard worker, clean passer and pretty nifty from the dead ball situation. That type of player. Always giving 100 per cent and never afraid to shirk a tackle, Bullard is the stereotypical English midfield dynamo.

The fact that City have been able to attract a player of this calibre who recently broke into the England squad, is proof of Paul Duffen backing his manager and Phil Brown being able to persuade the player to join. Bullard's press conference was also mightily revealing – *"I knew within ten minutes I was coming to the right club."* Wow!

At 30 years old, Bullard has been signed for a deal spanning four and half years. Bullard is a player that will keep us in the Premier League for sure. Indeed, even should the worst happen and City fail to build on their good start, Jimmy will prove to be the man.

Why? Well, the midfield ace came back from a horrific injury while at Fulham, to rescue a seemingly doomed club from relegation with three months of the season to spare. Bullard was instrumental in guiding the Cottagers to safety on the final day with a 0-1 away win at Fratton Park, Portsmouth, following a string of hugely influential performances that gleaned a run of victories for the London club – and ultimate safety. Bullard is the type of player that Hull City need. Here is a man primed for the worst, but could well propel us towards the very best. At £5m and a huge wage it could well be seen as a gamble. But the only gamble is; how big we now dare to become. Survival? The FA Cup? Europe? Bullard will be party to them all this season.

Welcome to Hull City, Jimmy. We all hope you're very, very, happy here and your career takes you were you want it to go – and where the club are daring to dream to go.

Ten years ago, we the supporters were chucking money into buckets, fighting to even get inside the ground and facing the prospect of non-league football. Meanwhile, a young East End decorator was putting in the graft with his father ten hours a day, six days a week for the family business.

Today, following hard work and a determination to get to the top by both the club and the player – down very different routes – it is a meeting of likeminded individuals coming together at the Circle in Hull this January. For the Tigers, it is to cement their place in the top league. For Bullard it is to earn those England caps and succeed in his preferred profession of football. It's no joke to describe it all as fairytale stuff.

And we all live happily ever after.

FRIDAY 23RD JANUARY 2009 – HULL CITY V MILLWALL – FA CUP 4TH ROUND PREVIEW

The battle of the big cats. A home clash with League One side Millwall has arrived as the FA Cup fourth round takes centre stage. Is everybody excited? The FA Cup fourth round is here! Come on, we haven't been able to say that for 20 years now! So if you're not, you should be - and grateful that this game has arrived to allow Phil Brown another golden opportunity to see those on the fringes of his squad and precisely who is and who isn't up for the Premier League fight. The last time Hull City were at this stage of the competition was when travelling to Bradford City in 1989 for the memorable 1-2 away win at Valley Parade. A game memorable personally for me – not for the stunning Whitehurst and Edwards attacking combo – but by virtue of missing the sodding thing! Bah! A rarity indeed.

Of course, Liverpool were waiting in round five and despite City leading 2-1 at half time, John Aldridge scored two goals in a minute and wrecked any hope of a cup shock. Eee, those were the days. The days when the FA Cup really did matter before Manchester United became selective, the cup wasn't sponsored and the competition wasn't usurped by the unborn Premier League. Changes, changes…

Yet now, the boot is on the other foot - and who would've thought that all those years ago? Premier League constituents as we are - sadly the overwhelming number of our support would all now openly declare that devilish sentence… *"The league is far more important."* Treacherous words indeed.

Worse still, is the blase post match attitude adopted in the event of a Millwall victory. Nobody will be bothered, it won't be a cup shock anymore - what is these days? No, instead it will be… *"Now we can concentrate on the league."* Or… *"It was only our reserve side, who cares?"* 'scuse me, actually I do care!

I want a full strength side. I want passion. I want commitment. I want a full to the brim Circle rocking with some wicked terrace banter. I want my £20 worth! It's not a great deal to ask is it? Millwall it may be, but at least it's not a plastic club, here's a proper old-school outfit if ever there was one. So let's have it!

As good as his word, Brown kept faith many of the fine performers up at Newcastle United that triumphed 0-1 in the replay and earned their chance for a starting berth against Arsenal last week. Once again, the City boss is likely to make changes for the visit of Millwall - major ones at that all being well.

Phil Brown can call upon newly signed defender Kamil Zayatte - back from a ban and fresh from agreeing to make his loan permanent from Swiss side Young Boys Berne for £2.5m. In a second boost for the Tigers, full back Andy Dawson is expected to make his first start since his Achilles injury suffered back in November versus Bolton.

Craig Fagan will not figure for City due to a one match ban courtesy of amassing five bookings. Kevin Kilbane is cup-tied, but record signing in waiting – Jimmy Bullard – is not. However, the midfield ace is not expected to play despite the fee, and personal terms being agreed, plus the medical being passed. The 12 o'clock press conference on Saturday is the giveaway.

In form Millwall travel to Yorkshire boasting eight wins from 13 games. The Lions are unbeaten in their last four outings, sitting fourth in the League One table. Team news sees Zak Whitbread banned and Danny Spiller injured. Tony Craig should fill in at the back, while strikers Tresor Kandol and Izale McLeod should lead the line for the Lions.

Saturday will see the first ever clash of the Tigers v Lions in the FA Cup. To be honest, the nearer the game gets, the more enticing the fixture is becoming. Come on City; let's get ourselves booked into the fifth round. Whatever our side turns out to be, at home, the Tigers have to be firm favourites.

That said, I'd settle for anything if it's a good game. Providing it doesn't go to a replay of course. A replay? *shudder* perish the thought... Ye gods, NO! London three times in 10 days is enough to put you off for life, methinks. On second thoughts, scrap that, give me a dour game with an own goal winner for either side in injury time. Ta!

SATURDAY 24TH JANUARY 2009 - HULL CITY 2-0 MILLWALL - FA CUP 4TH ROUND REPORT

It was like a step back to the 80s. Seats flew, fans surged like they did on terraces of old and the atmosphere bubbled along uneasily. And apparently, there was a football match going on as well. Who says the FA Cup has lost its magic?

Premier League Hull City beat a path to the last 16 of the FA Cup this Saturday, against 'cultured' Third Division opponents Millwall, who have clearly lost none of their charm and habitual terrace mannerism in the ever-increasing number of shiny new all-seater stadiums springing up all over the country.

And to be honest I like that. If you want banter with Millwall, you've got it. If you want to see a team try to play football, again you've got it. If you're looking for trouble, once again - you've guessed it - you've got it. Millwall are the quintessential icon of old fashioned football from the 80s. Times change, football's changed, thankfully Millwall traditions have not. Not sure our local plod would agree, mind...

Billed as the FA Cup tie pairing the Tigers and the Lions, the game was perfectly scripted for the stereotypical scrappy affair. It wasn't particularly pleasing on the eye, the football at times was primitive to say the least, but like all good cup ties it was close enough to keep everyone on tenterhooks until the dying minutes. This was a good old fashioned cup fixture - if lacking a little class.

Brown went half and half on the team selection with first teamers like Cousin, Turner and Ashbee pressed into action. Yet fringe players like Garcia, Halmosi and goalkeeper Tony Warner - facing his old club - also got a game. He included young Nicky Featherstone on the bench.

Record signing Jimmy Bullard was introduced to the crowd prior to kick off - and as it turned out - the £5m midfield ace had been signed in time to play and is not cup-tied. However, it proved a wise decision to leave City's newest signing out and save him for West Ham United away on Wednesday. It was brutal out there at times.

Credit goes to Millwall for having a go. 2,500 fans made the long journey north and tried to join the majority on numerous occasions. Such friendly fans. They were even prepared to bring their own seats with them. Only Millwall could be so considerate. The cheeky, chirpy cockneys have lost none of their charm since we've gone all Premier League on them, after years of slugging it out in the lower leagues with the south Londoners.

The Tigers for their part had much of the ball and territory - as you would expect being Premier League. Chances were still hard to come by though, as Millwall defended well. Going forward, the Lions gathered numbers to cause a threat, but the final ball or the shooting opportunity was rarely fashioned. City always looked in control.

As we've learnt in the Premier League during our short existence in the top flight, when you make a chance you have to take it. Finishing is the key difference between those at the pinnacle of the game and those further down the league ladder. Millwall were guilty as charged this afternoon at the Circle, I'm afraid.

City took their chance when Sam Ricketts was scythed down just outside the box. The resultant free kick found Michael Turner unmarked at the back stick to head home - the outcome of Turner/free header/goal was never in doubt. 1-0 City with probably our first real chance of the game, Halmosi's long distance drive apart.

Millwall's response was excellent. Three great chances were created; the first saw Izzy McLeod jinking goalwards with a mazy dribble in the City box and making a clear path to goal, but the shot was tame and Warner easily snaffled up the weak effort.

But controversy was just minutes away. Warner produced a huge gaffe when slipping trying to clear a backpass. Millwall's Harris looked like he'd got a touch and Warner did brilliantly to leap back and pounce on the ball, but calamity 'ghost goal' referee Stuart Attwell gave an indirect free kick in the box for supposedly collecting a back pass.

Millwall slammed the eventual shot just wide of the post. The best chance for the visitors - and arguably their last - came right on the cusp of half time. Neil Harris had shaken his marker and swivelled round for a free shot from six yards, but the ball went agonisingly wide, when it really should have dragged Millwall level. A golden chance missed by the Lions.

And that was about the sum total of Millwall's challenge. In the second half, City ran the show without, to be fair, being particularly creative. Daniel Cousin had a fine game up front - his best since signing - and the overlapping full backs of Ricketts and the returning Dawson from a massive injury lay off pegged Millwall back time and again.

Millwall refused to buckle and the odd corner brought nervous thoughts of the dreaded replay, but City always looked like they had another goal in them if they applied themselves correctly. The match had become bitty and the tackles flew in. But it was well into the second half before referee Stuart Attwell started doling out the yellows. Surprising really, especially with Dawson and Zayatte both needing lengthy treatment for elbows to the head in the first half.

As Millwall ran out of steam – even with a warm reception for ex-Tiger and Lions substitute Gary Alexander – the second goal was imminently coming. It came from a well worked move round the back of the visitors defence and the ball was teed up for skipper Ian Ashbee 20 yards out. And the customary once-a-season screamer arrived with a bullet into the top corner and squarely settled this fourth round tie. It was all about the finishing. That was the difference.

The game petered out from what had been a pretty ferocious encounter, though lacking the fluency to make it truly appealing. The fans traded seats, coins and water bottles in a rather surreal manner, before waving each other off at the final whistle. The FA Cup was firmly alive and kicking in deepest, darkest East Yorkshire on this evidence.

So, not quite the routine 2-0 home win the score may suggest, but undeniably the best team did win the tie and deservedly go into Round 5 of the FA Cup. As for Millwall, if they can get that finishing sorted, they could be in the Championship next year. Let's hope we aren't. As good as this cup run is, West Ham United on Wednesday in the Premier League is now foremost in our minds. Staying up is the priority. The FA Cup is fast catching up though.

Let's see what tomorrow's draw brings, eh?

MATCH STATS:
- Hull City: Warner, Ricketts, Turner, Zayatte, Dawson, Garcia, Ashbee, Marney, Halmosi (Featherstone 66), Cousin, Manucho (Folan 75). Subs Not Used: Duke, Doyle, Geovanni, France, Mendy.
- Booked: Folan.
- Goals: Turner 15, Ashbee 84.
- Millwall: Forde, Dunne, Robinson, Craig, Frampton, Grabban (Hackett 77), Laird, Abdou, Martin (Grimes 77), Harris, McLeod (Alexander 74). Subs Not Used: Pidgeley, Kandol, O'Connor, Fuseini.
- Booked: Martin, Harris, Dunne, Grimes.
- Att: 18,639
- Ref: Stuart Attwell (Warwickshire)

TUESDAY 27TH JANUARY - WEST HAM UNITED V HULL CITY PREVIEW

Here's a trip for the proper hardcore uproar City support. Wednesday night, end of January, in the east end of London? Allow me to explain, it's not one for the faint-hearted among Hull City fans.

Back in the summer when the fixtures were drafted up, this game was always going to separate the men from the boys. Back end of January, money is tight and a trip to the capital in midweek would hardly signal the merry band of newcomers to flocking down in their droves.

Me? I was grateful a small corner of the Premier League campaign would be reserved for the proper hardcore element of Hull City's support. You know the ones, the faces from Macclesfield, Rochdale and Southend on a Tuesday night, never mind a traditional top flight stalwart like West Ham United.

I've been looking forward to this trip for ages - and as it's turned out - it's going to be an overnighter with hotel, and trains booked Wednesday and Thursday so we can all get completely leathered. Just the sort of trip to perk you up from the January blues. Who says the fixture computer is ridiculous? It's perfect.

Indeed, with the Sky cameras in attendance for the evening, it is likely to be our lowest attended league game. I don't mind that, I'm looking forward to catching up with a few old faces from the south who have struggled to get away tickets in this new found era of loyalty counts for nothing. Sorry Mr Duffen, but it needs to be said.

The timing of the fixture is almost a carbon copy of the corresponding scenario back at the Circle in October. The home team were bang in form, the away side were spluttering and a tight encounter produced a narrow 1-0 victory for the Tigers courtesy of Michael Turner's header. I'm expecting a similarly tight encounter this Wednesday.

City are desperate for a victory in the Premier League, just one win in 13 it is now. Yet another picture shows two victories and two clean sheets out of the last three games. Massively in-form Arsenal, sandwiched in between, being the only blot on the more recent landscape when taking a 1-3 win from the Circle.

It sounds almost churlish to state after making such provisions for this game, but I'd be happy with a point out of West Ham. I'd go further and settle for a 0-0 draw and another clean sheet. Clean sheets are imperative. Between both sides, just six have been managed in 44 games this season.

Phil Brown rested some of the first team for the match with Millwall in the FA Cup on Saturday and players in the ilk of Geovanni, Bernard Mendy and Boaz Myhill will be pushing for a recall at the Boleyn Ground. The match is massive with eighth hosting ninth before this latest round of staggered midweek Premier League matches got underway.

Of course, all the talk in the away camp is about City's record transfer signing Jimmy Bullard. The £5m signing is set for a debut against his a club with whom he had a two-year spell between 1999 and 2001. An East End lad – and Hammers fan – destined to make his Hull City debut against his boyhood club. Having trained yesterday, the earlier virus will not keep him out.

On Bullard signing Brown stated – *"Today he [Bullard] was on the training ground for the first time and he was outstanding, a different class, a breath of fresh air to everybody. He plays football the right way, even with the circumstances we have got to suffer at the moment with the training ground knee-deep in mud."*

Before adding – *"Hopefully that will be infectious on the squad in these pressure moments. There are a number of massive games between now and the end of the season. There are games you earmark as potential ones you can get something from. I would put this in that category."*

Hammers boss Gianfranco Zola is set to parade his own new record signing, when fielding little-known Bescia striker Savio Nsereko for £9m, after signing yesterday. Kieron Dyer is likely to be out with a muscle injury, but defender Matthew Upson should return to the West Ham United line-up.

Zola commented on the fixture with the Tigers – *"It is a crucial game and gives us the opportunity to put some more space between us and the clubs behind. It is going to be tough because Hull are very well organised."*

So, let's have it then. A critical Premier League encounter that both would dearly love to win, but neither can really afford to lose, such is the intensity and tightness of the top flight this season. Like I stated prior, I'd take a point now. The one thing that's become apparent in the Premier League over the last few months, a point away is truly massive.

Now, about that 100 per cent record in London this season...

WEDNESDAY 28TH JANUARY 2009 – WEST HAM UNITED 2-0 HULL CITY – REPORT

Yeah, about that 100 per cent record in London in the Premier League. About being contented with a point. Hell, City never looked remotely like getting either and that, sadly, is six top flight losses on the spin. It's the early hours of the morning. The traffic is rumbling outside my hotel room somewhere in the vicinity of Kings Cross. I'm drunk. I've left this Irish bar with my friends still inside. I'm worn out from berating and chastising those I've travelled with, I need to get this West Ham United game out of my system and written down, done and dusted.

We'd made good time, hit the smoke late afternoon, freshened up and then arrived at Upton Park ready for a skinful. I was in the Queens - proper West Ham pub and then some - with all the Hammers greats adorning the wall from yesteryear. Bobby Moore, Billy Bonds and err... Paul Konchesky? Aye...

The thing was; we'd made too good time. We got beer, then some more and then the shorts in with every round. Steamed? Fairly. So trooping out this bizarre drinking den - the regular chime of 'Irons' ringing periodically - it was on to Upton Park. A strange ground it has to be said, hidden away on a high street of all places.

Of course, getting there and getting in was a whole new ball game. Queues for the away turnstiles wound up to be surprisingly long. We were going to be let in late, such was the scramble. It was Leyton Orient all over again. Only the fourth division side did a much grander job of getting us all in speedily. And what a turnout from City for a Wednesday evening at the back end of January - live on the telly, I might add. Comfortably surpassing anything a reverse fixture would have brought, I'm sure.

Brown had elected to keep new record signing Jimmy Bullard on a strained leash for the clash. Recalls for Geovanni, Dean Marney and Kevin Kilbane arrived, with Matt Duke the surprise choice between the sticks. The game was in full flow by the time I'd got in and it was all West Ham from the second I took my seat. Well, I say seat, I happily stood for the entire 90 minutes, hurrah! But, perhaps I shouldn't have bothered. There was nothing to get excited about.

Indeed, City looked bereft of a cutting edge and did not have enough of the ball to trouble the home side. West Ham poured forward in numbers and cleverly 'played' Howard Webb for every decision. City are distinctly naïve at this Premier League gamesmanship malarkey and as a consequence will continue to get rolled over for being an honest, hard working northern side in this division. Wise up City!

It was all West Ham and Di Michele smacked a post while Jack Collison put a free header wide. Carlton Cole was falling like a sack of spuds when anyone got within two yards of him and he bought referee Mr Webb cheaply for a penalty that was just plain cheating. A big lad like that, stumbling like a girl in the box? Cuh! Incredibly, like at Swansea, (I was there) Duke pulled off a magnificent save to his left and the score remained 0-0.

But the Hammers were rampant. Wave upon wave of attacks came into the City defence and another post was smacked with Duke desperately scrambling to cover lost ground. It was all just a matter of time. When the opener came, a cross from the City right was drilled across the six yard box and Duke pushed the fizzing ball out. But Di Michele was charging in at the back post and couldn't stop himself to have any sort of control and the ball cannoned off him and into the roof of the net with an element of fortune.

Not that City could complain. Indeed, if it had been 4-0 I couldn't complain. City were simply not at the races and turned in a shocking performance going forward. To be fair to Cousin and Manucho, neither had the service and were left isolated when the ball did finally reach them. The half time whistle came to end the relentless Hammers attacks and City could count themselves fortunate to be just the one goal down. In the second half, City improved drastically and attempted to make a game of it. They could hardly have been worse. And although the early possession was City's, West Ham were crashing in the second of the evening courtesy of the lively Carlton 'blow me down like a feather' Cole, when cutting loose within five minutes of the restart. Game over, surely? If it was me, I probably wouldn't have bothered giving Jimmy Bullard his debut from hereonin. This game was lost. But Brown did. Excellent passing and a lively energy were brought to the table with his £5m presence, but the service to Cousin and Manucho – then Fagan – in general was poor. Within five minutes though, Bullard had rifled in a stunning low volley from distance and drawn a stinging save from Robert Green. Was there hope after all?

Well, sad to say, but no, not really. As good as the visitors were second half, the ruthlessness to force a goal was distinctly absent – and West Ham always looked mighty dangerous on the counter. The hosts were seemingly content to let us have the ball and 'do our worst'. City were never really in this game at any point.

It's difficult to evaluate what positives you could possibly draw from the performance. Matt Duke's constant heroics was one, I concede – the keeper is simply getting better and better with every first team appearance. But our frailties in defence are fast becoming endemic. There's much work to be done there.

With West Bromwich Albion arriving on Saturday at the Circle, if the game wasn't must-win before tonight, it certainly is now. City simply cannot afford to be dropping points at home to teams in the drop zone. But who knows what City team will turn out for that critical encounter? It better not be this one.

I'm tired, I'm drunk, my eyelids are sagging. I might wake up in the morning and this will all have been a terrible dream, although I couldn't be that lucky. One hangover is firmly in the post after this midweek capital escapade. Deserved or not, it's coming...

MATCH STATS:
- West Ham: Green, Neill, Collins, Upson, Ilunga, Behrami, Parker, Collison (Faubert 71), Noble (Boa Morte 84), Di Michele (Nsereko 86), Cole. Subs Not Used: Lastuvka, Tristan, Tomkins, Sears.
- Goals: Di Michele 33, Cole 51.
- Hull: Duke, Ricketts, Turner, Zayatte, Dawson, Marney (Mendy 73), Ashbee, Kilbane, Geovanni (Bullard 53), Cousin, Manucho (Fagan 53). Subs Not Used: Myhill, Garcia, Halmosi, Folan.
- Booked: Marney.
- Att: 34,340
- Ref: Howard Webb (S Yorkshire)
- **Premier League position: 10th**

THURSDAY 29TH JANUARY 2009

With the speculation reaching fever pitch ahead of the January transfer window's imminent closure, more rumours are breaking about precisely who the Tigers are planning to land. The transfer window closes on Monday February the 2nd, with the latest name reported to be Albania's talismanic forward Erjon Bogdani.

Bogdani is currently playing in Serie A with Chievo, but the 31 year old is supposedly ready for a move away from the Verona based club – and two of Italy's premium clubs are reported to be interested, as well as Hull City.

Speculation suggests that Serie A super clubs Lazio and Roma – fierce rivals from Italy's capital – are set make bids within the next 24 hours. The Premier League interest is rumoured to be from Hull City, after ambitious Championship side Queens Park Rangers were turned down.

The Albanian international has won 12 caps – scoring three times for his country – and comes with plenty of top flight football pedigree on the continent with spells at Reggina and Sienna before signing for Chievo in the summer of 2006.

Hmmm...

Later in the day another transfer breaks. Apparently, City have completed the signing of promising French Second Division defender Steven Mouyokolo from Boulogne. But he's been immediately loaned back out... to Boulogne! Weird...

Bizarrely, it is believed it was the only way manager Phil Brown could ensure the £1.8m deal was secured for the promising 22 year old. He's our player, we've just signed him, but he's not going to play for us. Eh?

Allow Boulogne president Jacques Wattez to shed a bit more light on this bizarre signing – *"There is a time when we can no longer block the progress of a player. If Hull had not accepted our request, it wouldn't have happened. But we need to consider the future of our club."*

The Boulogne chief continued with - *"Of course we lose a good player, but his departure will enhance us. We could have waited until the end of the season, but sport is not immune from injury, in this case there would then have been no transfer."*

Righto... Anyway, all that aside, a defender and a striker are still rumoured to be on the agenda to arrive before Monday's 5pm transfer deadline.

Meanwhile, the intensity on transfer rumours continues to increase with another transfer 'story-jackanory' emerging. Apparently, Hull City goalkeeper Boaz Myhill – a noticeable absentee from the starting line-up last night at West Ham United – may well have a good reason for being left out of the starting XI. Get this for a rumour, don't you just love 'em?

In the north west of the country, Manchester City were hosting crisis club Newcastle United – a match in which Magpies owner Mike Ashley kept a low profile by watching in the executive suites. Toon manager Joe Kinnear selected Steve Harper in goal for the game to accommodate regular no.1 Shay Given's distinct absence. Indeed, the Republic of Ireland keeper is reported to be the subject of a £7m bid from the Eastlands club amongst press circles and to avoid a conflict of interests - and undoubtedly speed up the move - Given did not travel with Geordies to the match.

Now, should that move be pushed through, Newcastle United will be desperately searching for a new goalkeeper and guess who looks like he's been lined up? Interestingly, Phil Brown has blocked a move by League One side Crewe Alexandra to take Tony Warner on loan. The plot thickens...

But surely two and two make... five?

FRIDAY 29TH JANUARY 2009 –
HULL CITY V WEST BROMWICH ALBION PREVIEW

Six games in the Premier League without a point. Confidence sapping by the game? Morale plummeting ever lower? Luck seemingly deserting us? What better fixture to revive all of that than bottom of the league at home, right?

Yes, bottom of the league at home. Although West Bromwich Albion have rather unsportingly had a recent renaissance of sorts – well until the champions Manchester United came into town and dished out a 0-5 home thumping in midweek. Jeez, we all know how that feels, eh? Only, ours was against Wigan. *cringe*

Hmmm, some time has passed since then. A rousing recovery was summoned by the Tigers and a blistering run of form followed. Form that includes a 0-3 walloping of West Bromwich Albion at The Hawthorns back in October. Eee, happy days they were, happy days indeed. Hey up! Those Baggies better not be getting any ideas...

Indeed, however you dress this Saturday's encounter up, it's simply massive. A sure fire 'three points a must and circled in red pen' this was on both club's fixture calendar, well before a ball was kicked, I suspect. And as it turns out, with good reason, as just six points separate the sides in the tightest Premier League ever.

Yep, a relatively catchable six points it may be, but a whopping ten places is the stretching distance between the respective sides as things stand. It really is compelling for the neutral observer this season. Credit must go to all the promoted sides for attempting to make a fist of Premier League survival this season.

Wednesday's away game at West Ham United once again showed City's lack of creativity and goal scoring chances. Well, until Jimmy Bullard and Bernard Mendy came on. Surely, both have to start against an injury ravaged, patched up, makeshift Baggies side? How can we win if we don't score?

Yet manager Phil Brown has problems. The risk bringing on Bullard for a debut may have backfired with the £5m man taking a whack against the Hammers and is considered a fair doubt. Daniel Cousin at the head of the field is another and is rated at just 50-50 for the clash. The impressive Matt Duke looks set to continue in goal, but this really is a game that a clean sheet is a must. In the Duke we must trust.

Striker Caleb Folan - who has withdrawn from the Ireland squad to build up his fitness at the Tigers - claimed ahead of the game with the bottom club - *"It's a game we must not lose, but I think it is a must win game for West Brom."*

The forward – who would have had a fair shout of a starting place had he been 100 per cent fit – continued his comments with – *"As tight as the league is this season, we're still in a great position. We just need to get that belief back and that will come with a win in the league."*

Meanwhile, by contrast, West Bromwich Albion manager Tony Mowbray is to throw caution to the wind with his team selection. Jonas Olsson, Leon Barnett, Abdoulaye Méïté and long-term casualty - and ex-Tiger - Neil Clement are all ruled out through injury, meaning gambles will be made on undercooked Pele and Ryan Donk, who have troubling groin injuries. Ouch...

Mowbray ahead of the trip to East Yorkshire reminded us all - *"We've been there in the last two seasons and got good victories. We've got to go there and try and make it a hat-trick of wins at a relatively new stadium."*

Adding - *"It's a huge game that, first and foremost, we don't want to lose. They could go nine points away from us which could be a big ask [to make up]. It's a big game for Hull because if they were to lose they'd be three points ahead of the team sitting bottom. That shows the tightness of the league."*

Aye, thanks for reminding us all Tony, cheers for that. This is massive. If you're one of the sell out members of the home crowd tomorrow, do not fail your team. You have a duty. Your Hull City needs you. Each and every one of you have been called to arms. This is 'must win' territory now. You have been squarely warned. Right, let's have it!

SATURDAY 31ST JANUARY 2009 – HULL CITY 2-2 WEST BROMWICH ALBION – REPORT

How did Hull City not win that? Despite key injuries to striker Daniel Cousin and Jimmy Bullard, a makeshift Tigers batter West Bromwich at the Circle and once again fall victim to another key refereeing decision.

Stunned. Muted applause greeted the final whistle, with an air thick with bemusement, shock and a hint of resentment all rolled into one. One point gained? Or two lost? Maybe I'll work that one out before I finish scribbling.

Ahead of the game, it is was clear this was a huge test lying in wait for City, particularly after learning of Jimmy Bullard's likely non-appearance courtesy of a knee injury and Daniel Cousin tearing a cartilage on Wednesday against West Ham United. Indeed, the team had a very makeshift and workmanlike look about it.

In came Craig Fagan and Richard Garcia to spearhead the attack, while Bernard Mendy earned a recall to the starting line up in a much more orthodox 4-4-2 shape to the Tigers. Many of us raised eyebrows at such selections, but my only concern would be how we would hold the ball up. Not that I needed to worry as it turned out. Garcia and Fagan did not disappoint.

Yet the rumours sweeping the stadium and overshadowing affairs were that a certain Italian defender was indeed at the Circle and reportedly due to sign. It was Christian Panucci. Me? I'd heard a whisper a certain Fraizer Campbell was back on the agenda up front. I tore myself apart when Burnsy asked me live on air to give a name before selling fanzines. Do I, don't I? I opted for the latter. It seems though, that story made the airwaves after all. It could've been my exclusive! Damn!

But enough of all that, freezing brass monkeys it was and after packing up shop at five to three I was primed for an afternoon of hollering for a massive game ahead. This is what the Premier League is all about; never mind your Liverpools, Manchester Uniteds, Chelseas and Arsenals.

It was a fervent atmosphere conjured up by the home crowd and it needed to be. Pat on the back to all concerned. The effort on show from the Tigers was first class and City were getting to everything. The visitors simply had no answer and the pace of Fagan and Garcia's vastly underrated aerial ability were posing a mite too tricky for the Baggies to feel comfortable.

Throw in Mendy's blistering pace and all the ingredients were coming together nicely for City. Most of the ball, much of the territory and a visiting back four creaking under a 'one footed' disadvantage, was only fuelling the philosophy the hosts were on top and a lead was imminent.

Fagan had tried twice from distance and two throw-ins were scrambled clear by the wobbling West Bromwich defence, as the pressure continued to build. Richard Garcia had the best chance when Kevin Kilbane's exquisite cross picked out the makeshift Aussie forward but he headed inches over the bar when he really should have scored.

Carson was much the busier and fielded more efforts from range from the pacy Fagan and another from Dean Marney. Another back header had Carson back-peddling furiously to paw out. But it was coming, it was surely coming... With half time rapidly approaching and City wishing it was further away, Ashbee looped a ball over the high Albion back line and Mendy set off like a hare.

Albion hadn't read it! The Frenchman was off! Away and clear, scything in from the wing and making a beeline for the goal. Carson came out to meet the speedy winger, Mendy deftly waltzed round him and calmly rolled the ball into an empty net. YYYEEESSSS! At last. At bloomin' last! At that moment, my phone buzzed... it was the wife in the bath – **"Have you just scored? I heard that from here!"**

Aye, it was a massive goal indeed. Perfectly timed before referee Peter Walton blew for half time and fully deserved. The confidence was soaring. The atmosphere was bubbling along nicely. The beginning of the second half epitomised that belief. City roared out the blocks. Mendy and Fagan linked brilliantly for another chance, while Marney was thwarted by a flailing Carson arm.

It was all City and in a ferocious spell of pressure, Garcia tested Carson before Turner was denied with a header from another corner. So it was somewhat sickening to see what followed next. James Morrison ran at City, twisting, turning, reaching the box...a ricochet to Jay Simpson... wham! It was 1-1! You have got to be joking! First shot on target and it's a goal. A well worked goal admittedly, even with an apparent touch of fortune. City were rocked. But credit to the home team, back they came. Albion, encouraged by their goal, summoned enough spirit to try to make a game of it. For a short spell, anyway. The home side soon put that right with more swift passing and a break at speed. Mendy was again instrumental with a burst of pace and belting cross that Fagan refused to pass up. A searing header beats Carson and it's 2-1 to City. Order is restored once again. You couldn't argue.

Yet with the game seemingly well beyond the Baggies now, a lifeline was seized. Duke saved a stinging drive and Koren collected the rebound. With Zayatte challenging, the Baggies midfield hurled himself headlong to the ground and referee Peter Walton bought it. Penalty! Brunt smashed the spot kick under a despairing Duke and it was incredibly 2-2. What the...? How?

What was even more galling was; after watching the Baggies cling on desperately to our coat-tails all afternoon, Baggies boss Tony Mowbray now decided to throw caution to the wind and go for our jugular by wheeling out the strikers from the bench in Pele and Bednář. Jeez, he's got more front than Blackpool! Yet you couldn't really argue. On this performance, West Brom's plight in the top flight is serious. They have injuries, admittedly, but teams only marginally better than us will rip them asunder more often than not. The game was stretched to silly proportions for the final ten minutes, before the four minutes came up to warn everybody how long was left.

Common sense then prevailed from a City perspective at least. Sure, we're disappointed not to be winning this game, but let's not throw away the point we hold. We haven't had one for six matches, remember? And anyway, West Bromwich Albion wouldn't be gaining on us at the very least, in a game they undoubtedly targeted for a win.

And therein probably lies the answer. The Baggies really did have to glean a victory from today, while our points already accrued, suggest perhaps we could get away with not having to feel under the same pressure. A point being better than nothing. Remember the Aston Villa killer?

The critical encounter this match was billed as, produced a result that wasn't ideal, but neither was it too bad in context of the bigger picture. And the performance? Well, if that level of commitment is on show between now and May, we'll be right. West Brom couldn't beat the team in the worst form of all in the Premier League. That's got to bode well for us in the long run, surely?

MATCH STATS:

- Hull City: Duke, Ricketts, Turner, Zayatte, Dawson, Mendy, Garcia (Folan 81), Ashbee, Marney, Kilbane, Fagan. Subs Not Used: Myhill, Doyle, Geovanni, Hughes, France, Manucho.
- Booked: Dawson, Mendy.
- Goals: Mendy 44, Fagan 69.
- West Brom: Carson, Zuiverloon, Donk, Méïté, Robinson, Morrison (Kim 76), Koren, Borja Valero (Pele 88), Brunt, Fortune (Bednář 75), Simpson. Subs Not Used: Kiely, Hoefkens, Čech, Filipe Teixeira.
- Booked: Robinson, Méïté, Morrison, Zuiverloon.
- Goals: Simpson 53, Brunt 73 pen.
- Att: 24,879
- Ref: Peter Walton (Northamptonshire)
- **Premier League position: 11th**

SATURDAY 31ST JANUARY 2009

It now appears the Christian Panucci rumours are gathering pace after the West Bromwich Albion game. Hull City are set to carry out a medical on the player at the KC Stadium tomorrow if all goes well.

Everyone knows Phil Brown is in the market for a defender and a forward before the transfer window shuts at 5pm on Monday. Although, reports cannot be confirmed, neither have they been denied.

Meanwhile, with just two days to go before the window shuts, City are also in the market for a striker, and as we have been told already by chairman Paul Duffen this week, the club are attempting to engineer a real coup 'a blow your socks off'-type signing. But then, surely that's Panucci? Who actually knows with Premier League Hull City these days?

We await with interest...

CHAPTER 7 – THE BRIDGE OVER TROUBLED WATERS

SUNDAY 1ST FEBRUARY 2009

More, more, more! How do you like it? How do you like it? Come on, only two more days to go, chin up everyone, you'll miss it when it's gone, honest! Yes, the transfer window has just one more day left for trading.

The Sunday morning paper round up tells us out of favour Tottenham Hotspur striker Darren Bent is apparently is on the Hull City radar, with Phil Brown confirming a pacy striker is on the agenda. But then, that's the News of the World for you.

The Sunday paper is also claiming Brown wants to take the forward on loan, but Tottenham Hotspur boss Harry Redknapp is keen to sell the striker for a fee, as the Spurs gaffer looks to add funds that can be put towards a bid for Blackburn's Roque Santa Cruz.

Ironically, after stinging criticism from his manager in the past week, Bent came off the bench as a second half substitute to grab both goals against Bolton Wanderers this weekend. However, Tottenham went on to lose the game 3-2 with a goal for Gary Megson's men arriving five minutes from time.

This is how the transfer window works in England. It's great isn't it? It's just one big pile of ludicrous hogwash until the official statement appears on the official website.

MONDAY 2ND FEBRUARY 2009

More transfer deadline day silliness. It's in print, so you know it must be true... or more probably, it's just transfer deadline day guff again. With just hours to go, brace yourself City fans, brace yourself. This could be a long day.

Try this rumour on for size...

Barcelona's Eidur Gudjohnsen is in Hull after staying in the city overnight to talk about a transfer to the Tigers and boost Phil Brown's attacking options later today – and all this before the transfer window closes at 5pm.

And it must be true, because it's in print alongside the 'Robbie Keane to Spurs' story that probably has some genuine credence as one of the bigger stories that could well happen later in the day.

The big question is; which hotel did Eidur Gudjohnsen stay in? And was it a traditional full English breakfast on offer, or the more favoured continental fare offered by the more established hotel chains?

Of course, if this deal doesn't come off, we now know where the blame clearly lays. Cutting corners on hotel bills will not go down well with a regular first team Barcelona star in the hunt for a La Liga title, especially one that is in the last 16 of the Champions League.

"You heard it here first" Is the common phrase bandied around on transfer deadline day. It's now 4.59pm. It is quite clear the Eidur Gudjohnsen story was a complete fabrication. No, really! You thought it was true? But anyway, as the clock strikes 5pm I'm still sitting in the crash position with my socks firmly ON.

There will be no 'blow your socks off' signing for Hull City and we will be battling for Premier League survival with what we now have. Yes, Premier League survival. It's taken since February to acknowledge that fact, but then, I guess we always knew it was all about survival right from kicking off against Fulham way back on August 9th.

If only we had Eidur Gudjohnsen now...

WEDNESDAY 4TH FEBRUARY 2009

Hull City chairman Paul Duffen is an angry man. Supposed 'supporters' of our fine club are currently criticising manager Phil Brown. Angry? Irate? You better believe it. Who are these fans? They're not real fans, surely?

There is a new breed of supporters that have clearly riled our greatest chairman into a stinging rebuttal of the 'fans'? These are the 'supporters' duly having the audacity to question our greatest manager in the club's history – namely Phil Brown? This isn't Championship manager on your PC, you know? This is REAL!

But the criticism is now vocal enough for Paul Duffen to feel compelled to issue a cutting response to certain sections of the City support that are questioning Phil Brown's current team selections. And do you know what? I fully endorse the criticism meted out towards these alleged 'fans'.

In a statement full of passion, Duffen made the following comments aimed at those criticising the manager.

"I can't understand why any Hull fan would question the ability and the decisions of Phil Brown. I think it is disgraceful. Fans have to trust the manager. I do think it is a vocal minority. But I find it shocking that some fans have already forgotten how well this football club is doing.

People following the club now are privileged to be doing so, because it is the most successful period in the club's history. For some fans to be taking that for granted is a great shame. Fans need to support the manager, whatever happens this season."

Well I agree with Duffen. Sort yourselves out Hull City fans; this is completely unacceptable in our greatest ever season.

Meanwhile, on a topic not quite as close to home, Duffen has called for the transfer window to be scrapped once again, following the latest closure for trading between clubs on Monday 2nd February.

Duffen openly criticised the trading window at the end of previous dealings in the summer of 2008 – and nothing has changed in the chairman's mind that the window is doing the game any favours.

In his latest opinion on the controversial subject, Duffen explained – *"I think the January transfer window is an artificial market place and because of that I don't think it serves anybody at all. I think it is a very bad thing. There is a growing support now that the whole issue of the January transfer window has to be looked at again."*

Adding – *"A lot of transactions do happen at inflated prices in January but I'm not sure that does legislate in favour of the smaller clubs. Very often the smaller clubs want to hold onto their prized assets to ensure they retain their Premier League lives. Smaller clubs unfortunately tend to be buyers in that market because they are trying to do something to improve their fortunes."*

Duffen's actually right. Either that, or he's still peeved at not getting Eidur Gudjohnsen booked into the right hotel in Hull. One of the two.

FRIDAY 6TH FEBRUARY – CHELSEA V HULL CITY PREVIEW

The final away test against one of the 'big four' in the Premier League this season. My, the season has flown by, hasn't it? But this fixture gets me all misty-eyed about a trip to Stamford Bridge this weekend. I can't help it.

Amid the fall out of the transfer deadline coming and going last Monday, certain frustrations that were bubbling under at the club appear to have surfaced. Some fans wanted a deadline day signing - the 'blow your socks off' type - while the club refused to be held over a barrel finance wise. Such circumstances, rightly, prevented such a star name arriving. We should not waver in our beliefs.

Incredibly, this has prompted chairman Paul Duffen to appear on most of the Hull City websites this week in videos slamming everything within his eyeline. Including the fans. And the transfer window. And the supposed critics of manager Phil Brown. Believe me Mr Duffen, those that fall into the latter category are not fans of Hull City and are such a minuscule minority among the backdrop of the majority. Those 'fans' are hardly worth bothering about, in my humble opinion.

For me, though, let me reiterate I do completely condone the chairman's comments. I just question if they were needed? Just who are these 'fans'? Yet it does seem more and more clear that the chairman has snapped at some stray comments made by an isolated group, rather than a wholesale belief amongst the supporters that Brown needs to go. Jeez, just take stock of that for a minute. What are these people thinking? How short are some people's memories?

The football club are about to take on the European Cup finalists in their own backyard on equal terms. Erm, in terms of us both making up the 20 best teams in England, I mean. This is Chelsea. The big spenders, the movers, the shakers of the Premier League. This is the team that muscled its way to the pinnacle of English football with a little help from a wealthy Russian backer. Today, Chelsea are one of the Premier League's glitterati - indeed the quintessential icon of such. Chelsea ooze continental stars, unfathomable wealth and a daring flair in abundance. Chelsea have become the glamour London club, upsetting the traditional heavyweight challengers from 'oop north'.

But it's not always been the case. My Grandad – god bless him – was Streatham born and bred and became 'Chewsie man and boy' (as they say darn sarf) despite seeing out the overwhelming majority of his life in Hull. A time that afforded great affection towards the Tigers it must be stated, but he was a blue boy first and foremost. Always Chelsea. I'll be sparing a thought for him tomorrow come 3pm. 'Go easy on us, eh?' is the message. We will Grandad, honest.

In many ways, I'm thinking the trip to the Stamford Bridge is a 'free hit'. As ever, the Tigers can expect zilch, but will go into the game with a plan geared to attack. Fans of Arsenal, Manchester United and Liverpool – the other three of the big four – all welcomed our approach pre-game over a pint. *"That will suit us"* they say. Will it really?

Well, Arsenal fans were stunned when we came from behind to beat them 1-2. Manchester United thought they could take their foot off the gas at 1-0, soon becoming 1-1. Ok then, have that, 4-1. But these Tigers keep prowling. 4-2, 4-3... begging for the final whistle, they were. And Liverpool? The Reds were 0-2 down inside 20 minutes. Have some of that. They couldn't beat us either, it ended 2-2. Do Chelsea really want that? With their 'suspect' home record?

It's what we'll set out to do. Attack, attack, attack. There will be no hidden agenda. At the big four, you have to try to at least attempt to win the game, than die wondering. And to think some people want Phil Brown out! How many of the 'out' brigade will be at Chelsea? I bet... none. So far, we've not be humbled by any of the big guns in any of our games. A theme I hope we can continue to boast this weekend against the Blues - and all thanks to Phil Brown.

Team news sees Jimmy Bullard rated at 60-40 according to the manager, irrespective of what the scan results turn out to be. Striker Daniel Cousin is out after undergoing a minor operation. Unluckily, in form Bernard Mendy is suspended after collecting five bookings. At a guess, Ryan France and Bryan Hughes will be knocking on the door for the Frenchman's shirt in an 'as you were' type line-up employed against West Bromwich Albion last week.

City boss Phil Brown is wary of the task ahead and remained brutally honest - *"Chelsea have a wealth of experience and talent and so there is never a good time to play them. But we are going there buoyed by a couple of goals and a good performance in our last match against West Brom."*

Adding - *"We got a point which got us off the run of going six matches without getting a point. We are going to Stamford Bridge with our own game plan and with our own confidence levels renewed."*

So, on to Chelsea. Frank Lampard plays after rightly having his ludicrous red card overturned from the 2-0 defeat at Anfield last week. John Terry's yellow card comes into effect after the Hull City game - damn those Sunday Premier League fixtures and the seven day incubation period. Quite how Jose Bosingwa is eligible remains a mystery to the football world though, after referee Mike Riley appears to be the only human on earth that missed his outright assault on Liverpool's Yossi Benayoun. Then, you look at Manchester City's Shaun Wright-Phillips at Stoke getting pulled by referee Martin Atkinson after watching tv replays, it's all wrong. One rule for sixteen, one rule for the big four? Oh well, this is the Premier League, we all wanted to be here, didn't we?

The last time the two sides met, it was incredibly a challenge for top spot at the end of October. Predictably, Chelsea are still there now it's February and we've, erm... slipped a little. But Blues boss 'Phil' Scolari openly declared 'he loves this team' when speaking about Hull City last time around. I hope we can give him second thoughts come 4.45pm on Saturday. No, wait... until the game is over, I mean. Weren't Stoke winning at that time and still lost? Welcome to Chelsea!

SATURDAY 7TH FEBRUARY 2009 - CHELSEA 0-0 HULL CITY - REPORT

Leaving Stamford Bridge with a 0-0 draw and feeling... disappointed? Erm... well actually, yeah! Hull City could - and perhaps should - have won this game. No, really!

It's a six o'clock knock for the trip to Chelsea. It's cold, it's dark, it's going to be a game, where despite all the odds, we're going to get something. Yes, Hull City at the European Cup finalists and I'm thinking we could get something. Brain freeze in frosty conditions? Nah. I was unusually optimistic.

And it wasn't just blind faith either. At the big four this season, we've won one, drawn one and narrowly lost one. Plus, the word on the King's Road is; there's trouble at the Chelsea mill. Quality yes, but teamwork? That's open to question and recent results provide the evidence, it seems.

A tube in, then turfed out at Earl's Court for a pre-match bevvy. The mood was lively, positive and with a hint of carefree abandon. Who cares? This is Chelsea. We're supposed to be hammered out of sight, aren't we? Round our table we joked who would score quicker at 3pm, Chelsea or the West Indies in the cricket.

Making my way into the ground - albeit for the first time - even I could tell the place had changed radically. The famous open terraces and the tilted shed in the corner had all gone and were replaced with modern three-tiered affairs down the sides and double-tiered stands behind each goal. Sadly, the Bridge is now shorn of character from what it was. It's what money does for you.

The ludicrous press reports surrounding Phil Brown not being popular among some of the fans was soon put to bed. 'Phil Brown's black and amber army' rang round loud and proud. No offence Mr Duffen, but the fans love Phil Brown. Here is the proof.

Today, the City gaffer had stuck almost to the same side that drew 2-2 with West Bromwich Albion, with only Geovanni replacing the suspended Bernard Mendy. It was a more fluid formation than the rigid 4-3-3 we traditionally adopt when playing the big four. Garcia and Fagan led the line, Geovanni floated freely behind.

Referee Lee Mason gets us going, hold your breath, we're going in... Within a minute, the entire tone for the game is set. A dangerous cross comes in at the far post, Duke beats the ball out and it fell straight to John Terry two yards out. He can't miss... holy cow! He can! Think Amir Zaki, think Darren Bent, this is the miss of the season. Unbelievable!

While City fans were still reeling from that escape, Chelsea were fussing over possession and territory and calling the early shots - as you'd expect. But the travelling support was in full gusto. No let up in the stands and the players responded on the pitch.

City worked immensely hard to close down Chelsea. Ashbee and Marney were the passionate lungs of the team, the front pairing worked hard and Fagan was an outstanding menace unsettling the home back four and winning his fair share of the ball.

Chelsea were getting impatient that they weren't already 2-0 up, as a full 15 minutes had passed by this point. But clear cut chances were proving difficult to come by. Kalou drilled in a shot from an acute angle that was scooped out by Duke and/or Zayatte to keep the game at 0-0.

Home debutant Quaresma hit a dangerous shot that Duke tipped away, and shone brightly until a stiff tackle from Ricketts kept him quiet. Lampard shot wide from distance and a hotly-contested free-kick, given against the heroic Andy Dawson, was blazed by Ballack into the side netting. Another free-kick from a similar position saw Kamil Zayatte taking one in the nether regions for the team. Good luck finding the other one Kamil... Hey, but let's get this right, City had their chances too.

Indeed, Michael Turner had a goalbound effort scooped off the line and Geovanni had been on a mazy run, got tripped and blazed over the resultant free kick from just outside the box. Dean Marney also capitalised on some slack defending to hare in on goal, but dragged his shot wide.

Star of the show though, was Fagan. As the full back duo of Ashley Cole and Jose Bosingwa pushed onto our byline for every attack, that left Garcia with Geovanni looking for the busy forward, who was pulling John Terry and Alex all over the park.

It was either supreme confidence, or a tad too attacking from Chelsea - possibly even disrespectful - and it gave City much room to exploit. More than a few times, Chelsea were caught and Fagan had nipped in between the central defensive pair. Seriously, it could have been 0-1 to us at half time - especially when Kilbane headed just wide.

The vibe on the stadium concourse was bouncing in the away end. We could do this - hell, we could be even winning the game! For the second half, Chelsea were probably going to be really angry, get even madder and probably score. Brace yourself. But, you know, I'd seen enough to have me thinking... hang on a minute here...

The second half followed a similar pattern. Chelsea had lots of possession and territory, but failed to carve out clear-cut chances. Kalou scooted another shot wide from inside the box when well placed, but incredibly, the main threat of a goal was occurring at the other end.

As the hosts began to get frustrated with City's tenacity, togetherness and audacity to attack, gaps appeared more frequently at the back and the break was always on. Two on two, three on three, Chelsea were playing a dangerous game when pouring forward.

But the balance was all wrong for Chelsea to penetrate. That would be my observation. Why was Anelka so deep that he was collecting the ball in his own half? How come time and again the furthest player forward was Ashley Cole? Why did Chelsea only look seriously like scoring when leaving just Alex at the back?

City took full advantage. Yawning space was exploited as the visitors broke on the counter and at speed. The experience of Kilbane, the energy of Marney and the pace of Fagan stretched Chelsea. City looked like they could score.

Next, Fagan had slipped Alex and was left one on one with Hilário to beat. The pacy forward attempted a lob and was inches away from clearing the Portuguese keeper who just managed to claw the ball away.

And the attacking trio fashioned another lightning-quick break against a short home defence. Marney was played in by a delicious reverse pass from Geovanni and square on goal, shot across Hilário and missed the corner of the net by millimetres. Agonising.

More swift counter attacking saw Kilbane flattened and Geovanni lining up a free kick. But sadly, it was placed just over. Chelsea responded by chucking on Balletti, Drogba and Deco, yet the tempo remained the same. City stood resolute in defence and in fairness, Duke was rarely tested.

Indeed, only Kalou wriggling free was classed as a clear chance. Duke smothered the shot comfortably to heighten Chelsea's frustrations. A desperate appeal for a penalty than screeched from the home stands when a ball clattered Dawson, knocking the full back clean off his feet, but even if it had hit his hand, there was no intent at all. No penalty.

As the game ticked ever closer to full time, each team had one last chance to win the game. Chelsea had a free kick that was disappointingly well wide of the target from Drogba and surely ended their chance of winning the match. But City... they earned a corner after Fagan slipped Alex again - a theme of the day - deep in stoppage time.

It was swung into the mixer and beat everyone, Ashbee was at the back post to collect and smash a half volley... just wide! It could have been the winner. And if it had been the winner, Chelsea could not have complained. They'd been given a right game.

At the whistle, the heroic cheers in the away end were drowned out by the audible and disgruntled boos in the three and half home stands. Not happy bunnies, it would seem. Seriously, Chelsea were lucky they had a point to show for their inadequate efforts. All that money...

Leaving the ground you were delighted to pick up a point at the European Cup finalists, yet genuinely tinged with disappointment we hadn't won the game. And people say Brown out! And Ashbee should be dropped. And we've lost the team spirit. And we're going down... who are these people?

So, a point a gained, but dare I say, two points dropped! Okay, I'll save you Chelsea fans from that ignominy this season, seeing as it is our first.

On this evidence, it won't be our last though, either. A victory for confidence, self-belief and positive vibes in Hull City's squad. We didn't get all the points, but we're not going down on this evidence, trust me.

Grandad would have loved it.

MATCH STATS:

- Chelsea: Hilário, Bosingwa, Alex, Terry, Ashley Cole, Mikel (Belletti 57), Quaresma (Drogba 63), Ballack (Deco 73), Lampard, Kalou, Anelka. Subs Not Used: Taylor, Ivanovic, Di Santo, Stoch.
- Booked: Mikel.
- Hull City: Duke, Ricketts, Turner, Zayatte, Dawson, Garcia, Ashbee, Marney, Kilbane, Geovanni (France 81), Fagan. Subs Not Used: Myhill, Doyle, Barmby, Hughes, Halmosi, Manucho.
- Booked: Ashbee, Garcia.
- Att: 41,802
- Ref: Lee Mason (Lancashire)
- **Premier League position: 12th**

WEDNESDAY 11TH FEBRUARY 2009

England calling? England calling Hull City? England calling Hull City for not one, but two of our players? This is madness! Yet Hull City pair Michael Turner and Jimmy Bullard are in contention to become part of Fabio Capello's England international squad according to manager Phil Brown, after the Italian watched the match between Chelsea and the Tigers that ended 0-0.

After a chat with England physiotherapist Gary Lewin, Brown revealed - *"I had a casual conversation with the England physio at a dinner last Thursday and he said Fabio Capello was interested in Jimmy and Michael."*

Brown added - *"It was a conversation to gauge if the players were fit enough to play against Spain. Fabio Capello was at the game on Saturday and as far as Michael was concerned, he gave a performance worthy of interest."*

Before divulging after the Chelsea game - *"We got a phone call from Gary Lewin at 6pm on Saturday evening to say that Michael would not be required. But just to be in the thoughts of the England set-up is massively encouraging. Fingers crossed, Michael will continue to show the form he has done all season and who knows?"*

FRIDAY 13TH FEBRUARY 2009 – SHEFFIELD UNITED V HULL CITY – FA CUP 5TH ROUND PREVIEW

City are on the brink of sailing into uncharted waters in the FA Cup for at least a generation's worth of fans. Standing in the way of the passage to the quarter finals is arch enemy Sheffield United. But we never win at Bramall Lane...

The FA Cup fifth round is here again - and we've not been able to say that since we hosted Liverpool at Boothferry Park in 1989. Ah, what a day that was. 0-1 down to 2-1 up at half time thanks to Billy Whitehurst and Keith Edwards. A second half John Aldridge double in the space of a minute killed us. But this is what the FA Cup is all about!

After praying the fifth round draw would be kind following the Millwall 2-0 win with a home tie - a Valentines Day summons has been issued by the missus, see - thankfully, an away tie to Sheffield United was the next best thing to get me back in Hull in time. It's all right love, I'll be back. Generous offer from Chaz Cabs duly noted.

Of course, the close proximity of the fixture is great for personal reasons, but for progressive reasons, is a draw the best we can hope for here? Not since 1971 have we won away at the constant bane of our football supporting lives that is Sheffield United. A famous game, a 1-2 City victory, the top flight beckoned... until a ghastly run of form scuppered that particular notion nearly 40 years ago.

Since then, Sheffield United have pretty much yo-yo-ed up and down the leagues in tandem with ourselves. Rarely has there been a season or two keeping us apart. Sure, this is not a pure derby, but it is a Yorkshire derby and it is one that certainly sits awkwardly, and it traditionally sizzles between the fans.

Sheffield United are always there. Always pipping us to something. Always scraping together a win against us. Always keeping us in bloody check. Irritating club they are. The 83-84 season that ended with an out-of-season finale at Turf Moor being a case in point. That night City needed to win 0-3. Sheffield United fans turned up in numbers to see the Tigers win... you guessed it... 0-2. The significance? Promotion handed to the Blades by virtue of one single goal to the old Second Division. It wouldn't even be allowed to happen these days. Football has gone all politically correct - much for the worse.

Yet two seasons ago, the atmosphere at Bramall Lane fizzed in proper fashion as City - once again - were undone by an injury time winner 3-2 in a match that we really should've won, should've had a certain penalty, definitely played better, blah, blah, blah... it's always the way at Bramall Lane. City never win there. Ever. Well not in my lifetime of 37 years we don't.

Last season, even as favourites during our romp to the play-offs, City turned in a woefully out of character performance for just one game in that unbeaten series. You guessed it, it was at Bramall Lane. We lost 2-0 this time. Against ten men as well. What a let down. The Blades seem to revel in Tiger heartache. That has to change this weekend...

Now, Premier League Hull City will square up to injury ravaged, out-of-form Championship side Sheffield United, fresh from embarrassing back-to-back home losses to local rivals Sheffield Wednesday and Doncaster Rovers. Surely, not this time. Not now, not after all this time, City simply have to win this contest outright. Sheffield United are due their beating. It's got to happen.

A sell-out within hours for City fans will see the full 5,000 plus quota arrive at Bramall Lane. Phil Brown will likely rest record signing Jimmy Bullard rather than risk playing him in the cup, but Anthony Gardner and Nick Barmby are due to play following their long term injuries.

The Blades will be missing striker Darius Henderson who is banned, as well as cup-tied trio Jamie Ward, Leigh Bromby and Arturo Lupoli. On the injured list, Chris Morgan is a major doubt with a hamstring strain, while experienced Gary Speed, Ugo Ehiogu and Derek Geary are all sidelined for the clash.

Surely, our time is now? Surely Sheffield United are going to be licked by the Tigers at Bramall Lane for the first time in 38 years? Surely we'll never get a better chance? Feel the love, it will be Valentines Day after all. It better not be a bloody one... Oooofff!

SATURDAY 14TH FEBRUARY 2009 –
SHEFFIELD UNITED 1-1 HULL CITY – FA CUP 5TH ROUND REPORT

The curse of Bramall Lane strikes once again. Lucky Sheffield United get a goal that probably never should have been, but hey, as previously stated, we're at Bramall Lane. It's now 38 years and counting since victory, but at least we're still in the cup.

Chaz Cabs were right on cue. The big cat was wheeled out to whisk us away to Bramall Lane for the FA Cup fifth round tie and the passengers were treated like kings by chauffeur Charles. The kid knows how to travel - and travel in style. And there was no tacky, fake 'executive' misapprehension emblazoned down the side of this carriage. Goody bags were present for all including beer, sandwiches and pies. One bag for each!

The now traditional away day football quiz undertaken in one of the less reputable dailies returned an astounding 88 per cent conversion rate - almost a season best - surely, we were set to beat 'them' at Bramall Lane. Finally! Especially with a lucky green Brian Clough jumper on. Newcastle, Arsenal Tottenham, Liverpool. Unbeaten in it, I am. Now was our time. It had to be. And then, parked within yards of the stadium for free, driver Charles treated us all to a royal fish and chip supper to crown the day, the cherry on top had to be booking our quarter final berth. Let's 'av it!

Arriving at the ground, we went in search of our seats but ended up waylaid at the £1 a bottle offer that curiously was only at the kiosk at the far end of the concourse. Ssssh! Some things are best enjoyed quietly. 'Tis Bramall Lane after all, weird place. And neither has it lost any of its irritating features, cramped seats, poor viewing in the lower tier and that god awful John Denver wailing pre-kick off. I hate it here.

When the dirge finished and the game did commence, City looked like they were still on the plane back from Dubai, Dawson in particular having a torrid time against Dave Cotterill - a theme for the game. No captain Ashbee saw Dean Marney as the surprise choice as skipper and he was partnered with Zayatte in the middle. Yep, Anthony Gardner had finally returned from injury to partner Michael Turner. It was a sight to behold!

Meanwhile, the final change from the Chelsea match saw Caleb Folan gain a rare start up front. Despite the endeavour, Folan never fills me with confidence that he's actually going to score. Sadly, today was a case in point. What was apparent was how much we missed Ashbee. Sure Zayatte was getting familiar with his role but the Blades were lauding it, on what would have been Ash's manor. Not good...

The first goal was soon to arrive, predictably against us (as is always the case here). Bah! Cotterill flung in a far post cross and makeshift striker Greg Halford clearly pushed Sam Ricketts to head in freely at the back post. Foul ref! Foul! Not given. It was a shocking decision by referee Andre Marriner and another decision that robs City. But then, we're at Bramall Lane, so what did we expect? It never works out here. The highlights will vindicate me.

Sheffield United were lifted and City were sluggish by reply. If the Blades could only finish – and Billy Sharp in particular had more than running around like a headless chicken to his game – the home team could have been out of sight. But despite clearly raising the performance for our visit - Blades fans' comments upon leaving the match, not mine - City were given a foothold to remain in the game due to a poor final ball from the hosts.

A clearly unfit Chris Morgan was substituted by the Blades early in the game and that provided the catalyst for a City revival and the visitors started to look like they were the higher-placed side now. An equaliser came from a free kick. The expert delivery from Dawson found the now settling Kamil Zayatte in the box to head home. Get in! Now let's win it. For once, let's do these bleeders on their own patch. COME ON!

City indeed had renewed vigour. Folan pressed a woeful back pass to Paddy Kenny and almost clattered the ball in as the Premier League visitors showed more assertiveness. Just bide your time City, it will come... Marney flashed a shot wide and Geovanni did likewise, it will come. It's got to. But the interval arrived in untimely fashion as City were really pressing. So 1-1 at the break it was, not particularly pretty, but a game certainly for the taking.

Second half, City upped the pace again. The Blades struggled to hold City's more accurate passing and Paddy Kenny was hurriedly shovelling out a low shot to keep parity. But the Tigers smelt Blades' blood. The screw was turned and a delicious cross from the right found Garcia free, six yards out... on target... no! Again Kenny pushed it out.

The tempo was notched up further. Mendy's pace and trickery saw him scythe in on goal, a drilled effort at the near post was beaten out by Kenny once again, it just would not come for City. Sheffield United had weathered the storm. As City began to feel it wasn't going to be their day at Bramall Lane yet again, the Blades crept back into the game.

Although Myhill was kept pretty much trouble free as the game moved into the last quarter, United were enjoying the ball and territory now. It had 'late Sheffield United winner' written all over it. Here we go again... Yet thankfully, it never arrived. Very unusual. But as predicted in the preview, a draw would always be about the best we could ever hope for at this godforsaken place. Why here? Why always? Grrr...

On the positive, Gardner got a full 90 minutes - let's see how long he can stay fit for. Marney did a half decent job as skipper of the side and Zayatte eventually grew into his new role come the end, even if communication is a glaring miss from his game. But that Blades curse still remains. 38 years and counting since we last tasted victory here. When we won in 1971, did we have Pele on loan for that month or summat? How the hell did we do it? Probably the greatest ever football mystery - and still unanswered!

I can't really moan. I have been treated like royalty by chauffeur Charles today, travelled in luxury with a genuine old-school Tiger who bleeds black and amber and looks after his fellow kind. Charles is a true gent, a scholar amongst men. A genuine and generous man. I definitely owe him a bottle of claret or two for a top away day service; he wouldn't even take my travel share!

No need to beat ourselves up here. We're still in the cup, admittedly the prospect of three games in six days isn't exactly ideal, but we are in the hat. Plus, I'm back in time to type this up, get in a less salubrious cab and take the good lady out for an evening of romance, fine wine and good food.

So, grateful for another disappointment at Bramall Lane? You bet. This could have been Swansea away. I could have been divorced if the cup draw had allowed that to happen... Thank you ball six and ball three for coming together three weeks ago. You probably unknowingly saved a marriage. Damn! Is that the time? I gotta scoot!

MATCH STATS:

- Sheffield Utd: Kenny, Jihai (Naughton 60), Morgan (Webber 31), Kilgallon, Naysmith, Cotterill, Montgomery, Quinn, Hendrie (Howard 73), Halford, Sharp. Subs Not Used: Bennett, Walker.
- Goals: Halford 7.
- Hull City: Myhill, Ricketts, Turner, Gardner, Dawson, Mendy (France 88), Marney, Zayatte, Garcia (Manucho 79), Geovanni (Barmby 73), Folan. Subs Not Used: Warner, Doyle, Halmosi, Featherstone.
- Booked: Mendy, Turner, Garcia.
- Goals: Zayatte 34.
- Att: 22,283
- Ref: Andre Marriner (W Midlands)

TUESDAY 17TH FEBRUARY 2009

and then for the two weeks I don't play I can say that at least we got a good result there and that gives us a bit of breathing space."

It's a finely balanced match with much at stake. Should Spurs win, it's a clear sign they are moving in the right direction and ultimately to safety from the ignominy of relegation. Should City win, possibly two more victories would see the Tigers back for another season of top flight football.

This may be 13th versus 16th, but in the top division in England, the stakes are always high. Very high. It's about time our excellent recent performances got rewarded with all the points. Let's hope tonight heralds our first Premier League 'double'. COME ON CITY!

MONDAY 23RD FEBRUARY 2009 – HULL CITY 1-2 TOTTENHAM HOTSPUR – REPORT

Hull City end up on the wrong side of an odd goal, in a tight encounter with Tottenham Hotspur, that neither side could truly claim they deserved to win. But if there was going to be a winner at the Circle, it's now apparent the way the season is going it's very unlikely to be us. Well, that felt like a defeat. Oh dear... that's because it was. But it never should have been as two sides produced a relatively exciting encounter, but neither looked to have the guile or gumption to win the game. Until someone did, of course...

The winners were Spurs, but on this evidence, you would hardly say richly deserving of all the points. Both teams worked hard even if the football wasn't the prettiest, but the nature and intensity of the game made it a watchable match.

Pre-game I'd met our Belgian guests for the evening in Hop and Wes and downed some ales. A brisk walk to the stadium from the Admiral of the Humber ensured we made good time for kick off at 8pm - aye, Setanta were in town.

On the walk up, the conversation was all about the pace of the game compared to Belgian Juniper League football and the necessity to take your chances. Because in the Premier League, if you don't, your opponents will. See? Top flight newbies we may be, but we're learning.

Brown chose to thrust both former Spurs players Gardner and Marney into his starting XI, as well as handing a first start since injury to Daniel Cousin. Richard Garcia was the surprise starting partner in favour of Geovanni. The Brazilian was surprisingly left on the bench after tearing Spurs apart with a wonder goal at the Lane earlier in the season.

Of course that meant Kamil Zayatte was left to beef up the midfield alongside the returning Ian Ashbee. The side had a workmanlike look to it, but as correctly pointed out by Hop post-match, lacked the creative edge to test Tottenham.

But that wasn't apparent early on, as City roared out of the blocks. The possession, the desire and the will to win the game was the home team's. Much of the territorial advantage was Hull City's and a succession of corners were pegging Spurs back.

So it was somewhat a slap in the face - and squarely undeserved - when Spurs took the lead. It came from a short corner and City's insistence on posting just one man in defending it caused the problem again. The ball was played into Lennon. A mighty thud when given time and space saw itl arrow in for 0-1.

Sick. Sick of watching the predictability of it all in truth. Come on City, we're better than that. Time and again we defend this way. It's really beginning to irk me now. And here we are 0-1 down to a team who have barely got out their own half after 16 minutes.

City refused to lie down, much to their credit. Unrelenting, the justice of an equaliser was surely coming. Zayatte forced a save from the edgy Cudicini but Spurs would not be so lucky to emerge unscathed from City's pressure.

The visitors had laboured to clear every City corner but their fortune ran out when a failure to clear another in-swinger from Andy Dawson, saw defender Michael Turner rifle the ball into the roof of the net for a deserved leveller. Spurs couldn't complain, City had been well on top and Daniel Cousin's blistering drive could have seen the Tigers leading the match had it not whistled narrowly wide of the target. The best team had restored parity, but could've been winning this game.

Yet the second half saw a shift in power, for the early part of the half at least. Now it was Spurs making the early running of the second period and a succession of corners saw the pressure building. Wilson Palacios saw a powerful drive blocked that looked goalbound, too.

Spurs' pressure culminated in Ćorluka heading onto the bar, but then City took over. The Tigers put the visitors in a sweat from every corner - a real theme for the evening - and this time Kamil Zayatte headed downwards against the base of the post when it looked like being the winner.

City stepped up the pace and substitutions that brought Mendy and Manucho into play gave the hosts new impetus. But once again, it was to be another slap in the face for City with just six minutes remaining.

A Spurs corner unusually put the City defence all at sea in contrast to how the game had panned out. Anthony Gardner was left closing down a cross instead of marshalling the centre of defence. Cross came in, Woodgate dwarfs Dawson, goal. You have got to be joking! What a choker.

Spurs could barely claim to be worthy winners. City, far from being their best, were certainly not losers. But as the record books clearly show, they are and will be as far as this match is concerned.

City struggled to mount a serious challenge in the brief time that was left. Instead, the hosts looked shellshocked at the turn of events and with the stuffing knocked from them. In a way, I'm glad the Sheffield United cup game at home is in three days' time. Less time to dwell on events versus Spurs...

This Premier League malarkey, it's brutally harsh. Beating Blackburn on Sunday is now a must. And after tonight, frankly, I couldn't give a monkey's chuff how we do it or whether it's deserved or not. Let's just do it.

MATCH STATS:

- Hull City: Duke, Ricketts, Turner, Gardner, Dawson, Marney, Ashbee, Zayatte (Geovanni 87), Kilbane, Garcia (Manucho 79), Cousin (Mendy 67). Subs Not Used: Myhill, Doyle, Barmby, Halmosi.
- Booked: Dawson, Ashbee.
- Goal: Turner 27.
- Tottenham: Cudicini, Ćorluka, Woodgate (Dawson 89), King, Assou-Ekotto, Lennon (Zokora 87), Jenas, Palacios, Modrić, Keane, Bent (Pavlyuchenko 72). Subs Not Used: Gomes, Bentley, Huddlestone, Chimbonda.
- Booked: Modrić.
- Goals: Lennon 17, Woodgate 86.
- Att: 24,742
- Ref: Lee Probert (Wiltshire)
- **Premier League position: 13th**

TUESDAY 24TH FEBRUARY 2009

A fans forum hosted by Hull City, broadcast live on BBC local radio, has revealed the club has been courting the attention of interested parties looking to buy the club from Paul Duffen and his consortium.

Duffen, who along with Russell Bartlett and Martin Walker is the public face of the Essex based property developers that own the club, was asked if the club had been seeking interest from 'wealthier parties' to buy the club since promotion to the Premier League.

The chairman refused to answer after a long period of silence, but the question came up again at the end of the forum. Duffen then ventured a little further referring to a historic quote that had the chairman metaphorically describing Hull City as - *"The prettiest girl in the Premier League playground right now."*

When pressed, Duffen finally relented to reveal that interest has arrived at the club's door from potential suitors, but was then quick to state - *"It depends what you mean by interest. In terms of selling, we're not even vaguely interested."*

WEDNESDAY 25TH FEBRUARY 2009 –
HULL CITY V SHEFFIELD UNITED – FA CUP 5TH ROUND REPLAY

Hull City face up to part two of their trilogy of three matches in six days on home soil, when facing Sheffield United in an FA Cup fifth round replay. The last time these two sides met – just 12 days ago – I wrote that probably the best Hull City could hope for was a draw, considering our abysmal record at Bramall Lane. And so i came to pass - now it's no win in 38 years' worth of attempts now at the South Yorkshire venue.

But in truth, although nobody from either camp will come out and say it, neither team really wanted a replay. Sheffield United certainly didn't judging by the urgency shown at Bramall Lane to get the job done on the day, while Hull City didn't fancy clogging up the fixture list.

Yet where the magic of the cup still reigns for me is that despite all of that, neither team was prepared to lose the game without a fight. Both teams wanted the tie at Bramall Lane. Sure it wasn't a classic, but it was fought for with integrity and commitment.

And whatever sides take to the field this evening, you can expect the same. Tonight, a winner will be found by hook or by crook. Another piece of the FA Cup jigsaw will be resolved, leaving just the Arsenal v Burnley fifth round tie to be decided. The winners of this game will face the winners of that one in the quarter finals.

Yes, the quarter finals. How many times have Hull City been able to say that? I've never seen our club in the last eight of the competition. Many fans won't have either. It's been 38 years since the Tigers prowled in the last eight of this grand old tournament. It matters.

Changes are expected from the late and heartbreaking Spurs defeat in the Premier League on Monday. Ian Ashbee is carrying a knock and is unlikely to start. Boaz Myhill is likely to replace Matt Duke in goal. Meanwhile, Anthony Gardner is almost certain to be rested now he has returned from a five month injury lay off.

Of course, City cannot play Kevin Kilbane, who is cup-tied, or Craig Fagan, who is recuperating from minor knee surgery. Caleb Folan is expected to step into the breach up front and Ryan France may be pushing for a recall to the first team in midfield.

On the tie, assistant manager Brian Horton warned – *"If I was a footballer and I was left out tomorrow night, I'd be aggrieved. I'd want to play. I wouldn't even be thinking about playing Blackburn, I'd want to be out there in front of a packed house playing in a cup tie."*

The City no.2 added – *"This is a massive game for the football club - the chance to get into the quarter-finals for the fans, players, staff, board. It's been 38 years, that tells its own story. And it's massive because it is the next game. The next game is always important to players. Any game you are involved in as a player, manager, coach, you want to win. There is plenty of recovery time before Blackburn."*

Once again Sheffield United have selection problems for the tie. James Beattie, Arturo Lupoli, Leigh Bromby and Jamie Ward are all cup-tied. Ian Bennett, Matthew Kilgallon and Brian Howard are all injured, but skipper Chris Morgan is expected to be fit enough to play again.

THURSDAY 26TH FEBRUARY 2009 – HULL CITY 2-1 SHEFFIELD UNITED – FA CUP 5TH ROUND REPLAY REPORT

Hull City beat Yorkshire rivals Sheffield United in the fifth round of the FA Cup following a replay, but the passage through to the last eight will undoubtedly be debated long and hard as for once, a refereeing decision goes in favour of the Tigers.

Finally, the tables are turned on Sheffield United. Since the final game against Burnley of the 83-84 Third Division season, the Blades have long lauded it over the Tigers. Yep, it's long stuck in my throat. I hate Sheffield United for that. Always have, probably always will.

For the younger generation, City needed to win 0-3 at Turf Moor to secure promotion at Sheffield United's expense. You guessed it, a 0-2 triumph wasn't enough and the Blades – making an unwelcome if somewhat surreal third presence at the match – celebrated long and hard on a dark Lancastrian evening. It still rankles.

Snap back to tonight and the teams had been called to arms for the second time in this fifth round FA Cup tie, following a 1-1 draw at Bramall Lane 12 days ago. Probably a fixture neither side truly wanted, but one that certainly wasn't going to be given up lightly by either team.

Phil Brown didn't pick his strongest side by any stretch, but you always felt it was enough to beat the depleted Blades. Boaz Myhill got the gloves, Nathan Doyle was in the right back berth, the midfield included Bernard Mendy, Ryan France and Peter Halmosi. Nick Barmby and Caleb Folan were up top in a side totalling seven changes from Spurs.

City roared out of the traps and dominated the match in terms of territory and possession. Both wide players impressed, in particular a rejuvenated Peter Halmosi who had the consistent beating of his full back. Indeed a cross fired into Nick Barmby's path could well have opened the scoring, but the local lad blazed over.

The hosts kept pushing and Sheffield United laboured to even get out their own half as it was one-way traffic. Zayatte headed a near post corner just wide as the Blades struggled to draw breath. But when the goal did arrive, it came with much consternation from a Sheffield United point of view. A cross from Mendy had the Blades defence scrambling and Kyle Naughton inexplicably met the ball with a bullet like header towards his own goal. What on earth was he doing? The ferocity of such crashed the underside of the bar, bounced down and out, but it looked over the line on first impression at real time. However, the big screen replay left it inconclusive. Ah, balls to it. It was over.

I was jumping up and down and screaming like a banshee long before the linesman went Russian and gave us it. Like I bloody care whether it was in or not - the linesman gave it! COME ON! GET IN! In fairness it had been coming. Sheffield United hadn't been at the races, it was all City and the goal had been imminent. We owe 'em. Big style.

But the goal sparked life into a flaccid Sheffield United side. Rare trips into the City half began to sporadically punctuate the match and with United's first shot on target, sickeningly a goal arrived soon after. Greg Halford's cross found Lee Hendrie to head back across goal and Billy Sharp poked the ball in from three yards. The curse of Sheffield United was alive and kicking once more.

It's fast becoming an irritation now. Like a tick you haven't quite crushed yet. I wouldn't mind, but it was hardly deserved. Yet the Blades' confidence levels had increased as a consequence and the game evened out into a much more level contest.

That said, Bernard Mendy should really have done better when arrowing in on goal, but only finding Paddy Kenny with a ferocious near post drive. Sheffield United claimed loudly for a penalty when Billy Sharp flatlined himself in the box - all to easily under Kamil Zayatte's challenge it must be said - and referee Peter Walton booked him. Quite right. What a fairy.

In truth, the half time whistle came at the right time. Brown calmed his side down and sent them out again like they had started the first half. And the Tigers did just that by taking charge of the match once again. You felt a second goal was coming for City...

And it did. Excellent work by Nick Barmby saw a devilish cross pick out the unmarked Peter Halmosi and the Hungarian winger steered the ball in for his first ever Hull City goal and capped a fine performance in doing so. It was deserved, despite any lingering controversy in this game, The Tigers were rightly leading.

But the second half almost mirrored the first, as Sheffield United were once more stung into action. An increase in possession for the visitors saw the game become scrappy, but United were guilty of being hasty with the ball and mistakes were preventing the visitors from building up genuine pressure.

City seemed to have the measure of their Championship guests without too much of a defensive fuss made and despite a flurry of late Sheffield United substitutions and balls launched into the box, the Tigers stood firm and soaked up the pressure - pressure that failed to draw a save from Myhill.

Desperation set in and Blades goalkeeper Paddy Kenny joined the attack twice during injury time in failed attempts to gain parity. Both times City could have scored with Dean Marney shooting from 50 yards, but the keeper scrambled back and Bernard Mendy wasted a glorious three on two opportunity shortly afterwards.

But when the whistle came, victory – finally – was Hull City's. Whatever Sheffield United will argue, simply put, they weren't deserving of winning this tie. For once, the better team triumphed. Good prevailed over the evil Blades. And tonight, revenge is sweet. Even if it has been 25 years in waiting.

It's Arsenal or Burnley next in the last eight of the FA Cup now. And we haven't been able to say that in my lifetime. 38 years in fact. You try telling me the magic of the FA Cup is lost. I've got beer, I've got a big smile on my face and the loathsome Sheffield United are beaten and out. Put out by the Tigers. Nice... The world is all right again...

MATCH STATS:

- Hull City: Myhill, Doyle, Turner, Zayatte, Ricketts, Mendy, France, Marney, Halmosi, Barmby (Garcia 73), Folan (Manucho 65). Subs Not Used: Warner, Geovanni, Cousin, Featherstone, Gardner.
- Booked: Marney.
- Goals: Naughton 24 og, Halmosi 56.
- Sheff Utd: Kenny, Naughton, Morgan, Walker, Naysmith (Jihai 88), Cotterill, Howard, Stephen Quinn, Hendrie (Tahar 90), Halford, Sharp. Subs Not Used: Bennett, Keith Quinn, Starosta.
- Booked: Naughton, Sharp.
- Goals: Sharp 32.
- Att: 17,239
- Ref: Peter Walton (Northamptonshire)

CHAPTER 8 – CUP CLASHES

SUNDAY 1ST MARCH 2009 –
HULL CITY V BLACKBURN ROVERS PREVIEW

Who would have thought a home game with Blackburn Rovers would prove to be one of the most significant of the season? Err... well, I did actually. Hull City v Blackburn Rovers is your Sunday lunch appetiser this weekend.

As soon as the fixtures come out, this was one of those ringed in big red pen for victory. To survive, Blackburn Rovers at home is 'must win'. No offence to Blackburn Rovers of course, I'm sure over in Lancashire, Blackburn fans were doing likewise. Hull City away? That's a three point certainty.

And this is what the Premier League is all about for those of us unable to compete with the vast millions and billions away from the big four. This, is the real Premier League. The one where teams compete on relative parity and strive for the prize of... being here next season? Um... yeah...

It's actually a tad more glamorous than it sounds, honest! The Premier League is the best league in the world - bar none. Our season objective this year is stay in it. Since winning the play-offs, it was target 40 and above points in the end column, Blackburn Rovers had to be a match to target three of those for the tally.

This is Hull City's very first shot at the big league. The club is under no illusions as to the scale of the task. It's going to be hard, very hard in fact, but 29 points have arrived so far, so City can't be making that bad a fist of it in the top flight. From Wembley play-off winners to... Premier League survivors? It's some leap, let me tell you.

Yet City have done well. True, form is sketchy at the moment, but it hasn't always been. Endeavour has been an ever-present for us and I'm a big believer that you always get out of life what you put in. Hull City have been 'putting in' in spades. The same attitude, approach and mentality and we'll survive. Trust me.

This Sunday is not 'must win' territory for City just yet. 'Must not lose' is more accurate. A point for Blackburn will do little to ease relegation fears for them when sitting in the bottom three - game in hand or otherwise. It's points in the bag that count. City can put a nine point gap between themselves and Rovers with a win. How's that for motivation?

Phil Brown will be squaring up to his old boss this Sunday lunch - and I bet they've enjoyed more relaxing ones than this. Browny will be itching to put one over his mentor, while Sam Allardyce cannot afford to lose face by being beaten by his quick-learning apprentice. It has some special ingredients, this Sunday lunchtime encounter...

The match is the Tigers' third home game in six days, following defeat to Spurs and then a 2-1 cup victory over Sheffield United on Thursday. Changes are afoot for City for sure, but Ian Ashbee may miss out with a calf injury. Caleb Folan has a groin strain and is also considered a doubt, but Craig Fagan could well come back into contention to partner Daniel Cousin. The apprentice in this encounter – Hull City boss Phil Brown - stated – *"We'll both be going for the jugular for 90 minutes. I can't see any team pulling out of tackles, challenges or headers. I think there will be a little blood spilled because there will be that much commitment on show. But that is a typical Hull City performance and if Blackburn can match that, then we are in for a good game."*

Blackburn Rovers have been left smarting by a midweek 1-0 defeat to Championship side Coventry City at the Ricoh in the FA Cup. Two players are struggling to be fit with Vince Grella and David Dunn both facing late fitness checks before kick off.

Brown's management tutor Sam Allardyce warned – *"We have a group of players who are trying very hard to get themselves out of the position they are in. If we put that amount of effort and commitment into games from now on, then that will give us victories. But if we let our standard drop just because the team we are playing is not Manchester United, then we will be in big trouble."*

It might only be Blackburn, but the anticipation grips me. This is the Premier League at its most genuine. This is what it's all about. Bring it on! And all the trimmings too. Sunday lunch has never been this good. COME ON CITY!

SUNDAY 1ST MARCH 2009 – HULL CITY 1-2 BLACKBURN ROVERS – REPORT

It hurts. A huge blow is suffered by the Tigers with a less-than-effective Blackburn capitalising on a Hull City performance lacking quality and the visitors duly waltz away with all the points from the Circle this Sunday lunch. My mother has always done better than this, I tell you...

All in, this is a sickening blow to Hull City. Truly awful to take. Not necessarily because of Blackburn's brilliance because there wasn't much, more to the do with the fact we became architects of our own downfall in a Premier League clash that genuinely mattered, and the result of which has left City in a precarious place.

Once again, it's difficult to fault the endeavour, commitment and will-to-win, but the lack of quality is now beginning to bite. And in truth, it should not be left to our heroic captain to pick up the pieces and bang in the goals for the cause.

Yet the defeat was brought about by an intricate and complex series of events from all quarters. The manager may want to look at a side picked that had no strikers, the players have to look at their composure at key moments – and the least said about referee Martin Atkinson the better – but most shocking off all, were the fans.

Yes, the fans. Perhaps, even you reading this. What was that all about? Boos at half time, boos at substitutions, boos at the end? You may see events on the pitch you don't like, you might disagree with selections and tactics made, you could be frustrated at the lack of luck on the pitch. But hear me, don't bother coming if you want to boo. Seriously, you're not welcome.

To those who don't fall into that bracket, I salute you. I'd like to wager, that those that didn't boo will make up 99 per cent of the away crowd at Fulham this Wednesday, too. Good. Proper fans, decent people, genuine supporters of the club. And if we get a result – or not – you won't hear such despicable noises as heard this Sunday.

Everybody – and I mean everybody – will be disappointed by this 1-2 home loss. Players, manager and fans alike. We're all gutted, don't believe for one minute we aren't. But who are these people that turn up, boo and then bugger off ten minutes, sometimes 15 minutes, before the end? Please, just don't come. Oh yeah, the game. Well, Brown picked Geovanni and Garcia upfront, Mendy and Kilbane were included to provide the width with Ashbee and Marney in the middle. Doyle got a start at right back, Turner and Zayatte were in the middle, Dawson took the left berth with Duke in goal.

City began the game on the offensive with Geovanni having a glorious chance to open the scoring when sent clear, but incredibly his first touch was like a brick wall and the chance was gone. Another header was flagged offside, like another break was too, but I was hardly surprised, Geovanni is not exactly an out-and-out striker, is he?

Garcia, on the other hand, is a wide midfielder full of endeavour and nothing more than makeshift in the role. Yes, Garcia worked his socks off, but getting a goal always looks unlikely. Cousin, Manucho, Fagan, Barmby… forwards all looking on from the bench… ouch!

It would cost. And it did. Let's ignore the fact Santa Cruz looked a mile offside – stupid 'not active' rule indeed – and play seemed to stop. But it hadn't, and a pullback provided an open goal for Stephen Warnock.

And before City had chance to come to terms with a goal arriving against the run of play, Blackburn were cashing in again. This time an unpunished foul on Michael Turner helped Blackburn profit for a second time much to the ire of the home crowd. Warnock galloped through to turn provider for ex-Tiger (typical eh?) Keith Andrews to net from mere yards.

At 0-2 down in a matter of seconds, I refused to believe the game was up, but knew a mountain needed scaling. Blackburn had offered practically nothing, ridden their luck and took probably their only two chances of the game, both with a good dash of fortune.

When you expected Browny to change it at half time, he didn't. City again started brightly in the second half, but nothing was really forthcoming. A double substitution came in the guise of Barmby for Kilbane which was right with the latter having a shocker, but Cousin's change for Geovanni prompted an ill wind from the crowd.

A chorus of boos rang loud, as well as an unbelievable chant of 'you don't know what you're doing'. What? Phil Brown? That man who saved us from demotion to League One, took us to Wembley and got us into the Premier League? Him? He doesn't know what he's doing? Why don't you all get screwed? More to the point, YOU don't know what you're doing. Booing Brown and the team? Get lost!

It was probably the lowest point of all our time at the Circle. And directed at our greatest manager. Truly a disgrace. Hang your heads in shame if you took part. It was a sick moment in dire circumstances. Not exactly a show of 'support' from the massed ranks. And then it all then went horribly wrong. With frustrations boiling over on all fronts, Dean Marney lost his cool in a challenge with Morten Gamst Pedersen and proceeded to kick him in the gonads afterwards. It was a straight red card – and not one player protested. Uncharacteristic, but... deserved.

Incredibly, despite rubbing his crotch vehemently, just minutes later Pedersen himself was seeing red for a second bookable offence. Tempers were flaring and it was a late challenge on Zayatte that induce a second yellow. Both sides were losing it and its times like these that you can see both sides will end up in the mire come the end of the season unless addressed.

Blackburn's chance to see the game out comfortably was passed up and skipper Ian Ashbee set up a nerve jangling climax when crashing in a half volley from a corner with a little over ten minutes to play. Ten versus ten meant space was now available but in truth, City failed to capitalise.

And for all the effort, the best two chances came right at the death with Michael Turner swivelling on the edge of the box to crash a shot just wide and then Andy Dawson drawing a sprawling save from substitute goalkeeper Jason Brown, but the game was up, defeat was upon us.

A final and deeply irritating chorus of boos greeted the final whistle and that left my blood boiling more than the actual result. In the pub afterwards, a depressing mood swept the bar room floor. With 11 games to go - and City not even in the relegation zone - we're going down.

Undoubtedly the people saying this were the same that booed. When a siege mentality is needed, it seems our support crumbles under the merest fraction of pressure. To say I'm disappointed is an understatement. I'm mortified by some of our fans, I really am. On to Fulham on Wednesday, and I'll be there. Along with all the other loyal supporters. COME ON CITY!

MATCH STATS:
- Hull City: Duke, Doyle (Fagan 67), Turner, Zayatte, Dawson, Mendy, Ashbee, Marney, Kilbane (Cousin 53), Geovanni (Barmby 53), Garcia. Subs Not Used: Myhill, Halmosi, Manucho, Gardner.
- Sent Off: Marney (64).
- Booked: Turner, Dawson.
- Goals: Ashbee 79.
- Blackburn: Robinson (Brown 46), Ooijer, Nelsen, Samba, Givet, Diouf (Mokoena 83), Grella, Andrews, Warnock, Pedersen, Roque Santa Cruz (Roberts 86). Subs Not Used: Kerimoglu, McCarthy, Treacy, Villanueva.
- Sent Off: Pedersen (70).
- Booked: Warnock, Pedersen, Diouf.
- Goals: Warnock 34, Andrews 37.
- Att: 24,612
- Ref: Martin Atkinson (W Yorkshire)
- **Premier League position: 13th**

TUESDAY 3RD MARCH 2009

That Geovanni incident versus Blackburn Rovers on Sunday? You know, the one that caused all the consternation – even booing – well it's all sorted. Phil Brown, the manager of our fine football club has sorted it once and for all... All hail Phil Brown. This is what the manager has confessed as being his biggest managerial test to date. But you know what? He's come through it already. Geovanni will not be fined. Geovanni will be party to events at Fulham. Geovanni has destiny in his own hands. Take a bow Phil Brown...

The City boss explained on Geo-gate - *"He was very apologetic for his actions. But as far as I was concerned his actions were those of an angry man, as opposed to a composed man, and that's what I'm looking for."*

Adding - *"I'm looking for players who go across the white line and compose themselves, and can respect the decision (to substitute him) for the reasons it was taken. It was taken for the right reasons. If I printed the stats it would be there for everybody to see. But I'm not going to wash dirty clothes in public."*

The City boss continued - *"It's not written in his contract that if he storms off and gets the huff that you can fine him. I'm a big boy, but he won't be doing it to me again - that's for sure. But it's between me and Geo, it's in-house, it will remain in-house, and he's got an opportunity on Wednesday to do something about it."*

And on Geovanni's golden chance versus Blackburn - *"Composure is absolutely key at the moment. Probably the best 'touch' player at the club had the best opportunity to score the opening goal. It was probably the heaviest touch I've seen him have since he came to this place. But I know there's still a player in there who has something to offer between now and the end of the season but it has to come sooner rather than later."*

And on the fans that booed the decision to haul the Brazilian off - *"Of course it hurts. But we're big boys and that's what we're in the game for, making big decisions. You've got to make them. Them [fans] venting their anger against me - I'll take that all day as long as they keep it away from the players."*

Phil Brown - Hull City manager - Football genius. Poodles take note.

TUESDAY 3RD MARCH – FULHAM V HULL CITY PREVIEW

Testing times, trying circumstances, tough fixture ahead. All made for Phil Brown's Tigers, isn't it? Expect the unexpected by the Thames this Wednesday evening is the message from me. Or die trying at the very least...

This is one daunting trip in difficult circumstances, I accept that. Travelling to Fulham on Wednesday evening is bad enough. Bloody London on a weekday evening, indeed? Stupid fixture list. But, you can't change it so we have to get on with it. And it will be all hands on deck by the Thames.

There is no hiding from the fact Sunday has left a rotten taste in the mouth. Losing on home turf to bottom three side Blackburn was a right kick in the gonads. But, if there is one thing about Phil Brown as a manager, he is a fighter. And each fan of our fine club - by and large – is too.

Never more so have we needed to see Browny's mettle than this week. What has now become a controversial substitution of Geovanni – when it really shouldn't have been because he was awful against Blackburn Rovers - has swiftly been resolved, effectively and with a level head.

Geovanni has to accept he had a shocker on Sunday and was rightly subbed. Petulance is not helpful during a fight to stay in the Premier League. Delivery of a performance is. Geovanni failed, hence the change was made. In a way, it was pleasing to see such anger, it shows the Brazilian cares. But Browny quite rightly had to pull the playmaker into line for such impudence.

The booing of the situation does not help, either. As is now abundantly clear, we are fighting for our top flight status for the first time this season. Splits between the fans, the players and the manager will do little to remedy the current slump in form. Thankfully, we'll see a hardcore four-figure following for what will be a mighty test against Fulham.

Those that venture to the capital will be the loyal hardcore who will be willing the team on in testing surroundings. Noise and passion will exude from the visiting enclosure. A battle cry will be heard by the Thames, a full blooded roar will greet the team. A chance to become one again for 90 minutes at the Cottage will arrive. It must happen. It will happen.

Undoubtedly, Fulham's home record has been nothing short of sensational. Just one defeat to West Ham United all season at home. But, this is when the Tigers have been at their sublime best this season. Cornered, stacked up against the odds and expected to earn nothing. Ask Chelsea, ask Liverpool, ask Arsenal.

To Brown's credit he has smoothed over the Geovanni incident in double quick time. No fines have been levied but a stern warning has been administered. Brown has asked Geovanni to prove himself and repeat the early season form like... against Fulham for example. What a goal! Geovanni will feature, Brown expects a positive reaction. No second chances now...

Injury concerns continue over skipper Ian Ashbee's calf strain. Bryan Hughes is likely to deputise if the captain fails to make it. Michael Turner is also a major doubt following his clash with England keeper Paul Robinson. Anthony Gardner is hopefully ready to step in. And Craig Fagan is still not 100 per cent following minor knee surgery. Daniel Cousin will surely start if the forward fails to make the grade.

Definitely missing is full back Andy Dawson with a one match ban, while Dean Marney has incurred a three-game ban for misdemeanours versus Blackburn Rovers that resulted in a red card. Untimely, to say the least. Matt Duke's mistake might cost him the gloves also, with Boaz Myhill hopeful of returning between the sticks. Changes they are aplenty it seems.

An indication to what commitment levels will be expected for City's fourth game in nine days is given by Phil Brown regardless – *"I'm looking for players who go across the white line and compose themselves, and can respect the decision [referring to substitution changes] for the reasons it was taken."* Expect a reaction, then. I hope we get one.

Fulham have no such concerns. Form is bountiful and the only injury problem for Roy Hodgson is defender Chris Baird who took a knock in the 0-0 draw with Arsenal. However, John Pantsil is back from a ban and will undoubtedly plug the gap if needed.

To the Thames we go...But, I'm sure there is something I forgot to mention, though? Hmm... It can't be that important. Had it been such an influence on our season I would've remembered, wouldn't I? Now what was it...Oh, never mind...

WEDNESDAY 4TH MARCH 2009 - FULHAM 0-1 HULL CITY REPORT

A double! The perfect shot when needed. Hull City overcome the problems of a depleted squad carrying injuries and suspensions to record their fifth away win of the campaign at fortress Fulham. How big this win could prove to be is yet untold, but for me it will be hugely significant, I bet.

There's snow on the M4 as we approach London. But we've made good time. We're in Osterley near the Sky nerve centre. A tube ride to the Duke's Head by the Thames beckons. Inside, among the raft of Amber Nectar travelling companions I'm with; is John from the City Independent messageboard community. Aha, some common ground after the journey...

I've never met the guy before tonight, but I won't forget him. John told me he missed our glorious winning Wembley goal. He was buying a Wembley burger for his nattering boy. As Windass heroically volleys in the most important goal in our 105 year history, at the home of football, to a crescendo of 40,000 City fans going mental, there's a little lad's voice on the concourse muttering *"It tastes horrible Dad."*

But, across the Thames and over Putney Bridge from the Duke's Head was destination Craven Cottage, lit up by the four pylons to guide me alongside the river. As John is my witness, I felt getting something from this quaint abode disguised as a fortress was possible. I dunno why, I just did. And I'd only had one pint of Bombardier so I wasn't drunk either.

After all the Geovanni hoo-ha Brown chose his Brazilian to start. Fears over Turner, Ashbee and Fagan's injuries were unfounded – or deemed risk worthy at least – as all played their part in what is best described as a disciplined away performance. Cousin started up front and Kilbane was reverted to left back, while Gardner also got a welcome recall to the starting line up.

It was a daunting task ahead. Fulham have been inspired on home turf and one defeat at home all season tells its own story. But as mentioned before the game kicked off, these are the precise circumstances that Phil Brown's Hull City relish. Practically written off before a ball is kicked, City had a point to prove. So let's prove it.

And the Tigers wasted no time doing so, backed by a vociferous following who kept banging on with the chants all game. Geovanni was lively from the outset and a constant thorn in Fulham's side, drifting here, floating there and popping up everywhere in fact. An early free-kick flashed wickedly beyond the post with Schwarzer well beaten. Geovanni was here all right...

City continued their promising start and a corner saw Daniel Cousin glance over, but Mr Jones refereeing, gave us another corner to keep the pressure on. Nice. But the man with a point to prove was Geovanni, demanding the ball, turning Fulham around and running at pace with flair and trickery. Fulham hated it. Another searing run brought about a free kick but it came to nothing.

The visitors had started with purpose and Fulham were wobbling. However Zamora headed a chance wide to wake the hosts up before Johnson cut across goal for Dempsey at the back stick, but captain Ashbee booted the ball clear of danger. Getting a feel for affairs, Etuhu then tried an ambitious long range effort for Fulham, but it sailed well wide.

Unquestionably, Fulham found a foothold and built upon it. A spell of pressure brought a series of corners for the hosts that caused brief panic, but City coped effectively enough to keep their sheet clean. City's attempts to get at Fulham predominantly came from Geovanni, who was now being persistently fouled to break up play, along with some fine defending from Konchesky.

Fulham finished the half much the stronger though, with Zamora pulling a pass back for Davies, but the shot was hammered into the ground and ballooned over the bar. Then, City's good work was almost undone on the cusp of the break with a defensive lapse from Mendy allowing Zamora to rob the ball and Johnson capitalised on the dithering - but the England man's strike was wayward and wide.

At the break you were left encouraged by City's performance. Sure pressure was beginning to mount, it was expected - Fulham's record at the Cottage deserves due respect - but the Tigers were in this game and threatening on occasions. It was a pretty fair reflection of the game to be tied at 0-0.

But Fulham were clearly angered not to be beating an out-of-synch visitors who have been laboured in recent months and pressed the accelerator for victory. You can see why Fulham are good at home. Clean passers of the ball, forward in numbers and composed in the danger areas. But so far, the sight of goal was somewhat out of line.

Shortly after, Duke saved brillianty from Johnson's dipping shot, falling backwards to tip it over after it had taken a cute deflection. The corner brought a free-for-all in the box but City escaped intact. Then Zamora appealed in vain for a penalty when challenging for an aerial ball, but it broke to Davies and a cut across the face of goal found Dempsey lurking at the back stick... side netting. Phew!

Fulham were now pouring forward for the opening goal and pushing City back with purpose. Clint Dempsey produced a carbon copy of Andy Johnson's earlier effort in the half, but again Matt Duke did a fantastic job to leap athletically and palm the ball over for another corner. From that, a flick on found Johnson at the back post to head in, but Mendy mercifully cleared off the line.

The hosts were in full flow and it was in danger of becoming an onslaught, as Fulham piled on the pressure. Konchesky this time driving from long range, but once again Duke denied the hosts tipping over for a third time. City needed some respite and a freak mix up in the

Fulham back four provided it - letting Fagan in on the byline. The cut back found Cousin, but the striker hammered the shot high and over the bar from a good position.

That though, did arrest the white tidal wave. City had weathered a mighty second half storm and came out from their shell a little. But not before neat play from the hosts fashioned a chance for Davies to drive across goal, with Turner just managing to get to the ball first and sweep away the danger.

Fagan progressed from nuisance factor to main outlet now for City and the visitors got better at finding the pacy forward. Geovanni cut inside and drove towards goal and that produced a City corner. The big guns of Turner and Gardner ambled forward but Schwarzer pouched the ball.

Geovanni was now back in the game and City's confidence grew. A good period of possession followed and the tide was beginning to turn as Fulham appeared to run out of steam as a barrage of windmilling attacks appeared to have dried up. Brown sensed it from the touchline and Cousin was switched for Manucho. His first touch was to swivel just outside the box and fire just over.

Now it was game on and the Tigers smelt blood. A well worked free kick saw Ashbee free in the box but, a scuffed shot when well positioned was easily claimed by Schwarzer. Still City came, though. Geovanni tore through Fulham's midfield and now a flurry of bookings came Fulham's way for persistently following the little Brazilian. This time the in-swinging free-kick flashed just wide of the far post.

Fulham broke up the building Hull City pressure when Dempsey forced a save from Duke and then Turner had a rare lapse of concentration and almost let Johnson in on goal, but the lanky defender recovered and just managed to toe the ball to safety when the home striker looked clear.

But Browny wanted victory. On came Richard Garcia and Nick Barmby for Mendy and the superb Geovanni. Garcia - like Manucho earlier - fired high and wide with his first touch of the ball despite just minutes of the game remaining. It was finely poised, but it was City in the ascendancy to win the game, no defenders off the bench here, it was all about striving for victory.

Garcia then collected a ball 30 yards out from goal. Turn, run, challenge, ball breaks loose and wide. Garcia refuses to give up the chase, gets there... hooks back a cross... Manucho steaming in... BLOODY HELL! GOAL! Incredible! Think Wembley, think Arsenal, think Tottenham. This feeling coursing through my writhing body is right up there with those. Manucho had bundled it in from six yards and it felt bloody terrific!

The Putney Stand went berserk. This was massive! Absolutely massive! People, fans, supporters who I'd never even met before capered with delight, hugging and cheering. It was an immense moment, deeply emotional and so, so, critical in our quest to survive the toughest league in the world. It was euphoric blood pumping round my veins. COME ON!

I couldn't even breathe. There were just seconds to go. But referee Mr Jones was not letting up yet. Fulham were mortally wounded. Everybody in white piled forward for the last seconds. A corner. Damn! No! Not now. It speared into the near post low, BANG! No, please no! Just wide from a deflection... phew! Here comes another... scramble... AWAY! Mighty roars go up! Then the whistle sounds. Get in! GET IN! City claim all the points!

The Putney End is awash with jubilation. A heroic test had been matched and then overcome. Fulham's record is awesome at home, but we came, we challenged and have now conquered. Dancing with delight, I just knew there was something in it for us. I just knew... and watching the players flock to the Putney Stand and Brian Horton and coaching staff join them, harmony, togetherness and unity of one was here again. Fans, players, staff. All deliriously happy!

The significance of this win in very trying circumstances cannot be underestimated. Fulham are rock hard at home and we beat them fair, square and deservedly so. A double has been recorded and these six points are going to be absolutely critical towards our final total. I've stated all along we can do this. More spirit and endeavour like on parade this Wednesday eve and we'll be alright. Trust me.

City have at last, moved on. COME ON! Going down? Not without a fight we aren't. Oh no... Make sure you have beer tonight and savour it. This was massive, absolutely massive.

MATCH STATS:
- Fulham: Schwarzer, Pantsil, Hughes, Hangeland, Konchesky, Davies, Murphy, Etuhu, Dempsey, Johnson, Zamora (Kamara 89). Subs Not Used: Zuberbuhler, Nevland, Gera, Dacourt, Stoor, Kallio.
- Booked: Hangeland, Etuhu, Davies.
- Hull City: Duke, Zayatte, Turner, Gardner, Kilbane, Mendy (Garcia 89), Ashbee, Ricketts, Geovanni (Barmby 90), Fagan, Cousin (Manucho 76). Subs Not Used: Myhill, Hughes, France, Halmosi.
- Booked: Geovanni.
- Goals: Manucho 90.
- Att: 23,051
- Ref: Mike Jones (Cheshire)
- **Premier League position: 12th**

FRIDAY 6TH MARCH 2009

Meh! You've got to laugh. Big club Newcastle United have tagged their next Premier League fixture away at Hull City as a 'cup final'. Surely some mistake? No, no, apparently not. Megastar Michael Owen says so...

Muhahaha! Is the pressure getting to the relegation-threatened Geordies? Apparently so! It's only March, but massive club Newcastle – battling to beat the drop – have targeted their next Premier League fixture against ickle Hull City at the Circle as a cup final! No, seriously they have! Michael Owen has said so! Prrrrffffttt!

Here's what the Magpie striker had to say on the impending fixture - *"The game at Hull City on Saturday week is at the moment shaping up to be our cup final - and the other games against teams around us, Stoke City, Portsmouth and Middlesbrough, could also be crucial."*

Wait, there's more - *"We've got some tough games coming up, yes, but we've also got some very winnable games - games which, if we do win them, will put our biggest rivals in trouble. There's no denying that we're in the middle of the relegation scrap, but myself and the lads have no doubt in our minds that we have enough quality to pull clear. However, this is now the time when we have to stand up and be counted - just like we did last year, when we put together a very good seven-match unbeaten run."*

And get this, we're even 'significant' now - *"That sort of sequence is well within our capabilities, and while we have some tough home fixtures in a row, which started against Manchester United and continues with Arsenal and Chelsea, it is the other games against teams around us that are going to be most significant."*

My, my, how the mighty have fallen! How could a massive club like Newcastle United ever consider an away trip to little old Hull City as a 'cup final'?

Oh, wait, Hull City must be a big club now, ah! Best get some winners and losers medals prepared then, sharpish… Indeed, have royalty been called? Yes, let's have majesty down at the Circle and make it a proper do.

FRIDAY 13TH MARCH 2009 – HULL CITY V NEWCASTLE UNITED PREVIEW

It's cup final time in the Premier League when Newcastle United visit Hull City. No really, it is. Look, just trust me, it is. Let me explain once more…

Tomorrow you need to have your 'cup final' ticket at the ready. Oh yes, its cup final day at the Circle, didn't you know? What's that? You didn't? Never mind. It's been quite amusing reading some of the press in the north east this week. Talk about setting yourself up for a fall…

Firstly, we have the euphoria of Michael Owen returning to the Newcastle side. The game in Hull is 'a cup final', the injury-plagued striker trumpeted on his expected return. I'm sure his team mates will love him for that comment. No pressure, eh lads?

And just when you think the Geordies might try to hush up the former England striker and sweep it all under the carpet... nope! Goalkeeper Steve Harper is getting all excitable now the Shay Given shackles have been removed and the keeper is first choice at the club.

Yes, the Geordie custodian cranked up the expectation on Tyneside with the 'biggest match in the club's' history' gaffe. What? Bigger than Wembley? Bigger than the Champions League encounters? What are you talking about, Steve? Someone's getting giddy with the gloves it seems...

Meanwhile, back on planet earth, Hull City have quietly gone about their business, well hidden from the media glare. It's been a notably low profile week in the Tigers' camp with little, if any talk, coming from City about the game ahead. Perhaps, a sensible approach in the context of the fixture?

It is true, this match should be a decent barometer to who is and who isn't going to be having a nervy time come the end of the season. But it's hardly definitive, is it? And it's not like with ten games to go, the damage is irreparable, either. Talk about overegging the cake. That's the Geordies for you...

City will be looking to record their second Premier League double in succession with victory over the Magpies. After a fine 1-2 victory in September, followed by a 0-0 draw here in the FA Cup and a 0-1 replay win up at St James Park, Phil Brown's team have certainly had the measure of Newcastle so far this season.

Buoyed by the magnificent 0-1 away success at Fulham last time out in the Premier League, the Tigers will have a timely fillip for confidence levels ahead of the game. Preparations could not have gone much better, in all honesty.

Manager Phil Brown will welcome back the services of left back Andy Dawson for the game after completing his one match ban. However, Dean Marney remains suspended and will miss the FA Cup quarter final clash with Arsenal at the Emirates on Tuesday as well.

Finally breaking his media silence since the Fulham game, the City boss came out like a Tiger with some bullish comments – *"There is a lot of fighting talk coming out of Newcastle and it is interesting to hear that."*

Brown then continued in the same spirited vain with – *"If they had that fighting talk all season they wouldn't be in the position they are in. As far as I am concerned, bring your fighting talk to the table at three o'clock and we'll get it on."* Oo-er, missus!

So, onto to Newcastle then. Chris Hughton seems deliriously happy to have Michael Owen back from injury. Nicky Butt and Damien Duff are hoping to shake off knee and calf injuries respectively, while Kevin Nolan serves the last match of his ban.

Caretaker Magpies boss Chris Hughton beamed on Owen's return – *"It's a massive lift. He is our club captain, he is a player with a wonderful goal scoring record and ability. One thing we have continually said is what we wanted to do is have a stronger bench. A stronger bench means a stronger team and also competition for places. That being the case, to have someone like Michael back involved in the squad is a lift for everybody."*

And when you chuck those comments in alongside Michael Owen's – *"The game at Hull City on Saturday week is at the moment shaping up to be our cup final."* and Steve Harper's – *"I said last year before the game against Birmingham that it was the biggest game in the club's recent history. I've got no problem about saying this game at Hull is just as big."* Newcastle sound a trifle flustered about Saturday.

Is this how a big club prepares for little old Hull City? Surely not? Funny though, isn't it? I wonder what will happen if the Tigers win? Yet again...

SATURDAY 14TH MARCH 2009 –
HULL CITY 1-1 NEWCASTLE UNITED – REPORT

A muted response at the final whistle greeted the end of this game. A poor Newcastle United side were there for the taking, but City let their visitors off the hook. It was clearly two points dropped, rather than one gained.

There is an air about Newcastle that reeks of 'we're too good to go down'. The truth is, had City won this game like they should have done, the Geordies would have looked doomed. Indeed, with their fixtures, they probably still are. Time and again City exploited the available space and a chance to glean all the points was genuinely in the offing. But...

All week Newcastle had been making a rod for their own back with 'cup final' this and 'biggest ever game' that, comments pouring out of their camp, while Hull City quietly went about their business. And from the outset you could see Newcastle had overcome themselves, drunk on all the hyperbole.

City boss Phil Brown picked a side that looked up for a fight with a heartily pleasing back four of Kilbane, Turner, Gardner and Ricketts. The midfield looked up for a battle with Ashbee and Zayatte in the centre, plus Mendy and Geovanni outside of them to provide pace and trickery. Cousin and Fagan started up top. A text was sent to the away end: Ready for your cup final?

And very quickly, it was City on the front foot. Yawning gaps appeared all over the park that Geovanni and Mendy both scampered into, while Newcastle looked like they'd all met for the first time on the coach on the way down. Fagan was the crucial nuisance factor in it all as the hosts set the agenda for the match.

City got some early reward when Fagan burst down the left in space and centred for the unchecked Geovanni. The little Brazilian was left with the freedom of the box to powerfully head home the opening goal inside eight minutes and the Circle enjoyed the '1-0 in your cup final' chant while celebrating. Brown's side continued to press with Newcastle at sixes and sevens and Geovanni running at the Magpies, producing several free-kicks, with the most pertinent being central outside the box. City's no.10 dusted himself down, curled a shot over the wall and just past the post, with Harper looking well beat.

Newcastle reminded us they had actually arrived when Martins turned in the box from close range but fired high and wide. City were winning everything in the middle with Ashbee and Zayatte central to all things positive, as the hosts enjoyed much of the possession. Cousin did brilliant to rob Coloccini and really should have done better to set up a City second, rather than firing wide and away from goal. Pressure was being applied and the need to make hay while the sun was shining was now apparent as Newcastle wilted under some superb closing down.

So it was a right royal pain in the Butt when a rare foray forward from Newcastle saw the aforementioned centre for the unmarked Steven Taylor to shin in an equaliser at the near post, across goal and into the net. Half time was in sight... How are we not still winning this game? It was a pretty low blow for City fans.

There was much consternation at half time. Newcastle looked ragged, City looked keen, but the score was 1-1. The second half then duly failed to live up to the first from a home perspective. After being let off the hook, the Magpies raised their game, but lacked composure in key areas.

City had left their fluency in the dressing room and pretty quickly the game developed a nervy edge to matters. It was not particularly pretty to watch and the better players failed to shine as petty free-kicks and general scrappy play began to win the day.

Mendy then cantered down the right clear and free and homing in on goal. Fagan followed at the far post in a replica of the first goal, but the Frenchman got caught in two minds and neither shot nor crossed as Harper easily pouched whatever Mendy had tried to do. It should have been 2-1, no question.

Brown changed on-field affairs by replacing Fagan - who was a little too pumped up for the game and skating on thin ice with a yellow card already against him - for Garcia and the latter almost broke the deadlock when battling with Bassong to emerge free in the box, but the Aussie was ajudged to have fouled the defender first.

Manucho and Barmby also appeared from the bench as City looked to grab a winner, but in fairness it was now Newcastle finishing the stronger. Martins once again spurned the best chance when tamely poking the ball into Duke's midriff. Chances though, were at a premium.

At the whistle, Ashbee belted the ball high in the air in a clear act of frustration. The skipper was clearly vexed City had not claimed all the points with their only defensive lapse and I knew exactly how he felt. Join the club mate. This is one point gained and two points dropped. Newcastle truly were there for the taking and City passed up the opportunity.

So, in this cup final there was no trophy. There were no medals. And the game ended all square. Not to worry Newcastle fans, if it had been, you would have lost the replay anyway. Four times now we've faced Newcastle and I've yet to see them look better than us. Baggies, Boro and Geordies for the drop? I'll be honest, I've seen nothing to change my mind today...

MATCH STATS:

- Hull City: Duke, Ricketts, Turner, Gardner, Kilbane, Mendy (Barmby 80), Ashbee, Zayatte, Geovanni, Fagan (Garcia 70), Cousin (Manucho 54). Subs Not Used: Myhill, Dawson, Hughes, Halmosi.
- Booked: Fagan, Zayatte, Garcia.
- Goals: Geovanni 9.
- Newcastle: Harper, Steven Taylor, Coloccini, Bassong, José Enrique, Smith (Ryan Taylor 75), Butt, Geremi, Gutiérrez , Owen (Ameobi 73), Martins. Subs Not Used: Forster, Duff, Løvenkrands, Edgar, Carroll.
- Booked: Geremi, Coloccini, Smith.
- Goals: Steven Taylor 38.
- Att: 24,914
- Ref: Howard Webb (S Yorkshire)
- **Premier League position: 12th**

MONDAY 16TH MARCH 2009 – ARSENAL V HULL CITY – FA CUP QUARTER FINAL PREVIEW

It was 38 years ago Hull City were last in the FA Cup quarter finals. Now, the Tigers are back in the last eight... err... five of the competition. Yes, five. There have been some delays getting round to this tie what with all the replays and adverse weather conditions occurring elsewhere.

This is all rather surreal. Here we are in the last five of the FA Cup, bidding to reach the last four of the competition for the first time since 1930 – and guarantee a second Wembley appearance in the space of 11 months, after previously never going there before in our 100-odd year history.

It should be absolutely massive. It is massive. Yet bizarrely, the chatter about this delayed FA Cup quarter final with Arsenal at the Emirates Stadium is not about the glories that potentially await. No. Instead, all the talk is about gaining a point at the very least from Wigan Athletic in the league on Sunday. You couldn't make it up!

Undoubtedly, it is accepted because of several replays and cancellations that Arsenal have faced to get here, the gloss of a quarter final appearance by Hull City is tempered by arriving on a Tuesday night. London is a pain to get to at the best of times and the current economic crisis is certainly biting hard. See my second job for proof. If I pull this ambition of mine off it will be incredible under the circumstances.

To be fair, I couldn't ask for a more supportive family to help me fulfil a lifelong dream of completing a full season and writing a book. Killing two birds with one stone sounds ideal, but it definitely feels like I am paying a hefty price on occasions like this one when having to trundle down to London in midweek for the second time in a matter of days. I do feel like this is the last major hurdle, though, for the season. Unless we get to Wembley of course! Hell, Wembley again!

But anyway, enough sentiment, the magic of the cup is here and those that will venture down to the Emirates to sample such wares will surely give it their all. Including the team, I hope. Buoyed by a victory already against Arsenal on their own turf this season (how can you ever tire of saying that?) the players will surely be hankering for a second chance to get to Wembley.

The prize this time is not promotion to the Premier League, but a chance to return to Wembley to reach the FA Cup Final. Yes, I know that's all a bit mad – and wrong if you want my honest opinion – but come on, facing Chelsea at the home of football to reach the greatest club final in the world is surely worth fighting for?

Now, Phil Brown is undoubtedly thinking the same. A full strength side will greet the Gunners, although it is unclear if the 4-3-3 formation that was boldly used in the Premier League to deservedly secure a 1-2 win over the Gunners will be used to hoodwink Arsène Wenger again. A more orthodox 4-4-2 is likely.

Kevin Kilbane cannot feature because he is cup-tied. However, Andy Dawson is almost certain to fill the gap after serving his suspension and sitting on the bench against Newcastle United. With Dean Marney serving the last of his three-game suspension, that should be the only change to the side that lined up against the Geordies on Saturday.

Assistant manager Brian Horton stated on the tie ahead – *"It is going to be a tough game, we all know that, but we have had two very good games with them. When they came to the KC they treated us with the utmost respect, as you would expect from a top club. They came and won late on but it was a very even game until late on."*

Adding on the prospect of revisiting Wembley – *"To go back again would be unbelievable. The people of Hull had never been there, a lot of the players had never been there. Someone has said the league is the priority - of course it is. It is important - but not tomorrow night it's not."*

And do you know? It's true. Arsenal haven't been to the new Wembley yet. The team standing in their way is team that already has - and are one of only two sides that have beaten the Gunners on home soil. You just know they'll be itching to do us over as a consequence. But so what? It's when Hull City are at their premium best as we have all seen this season.

Manager Arsène Wenger will place Lukasz Fabiański in goal with Manuel Almunia injured. The Gunners boss is also considering resting Gaël Clichy so Kieran Gibbs may get a start. Andrei Arshavin has had eight stitches in his foot and is considered a doubt for City's visit.

Right. Enough of this talk that Wigan is this and more important than that. The chance to get to Wembley is here – rightly, wrongly, or morally – and the next time that chance comes along may be another 38 years away. This is the FA Cup. It's magic. Drink it all in...

TUESDAY 17TH MARCH – ARSENAL 2-1 HULL CITY – FA CUP QUARTER FINAL REPORT

What a stormy encounter! This quarter final of the FA Cup at the Emirates Stadium is settled in highly controversial fashion late in the game – and laced with a huge amount of ill-feeling to boot. One thing is certain; this game will not be forgotten in a hurry... London calling. Tuesday night, FA Cup, a place in the semi-finals is at stake. A call to the offy is needed. Being a Tuesday night game, a bizarre ritual has been developed over the last season or two. Glasses are charged with copious red wine all the way down the M1. Mmmm...

With memories of the league encounter still burning brightly, there was no reason to change the routine of parking at Cockfosters, taking the tube into Finsbury Park, hitting the Twelve Pins again and taking the short walk to the ground. A crisp, clear evening greeted our arrival... and a cordoned off street. 'Must have been a shooting', I muttered to my group of travelling companions.

In the Pins, beer flowed and one of our party came back from a venture down the high street with a bag of chips in tow. Firming up, *"Yeah, there's been a shooting."* No, really? I should be surprised, but bizarrely, I'm not. It's around 5pm, it's broad daylight, its London. All very sad, indeed.

As kick-off approached, the atmosphere livened up in the boozer and some banter was finally had with the Gunners. A little more wary Gunners though, it had to be said, following our successful conquering last time here. City fans won the verbal exchange come the end with 'We scored your goal for you', harking back to splendid times of yore at the Emirates in late September.

Onwards. Yet sadly, a couple of cockneys tried to 'mix it' on the approach to Emirates. Sensing we were Hull lads (and one girl – our driver Coreana) sly kicks and trips were delivered with a half-baked push in the back to welcome me. Trying to provoke an 'off' on your own manor with 'little Hull'? Classy Arsenal, classy... It was laughable.

In the ground, an assortment of travellers had beaten the path to the Emirates. A few southern Tigers were on show. Pompey Pete tried palming me off with 50p for his ill-conceived debts – and I was having none of that. Interest Pete, interest... you still owe me.

Also, the closet Tiger that frequents (plagues?) the City Independent messageboard – namely Essex Gull – well, it appears the salacious one had clearly concluded business at the Square Mile for the day to unexpectedly drop in. Yes I know what you're thinking. Torquay, incredibly, are not in the last eight, err... five of the FA Cup. How strange?

But on to the game. Look, right, I'm slaughtered at this point so in depth analysis is not going to be found here. Alcohol/memory deficiency reigns supreme. I recall City getting off to a magnificent start and being clearly up for the cup. I'm thinking 'Hello... here we go...'

Andy Dawson played in Nick Barmby and the diminutive ex-England man looped the ball in to give City a surprise lead. The hardy souls on the terraces (yep, stood up all game - cheers stewards, common sense prevails) go berserk - and I'm in the joyous writhing mass that's celebrating. Unbelievable! We're winning at Arsenal! Again!

Geovanni then whistles in a wicked free-kick, but a sprawling Fabiański just manages to claw it away. Kinnel! We've got Arsenal rocking! Then, the unthinkable happens, I'm watching Nick Barmby rifle in a second! No... a linesman's flag scotches what would've been a 0-2 lead. Damn! Arsenal decide this is actually going to be a contest and wake from their slumber. Hull City, clearly, are not just going to roll over and go quietly. New £15m signing Andrey Arshavin drills a shot wide on the volley. But at the interval (already?) it's 0-1 Hull City. Chatter on the concourse is all about the seemingly impossible occurring once more. Could it really?

The second half saw a clearly vexed Arsenal saturate City. It was red wave after red wave of attack. Chances for Song, Diaby and Arshavin all passed up and it really was a backs to the wall affair. And Ashbee was... where was Ash? Injured? Manfully, City braved the onslaught, Ricketts in particular throwing life and limb at everything that hinted the threat of a goal. It was coming though. Bendtner finally cut through the City defence with a slice of fortune and squared across goal, the ball deflected to Arshavin and a lay off to Van Persie was smashed in by the Dutchman. 15 minutes left, finally it was 1-1 – and on balance, you couldn't really complain.

Incredibly, Geovanni then lashed a vicious shot just past Fabiański and the post as the Tigers almost had the audacity to take the lead straight back. It was a light reprieve.

Arsenal piled on the pressure. There were five minutes left. A replay, I'll settle for a replay...

Nope. Nasri launches a free-kick into the heart of the City box. Myhill looks to punch but appears impeded. Diaby flicks on... Gallas heads in... doesn't matter he's miles offside. Linesman... Linesman? LINESMAN! You utter ****! What the? How on earth can that stand! Joyous writhing cockneys engulf us. Sick...

Protests are all in vain. The Emirates boom is piercing. It's a right kick in the nuts. It hurts. It really hurts. Mike Riley, refereeing this debacle rolls out his pièce de résistance by gifting the Gunners their path to a Wembley semi-final by allowing an atrocious decision in a high profile game to stand. I hate him. Six bookings for us, not a decision going for us all night. Typical Wessie.

And it was the killer blow. Arsène strides straight down the tunnel in typically arrogant and ignorant fashion, Arsenal celebrate like they'd actually won the sodding cup, never mind laboured to overturning us with an illegal goal late in the game. It's all pretty wretched to watch.

Calls and texts rain in. It's all going off backstage. Browny disgusted with Arsenal, Cesc Fàbregas allegedly spitting at Brian Horton, Arsène Wenger's behaviour, Mike Riley... the list goes on. Like me, Browny is clearly angry and hurt. But what can you do? Mike Riley FC has done us up like a kipper. ****!

There's good and bad to come from all this. The bad is; Ashbee injured, Gardner injured right at the end and looking quite serious and we had no Turner, who apparently underwent a scan. The defence to face Wigan on Sunday appears decimated.

On to the good, though. No way on earth are we going down after watching that! No way. We'll be back at the Emirates once again in the Premier League, you just know it. Indeed, I've never been more confident. I'm proud of my team. My team! Your team, our team. I'm proud... Our spirit and fight is first class. It's 3am eternal towards Hull... get me out of here... A little piece of me is glad we won't have to come back to London again this season...

MATCH STATS:
- Arsenal: Fabiański, Sagna, Gallas, Djourou, Gibbs, Walcott (Eboué 82), Song Billong (Bendtner 64), Diaby, Vela (Nasri 64), Van Persie, Arshavin. Subs Not Used: Mannone, Touré, Denilson, Silvestre.
- Booked: Gallas, Nasri.
- Goals: Van Persie 74, Gallas 84.
- Hull City: Myhill, Ricketts, Gardner, Zayatte, Dawson, Ashbee (Hughes 46), Barmby (France 76), Geovanni, Fagan, Manucho, Halmosi (Mendy 67). Subs Not Used: Duke, Garcia, Folan, Featherstone.
- Booked: Halmosi, Myhill, Dawson, France, Manucho.

- Goals: Barmby 13.
- Att: 55,641
- Ref: Mike Riley (Yorkshire)

WEDNESDAY 18TH MARCH 2009

As expected, but certainly unrealised by myself at the time by being in London and trudging away from the Emirates, it really did kick off post-match. I was stuck in a car blissfully unaware of what had actually taken place, gorging on the fine red wines from Chile we'd stashed for the car journey home.

However, checking back on the post-match comments, it seems there was more than just the refereeing decisions and result that made for a very heated press conference at the Emirates.

Hull City manager Phil Brown and Arsenal manager Arsène Wenger gave their opinions on a stormy FA Cup quarter final encounter between the two sides at the Emirates Stadium on Tuesday evening. I let you decide for yourself...

Brown – post-match press conference v Arsenal (a) - *"You know you're not going to get the rub of the green when you come to places like this but for their club captain, Cesc Fàbregas, to spit at my assistant manager tells you what this club's about.*

It's an absolute disgrace.

We haven't been beaten by Arsenal, who are fourth top in the Premier League; we've been beaten by a linesman's decision and a referee's decision. It's as simple as that."

Meanwhile, here's Arsenal manager Arsène Wenger on William Gallas' extremely dubious offside winner - *"The goalkeeper touches the ball, so he's not offside. For me, it is a goal because their goalkeeper deflected the ball."*

Perhaps Arsène Wenger's stock line of – *"I didn't see it"* would have been far more appropriate under the bowing evidence of television replays. Seriously, Arsène, you look foolish if you truly believe that.

As for Brown's post-match accusations against Fàbregas, Wenger claimed - *"It's completely new to me. I don't know about that at all."* Yes, that's much better and so much like the loveable Frenchman we all endear ourselves to.

Wenger continues when asked if he was concerned that Horton may make the allegation official, Wenger stated – *"No, frankly."*

However, this is big news. And the media are crawling all over the story. Bad news, ugly stories and a nasty edge sells.

Yet the bottom line is; Hull City assistant manager Brian Horton was allegedly spat at by Arsenal club captain Cesc Fàbregas at the end of a turbulent tie. This is not likely to go away in a hurry, whatever the case may be. Indeed, Tigers boss Phil Brown has backed his assistant manager Brian Horton in whatever course of action the City no.2 chooses to take.

Brown revealed insistently – *"Brian will receive the full support of the people of Hull, that includes my chairman, who we had a long conversation with this morning. We'll go down the right channels and support Brian Horton."*

Adding – *"It just shows how we've got up the noses of the Arsenal hierarchy. He wouldn't shake my hand when we beat them fairly 2-1 at the Emirates, he wouldn't shake my hand when they beat us, fairly, 3-1 at the KC Stadium."* Reflecting on the game itself, Brown felt his side were harshly on the wrong end of the officials to claim – *"There is no excuse for the first goal, it was definitely a mistake by us, no excuse about the second goal, it was definitely a mistake by the officials."*

Continuing – *"That is why we are out of the FA Cup. Ask Mr Riley how much that will cost to the city? I don't think he'd understand and I don't think he'd care."* Brown stopped short of saying his players had been cheated but did make a clear point when vehemently arguing – *"I can't use that word but that is the case."*

Meanwhile, back in the Arsenal camp, the man at the centre of the row Cesc Fàbregas has denied any allegations of spitting, but Horton has held talks with the League Managers Association about the incident and it looks as though we won't be hearing the last of this for some time.

SATURDAY 21ST MARCH – WIGAN ATHLETIC V HULL CITY PREVIEW

Much water has passed under the bridge since the Tigers and the Latics last clashed at the Circle one sunny day back in August. Now, the two sides are preparing to meet again – and arguably I am even more wary of the challenge ahead...

Back in the heyday of summer, Wigan came to town. Unlike many fans back then, I wasn't as forthright with the opinion that this was going to be one of those 'three point bankers' that we would need to secure our ultimate Premier League survival. Or not, as the case may be.

Wigan have been in the Premier League for four seasons now and continue to make a mockery of the 'little clubs should be relegated' mentality that predominantly sweeps through the top flight, and we ourselves have encountered along our rollercoaster ride this season.

Indeed, dare I say it, Wigan are perhaps a benchmark club that we would do well to take a leaf from when it comes to surviving, building, progressing and hell, who knows, getting into Europe? Well, the Latics are not a million miles away from such achievements, are they?

Back in August, I had hoped our spirit, commitment and endeavour would reward us against Wigan. I had expected a close game. Shows what I know after 30 odd years watching us, eh? Roundly walloped with a result that still makes me wince to this day. It was embarrassing. But playing ten Championship players lacking Premier League experience? Was it hardly surprising?

Now, it's something of a role reversal. Wigan would be the first to admit they got off to a wretched start. Yet once again, the Latics are mixing it at the right end of the league and deserve respect. And they'll get it from me. Pace, power and an honest work ethic, that's Wigan. Seriously, like I say, it's a good example to follow.

Yet hopes of righting the wrongs of the awful misdemeanours that took place in the summer, is once again set be a tough challenge. Back then, injuries decimated our side. This Sunday, following the midweek FA Cup quarter final tie at Arsenal, it seems the curse has struck again pre-Wigan.

The defensive triumvirate of Ian Ashbee, Anthony Gardner and Michael Turner are in serious jeopardy of missing the Latics clash and that would literally rip the heart out of our side. Ashbee has a hamstring strain and was removed at half time against Arsenal, Gardner hobbled off at the end of the game, while Turner missed out altogether after undergoing a scan. This is all rather worrying.

Marginally better news will see Dean Marney's timely return from a three game ban and Kevin Kilbane restored to the squad after being cup-tied on Tuesday. It is hoped those two and the aforementioned trio can figure for the side, to give City a sporting chance of getting some points.

Of course, manager Phil Brown has been in the news much this week, particularly after events at the Emirates. Thoughts that our manager was caught up in a higher state of consciousness and in the heat of the moment are perhaps wide of the mark, though. Brown stated – *"We seem to be getting up people's noses. Hopefully we can do that on Sunday against Wigan."*

And continued with – *"We conduct ourselves the way we conduct ourselves, and have done throughout the season. If you don't like it then it's your problem to get over. We're in nine battles and I suppose a siege mentality is important, not just the 11 players who go out but the whole changing room and the city of Hull."*

So, it appears, the manager is still seething from events four days ago. How that will translate to events on the pitch this Sunday lunch is anyone's guess. Yet it's probably fair to surmise that a performance full of passion is coming Wigan's way. But will it be enough? Will it be controlled aggression? We'll soon find out...

Wigan manager Steve Bruce has one injury concern to deal with as winger Antonio Valencia has reported a hamstring strain, but may still play. Lee Cattermole will definitely be out of contention as he serves the second of a two-match ban.

So, can City stop Wigan from completing a double over us? Well, our impressive away record is surely going to be tested to the maximum, and with results elsewhere doing us little favour, a defeat again to the Latics will leave us with much food for thought. Here's hoping we don't get beaten.

SUNDAY 22ND MARCH 2009 – WIGAN ATHLETIC 1-0 HULL CITY – REPORT

The predictable tough test at Wigan this Sunday lunchtime came to fruition. However, the manner and nature of the defeat is pretty difficult to stomach and serves as a stark reminder there is much work still to do if Hull City are stay the course in their inaugural Premier League season.

Taking the train to Wigan, I was pretty surprised to hear the rabid positivity among our group. Nearly all our party were in agreement that City would go to Wigan and win. The exception? Well if you read the preview, that was me. Sometimes, it's not good to be always right...

It was a bright if somewhat breezy day and the customary *"Yorkshire!"* chant that greets our opponents from the wrong end of the M62 failed to materialise. On a Sunday lunchtime that really is quite unforgiveable. In defence, I suppose everyone had other things on their mind rather than the trimmings that accompany a Sunday roast.

However, ultimately this game turned out to be a pudding for us Yorkshiremen. Indeed, the game itself was pretty much a slow, painful death that surely wouldn't have spoiled anyone cooking dinner at the time. You can bet the rush to peel the spuds was far more appealing than watching this match.

Brown had to deal with the loss of influential duo Anthony Gardner and Ian Ashbee but we looked a soft touch because of it. Of course it couldn't be helped, but naming Kevin Kilbane as our captain on his first return to the JJB Stadium was probably a bit rich. Particularly with Dean Marney reinstated to the midfield following his ban.

So City lined up with Duke in goal, Ricketts, Turner, Zayatte and Dawson in defence. Mendy, Marney, Geovanni and Kilbane held the middle while Manucho and Fagan were up top. Whatever the initial game plan was, it failed to materialise as Wigan dominated the start, indeed the half.

The hosts play on a massive pitch and exploit its size to the maximum. Spreading play as wide as possible, clearly looking to isolate City in key areas and pounce on mistakes. It sure works. Of course, a strong worth ethic and pace is also required, but Wigan had these traits in spades. However, what the Latics clearly lack is finishing prowess.

Take the two-yard sitter Ben Watson failed to convert in front of the away fans. Check Mido's wild drive, high and wide, after a fine move and being well placed. See the free header from three yards inexplicably headed back across our goal rather than towards it. A team lacking in confidence? Strange.

City couldn't enjoy any sustained spells on the ball nor mount significant attacks. The most dangerous City ever looked was from a set-piece on the rare occasions Brown's side breached Wigan territory. It was telling though, there were no shots on target from us. A forgettable half from our prospective, no doubt.

By contrast, Wigan will be wondering how they were not leading the game at the interval, especially after drawing a fine save from Matt Duke, who then had to respond to the rebound which he beat away for a corner. City could surely not turn in a more tepid performance in the second half, surely?

Thankfully not. Garcia was now involved in the play and the substitute injected a fresh impetus to City's attacking play. The game shifted balance after the interval and it was the Tigers who were looking much dangerous. Territory and possession swung City's way and for the first time this afternoon, the match was actually a contest.

But critically, Brown's side could not make their new found wealth work. Fagan probed and irritated the home fans. Geovanni's direct running caused problems. Manucho held the ball up admirably, but the end product? What end product? It just wasn't apparent. Marney blazed over from a good position. A corner swung into Manucho at the near post brought a fine reactionary save from Chris Kirkland in the Wigan goal and then Marney again dragged another chance well wide. Nope, for all the effort and intensity, City looked blunt.

Wigan, meanwhile, were seeing the whites of Duke's eyes less and less. A scramble was thwarted again by the City keeper and then a header saw the base of the post rapped, but it really did look like it was never meant to be. For either side. The match had 0-0 written all over it – and in truth, I was inwardly quite happy about the fact. Until...

Such selfish thoughts were rudely interrupted with an untimely error. Ah yes, the old 'human error' factor had not been filtered into my equation. Dean Marney was caught buggering around with the ball in his own box with six minutes remaining. Just welly it! Welly it anywhere! But no. Ben Watson robbed the midfielder and crashed in off the underside of the bar.

Oh dear. You knew that was game up. Pack it up and head home folks. It had been a woeful game, spoiled further by Watson's late goal. I wouldn't begrudge Wigan the win having certainly looked the most likely to score, but it was harsh on City who were punished for their only mistake in the 90 minutes.

In hindsight, this was one of the remaining fixtures I wasn't expecting anything from. But having had time to reflect on the events, perhaps smuggling a point out of Wigan could just about be argued as fair. Downhill and a backwind prevailing of course.

The second half fight-back left me encouraged City still have the desire to stay in this league, no doubt. But heed the warning of this first half showing. There is the answer why we sit precariously over the drop zone with just four points as a cushion. Work is still to be done. Portsmouth at home and Middlesbrough away – our next fixtures – are now clearly massive.

MATCH STATS:
- Wigan: Kirkland, Melchiot, Bramble, Boyce, Figueroa, Watson, Brown, Scharner (Kapo 77), N'Zogbia (De Ridder 46), Rodallega, Mido (Zaki 72). Subs Not Used: Kingson, Pollitt, Edman, Cho.
- Booked: Bramble.
- Goals: Watson 84.
- Hull: Duke, Ricketts, Zayatte (Folan 61), Turner, Dawson (Garcia 38), Mendy, Marney, Kilbane, Geovanni, Manucho, Fagan (Halmosi 82). Subs Not Used: Myhill, Doyle, Barmby, France.
- Booked: Ricketts, Mendy, Fagan.
- Att: 17,689
- Ref: Andre Marriner (W Midlands)
- **Premier League position: 13th**

THURSDAY 26TH MARCH 2009

Veteran striker Dean Windass has posted his last ditty on his tumultuous ITV internet blog, after returning to Hull City full time from a shortened loan stint with League One side Oldham Athletic... The ageing striker has called time on his blog after the forward returned from his loan stint with League One Oldham Athletic early (a deal taken out in January and supposed to last the rest of the season) with rumours of discontent reportedly sweeping through the Latics camp.

Windass was due to stay with the Lancashire club until the end of the season – including any play-off games that may come Oldham's way – but the 39 year old striker chose to end his spell early following the unrest in the Boundary Park camp and take an opportunity to coach the Tigers' youngsters.

But the controversial blog that has landed the experienced striker in hot water with Hull City manager Phil Brown on numerous occasions this season has now also been pulled by the player's own choice. Err...I think it's a bit late for that now, Deano! Stable door, horse and bolted springs to mind.

An ITV a statement on their website sounded devastated when claiming - *"Dean's loan spell at Oldham has now been terminated and he has returned to Hull where he will be concentrating on coaching the club's youngsters and playing for the reserves. Sadly his deal to return to the KC Stadium stated he could no longer continue with his media work which means there will be no further updates to this blog."*

As an aside, Windass is not eligible to play for the Hull City first team under the terms of his loan, but has made a scoring return for the reserves, helping City's second string to a 2-0 victory over Bolton Wanderers.

MONDAY 30TH MARCH 2009

Yadda, yadda... Former England and Newcastle United winger Chris Waddle has stated Hull City are in freefall and will be relegated from this season's Premier League. Funny though, cos the Geordies will just about survive. Yawn...

You know when you're getting older; you start to lose your marbles. Well, Chris Waddle is possibly at that stage in his life now. Apparently, Hull City are in freefall and destined to be relegated. Yet incredibly, Newcastle United will survive a drop into the Championship in a surprise claim! That team who we've played four times and not lost once against...?

Here's what he had to say on matters regarding Premier League relegation, the expert that he is – *"It looks to me as though Hull are in freefall, and I fear nothing can save them. People say they have had a great season, but that is not strictly true."*

Continuing – *"What they had was a great start to the season, and they certainly shocked and surprised some of the big guns with the way they set about them. They attacked all opposition, were not respecters of reputations, and full credit to them for that. They also had their Brazilian Geovanni banging in spectacular goals, and delivering from set plays."*

Before concluding – *"But now they have been found out a bit. They are finding out you cannot get away with making as many mistakes in the Premier League like you could down in the Championship. Their goal difference is not good either, and I think that will work against them in the final analysis."*

CHAPTER 9 – LOOK NORTH WHILE HEADING SOUTH

FRIDAY APRIL 3RD 2009 – HULL CITY V PORTSMOUTH PREVIEW

The Premier League swings into action once more following an international break with Hull City hosting Portsmouth. Striker Craig Fagan has been asking the home fans to be vocal, but one thing is assured, the visitors will be.

When your striker comes out in the media and asks the home fans to make a racket and get behind the team, I'm actually quite disappointed. Not with the player, more with myself and others around me. In fact, all of us attending. We may think we're doing a good job, but are we?

You see, if us fans were doing being vociferous enough, why would Craig Fagan come out and ask for more from our support? And if you think you're one of the vocal ones among the City ranks, what are you doing to encourage others? This is a joint effort, not a personal crusade. If you're reading this and you don't make a noise, change that habit tomorrow.

In the corresponding fixture back in the autumn, the sold out away end was putting the revered home support to shame, despite some officious stewarding in archaic (seats chucked on traditional terracing) facilities. Granted, hardly Portsmouth's fault - the terracing, I mean. But City fans can do it and against some of the louder groups of fans too. We must be ready to do it again.

Indeed, Portsmouth fans were probably embarrassed by the ridiculous 'Punch and Judy' show prattling on adjacent to the away fans, making a god-awful din with cowbells and such. The home support were no doubt cringeing at the opposite end. It stifled what was supposed to be an atmospheric Fratton Park, let me tell you.

In fairness, those travelling north this Saturday for such a critical fixture will enjoy a role reversal if we're not careful. Unquestionably, the Portsmouth fans housed in the North Stand will make a row – and it could humble us. City fans have to recapture that early season atmosphere again in the Premier League and bellow out some pride.

It really is at the stage of the season where everything counts. And I mean everything. Me, you, the bloke stood next to you, those in the South Stand and the rest of the ground have to stand up and be counted. Be loud, proud and there for the team. It's paramount.

We fans have a duty tomorrow. That duty is to recreate those heady days when we could generate an intimidating home atmosphere against the ilk of Swansea on Tuesday night with just 100 away fans rattling around in the North Stand. We've done it before, we can do it again. Now is our time. Let's not have these southerners lauding it on our manor. Stand up if you're Hull City.

Getting off my soapbox; the game. As for team news, Daniel Cousin is not going to start the match, but may be fit enough for a place on the bench. A late fitness test will determine the fate of the Gabonese striker. Richard Garcia arrived back at the club only today from Australian international duty and will also be assessed for reasons of fatigue.

What will be a major boost to manager Phil Brown and the rest of us with Hull City interests will be the return of influential skipper Ian Ashbee, after overcoming a hamstring strain. Plus, with England prospect Michael Turner and Guinea international Kamil Zayatte both fit to feature for the Tigers, a much steelier looking side will take to the field for a surefire battle.

On the match, Brown claimed – *"We probably need to win three out of the last eight – if we do that, we are probably looking at a top-half finish. Everyone is feeling the pinch, but if you had given me this position at the start of the season I'd have taken it. Seven teams are worse off than us, we are four points clear of the bottom."*

The visitors travel to the Circle with a fully fit squad to choose from. Peter Crouch is a picture of health despite fears while on England duty and will play, as will Glen Johnson and David James. Cheered them on Wednesday, we'll probably boo them tomorrow. Mad or what? Jermaine Pennant also returns for Portsmouth, after a recent thigh injury had kept him out of action.

Manager Paul Hart is wary of the trip north stating – *"It is a really tough game on their patch. Hull's players and the manager have done really well but they are scrapping for points just like we are. It would be a big boost to beat them and climb the table again but equally we don't want them strengthening their safety net by beating us."*

And if the Portsmouth manager is saying that before the game, then we – the home fans – have to make our advantage count during the game and prove Paul Hart correct. Hull City is a tough place to visit. Should we do so, the odds of a vital victory will surely swing in our favour. Come on City fans, it really counts now, it really does... Let's win it for the team.

SATURDAY 4TH APRIL 2009 - HULL CITY 0-0 PORTSMOUTH - REPORT

It wasn't the prettiest or the most fluent game in the Premier League this afternoon I'm sure, but it provided another point towards top flight survival and increased the gap to the bottom three. Under the circumstances, that will do.

You wouldn't exactly say 'job done' but this fixture could have ended far worse. As it is, a 0-0 draw proved to be about right with neither side truly testing their opposing keeper and clear cut chances at a genuine premium. A clean sheet never does a team any harm and today will leave both sides relatively confident of surviving the drop.

For the fans, well it wasn't the greatest spectacle on earth. The action was honest, even incident was sparse. In some ways, that was probably for the best from our point of view, because our penchant for leaking goals is apparent. Yet today, that never really looked like being the case.

The sun shone brightly, it was a pleasant afternoon at the Circle and, to begin with at least, the atmosphere was raucous. Once again though, the fabled enthusiastic Portsmouth support was found wanting. Perhaps Premier League-itis has finally caught up with Portsmouth? Would a trip back to the Championship do them any harm? As long as we're not joining them...

Portsmouth are a funny side. It's abundantly clear their squad has talent. But when you have three managers in a season, it's clear the players sometimes are not sure of their arse from their elbow. The visitors started brightly - Peter Crouch wasting an early free header with a pass back to Duke in goal - but something clearly is missing.

City had decided width was the key and adopted an attacking 4-5-1, assuming there is such a thing. Manucho was the lone striker but with a midfield of Fagan, Barmby, Ashbee, Geovanni and Mendy, attack was surely the name of the game. Dawson, Turner, Zayatte and Ricketts completed the side and the hosts looked reasonably set. Indeed, Brown's side perked up after the early Crouch header and Manucho drilled a shot wide at the near post when getting ahead of his marker. The main focus though, was on Glen Johnson. A wild challenge brought a booking and seconds later a rash lunge on Geovanni could well have seen a second booking, but referee Chris Foy called visiting skipper Sol Campbell over for a calming word.

To be honest, Johnson was a hothead all game. It was only heading one way... City perked up and enjoyed the territory and possession after Portsmouth's early show, but chances were still hard to come by. Barmby in particular having an effective game. It wasn't exactly lifeless as a contest with much at stake, but neither side were prepared to seriously gamble on winning the match it seemed.

At half time, you felt City's best way of triumphing in the contest would be from a set-piece. A corner, a Geovanni freekick, something pre-meditated. A strike from open play was looking less likely and with Portsmouth snuffing out the wide play from Mendy and Fagan - and the threat of their pace - City appeared out of ideas after the break.

But that said, Portsmouth were still pretty much predictable going forward and Turner and Zayatte covered everything, while Duke looked steady and untroubled barring a couple of 'choice' leaves. Either it was excellent goalkeeping, or the City stopper had been beaten all ends up. The jury is still out.

The best City chance of the second half came when a mix-up between goalkeeper David James and his defenders saw Craig Fagan nip in, prod the ball goalwards, but an acrobatic recovery from James saw the keeper palm the ball wide. Portsmouth then had Nico Kranjčar drill across the face of goal and any touch would have seen the visitors leading.

Then, a key moment saw Glen Johnson lose control of the ball and lunge in on substitute Dean Marney with ten minutes remaining, and that saw the England man booked again and sent from the field of play. Admittedly, time was short, but a chance was now presented to us to earn victory.

Sadly, City wasted their numerical advantage, rarely threatening to exploit it. Shots from distance by Ian Ashbee had been our only other sniff of goal and it didn't look like changing any time soon with the Tigers dilatory in their approach.

Incredibly, right at the death, Portsmouth won a free kick in the City half and almost snatched a late winner. Floated to the back stick, Hreidarsson looped a header back across goal and Duke left the ball... to strike the base of the post. Jeez! Too close for comfort. City hacked it clear and that was that.

At the whistle, half of me was pleased with the clean sheet and the point, the other half disappointed a chance to push on was spurned, particularly with the bottom three teams all losing. But then, that is the key. At the end of the day, it proved to be a point gained and one more fixture has been chalked from the list.

Overall, it's a true gain. Five points clear and just seven games left, we'd take that, we all would. Just ask those in the bottom three for proof of that point. Middlesbrough away next Saturday now looks increasingly important. Come on City, let's make it count. We're still on course for survival and that's all that really matters at this stage.

MATCH STATS:
- Hull City: Duke, Ricketts (Folan 85), Zayatte, Turner, Dawson, Mendy, Ashbee, Barmby (Marney 74), Geovanni, Manucho, Fagan (Kilbane 71).
- Subs: Myhill, Garcia, Halmosi, Featherstone.
- Portsmouth: James, Kaboul, Campbell, Distin, Hreidarsson, Johnson, Mullins, Hughes, Nugent (Kanu 64), Kranjčar (Belhadj 76), Crouch.
- Subs: Begovic, Pennant, Belhadj, Basinas, Pamarot, Utaka.

- Sent Off: Johnson (80)
- Ref: Chris Foy (Liverpool)
- **Premier League position: 15th**

THURSDAY 9TH APRIL 2009

With the bottom of the Premier League really tightening up, the impending game with Middlesbrough is crucial. Phil Brown says he will do everything to cover off any attempts to sabotage Hull City's quest for three points by former loan star Marlon King – now he's at Middlesbrough...

It would be some irony. Marlon King netted the winner for Hull City against Middlesbrough in the Premier League at the Circle back in December, with a late penalty that provided a welcome 2-1 over Gareth Southgate's side. Now, the Jamaican is at the Riverside, but Phil Brown appears unfazed by the fact.

Brown explained – *"I think the reason we let him go was because he wasn't bringing to the table what he brought to the table at the start of the season. It is as simple as that. The situation moved on; we moved forward fairly quickly - and Wigan moved forward fairly quickly. Middlesbrough acted upon it and the rest is history."*

Adding – *"I don't know what Marlon's record is since he's gone up there, but he hasn't played regularly for them. Would he have played regularly for us? He wasn't in the team when he left, so the answer is probably no. I think every time players cross the white line, if they have got anything about them, will have a point to prove. The game is not about Marlon King or me - it is about Hull City getting three points. If Marlon King stands in our way, he's got to bring his best game to the table."*

Before concluding – *"Whether they start with Alves and Tuncay, whether Marlon King is on the bench, it doesn't matter. Whatever team they put out, they'll be fighting for their lives. We have to make sure we keep that quiet, we choke it as much as we can, keep a lid on it and play some football. If we get those things right we've got a chance of winning the game."*

FRIDAY 10TH APRIL 2009 – MIDDLESBROUGH V HULL CITY PREVIEW

For some time now – and perhaps even at the cost of results against other teams before this fixture – the Middlesbrough match has been hoisted up high on to a pedestal.

Maybe our eye has been taken of the ball over the last couple of weeks. In the background - lurking menacingly - is this vital clash. The North Yorkshire outpost side has been struggling for form since surprisingly rolling over Liverpool 2-0 back in February.

As a consequence, our hosts are now languishing in deep, deep relegation trouble - and in truth, nothing short of victory against Hull City will suffice after a poor series of results have left Southgate's side five points adrift of safety and further two points behind us.

By accident or clever design, Hull City have kept a remarkably low profile leading up to this game. Hardly any media soundbites have been coming from the Tigers' camp. It's almost as if the shop has closed for Easter early. The dialogue coming out of the club has been as barren as I can remember this season. With good reason? Are we happy to let Middlesbrough hog the limelight? It would appear so.

Predictably, up in the north of the county, that most certainly has not been the case. All manner of voices have been clamouring for the media spotlight this week and one almighty din has been pouring out of the Riverside from all corners that have homogenised into a big messy dirge.

Firstly, the club, the players and the fans all seem to be at loggerheads with each other and rumours of Gareth Southgate losing the dressing room are rife. Beginning with the fans, they are angry with the Boro boss for performances and results, the players for not 'wanting it' and the chairman for not sacking the beleaguered manager earlier. Protests are abound for our visit against all of the aforementioned.

Meanwhile, Southgate has been banging the Boro drum all week and placing huge emphasis on the importance of victory against Hull City. The manager has built this game up into one of huge importance and is in danger of taking the hyperbole to new and unreachable limits. While the message is clear, the incessant nature of putting such thoughts across is surely piling enormous pressure on the team? Mind you, his players have been doing likewise, are they just setting themselves up for a fall?

It's a fair question to ask; are Middlesbrough able to cope with such internal pressure placed on them? This is the crux of the entire fixture for me. Middlesbrough have more often than not failed to deliver when it matters. Results have been poor for some time; the team are lacking fight and tenacity. The mindset appears to be far from one groomed and primed for a relegation scrap.

Indeed, therein probably lays the problem. Middlesbrough do not seem to have the heart for a fight. Players are probably past caring what happens, the better ones will be picked off by other Premier League clubs if the worst happens so won't care anyway, others will have release clauses built in. Where is the stomach for a fight in the Boro camp in such circumstances?

This does play into City's favour. As fledglings of the Premier League, the hunger and desire for a scrap still burns brightly for the top flight's newest club. Phil Brown's side may lack the depth in (fit) quality, but will not be allowed to cross the whitewash without desire to fight for every ball, strain every sinew for the right result, or turn in an abject performance without serious consequences.

If there is one thing I'm certain of, we'll have the right mentality for what I reckon will become a war of attrition that we can win. And would be favourites to win in my opinion. Guts and determination are not traits I'm seeing in the Middlesbrough camp. Quality – if it can be bothered – are what I see in the hosts. But can Southgate motivate his side for the game, though? Do the players want to be motivated for a team who will greet them with blood and thunder?

Phil Brown will probably be without Daniel Cousin once again, as the niggling back problem continues to plague the striker. Richard Garcia may earn a recall after starting on the bench against Portsmouth following international duty with Australia. But the best news of all is George Boateng returning to bolster the midfield after three months out. Although, this week at least, he will probably start on the bench.

In a rare soundbite before the game, Phil Brown commented – *"I think we have to keep faith with the team that's tightened up. People might class last week against Portsmouth as a boring 0-0 draw, but it was far from that in the first half."*

And continued – *"To keep a clean sheet was key and clean sheets are going to be paramount in the last seven games. If we can get one on Saturday, that means we will have a point or three. That will put further space between us and Middlesbrough."*

So how will Middlesbrough be squaring up to the match? Well, unluckily for them, Emmanuel Pogatetz has a knee injury and will be a huge loss; Gary O'Neill is suspended and Adam Johnson is battling to overcome an ankle injury and will need a late test. Ex-Tiger - and matchwinner for Hull City at the Circle - Marlon King will likely start from the bench.

Gareth Southgate warned anyone who would listen – *"You have to fight right to the end and there is nobody at the club who accepts that we are down. While there is hope you keep battling although we understand how difficult it is going to be."*

Adding – *"On Saturday we have a great game. It's a bit of a local derby - Hull will bring a big crowd with them but it is an opportunity for us to get back into the fight because at the moment we are a bit out of it. The win could take us back into it."*

And the Middlesbrough boss is not wrong. A 4,000 travelling sell-out will arrive at the Riverside to add to what is already being touted as a tinderbox atmosphere, due to the expected protests from the locals. The fixture is probably the most anticipated match of the season – and was already one to look out for when the Premier League fixtures first came out.

There is much debate about this being a proper derby, but what cannot be denied is two traditional working class locations, steeped in Yorkshire heritage, clashing once again. In days gone by, this fixture has caused fireworks. Saturday is unlikely to be an exception to the standard rule.

SATURDAY 11TH APRIL 2009 –
MIDDLESBROUGH 3-1 HULL CITY – REPORT

Hull City turn in an uncharacteristically abject performance at the most unwelcome of times and allow themselves to be reeled back into the relegation melting pot, when gifting Middlesbrough a top flight lifeline...

I had to be up early this morning to catch the train. Miscalculation of the bus times by someone who shall remain nameless – but he's a co-editor of this heavy bag full of fanzines I'm labouring up the street – meant there wasn't a bus at all. I'd got up early, walked miles to the bus stop, only to find 'NS' means 'Not Saturday' and not 'Not Sunday'. So, like Jesus' penance with the cross before crucifixion, here I am this Easter Saturday toiling my way onwards to town with a bag that was nailing me. And worse still, the stupid trains weren't running directly to York then Middlesbrough. Oh no. To Leeds, back on the bus to York, then Middlesbrough. Bah!

Eventually beer passed my lips on the train in towards our destination. The traditional Daily Star sports quiz was pathetically amassed to a below par 74 per cent and all the ingredients were beginning to stack up towards a horrible day. Now is not the time for horrible days. Welcome to the business end of the Premier League season.

A sell-out 4,000 following shows the people of Hull recognise how important this fixture actually is. Yet critically, they didn't shout about the matter enough, indeed hardly at all. As tame an atmosphere I can remember this season from our away following and another contributing factor to what eventually turned out to be a pitiful day. And yes, I take a small amount of blame for being amongst the muted 4,000.

It appeared as though the teams had swapped shirts from the first whistle. All day long countless Boro fans had warned us 'we always say we're up for it, but we never are'. This was possibly an 'in joke' to hoodwink us Premier League newbies. Well, it certainly worked. No sign of any supposed protests either, before, during or after the game. Hmmm... something fishy is going on here...

And with Boro 'not being up for it' Tuncay was ramming the ball in from the angle after keeper Matt Duke spilled Afonso Alves shot into his path inside three minutes. Great. Just what we need. The Riverside was now alive. And as for those protests? What protests? I kid you not, *"One Gareth Southgate!"* Fickle? You couldn't make it up!

For a brief spell City recovered from the short, sharp early shock. Manucho was towering in the box to leap highest and plant a firm header into the top corner and parity was restored by the ninth minute. At this point, the Tigers looked alive with Nick Barmby running on pure adrenalin and really pumped up for the occasion.

But you did feel, this had to be City's time. This had to be the moment to puncture Boro again. While they're down, while they're wounded. Geovanni was good surging forward carrying the ball, but the delivery from wide was sub-standard. Craig Fagan sparked a scramble in the box when dalliance in the Boro defence was almost punished, as City's no.7 nicked in ahead of keeper Brad Jones – but the ball was pushed far too wide to turn in.

A moment of real controversy then arrived. Tuncay battled with Dawson for the ball and the defender cleared. But a corner was signalled with ball clearly still in play. Skipper Ian Ashbee earned a booking for vehement protests - and then still chuntering – lost his cool from the corner and lost marker as well, leaving Matthew Bates to sweep in from six yards. What an absolute choker.

Two shocking mistakes. And it doesn't matter who you are at this level, such mistakes will be roundly punished. It's not like Middlesbrough had been made to work for their goals either. For all their huffing and puffing Boro's rich rewards were presented on a silver platter by us and it was now becoming evident this wasn't going to be our day.

I'm sitting there smouldering at our ineptitude, but restraining my swelling ire by reminding myself I am determined to enjoy our Premier League ride come what may. And consoling myself the second half couldn't really get any worse, of course. Well it couldn't, could it? Greeting me for the second half was Dean Marney. Was Mendy injured? Actually, had Mendy been on the pitch? Oh dear.

City tried to get themselves back into the game but never truly got among a pretty rickety back four the hosts were presenting. The width wasn't enough, penetration was poor and the final ball was lacking quality. It was interesting to note that Tuncay, Alves and Aliadiere were adept at earning easy free-kicks when any City defender went near them. Inviting the tackle and then hitting the deck instantly. Yep, Boro are wizened on the Premier League's ways.

By contrast, City do this mad and frankly ridiculous 'honest English' approach, far more suited to the Championship standard of gallantly attempting to win the ball, as opposed to just accepting a soft free kick would be forthcoming. It's the finer points like these that are going to unpick our chances of survival and boost our relegation rivals. We're simply too green.

I'm watching Marney power a header over, then David Wheater head off the line from Manucho again, but City lack the creative ideas to put Middlesbrough truly under the cosh. Unless we get a free kick or a corner, we haven't got a prayer of scoring. Hang on, a corner! Marney - who had a mare to be honest - wafts in a flag kick way over everyone and the chance is spurned. Middlesbrough are getting tense now. George Boateng is now on the field for City to warm applause from all back at his former club, after a three month lay-off. I'm inwardly reassured our midfield has experience, stability and the bite is there again for the remaining six matches. George even fires in a decent effort in, but it's high and wide.

City are desperate, pouring forward with little or no effect and leaving huge gaps at the back now. Just before the 4 minutes warning to end the game arrives, it all goes horridly wrong. Boateng has a mad moment trying to be clever instead of just hacking clear, tangles himself up, loses the ball, allows Marlon King in... goal. Well, that's that, then. 3-1 Boro. Now, about that calming midfield influence...

I'm enjoying this, I keep telling myself. But I'm lying. Who am I kidding, eh? I know this team are capable of far better. But not today.

And if that's Boro's best game brought to the table, I'm sticking to my guns that West Brom, Middlesbrough and Newcastle are the three sides to fall from this league.

As for us, I doubt we'll win again playing like this. Fortunately, though, we might not have to courtesy of our great start. Boro won't get an easier three points this season, that's for sure. So, we have to park this result, box it off and move on.

Sunderland away next, I bet you all can't wait!

MATCH STATS:
- Middlesbrough: Jones, McMahon, Wheater, Huth, Taylor, Bates, Aliadiere (Emnes 90), Downing, Sanli, Alves (Adam Johnson 77), King. Subs Not Used: Turnbull, Hoyte, Shawky, Riggott, Walker.
- Booked: Sanli, Bates, Taylor.
- Goals: Sanli 3, Bates 29, King 90.
- Hull City: Duke, Ricketts, Zayatte, Turner, Dawson, Fagan (Boateng 71), Mendy (Marney 46), Ashbee, Barmby (Folan 62), Geovanni, Manucho. Subs Not Used: Myhill, Halmosi, Kilbane, Featherstone.
- Booked: Ashbee, Ricketts.
- Goals: Manucho 9.
- Att: 32,255
- Ref: Phil Dowd (Staffordshire)
- **Premier League position: 15th**

SUNDAY 12TH APRIL 2009

The word buzzing round the internet is Marlon King – ex Tiger loanee and yesterday's man of the match – rather pointedly sent Hull City manager Phil Brown his winning bottle of champagne. Yes, all very grown up Marlon.

FRIDAY 17TH APRIL – SUNDERLAND V HULL CITY PREVIEW

The second of our double-header to north eastern destinations takes places this weekend with a trip to Sunderland – a team below us in the table so naturally... well, you know the rest. You don't really need me to spell it out, do you?

Still enjoying this Premier League adventure, then? I am. It may well have taken us 30 odd games to get here, but we're finally in this relegation scrap that every man and his dog said we would be in. It's been a thrill getting here – and as I promised myself right at the beginning of this journey – I am going to enjoy this top flight trip come what may.

Almost immediately following the final whistle at the Riverside last weekend, the result was forgotten. There was no use crying over spilt milk, what was done, was done. So onwards we go and to Sunderland as we head for our second visit to the north east in a week.

But here's a thought for you all. The last time City turned in a performance as below par as the Middlesbrough one, was probably rivalling the debacle at Everton away in January. Next came Newcastle away in the FA Cup. The response from the team that day was first class. In recompense, the Tigers defeated the Magpies at St James Park 0-1. Food for thought...

City do need a reaction this weekend at Sunderland – a team languishing below us in the table. The lessons from Middlesbrough need to be learned and quick. Indeed, what happened at the Riverside will be a good indicator to what we can expect from the hosts this weekend. Only this time, we should be ready. We've done the dress rehearsal, as it were.

The Riverside experience should put us in better shape for the Sunderland game. If more of the experienced players come to the fore then maybe, just maybe, we can ride out the expected Sunderland storm and pick up valuable points. Preferably all of them. Here lays the key; experience.

Geroge Boateng is set to lead the midfield in skipper Ian Ashbee's absence. In what has been a largely flawless season, it is inappropriate for Ashbee to blot his copybook with a caution booking for dissent at Middlesbrough, which now means he misses the next two games. What was I stating about experience?

And again for experience reasons, I wouldn't be surprised to Matt Duke dropped after a mediocre and arguably error-strewn performance against Middlesbrough for Boaz Myhill. Then there is Kevin Kilbane. Maybe a timely recall against his former club will be considered in the hope of seeing a 'Marlon King' type of reaction against a set of supporters who had no time for him during his spell at the Black Cats.

With seemingly positive injury news to consider too, striker Daniel Cousin is reportedly approaching full fitness after a back problem and may well start. Bernard Mendy is another looking to get over a foot injury and must be a genuine consideration if City go up to Sunderland attempting to win the game.

Manager Phil Brown has warned ahead of the match – *"It's vital that we are more difficult to play against, we didn't work hard enough against Middlesbrough. I don't mind taking the rap if my players come off the pitch having given it everything, I'll take any criticism that comes our way then."*

Before adding – *"Against Middlesbrough we didn't put a shift in and that's not acceptable. I don't think there's a lack of belief, it's about using the knowledge of how we have won games in the past and getting back to the basics."*

On to Sunderland and boss Ricky Sbragia is in real danger of losing his job if his side don't beat us. Rumours are rife Alan Curbishley is about to take over if Hull City win this game. Weird, it only seems like a few weeks ago that old Ricky was the best thing since sliced bread. Oh... that's because he was. But now he isn't anymore. Aren't chairmen strange?

Sunderland are looking for four players to return to their side if all can prove their fitness. Those include Kieran Richardson, Steed Malbranque, Dean Whitehead and Andy Reid. However, George McCartney and David Healy will remain sidelined for City's visit.

Right, so here we go then. Middlesbrough has been parked for me and we head to Sunderland with a blank canvas. A reaction is due from the team and we really need one. Like everyone else with Hull City interests, I'm hoping it will be a victorious one. COME ON CITY! COME ON!

SATURDAY 18TH APRIL 2009 –
SUNDERLAND 1-0 HULL CITY – REPORT

Here we go again! More woes on the north east road and the uncomfortable realisation that the end to our first Premier League season is going to be dramatic and defining is now upon us. How are your nerves holding out?

Chaz Cabs arrived to collect me, on time as usual and ready for the road to our north east destination. The talk pre-match in the big cat that sped north up the A1 was similar to the train journey last week, namely this is 'must not lose' territory.

Seeing a better performance was an absolute must, but I could not hold my hopes up high as some. It had that horrible stench of an awful, scrappy, horrible 1-0 home win written all over it. On second thoughts, the performance is perhaps secondary. Getting the result is now everything. This is the business end of the season. Walking into Sunderland centre I met Dutch Ian for a pre-match snifter. The general consensus was our good start might save us, even if defeat comes at Sunderland. The theory being, one win for us before the end of the season means a likely three needed by Newcastle and/or Middlesbrough. And frankly, that's getting into miracle territory.

Leaving the William Jameson public house the team news that greeted us on entry to the Stadium of Light meant Mendy and Cousin would not be starting. This was disappointing and would mean only one recognised forward would be on the field in Manucho.

The key to this game was keeping the home fans quiet and the ball out of the net early on, if we planned leaving the Stadium of Light with points. After the early scares and exchanges and Djibril Cissé getting the wrong side of City's defence, a settled and composed City prodded the Sunderland defence intermittently.

What was evident once again – and worryingly it has to be said – was that the chances from open play were pretty much non-existent. Indeed, it has now become almost the norm to accept that City's best chance of a goal will come from a set-piece or a free-kick. Our threat from open play has practically vanished.

When those dead ball opportunities arrived, panic was apparent in the Sunderland defence, which did look edgy. More so than us it has to be said. But forcing Craig Gordon into a save just wasn't happening. Kevin Kilbane's shot being deflected for a corner and Geovanni's free-kick looping off the wall for another corner being our best chances.

Sunderland meanwhile, were not seeing as much of the ball as they perhaps would've liked for the home side. City had now quelled the crowd and kept the chances from the hosts to a premium and Myhill – like his opposite number – was rarely called into action.

As half time approached, the City fans chorused 'Just like a library!' to record the stony silence that was now greeting the home side. It was first half injury time though when a corner was poorly defended and Cissé was left unchecked at the back post. A deft header had turned the game around.

Suspicions of offside came to nothing, a good solid half of work was undone and City were trailing in a game they really shouldn't have been. All that good work was down the drain and I cursed my horrible pre-match prediction. Most annoying. And the Sunderland fans reminded us it was 'just like a library'. Fickle or what?

Phil Brown will have been gutted not to get the troops back in level and the difficult task in hand was now magnified. Form has not been pretty or filling anyone with confidence and you did wonder about the wider ramifications of this result if it stayed this way.

For the start of the second half, Myhill was called into action immediately to make a save from Cissé as Sunderland could and should have been 2-0 up. Tremendous goalkeeping had kept the Tigers in the game, no doubt.

But Sunderland had come out for the second period flying and Kenwyne Jones was nodding in a second for the hosts, but the flag this time ruled his effort out. It was hard to tell from the opposite end if this was right or wrong.

But what couldn't really be disputed was the fact Sunderland were leading. The reaction that was needed from City gradually came. Sunderland had begun to back off and the nerves had descended on the home team. That also transferred itself into the crowd. Phil Brown and the team had sensed this and now City looked to press their hosts and get back on terms.

Manucho had been winning a decent share of his headers up front, but the chase to the second ball was critically letting City down in the bid to force genuine pressure. The ball wasn't breaking for the visitors but actually making it break for us was an issue. The support from those around the target man was simply lacking.

However, the support in the away stand was not. The travelling contingent were doing their best to lift the team and territory and possession had swung round in City's favour. But crucially the chances had not. Sunderland appeared content to hit their guests on the break, but the final ball for both sides was proof enough why both struggle to score.

But Cissé's goal was shading matters and despite a flurry of substitutions from both sides, the game barely got above scrappy in terms of entertainment. That said, the Bernard Mendy and Kieran Richardson spat – he kicked me, he butted me, we never did anything ref, honest - was comedy gold.

And Mendy almost had the last laugh, much to the home crowd's ire, when making mincemeat of Richardson seconds later by turning him this way and that, but the dink across goal from the byline was cleared and the chance to draw level was gone.

Only Manucho blazing wildly, Dean Marney doing likewise and George Boateng's whistling drive had done enough to rouse City's hopes, but the most golden opportunity of the lot was Caleb Folan's free header from six yards, shamefully put wide with the goal gaping. It wasn't going to be our day.

At the death, with Sunderland praying for the whistle, a post was clattered by the hosts that would've lifted the end game tension in an instant, but as it was the home team had done enough, deservedly or otherwise. The jury is still out, but I'll stick my neck on the line here and say the winner was probably offside. No doubt Gary and boys on Match of the Day will put me right.

Whatever, City are once again looking for positives from a defeat - and it sucks to be honest. I suppose Sunderland - like Middlesbrough – never looked brilliant in victory and the threat looms just as large for them as it does us. And the performance was better by us than the week before, we are at least heading in the right direction in that respect.

But you know what? Stuff performances. I might well have mistakenly hoped for an improvement from the Middlesbrough game – and got one – but it's not about how well you play any more. It's all about results. I've revised my thinking. Give me getting outplayed, outfought and outclassed against Liverpool next week all for a dodgy own goal that wins us the game in the 90th minute.

We deserve it. And poor old chauffeur Charles does. Very quiet was the driver on the way home. I feel his pain. We're all in this together. Let's make it count, beginning next week at the Circle. We are not in the bottom three yet.

Let's not break the habit of our Premier League lifetime now. Chin up!

MATCH STATS:
- Sunderland: Gordon, Bardsley, Davenport, Ferdinand, Collins, Edwards (Malbranque 78), Leadbitter, Tainio, Reid (Richardson 76), Cissé (Murphy 90), Jones. Subs Not Used: Fülöp , Ben-Haim, Yorke, McShane.
- Booked: Cissé, Richardson.
- Goals: Cissé 45.
- Hull: Myhill, Ricketts, Zayatte, Turner, Dawson, Fagan, Geovanni (Mendy 74), Boateng (Barmby 77), Marney (Folan 68), Kilbane, Manucho. Subs Not Used: Duke, Doyle, Halmosi, Cousin.
- Booked: Turner, Kilbane, Fagan.
- Att: 42,855
- Ref: Mike Dean (Wirral)
- **Premier League position: 16th**

MONDAY 20TH APRIL 2009

Phil Brown is calling for those with genuine Hull City interests not to be lulled by the comments of some of the supposed Premier League expert pundits, confident his side will rise to the challenge and survive in the top flight...

The City boss has fired a warning shot across the bows of the pundits by claiming he and his players are ready for the challenge of the five games that will decide if their first ever season in the top flight is a success or a failure.

Brown began his comments with - *"We showed Champions League form in the first nine games but our form now has allowed some people to start writing about us. People like Mark Lawrenson have been coming out of the woodwork again to say they were right to write us off at the start of the season. We started as everyone's whipping boys and now people believe it again."*

Adding - *"The key is no one in our camp agrees. I still say the same thing - our destiny is still in our own hands. Liverpool is next up and we cannot hide from that challenge. They have 60 professionals who can play at this level so playing twice in five days means they have a squad to face Arsenal on Tuesday and us on Saturday."*

Before concluding - *"We are up against one of the better teams in the Premier League, there is no doubt about that. It is a challenge. People will write us off but I remember the commitment we showed at Anfield [in a 2-2 draw] when we could have got all three points."*

FRIDAY 24TH APRIL 2009

A month later, 'Spitgate' rumbles on... Arsenal's Cesc Fàbregas faces two charges of improper conduct following the recent FA Cup Quarter Final tie between the Gunners and Hull City, while Tigers boss Phil Brown will answer charges relating to post match comments about referee Mike Riley...

The turbulent FA Cup Quarter Final clash between Arsenal and Hull City at the Emirates Stadium in March has brought about three charges of improper conduct, following the FA Premier League's investigation to the stormy clash between the two clubs.

Cesc Fàbregas - accused of spitting at Hull City assistant manager Brian Horton - faces two charges following submissions of evidence from both clubs and video evidence capturing events. Meanwhile, Phil Brown has also not emerged from the fractious encounter unscathed.

An FA statement read -

"Fàbregas faces two charges of improper conduct relating to his conduct on the pitch following the game.

One charge concerns his behaviour in coming on to the pitch after the final whistle, the second charge relates to an alleged spitting incident. The charges are based on submissions from Hull City and video evidence.

Brown is charged with improper conduct and/or bringing the game into disrepute in relation to media comments made after the game concerning referee Mike Riley.

Fàbregas and Brown have until 12 May to respond."

FRIDAY 24TH APRIL 2009 – HULL CITY V LIVERPOOL PREVIEW

Title-chasing Liverpool roll into the Circle for a contest with survival-chasing Hull City, with the points a desperate necessity for both teams, albeit for vastly differing reasons.

You always got the impression when the Premier League fixtures were originally drafted up back in the summer of 2008, that the Liverpool match would have a lot riding on it. For both clubs obviously, but Liverpool's need to get points is now abundantly more acute than it was four days previously.

A quite stunning 4-4 home draw with Arsenal at Anfield has cast serious doubt on their title credentials, particularly with Manchester United managing a midweek home win over Portsmouth. The pressure at the head of the Premier League is now beginning to mount and replicate the trend the bottom half of the table – a trend that has prevailed for most of the season.

For quite differing reasons the game enters must-win territory for both clubs. Liverpool can kiss goodbye to ending two decades without a championship title if Hull City waltz away with points from this game. Especially as championship rivals Manchester United are three points clear and have a game in hand on the Reds.

Meanwhile, Phil Brown's side has won just once in the Premier League in 2009 – a 0-1 away success at Fulham in March – and as a consequence, City are painfully sliding at a slow but steady rate towards the trapdoor into the Championship. Such a pity, after a mind-boggling start to our inaugural top-flight season had seen the Tigers flying high in the top six when the club's last met.

Ah yes, that was December. It heralded our last home victory too. A 2-1 scratch affair with Middlesbrough that saw the Tigers fall behind with ten minutes remaining, yet showed amazing character to bounce back and win the game with two late goals. A week later, City rocked Anfield by racing into 0-2 lead before Steven Gerrard dragged the Reds back into the game to force a 2-2 draw.

It was an incredible afternoon. A 4-3-3 formation hit Liverpool hard, pushed the Reds backwards and stunned the most successful club in England. Bravery – or madness, depending on your opinion – had the Kop applauding come the final whistle. Liverpool fans' natural disappointment was overshadowed with a tinge of respect that a freshly-promoted side had actually had the gumption to turn up at Anfield and have a rare old go.

Walking out on to the Anfield Road that evening, I don't think I could be more proud of our manager, our team, our supporters. And thoughts of relegation? What the hell are you talking about? You would have been consigned to the loony bin had such thoughts been put into words.

And so here I am in the loony bin or the sanity ward - take your pick. Yes, I uttered such words to some Liverpool fans in the King Harry post-match. Comments of *"well played"* and *"you deserved it"* greeted us City supporters in our post-match (celebratory?) bevvy. I replied with *"Do you think we'll go down?"* *slaps forehead* Yes, 30 years of following Hull City does that to you. But worse... those words are now stalking me. Haunting me, in fact.

The Wednesday evening early in March at phenomenal home side Fulham apart, Phil Brown's side have struggled terribly since that splendid day in the red half of Liverpool. With just five games remaining, three points and two places are keeping us out of the dreaded drop zone – the urgency for a win is now painfully prevalent.

In many ways – and as ludicrous as it sounds – all the pressure is off us this Saturday. Like at Anfield, we are expected to get absolutely bugger all from the game. All our relegation rivals have written this fixture off as 'thank god Hull City have got Liverpool this week, no points there then.' And you know they have, because we all pontificate the same over Newcastle, Sunderland, Blackburn and Middlesbrough fixtures.

But we all know why the season has come off the rails. We haven't got three strikers fit to play 4-3-3 these days. Indeed, we haven't even got three strikers have we? Neither have we had the midfield personnel to do all the leg work with key players being ruled out for the season, or lengthy periods at the very least. And the defence has been constantly disrupted for exactly the same reasons. No doubt these are excuses, but facts all the same.

Thankfully, wily veteran George Boateng is back in the middle for the season's climax - which is timely - as skipper Ian Ashbee serves the second of his two-game suspension. Better news sees striker Daniel Cousin return from a back complaint and appears destined to figure somewhere at some point versus Liverpool. Plus, wide man Richard Garcia has overcome minor knee surgery and could return to Phil Brown's plans.

Hang on, with Nick Barmby about and primed to face his former club, we could piece together a 4-3-3 formation here... And what with the City boss talking about bravery from all those connected with the club... here, you're not thinking what I'm thinking, are you? Wow! That would be a bold statement. Hell, we could even chuck Caleb Folan into the mix... Balls to it! Why the hell not?

Now here's the kidology from Phil Brown. Or is it? The City boss on the game with Liverpool has warned – *"We'll try and frustrate them. We know we're not going to have much of the ball. They'll have a lot of possession, a lot of chances, a lot of corners, so we've got to defend properly. It's as simple as that."*

And then added – *"I've been talking about bravery all week. Bravery manifests itself in a number of ways. For the defenders it's about sticking heads in where the boots are flying. The same for goalkeepers. For strikers it's remaining calm in front of goal, or creative players remaining calm in the final third."*

Hmmm... Anyway, that's Rafa Benitez's problem. We're expecting nothing, as Phil Brown has indicated. Steven Gerrard will not be fit enough to rescue his side against the Tigers this time around, with a groin injury ruling the England man out. However, probably the best striker in the Premier League will be fit this time to face us, in Fernando Torres. Ouch!

Liverpool manager Rafa Benitez is wary of the battle ahead to claim – *"We know Hull are dangerous on set-pieces and hopefully we will not see the same situation we saw against Arsenal in midweek. They are a physical team and are fighting at the bottom of the table. Now they are in a position where they almost have to win every game as well so it will be tough."*

So, now the time for talking is done. It's all down to the two teams getting it on at a packed Circle and the best team going on to win the game. And believe it or not, I'm certain we will. I didn't just type that, did I? Pass me another beer...

SATURDAY 25TH APRIL 2009 – HULL CITY 1-3 LIVERPOOL – REPORT

Ten-man Hull City turn in a creditable performance against title-chasing Liverpool but end up with a slap across the chops for their efforts, with some highly contentious decisions surely getting an airing on Match of the Day later tonight. And I will be vindicated!

So here we are then, on a hiding to nothing but with everything to gain. Last night's beer and preview rambling deemed I'd foolishly written that we'd get something out of the game. When David Burns collared me for the BBC local radio build up I still hadn't changed my mind. I was still 'camped' in the 'we could get something' sector. As for Burnsey, well... it's not really my position to say...

But the media spotlight was trailing me far and wide. You could tell Liverpool were in town. Next, the polite and delightful BBC TV boys had waited patiently for a chat with me. Of course, I took a quick respite in my trailer before fixing my make-up in readiness for Match of the Day 2's Kevin Day. I must speak to my agent about getting my cut reviewed too...

Kevin was a warming character but led us both into the valley of no retreat by venturing Arsenal would've tired Liverpool out following the 4-4 at Anfield in midweek and 'we could get something'. Naturally I hurled myself headlong into Kevin's cunning trap and that prompted a *"Meet me after the game to discuss our prediction"* type closing. D'oh!

Entering the Circle, the atmosphere was as good as I can remember this season. The East Stand was boisterous and armed with the knowledge of MOTD 2's appearance, I was proud to be from Hull and proud to be supporting my team. A fact that was hurled vociferously at the Liverpool section penned in the North Stand. Right, this is it, what can my team do?

Let's be honest, motivation shouldn't be a problem. Indeed, taking anything off Liverpool would surely retire their title charge and duly set up a free hit against Manchester United on the final day, wouldn't it? Well, that was my theory anyway. Liverpool started brightly and the scale of the task was evident from early on. Benayoun looked fantastic and Torres sharp. Thankfully, the Spaniard blazed wide when well placed.

But the Tigers needed no encouragement to pour forward. Finding their feet after the opening exchanges and Benayoun clipping over the bar, Ricketts was tearing past Dirk Kuyt with consummate ease and the balls were certainly reaching the forwards. Caleb Folan found himself clean and clear but the recalled striker dallied, pulled the ball back instead of shooting and the chance was snuffed out.

The home crowd were encouraged and roared on their team. Boateng put in a big shift for the cause and reassuringly fills me with hope that his return could not have been timed any better for the scrap we now find ourselves in. Urged on by the buoyant home crowd, City kept coming with a strong work ethic and desire to reach every ball first.

Two cheap corners conceded by Liverpool threatened Pepe Reina's goal briefly but eventually came to nothing. Then Geovanni snorted a monster drive just past Reina's post from 25 yards and Liverpool now knew they were in a game. Midfield dynamo Dean Marney almost broke the deadlock when bravely heading in a goalbound effort but Arbeloa cleared off the Liverpool line. City were impressing.

With a fine half's work almost done, a contentious free kick was awarded by referee Martin Atkinson. Mascherano had scurried forward and then decked himself to con a cheap free kick that Martin Atkinson bought. Alonso drilled in, the wall did its job, but a perfect bounce back to the Spaniard allowed a second chance to hit it and you guessed it...

Unbelievable! How lucky was that? Call me cynical, but it wasn't even a free kick! Sure I may be setting myself up for a fall here when the Match of the Day boys mull over the decision from every angle and I'll wait to see if I'm vindicated. Or not. Whatever, I felt like I'd been kicked square in the nuts. City did not deserve to be losing this game and Liverpool were more than fortunate to be leading it.

At the break, it seemed the general consensus amongst the fans was that the Tigers were indeed luckless. I spent much of the 15 minute interval cursing myself for cursing us, by claiming 'Liverpool will come out all guns blazing second half'. Well, I thought it was going to be 0-0 at the time, didn't I? Bah!

It was evident Phil Brown's words had to penetrate a Hull City side distraught by the travesty of being a goal down. And sadly, the devaststion showed for the opening spell of the second period. Liverpool were now patiently dominating the possession but City were defending manfully. Sporadically, the hosts interjected with some swift counter-attack play, on the cusp of building up a head of steam.

Folan then hared after a long ball. It was 50-50 with Škrtel and the pair tussled in the box. Vying for the ball Škrtel just about got enough on the ball to divert it back to Reina and Folan did his usual kick into fresh air to mark his frustration as Škrtel flung himself to the ground attempting to gain another cheap foul. Why is he rolling around clutching his face? Referee Atkinson steams towards the pair. Red card for Folan! Whaaat? The atmosphere turned ugly and a crescendo of derision greeted the decision. Folan stood aghast, the crowd were smashing the atmosphere up with raucous boos. Never for one moment had it even looked like a booking incident let alone a red card. The Circle turned on referee Atkinson and booed Škrtel from this moment on. I can write this – and I will – it was blatant cheating. Again, Match of the Day can hang me if I'm wrong.

City had received a mortal body blow. Down to ten men and losing this game, Liverpool were hardly covering themselves in glory, not proving to the Hull public that they would actually be worthy champions of England. And wouldn't you know it, with City still shellshocked, Benayoun found Škrtel in the box and a poor header deflected most kindly to Kuyt, who could not miss from mere yards. And I haven't even mentioned Lucas handballing the thing in the build up. Frustration overload had just docked.

But for sure, I am proud of my team. Rather than recoil with ten men, roll over and die, Hull City roared like the Tigers they are and still went looking for goals. Geovanni hammered a free kick into the wall; a corner saw a mad scramble hacked clear by Liverpool desperately, as City roused themselves to first half levels looking to rectify the injustices served upon them.

Great work from Cousin on the right saw the returning striker, on from the bench, fox two defenders and pull back for an unchecked Geovanni – yes, unmarked despite only having ten men – to smash in an open goal and pull the score back to 1-2. The Circle was now in full voice and it was Liverpool doing the retreating as the depleted City side bravely looked to pile forward whenever they had the ball. Albeit limited as it was, as you would expect.

Indeed, Rafa Benitez was so coy about the precarious position he found his side in, off came attacker Yossi Benayoun and on came centre back Daniel Agger. Yep, the visitors were worried all right as an uncomfortable closing spell began to unfold. Liverpool did fashion a further chance for Torres, but the Spaniard crashed his header against the bar as obvious gaps now appeared for an ambitious home team.

Yet as brave as Phil Brown's team had been, Kuyt slammed in a second close range effort at the end to kill off any hopes of another shock 2-2 draw and the Circle vented their spleen at referee Martin Atkinson and Liverpool defender Martin Škrtel as the final whistle drew a veil over a highly contentious affair.

Now, reality dictates that we were never supposed to get anything anyway. But my hope had morphed into a decent atmosphere. In turn, that transposed itself onto the pitch. And then duly manifested into a top drawer performance from my team. My prediction may have been wrong – and now I have to go and have my chat with Kevin from Match of the

Day 2 – about how wrong I (we, actually) were, but I could hold my head high, proud of my team after that display.

At the meeting point, before the cameras rolled, Kevin felt certain Hull City would not be going down. Indeed, we'd been robbed with some atrocious decisions that will no doubt bear us out when the analysts tuck in later tonight on the telly. Either that or we'll both have even more egg on our faces, we concluded. But Kevin was encouraged by the mighty performance of our side.

And that for me was the 'something' I had hoped we could take from our encounter with Liverpool. Yes, we didn't get any points, granted. But the 'something' we did get was a performance, commitment, bravery, a never-say-die attitude, togetherness, a will to actually win. It may not have happened for us today, but I've never felt more confident that we will do this. Hull City will survive. There, I said it.

MATCH STATS:
- Hull City: Myhill, Ricketts, Zayatte, Turner, Kilbane, Fagan (Mendy 62), Boateng (Manucho 79), Marney, Geovanni, Barmby (Cousin 62), Folan. Subs Not Used: Duke, Hughes, Garcia, Halmosi.
- Sent Off: Folan (59).
- Booked: Marney, Barmby, Fagan.
- Goals: Geovanni 72.
- Liverpool: Reina, Arbeloa, Carragher, Škrtel, Insua, Kuyt (Dossena 90), Alonso, Mascherano (El Zhar 84), Benayoun (Agger 87), Lucas, Torres. Subs Not Used: Cavalieri, Riera, Aurelio, Ngog.
- Booked: Arbeloa.
- Goals: Alonso 45, Kuyt 63, 89.
- Att: 24,942
- Ref: Martin Atkinson (W Yorkshire)
- **Premier League position: 17th**

SUNDAY 26TH APRIL 2009

Just seen Match of the Day 2. Worryingly I look like a Liverpool fan with a red tracky top on. A grave faux-pas on my part on reflection. Worse, in a direct response to me telling Kevin Day that if those decisions by referee Martin Atkinson are correct and I – actually we – are wrong, maybe the BBC can conduct some neat editing. Presenter Adrian Chiles then warned me and the watching Sunday evening nation – *"Actually, no we can't edit those decisions."* Frankly, I find this is an outrage. What the hell do I pay my licence fee for? Pah!

TUESDAY 28TH APRIL 2009

Dean Windass' Hull City career now appears to be over with reports surfacing in the national press suggesting the 40 year old forward has been asked to leave the club with immediate effect, as the Tigers concentrate on Premier League survival.

Windass has been pretty much unsettled at the club throughout most of our top flight tenure and thoughts and feelings expressing as such via his ITV blog did little to appease manager Phil Brown's opinion.

The evergreen forward decided in January to team up with former team mate John Sheridan at Oldham Athletic in an effort to get the Latics into the League One play-offs, but a wretched and tumultuous two months coincided with a sharp downturn and in-house fighting at Boundary Park that has cost the club any chance of the play-offs.

Now, it is believed Windass has been told not to return to the club again this season by manager Phil Brown – seriously jeopardising chances of securing a coaching role in the future at the club – with a severance deal reportedly being sought.

In the meantime, speculation has been heightened with news reports suggesting the Hull born striker could be about to take over from under-pressure Bradford City manager Stuart McCall, after the Bantams missed out on featuring in the League Two play-offs this season.

CHAPTER 10 –
AND NOW, THE END IS NEAR...

FRIDAY 1ST MAY 2009

Yes, one time Liverpool legend and Newcastle United messiah for whatever year it was back then – Kenny Dalglish – has been roused from his pundits chair to assess the relegation scrap from the Premier League...

And guess what peeps? Yes! That's right! Hull City are going down! Again! No surprise that pundit king Kenny has plumped for former club Newcastle United to survive and we all know now that it's West Bromwich Albion, Middlesbrough and ourselves for the drop. You can all sleep easy, Newcastle are safe!

Here's what the former Newcastle management expert had to say - *"I think they'll [Newcastle] stay up. I think it was a difficult game against Pompey and maybe if either Obafemi Martins or Michael Owen put their chances away, they could've been sitting there with three points."*

Adding on the Toon with the 'BIG IF' thrown in for good measure - *"Obviously a goal gives everyone a bit of confidence. They've got two home games left - Bolton and Middlesbrough. If they win those two, they've got 37 points."*

Before claiming scientifically - *"Look at Hull. If they get three points against Bolton, it'll be them on 37. I don't see too many points coming for either Newcastle or Hull apart from that so Newcastle would stay up on goal difference."*

SUNDAY 3RD MAY 2009 - ASTON VILLA V HULL CITY PREVIEW

Hull City prepare for their Aston Villa test this Bank Holiday Monday with a free hit, as the rest of the sides above and below the Tigers in the relegation scrap failed to record a single point between them this weekend in the Premier League. Which is nice...

Before the weekend began, I freely admit I was filled with dread. Hull City had to travel to Villa for an 8pm kick off, potentially knowing we could be in the bottom three by the time the game arrives with all the other Premier League fixtures played before ours. And worse, there would be nothing we could do about it.

Then, should the damning actually arrive, we'd have to go to Villa and attempt to repair any sustained damage, under pressure, filled with nerves and relying on form that has been less than complimentary until perhaps the second half of the recent Sunderland away game and Liverpool at home last weekend.

If the green shoots of recovery are now appearing for us, I guess we'll find out for definite with our match against Villa. We have four games left to ensure our Premier League status – four games that will define our club. And quite possibly, change the perception of our Hull City for the long term.

But rewind to Saturday lunchtime. For the first time ever in 30 odd years of supporting City – be it by accident or design – I made a conscious (or subconscious?) effort to follow all our rivals over the net, on the telly, or on the radio while driving the car and doing the household chores that blight us all. I was kicking every ball for Manchester United at Middlesbrough. I punched the air when Ryan Giggs scored and belted out a very audible 'YES!' Then Ji Sung Park grabbed a second and made sure Middlesbrough would be beaten in the first Premier League game of the weekend. Well, we'll take that.

Anyone who knows me will be raising eyebrows right now, as they know I truly loathe Manchester United with a passion. But this is the Premier League. This is what it does to you. I'm resigned to cheering on Manchester United for crying out loud! I'm still coming to terms with this, it feels really odd. In fact, I think I need a lie down...

Results are flooding in on Soccer Saturday... West Brom lost... CHECK. Stoke City lost... CHECK. Blackburn lost... CHECK. Wow! Not bad, not bad at all. On Sunday, me, my wife Suzy and the kids pile back into the car after a day at the park. I turn the radio on and Liverpool have smashed Newcastle United 3-0. Excellent news! So now, here I am cooking tea in my kitchen with Sunderland v Everton crackling in the background on the radio.

Indeed, more by accident than design, I think I've stumbled upon the secret to making a good shepherd's pie. I'll let you all in on it...It's hearing Marouane Fellaini slamming in Everton's second against a woeful Sunderland (5 Live commentary, not mine) to wrap up the game at the Stadium of Light for the Toffees and leave the Black Cats teetering on the relegation brink, just one point and one place above us. Brilliant! And clean plates all round at the dinner table too! Told you!

So what a weekend it has proved to be so far. Scared witless before it all kicked off, here we are in the privileged position of knowing whatever we gain at Villa Park is making ground on our relegation rivals. And if, as pundits expect, we don't achieve anything, we've not really lost a great deal other than a game of football. And the whole shebang moves onto just three matches left with us three points clear of the drop.

For the first time in months, you could argue a case that Phil Brown's team can play with a little more freedom and little less pressure because of this weekend's flattering results sequence elsewhere. And Villa are not exactly setting Villa Park alight these days with just one home win in 2009. Wow! That bad, eh? Dare we suggest a point or more? I'll shut my mouth after my natter with Match of the Day 2's Kevin Day last week, I think...

City will travel to the Midlands without striker Caleb Folan who begins a three-game ban for his sending off at home to Liverpool. Daniel Cousin is likely to be fit enough to start and will be favourite to claim the shirt left by the Irish international. Left back Andy Dawson will also come into contention for a place, after being added to the squad.

And manager Phil Brown warned – *"On Monday we will have a game plan and hopefully we can get something from the game. Aston Villa have had a great season and have been pushing for a top-four spot this season. But they are on a slightly bad run of form as well, so it should be an interesting game."*

Indeed, Aston Villa are stuck in a rut form-wise and the hosts have lost their top four berth and have now slipped behind Everton to sixth in the table. Luke Young is struggling with a foot injury but may still play, while Gabriel Agbonlahor and Nigel Reo-Coker are hoping to overcome their respective injuries in time for the game with City.

Villa boss Martin O'Neill is aware of the sketchy form his side are now in, to relate it all to us, when stating – *"They had such a fantastic start, after nine or ten games they had more points than Manchester United. I am sure they thought because of the start they would get to about 40 points more quickly than they have done. What happens is you lose confidence. Then it starts to bother you. The league is unforgiving. It is difficult if you get on a losing streak."*

Now, I don't know about anyone else, but perhaps dear old Martin veered off on a tangent with that statement, forgot he was actually talking about Hull City and subconsciously reverted to type about his own club half way through his statement. Just a thought, like... Anyhow, here we go then, a 'free hit' for City is here and it's all on Sky. COME ON CITY!

MONDAY 4TH MAY 2009 – ASTON VILLA 1-0 HULL CITY – REPORT

Hull City lose at Villa Park and miss the opportunity to pull themselves further away from the drop zone, but perhaps can argue a case that for the second time in three games, the only goal should not have stood. This is sounding all too familiar this season...

A battle of two of the Premier League's off-form clubs. A Monday night escapade to Villa Park could be more appealing, but in light of everybody in the bottom half failing to win over the weekend, perhaps City could use such as a motivational tool to drag themselves out of this sorry rut we find ourselves in.

Yet Villa are from enjoying a purple patch of form themselves. Just one win in 2009 has seen the Midlanders slide from Champions League territory and into the UEFA Cup places after a downturn in fortune almost as severe as ours has been. Because of such, there was always hope.

Browny named a team that had a relatively balanced look about it with Andy Dawson and Sam Ricketts occupying the full back berths, while the midfield saw the return of Bluenose Ian Ashbee to skipper the side following a two game ban, plus Richard Garcia and Kevin Kilbane to provide the width. Daniel Cousin was a welcome sight up front with Geovanni.

It was a decent start by the visitors. Bodies were coming forward and a willingness to attack appeared present. Garcia in particular looked lively and George Boateng hammered in a piledriver that was blocked. It was encouraging stuff from City and certainly gave Villa something to think about.

Then a hammer blow for City. Fresh from his two-game ban, Ian Ashbee launches into a crunching 50-50 tackle and probably for the first time ever comes off worse. After lengthy treatment – and a clear desire to stay on the pitch – the City skipper lasts only another minute before admitting defeat and being substituted.

But the hosts were soon getting into their stride, looking for Ashley Young out wide and the impressive John Carew in the centre. The tactic was working but Myhill wasn't being worked over and the defence was just about holding firm to keep the scores level.

At the other end, the very theme of City's recent problems has been creating chances from open play and getting a shot on target to test their opponents. The Tigers are not doing this enough, meaning corners or free kicks are our only realistic chances of getting on the scoresheet. But you can't fault the effort... Villa were soon being frustrated and the home fans were soon silenced as things were not going their way. The spirited visitors may be in relegation trouble, but they were far from being the soft touch the hosts may well have been expecting. It made for a rather chanceless encounter and 0-0 was looking about right.

Yet that changed and then some with a hint of controversy to boot. Boateng lost the ball on the edge of the Villa box as City looked to fashion an attack and a swift break saw Villa advancing up the field at and alarming rate. As the ball came in, Carew appeared offside, but the flag stayed down and the side-footed effort beat Myhill and stood.

The goal gave a pretty confidence-shorn Villa a shot in the arm and Myhill was pressed into action just before the break to beat out another shot arrowing in on goal after a slip at the back by the City defence. Strong presence and fists from the City keeper.

Gutted. Here we go again. Now the task was massively uphill and City probably needed more than a little luck to get back into this even now, with half time approaching and a full half to play. As the half ended Geovanni blazed an abysmal free-kick high and wide and then became embroiled with a spat with Daniel Cousin at the half time whistle that needed the City backroom staff to intervene.

Oh dear, trouble at mill. They say it's good; it's a sign of passion. For me, it shows we are in disarray. All is not well, or why would the players be bickering in the first place? Manager Phil Brown certainly had his work cut out in the dressing room, what can City do to turn this around? Enter Nick Barmby. For Geovanni... is this the end of the little Brazilian?

Villa were less cutting in the second half, but City lacked genuine penetration to threaten the back four or even get a shot in Friedel's goal. It was looking increasingly frustrating, particularly as the hosts were getting more and more nervous as the match progressed. The need to conjure something, anything, was now becoming pressing.

But the best chances fell to Villa. Gareth Barry drew a magnificent save from Boaz Myhill and then from an outrageous free kick that should have prompted an offside flag for Agbonlahor, play was incredibly allowed to continue and the cross came in with the forward still offside and deemed inactive. His header produced an excellent save from Myhill. The boos were loud from City's fans.

It sparked the best spell of pressure by City as Villa retreated into their shell and clung on to what they had. Manucho was now on and the ball was sticking up top. A double free kick eventually forced Friedel into conceding a corner as City had their best moments from set-pieces.

The big Angolan headed downwards from one centre but Friedel covered it. There was not enough power to sneak it in, allowing the save. It was getting late, but City were much more advanced now and finishing much the stronger and Villa were now pushed back. A series of corners were won as the hosts desperately hacked away the inswinging deliveries.

With injury time now upon us, Myhill piled into the box to add to the pressure in the packed penalty area. But with time against City nothing came from the foray forward and referee Mike Dean blew for time to give a pretty relieved Villa all the points and only their second home win in the last four months.

Back at the bottom, still with the three-point gap as the rest of the bottom half laboured equally badly, but City are never going to get a better opportunity to stay in this league and must start taking charge of their own destiny. And if we're honest, we all know the next two games will truly be the pair that decide our seasonal fate – not what happened this Monday evening at Aston Villa.

Anyway, I still believe. Upon exiting a kindly steward reminded me to keep my chin up, because they want Newcastle relegated. And the Geordies are at Villa Park on the final day. *"Don't worry! We'll beat 'em for you"* was the parting shot exchanged between us.

MATCH STATS:

- Aston Villa: Friedel, Luke Young, Davies, Knight, Shorey, Milner, Petrov (Reo-Coker 90), Barry, Ashley Young (Gardner 90), Carew (Heskey 86), Agbonlahor. Subs Not Used: Guzan, Sidwell, Delfouneso, Clark.
- Goals: Carew 34.
- Hull City: Myhill, Ricketts, Turner, Zayatte, Dawson, Garcia, Boateng, Ashbee (Marney 9), Kilbane (Manucho 73), Geovanni (Barmby 46), Cousin. Subs Not Used: Duke, Doyle, Halmosi, Featherstone.
- Booked: Zayatte, Boateng.
- Att: 39,607
- Ref: Mike Dean (Wirral)
- **Premier League position: 16th**

THURSDAY 7TH MAY 2009

Hopes that influential Hull City skipper Ian Ashbee's injury wasn't as bad as first feared have been dashed with a set of damning scan results that ruled him out for the remainder of the season. This is devastating news for our chances of survival.

Ashbee is now coming to terms with the news after scan results revealed the midfielder has posterior cruciate ligament damage and will not be able to feature again this season.

It had been hoped the influential Tigers skipper may be able to recover from the crunching tackle with Aston Villa's James Milner on Monday night after being taken off, but manager Phil Brown has had to now reveal the injury is far worse than first feared with his latest comments on Ashbee's injury after a medical scan.

The City boss revealed - *"Ian is going to be out for a number of weeks with the injury. However, further investigation is still required. We can't actually go in to have a look because of the wound that is on his knee at the moment."*

Before lamenting further - *"But the results of the scan say that he has got a ruptured PCL [posterior cruciate ligament]. We'll have further information when we put a scope in there and find out a little bit more, but we won't be able to do that for another seven days."*

I have no idea what a posterior cruciate ligament is, or what it does. But what I do know is we won't be seeing our talismanic leader, inspirational captain and influential midfield general for the remainder of this relegation battle. Damn! This is a huge blow...

FRIDAY 8TH MAY 2009 - HULL CITY V STOKE CITY PREVIEW

This game was targeted for a win by both sides back in August. Nine months later, it still is. For Hull City, a win is desperately required to keep an arm's distance from the relegation places. For Stoke, survival can be achieved with a victory.

I knew when the fixtures came out that the timing and importance of this one would be hugely significant to our Premier League ambition. Unsurprisingly, so it has proved to be. Indeed, despite three games remaining and three points separating us from the drop zone, it is likely to be definitive of our future.

But I'm looking upwards. And I'm seeing Stoke. A team who have plumbed the depths of this division, courted the lowest of the lows and yet somehow, from somewhere, pieced together a run of form that has hauled the Potters out of immediate danger and in all probability away from relegation danger.

However, Stoke are not out of the woods just yet. It is interesting to note that should the Tigers cobble together a scratchy win against them, just two points separate the sides, with a six-point cushion spanning the gap between ourselves and Newcastle and Middlesbrough who meet on Monday in the battle between third bottom and second bottom.

It sounds great, but beware. Stoke are still going to be up for this match to guarantee their safety. Plus, let's remember Newcastle or Middlesbrough can cut the gap on us if we fail to beat the Potters. So no pressure then, we need a win. By any means, fair or foul (look at Villa's offside winner on Monday for a case in point) it really doesn't matter now. It's all about results.

Those coming to the Circle tomorrow need to understand this is our time. This is our game. This is when we supporters are truly are needed the most. You can't fault the endeavour of Hull City, but creating and scoring chances has been thin on the ground these days. Therefore, you may have to physically suck the bleeding ball into the net for us. Do not be found wanting. I hope you're all fit for the job.

The mission is a simple one, then. We have to win. By any means. We have to use all available resources and this includes you, the Hull City reader. Do not be leaving the Circle thinking you could have done more to support your side.

We are Premier League for the first time ever. Generations of fans have lived for and craved these days, don't let them down. But above all, don't let yourself down. Leave knowing you gave every ounce you had.

So, on to the game then and Phil Brown is likely to be able to call upon pacy winger Bernard Mendy after a foot injury. Plus, more pace should be at the ready with Craig Fagan reportedly back to fitness after an ankle problem. Caleb Folan is suspended and skipper Ian Ashbee has ligament damage from the Villa game on Monday, so Dean Marney looks set to continue in the middle. Manucho may get a call up in attack.

Phil Brown offered a Hull City perspective on how to play a workmanlike Stoke City side who are relatively direct to state – *"We are coming up against a team that is well drilled in a certain way of playing and we have got to combat that."*

Continuing – *"Of course we would like to win and of course we would like to put six points between us and the bottom three - these things are up for grabs on Saturday. A lot of people have made reference to how Stoke play but it is about how we approach the game."*

As for Stoke, well Tony Pulis has lost some key members of his squad that has seen the Potters lose their last two matches. Amdy Faye, Mamady Sidibe, Danny Higginbotham and Salif Diao are all out, while James Beattie and Liam Lawrence will need fitness tests before the game.

SATURDAY 9TH MAY 2009 - HULL CITY 1-2 STOKE CITY - REPORT

Hull City continue their winless streak against Stoke City at the Circle and the situation facing the Tigers for Premier League survival has now evidently reached critical status.

And then there were two games to go before the Premier League season ends. Today, unquestionably, turned out to be a missed opportunity. In all my born days I couldn't ever remember beating Stoke at home, but I wasn't exactly going to scream from the rooftops about that fact enjoying a pre-game pint or several in the Three Crowns beforehand.

For some time now, I've been of the opinion that our Premier League future rests in the hands of our games against Stoke City at home and Bolton Wanderers away. These results are ultimately going to determine whether will be asked back for a second sitting at the top table.

In all honesty, I wasn't particularly confident today – or next week for that matter. Shame on me. Two points of favour that I nursed in comfort before the game were Stoke had lost their last two; Stoke had won just once away all season. Counter balancing that was the realisation we simply haven't been scoring goals or even creating chances.

Today's team had one recognised centre forward in it – namely Daniel Cousin. For a match we probably had to win against opposition we had a realistic chance of beating, I admit I was a little perturbed. But, I wasn't going to fold that easily. Onwards, the team needs us.

For the first time this season, nerves had clearly descended on the players. The pressure of the Premier League was telling and everything the Tigers created was snatched, forced or hurried due to Stoke City closing down or our own habit of just not handling the situation particularly well.

This was a more than a tad concerning as Stoke clearly weren't world beaters by any stretch. But Stoke get credit for being organised, hardworking and hitting the danger areas as quickly as possible by any means. It's not pretty, but against us, it was effective.

Both sides created very little. It was not the quintessential advert for the Premier League and neither team would claim otherwise. Yet today wasn't about pretty football, or neat precision passes, it was all about the result. A result Phil Brown's team needed more than their visitors.

But it wasn't happening. Possession was marginally shaded, even territory was edged, but chances? Once again glaringly sparse. Indeed, Garcia had the best when turning inside his marker in the box, shoot! He did... tamely at Sørensen. In the Premier League, anyone else would have scored, simple as.

Zayatte and Cousin spurned gilt-edged chances from corners that didn't even test the big Dane in Stoke's goal – let alone find the target – as the Tigers looked distinctly shorn of ferocity. But let's get this into context, Stoke hadn't done anything themselves. Until Lawrence broke clear and saw his shot deflected just wide for a corner.

That changed everything. In came the corner, horrible scrap, ball pinging everywhere in the six yard box and thwack! Fuller slams in from mere yards to chalk up the first goal of the afternoon in game-fittingly scrappy fashion. One body blow of almost mortal proportions was absorbed. Where was the way back now?

At the break, Phil Brown didn't dwell on his team talk, sending his team out early. A more encouraging second half performance followed, but still that cutting edge was missing. Stoke, disciplined in their ways, continued to hit the ball long, deep into the danger areas and feed off the scraps of mistakes. It was working.

Manager Phil Brown knew his game plan was failing. On came Manucho and Mendy to spice affairs up before City really had to think long and hard on their options. Centre back Kamil Zayatte was stretchered off – and rightly, Brown threw caution to the wind and brought on Geovanni in a bid to rescue matters.

But while the hosts redressed themselves, Whelan saw a dipping drive go the wrong side of the bar with one effort, before a second effort shortly after, actually crashed the innards of City's post as a shaken home team held on grimly. Unerringly, the killer punch wasn't far away...

It came from a lightning counter attack. Fuller held the ball up well and fed Lawrence who scampered into acres of space. The shot was on and the winger took it in devastating fashion to lash home beyond Myhill and cull the fightback from the Tigers. It was a superb finish and gutted me and around 20 odd thousand others in one instant.

There was to be no way back now. Once more, for all the endeavour City put in, the output, creativity and goal scoring was minimal. We simply are not efficient as a team.

Stoke lapped up their position and the visitors laid into the home support with some venom and a wit, mostly directed at Phil Brown. Could I argue? Not really, they've now achieved safety, something we really should have secured months ago.

A small amount of credit should go to the Tigers for not folding and battling to the end. A free kick won by Geovanni deep in stoppage time was not taken by the little Brazilian – instead left back Andy Dawson took it. And scored, with a belting effort. But it was all way too late in the day to even comprehend a miracle come back.

And therein lays the problem. This dreadful run of form shows no sign of abating. City are now relying on other results within the Premier League to survive, because if Newcastle win on Monday evening, for the first time this season we will be in the bottom three.

I'm looking for a positive. I suppose points in the bag are better than games in hand? I guess the proof in the pudding will be Monday. We're not in the bottom three yet but strangely, it does feel like it tonight. I'll save the last comment for Stoke, well done on survival, as a newly-promoted club we definitely know how hard it is to survive. You certainly deserve your place in the top flight.

As for us, fate is worryingly yet to be determined...

MATCH STATS:
- Hull City: Myhill, Ricketts, Turner, Zayatte (Geovanni 67), Dawson, Garcia (Mendy 60), Boateng, Kilbane, Barmby, Fagan, Cousin (Manucho 60). Subs Not Used: Duke, Hughes, Halmosi, Marney.
- Goals: Dawson 90.
- Stoke: Sørensen, Wilkinson, Shawcross, Abdoulaye Faye, Cort, Lawrence, Delap, Whelan, Etherington (Pugh 85), Beattie (Cresswell 78), Fuller (Kelly 90). Subs Not Used: Simonsen, Olofinjana, Camara, Sonko.
- Booked: Etherington.
- Goals: Fuller 41, Lawrence 73.
- Att: 24,932.
- Ref: Howard Webb (S Yorkshire)
- **Premier League position: 17th**

MONDAY 11TH MAY 2009

It's a bleak day. Two of the bottom three meet when Newcastle United host Middlesbrough and a win for the Geordies will put City in the relegation zone courtesy of goal difference. I have to know what is going on. I decide to opt for the relative peace of the radio in a quiet room – at my Dad's. There's no such thing as a quiet room in our house. At 10 pm the wireless is switched off forlornly. Newcastle have won the game 3-1 and duly climb out of the relegation zone. Sliding into it are Hull City. For the first time this season – for the first time ever in fact – in the top flight at least. Will we get out of it? Bolton Wanderers away and Manchester United at home on the last day will provide the answers. I'm worried.

WEDNESDAY 13TH MAY 2009

This is quite remarkable. With City teetering on the brink of a return back to the Championship. Hull City manager Phil Brown is flattered by the response of the supporters renewing season tickets, as the Tigers go in search of the crucial points that can keep the club in the Premier League.

The renewal take-up from Hull City fans after the first discounted period ended has left the club with a staggering 19,000 plus season ticket sales – and all this despite the football club still being unsure as to which division they will be competing in next season! Never in my life have I seen such commitment from the fans come pass renewal time.

Even more so when you think the club fell into the bottom three for the first time in their top flight lives after Newcastle United forged a 3-1 victory over Middlesbrough to leave both clubs on 34 points with just two games left each to save their Premier League lives.

Yet the predicament has done little to quell the top flight fever gripping the City and leaving manager Phil Brown overwhelmed with the response to comment - *"The amount of season tickets we've sold already for next season is phenomenal and shows that the fans are behind us."*

Before adding - *"When I first arrived at the club, we were averaging 14 or 15,000 crowds with 12,000 season ticket holders. To have 19,000 fans behind us for next year is tremendous and shows what we've achieved in the last two years. It's up to us to make sure that they'll be watching Premier League football."*

Remaining season tickets will go on general sale from Thursday 21st May.

FRIDAY 15TH MAY 2009 –
BOLTON WANDERERS V HULL CITY PREVIEW

All week I have been telling myself to keep the faith, believe and we shall achieve. But the time for talking (or thinking) is over. Simply, the players have no more chances left. Being in the bottom three means the time for action is now.

Let's not dress this up. It really is do or die at Bolton Wanderers this Saturday. All this talk about not being in the bottom three yet and destiny is in our hands was firmly put to bed on Monday. Our 'luck' finally ran out as Newcastle United recorded the win over Middlesbrough on Monday to put us in the bottom three.

Now, this is a real test of character. And it will be interesting to see how manager Phil Brown and the players react to dropping into the Premier League relegation zone for the first time this season. Yep, incredibly that's right, the first time this season. It sounds remarkable to say and is a testament to some of our finer performances of a momentous season.

But the need for one of those finer performances has never been needed more so than right now. Not in the next game, not in the second half, right here, right now. And from the first kick at the Reebok Stadium to the very last. Victory has to be sought, a point is… well frankly, pointless with Manchester United at home to come, only a win will suffice.

In many respects we need a performance against Bolton like the one at the Circle. We were dominant in possession and territory. Battering the Bolton door down all game and only denied anything by a deflected strike against the run of play. Surely, not even Jussi Jääskeläinen can say he's performed better this season. We owe Bolton…

So, like a good statistician, we delve into the archives and look at our previous record at Bolton. Suffice to say, I probably wish I hadn't bothered. Of the 22 visits made to meet Bolton in the past, we've won once. And that was back in 1935 – a 1-2 win. Right, so we've not won against the Trotters for 74 years on their patch…

If ever a record needed breaking, then now really is the time to do it, City! There has never been a bigger stage or more important game to win than the one presently facing the club now. We've just got to win. However, by whatever means. Indeed, let's do a Bolton. Let's do to them what they did to us at the Circle, I don't care! Just win!

In typical 2009 fashion, yet another player has been ruled out for the season ahead of the game - and arguably the most motivated player for the Bolton fixture in Bernard Mendy. It is now clear we've clearly urinated on the Premier League god's chips, as our last hope for a blazing performance on Mendy's return to his old club has been snuffed out due to a fractured toe. The Frenchman joins stars of the ilk of skipper Ian Ashbee just eight minutes into his return, Jimmy Bullard 28 minutes into his debut and Anthony Gardner, five games into a five month lengthy lay-off. Not to mention George Boateng who has spent most of 2009 out, along with Daniel Cousin.

Then, we have to accommodate the likelihood that Kamil Zayatte is out with a head injury sustained last week versus Stoke, despite passing an independent consultant's assessment this week. Plus, striker Caleb Folan is banned to add to the growing list of absentees.

On the positive side, local lad Nick Barmby is aiming to secure his 100th career goal, and none of us need to remind anyone how appropriate delivering that goal would be now, least of all Nick himself. But if luck isn't going for you, then at least ensure hard work, endeavour and a desire to win the match still is. We must ensure we take those ingredients to the Reebok Stadium.

Phil Brown will be making a return to his old club looking for favours. Not that he'll get any, like, but hey ho. Still revered round these parts, most Bolton fans would be sad to see the former no.2 take the Tigers down, but neither would they want to watch their team roll over for him. And I doubt the Bolton fans will be singing his name like they did at the Circle this time round.

On the match the City boss warned – *"We're standing before the most important game in Hull City's history. The players are representing the hope and belief of 105 years of history and we need to find a performance that matches that. It needs to be inspired. We've got two massive games left and we have to make sure that we take it to the wire with a win."*

On to Bolton and the hosts have some good news and bad news. The positive news is Dan Shittu appears to have overcome a calf injury and is likely to break into the squad. However, Ricardo Gardner is definitely ruled out with a hamstring strain and misses the last two games.

Bizarrely, Bolton boss Gary Megson appears content to watch Phil Brown squirm. Megson claimed – *"It will be a big game for Hull - they will need everything out of that game and it is nice to be in a position to make or break their season."* Yeah, cheers for that Gary, talk about kicking a man when he's down.

And then added – *"We have got ourselves in a good position, secured ourselves and we should be proud even though we have been a bit stop-start at the end. Getting 40 points after 36 games is something we should be pleased about."*

But you know what? It's not about whether Manchester United clinch the title this Saturday lunchtime and rest a clutch of players before coming to us three days before the European Cup final. It's not about sadistic Gary Megson revelling in our plight. It's not even about Phil Brown or the players. Not performances, not luck, not the crowd.

It's all about winning. Nothing else matters. Hull City have to ensure it's them, deserved or otherwise. Everything else simply melts into insignificance. A 5,000 travelling contingent from Yorkshire are about to be mobilised. To battle we must go, only victory can be our saviour.

SATURDAY 16TH MAY 2009 – BOLTON WANDERERS 1-1 HULL CITY – REPORT

Out of the bottom three with a precious point gained at the Reebok Stadium and destiny pressed back into our own hands with just one game of the Premier League season remaining. Mighty relief is reigning supreme. Only world champions Manchester United can stop us now! It wouldn't be correct to say this was a day of destiny absolute, but realistically everybody knew leaving Bolton empty handed this Saturday would pretty much seal our fate. A victory was a must, a draw may prove to be acceptable, defeat doesn't even come into the equation.

A taxi came to collect me and whisk me to the train station. An early morning start it was and upon second collection, Kev was still wheeling out last years barbecue beer. Talk about scraping the bottom of the barrel? There was no shame as the dreadful Skol – the very last of it – was carrier bagged up and brought along. Trust me, I'd rather - and did - go without. Skol! I don't know who is more desperate our football club, or my mate Kev?

Getting to Manchester Piccadilly, it was time to acquaint ourselves with the Dublin Tiger Association led by big Chris. He's badgered one of his Emerald Isle clan into coming over purely on the basis he's never, ever, seen City lose. Bless, god loves a trier. As the beer flowed, old Dublin was looking for a straw before he could even clutch it, such was his anxiety to see our club survive the rigours of the Premier League.

The pub was filling up quickly. It was title deciding day in Manchester with the early Saturday lunchtime game showing Manchester United v Arsenal, the home team needing just one point from either today, or away to us on the final day. Bloody hell, they better do it today. The pace was crawling with Mancs, suitably friendly and understanding of our sub-motive for their desires.

We had to leave a rammed Waldorf at half time to scoot down to Piccadilly and catch the train to Bolton. Just. We arrived at the Reebok to see the closing stages of the second half and thankfully Manchester United clear one last corner to claim a point with a 0-0 draw and clinch the title in the process. Part one done at least. Now if we can just get something from Bolton…

It was a very peculiar concourse to be stood on. On the one hand, a cheer went up that Manchester United will undoubtedly now bring their reserves and kids to our place three days before heading to Rome to meet Barcelona in the European Cup final. On the other, the tense nature of our predicament was hardly brimming with optimism. I felt like I was rallying the troops before clambering out the trenches to go 'over the top'.

If I'm utterly honest, inwardly, I was in the 'que sera sera' camp. Let it happen. Come on Reebok, hit me with it. The teams came out, flashbacks of the Jussi Jääskeläinen show at the Circle came to the fore and you just knew it was going to be one hell of game to get something from. But we had no choice, time to go for it…

Zayatte was out so Kilbane filled in at centre back with Turner. Dawson and Ricketts flanked the pair. In the middle Geovanni, Barmby, Garcia and Boateng held court, while Manucho was paired with Fagan. Into battle we went. And it was soon apparent, Bolton frankly couldn't be bothered. By contrast, City looked edgy in their quest.

City's endeavour was clear. Chances to score were still trailing somewhere in the dim and distant though. We have no cutting edge. It's worrying. Bolton looked like a team in third gear and content to simply watch us create pretty much nothing. Only the set-piece and corner could save us it seems. A cross flies in, Manucho heads in from the back stick, Jääskeläinen covers it off.

Then, a horrible piece of slack passing saw City give the ball away on the edge of Bolton's box. A mightily swift counter attack took place and City were scrambling back. With everyone at sixes and sevens a neat lay-off to right back Steinsson and the defender stroked the ball in casually. I wouldn't mind but it was a full back from bloody 25 yards out rolling it into the bottom corner of our net. One chance, one goal.

It floored me. Incredibly, I could half forgive the players if it floored them too. Now what? How on earth are we going to do to get back into this? It looked like mission impossible. Text... 'Boro are winning against Villa.' Followed by 'Newcastle are losing at home to Fulham.' I'm far from comfortable about it all, I'll be honest.

Within seconds of Bolton's lead, Manucho should have levelled. A pull back was blazed high and handsome miles over the bar from 10 yards. Oh dear... head in hands time. A lot of ball, a clear work ethic and no question we 'wanted it' but we simply couldn't hit a barn door. Troubling. And then Barmby heads over...

At the break, searching for solace I genuinely thought this looks like it could be over. If we can't shoot – and get it on target – what chance have we got? A flat atmosphere on the concourse reigned. The second half begins. Cue Danny Shittu becoming our saviour. A horrendous defensive faux-pas saw the big defender get himself into an abysmal defensive mess one-on-one with Fagan – who got goal side – and shoots... round the impregnable Jussi... and... IN! Hell fire! We've breached Jussi! It's a miracle!

Within seconds of the half starting, all the despondency washed away, I wrecked my elbow on Andy's accommodating jaw in celebration and Tony rocked up, wondering what the hell had happened, with his interval fodder in hand. Bloody hell, 1-1! I rubbed my elbow, Andy rubbed his jaw, we both shelved the pain and continued celebrating.

The goal visibly lifted City. Texts now reigned in again. 'Villa have equalised' and 'Bassong sent off for the Mags' good, good... And City were now clearly in the ascendancy and ready for a comeback of all comebacks to win the game. Roared on by the 5,000 pilgrims the effort put in was first class.

But, it has to be said for all the pressure, the chances were still thin on the ground. City pushed and pushed. A series of corners were won, but Bolton had learned to stitch up Turner good and proper. Megson had done his homework. What now? A Geo free-kick? Something, anything... All the ball, all the pressure, no chances. Time ticked... Come on City!

Like buses, suddenly three chances arrived in quick succession for the Tigers. First, Barmby had a mis-timed volley fox Jääskeläinen and was heading in... inside base of the post and... no! Bounced away and out, booted into orbit by the rocking Bolton defence. What do we have to do to score?

Then, a Daniel Cousin header was brilliantly saved by Jääskeläinen - again - a man who clearly saves his best for us. soon after, a superb header across goal from Fagan looked in all the way... but no! Jussi was there yet again to somehow paw the ball away. It just wouldn't go in! Subs come on and still the crosses flew in. Two fizzed across the six yard box as City were relentless in their pursuit of a winning goal. But alas, like a boxer who had given his all, it wasn't to be.

A nervous last few moments were played out. Newcastle had lost, Boro could only draw. Referee Peter Walton blew the whistle, the fans cheered in the away end. We knew we had reached the safety of 17th. But the players? Some on haunches – they looked beat. It was instantly apparent they were unaware of events elsewhere, clearly ploughing all their efforts into getting a win from the Reebok. The fans soon put that right with their chanting.

As furore died down, I managed to cadge a lift back to Hull to pontificate this result and savour the moment rather than use the slow train. After thought in the relative tranquility of the car, it comes down to destiny being in our own hands - and you can't ask for more than that.

Now, there's one cup final against Manchester United in our own backyard. We're one point above Newcastle. We have one last chance to save ourselves. It really, truly, has been one hell of a season. Sunday, is now destiny day. Now it's a statement of fact. Let's do it. Or hope Villa beat the travelling Magpies. Either will do for me...

Actually, if I remember rightly, I'm thinking that Villa steward promised us a win on the final day. I'm holding them to that.

MATCH STATS:
- Bolton: Jääskeläinen, Steinsson, Cahill, Shittu, Samuel, K Davies, Muamba (Basham 82), McCann, M Davies, Taylor (Riga 82), Elmander (Makukula 89).
- Subs Not Used: Al Habsi, Hunt, Puygrenier, Cohen.
- Booked: Samuel.
- Goals: Steinsson 26.
- Hull City: Myhill, Ricketts, Turner, Dawson, Kilbane, Fagan, Boateng, Garcia, Barmby (Marney 72), Geovanni (Cousin 77), Manucho (Halmosi 83). Subs Not Used: Duke, Doyle, Hughes, Cooper.
- Booked: Dawson, Boateng.
- Goals: Fagan 47.
- Att: 25,085
- Ref: Peter Walton (Northamptonshire)
- **Premier League position: 17th**

TUESDAY 19TH MAY 2009

Hull City's talismanic central defender – Michael Turner – was decorated with the Official Supporters Club's Player of the Year award at a ceremony held on Monday evening to honour the players.

Turner has enjoyed a monumental season that has rocketed the former Brentford defender onto the very fringes of the England squad, with coach Fabio Capello keeping tabs on the City stopper's career in the top flight. The defender collected the main prize and a clutch of other regional honours that amounted to a total prize haul of 12 from the official supporters. Skipper Ian Ashbee claimed the runner-up spot, while striker Geovanni came in third.

Meanwhile, in the goal of the season competition launched by the Official Supporters Club, fans voted for Geovanni's equaliser at Arsenal's Emirates Stadium as the best goal, with the winning free kick at Spurs a week later coming second. Ashbee's pile-driver against Millwall in the FA Cup came 3rd.

THURSDAY 21ST MAY 2009

Hell fire! You can't turn on a radio, pick up a paper or see the TV without some ex North East legend/pundit/former pro sticking their oar into OUR last fixture against Manchester United! As chairman Paul Duffen states – *"Leave that to us!"*

And the Hull City chairman is quite right too in my opinion. The Tigers chief has responded to claims pouring out the from the north east about a 'weak' Manchester United side visiting Hull City on the final day of the season that will go some way to determine the future of ourselves and the three North East clubs involved in the fight for relegation.

Duffen responded wistfully – *"From our perspective I'm just delighted our rivals on Sunday are more focused on our opposition than their own. We're happy, we know what we have to do."*

And continued with – *"Whatever team Manchester United put out it is going to be a very tough ask for us. Even if they put youngsters out they could still field 11 internationals and we have to focus on winning the game. I feel we have to beat the side in front of us, I really don't worry too much about what other people are going to do and it is not an issue that is going to disturb us."*

The City chairman then added realistically – *"We have to go out and beat Manchester United. Whoever comes out of that dressing room wearing a Manchester United shirt will play their heart out for their club. We need to do the same to be better than them on the day."*

Before summarising – *"It is in our hands to stay in the Premier League. That was always our ambition this season, to secure Premier League football again for next year and I believe we can do that."*

FRIDAY 22ND MAY 2009

The long running 'Spitgate' saga that alleged Cesc Fàbregas spat at Hull City assistant manager Brian Horton appears to have come to an end following the Premier League's investigation into the affair.

And Fàbregas appears to have escaped FA punishment for the alleged spitting incident post the FA Cup Quarter Final tie with Hull City in March, by virtue of 'not enough evidence' to enforce a charge, according to one national radio station at least

An FA statement read – *"The FA can confirm that, at a regulatory commission hearing, two charges of improper conduct against Arsenal midfielder Cesc Fàbregas were found not proved. One charge concerned his conduct after coming onto the pitch following the final whistle. The second charge related to an allegation of spitting."*

Meanwhile, assistant Hull City boss Brian Horton refused to be drawn into further comment upon learning the news to state – *"I only found out this morning. Until I speak to the League Managers Association (LMA) there is nothing I really want to say about it at the moment."*

Arsenal manager Arsène Wenger was relieved to state – *"It is a relief because personally I always believed he was innocent. That it has been confirmed by the FA is very good news for us. You have to respect that if the FA comes out and says there is nothing about the whole inquiry to punish Cesc Fàbregas, then we have to respect that as well."*

Let's be clear about this; the FA statement categorically states the allegations were found to be "not proved". It does not say they didn't happen. We know the truth...

SATURDAY MAY 23 RD 2009 – HULL CITY V MANCHESTER UNITED PREVIEW

So, it all comes down to the final game then. Destiny is in our own hands. All that stands in the way of preserving our Premier League status is a win against this season's champions – and champions of the world – Manchester United.

A week has passed since the heroic performance over at the Reebok earned a point – that would have been all three if wasn't for bloomin' Jussi Jääskeläinen again – but, at least we have scrambled out of the relegation zone with our precious lot.

Now, with time to dwell on matters and work out the multitude of permutations that envelop us, Sunderland, Middlesbrough and Newcastle, I wouldn't want to change anything. We have what we have - and that's the power to forge our destiny.

Given this situation 20 minutes after we kicked off against Fulham on the opening day way back in August, hell yeah! I'd I've whipped your hand off. Much changed thereafter, mind. A steady progression morphed into a trailblazing opening three months.

It's quite remarkable now to consider, without such an incredible start, we'd have been relegated well before West Bromwich Albion were last week. Lest we forget how magnificent our start to Premier League life was. Indeed, it is still the difference between where we are now and the drop zone.

There is no reason our end to the campaign cannot finish with the same headline-making flurry. Claiming a place in the Premier League exactly one year ago to the day we play Manchester United – May 24th – it is almost surreal to think that on the very same day we were all at Wembley, celebrating Dean Windass' historic goal.

Sunday will see another massive game for the club in our acceleration through the leagues at breakneck speed. Last year a local lad was our saviour, this season we are looking for a new messiah. Someone to step up to the plate when it truly matters and provide a moment of genius like veteran Deano did one year ago with that splendid volley.

Candidates are aplenty. The weather is set fair and little Brazilian Geovanni is no stranger to netting wonder goals against Manchester United. Just ask Manchester City fans. Another is Daniel Cousin, a real big game player - and like Geovanni - a previous scorer at Old Trafford in a memorable 4-3 encounter during November.

Then, there is the hero of the opening day – Caleb Folan – who netted the winner to provide our first ever win in the top flight. Can the Irish international repay his debt with a recent and untimely ban that has robbed us of forward power for the last three games, with a welcome winner in our last game of the season that will guarantee Premier League survival? Starting with a bang, ending with a bang...

Yet perhaps most fittingly, bearing in mind our predicament - and on the first anniversary of the greatest day in Hull City's history - how about locally born veteran Nick Barmby? The ex-England man has been in scintillating form and currently stands on 99 career goals. Dare we suggest the 100th? By a Hull lad, for his home town team, in the biggest game of our lives. On May the 24th? *gulp* all the ingredients are there...

As perilous as the situation is that we now find ourselves in, no way would I swap it now. Yes, we might be facing the champions, but with Barcelona in Rome waiting just three days later for Manchester United, Sir Alex Ferguson (rightly) isn't going to risk anyone with a sniff of a chance of making that squad for a game that means nothing (to them) in Hull.

But Manchester United won't be weak. Neither will they be poor. And most certainly they won't be here for a jolly end of season outing. Sir Alex Ferguson has not become the manager he is today by accepting mediocrity. This is going to be a mighty test, whoever emerges from the tunnel in the red shirt of Manchester United. Anyone who thinks differently is just mugging themselves.

Motivation for both sides shouldn't be a problem. Both will want to win for obvious reasons. City to survive, Manchester United to put in one last performance to show why they are champions and hopefully impress the boss enough to be taken into consideration for the Champions League final. Make no mistake on that.

However, while we sit one point above the drop zone fate remains primarily ours. Middlesbrough are away at West Ham and need everybody to lose while they gain a five-goal swing. It is asking an awful lot, particularly without Stewart Downing.

Sunderland – a point above us – are in similar circumstances to ourselves. At home, against a Chelsea side preoccupied by the FA Cup final next week and certain to rest players. It is highly unlikely City can expect to gain an extra point on the Mackems and a four goal swing.

Newcastle meanwhile, head off to Villa Park. Aston Villa need a win to guarantee fifth place and avoid a protracted Europa League pre-season qualification route. With the Magpies below us by a point, simply, Alan Shearer's side have to do better than us. With seven wins from 37 games, it's asking a lot away from St James Park.

No. Nobody in their right mind would swap positions now with any of the teams below us. The pressure is on Middlesbrough and Newcastle now to overachieve. If it all goes catastrophically wrong for City, we could still survive. And that is some comfort, although certainly not to be relied upon.

Phil Brown will have a fully fit squad to choose from barring long term absentees Jimmy Bullard, Anthony Gardner and skipper Ian Ashbee. As mentioned above, striker Caleb Folan returns from a three game ban. Bernard Mendy and Kamil Zayatte are both fit to return to midfield and defence respectively. Full back Andy Dawson has overcome illness in midweek to feature too.

Brown claimed ahead of the game on the subject of the furore raging in the north east about Manchester United's team selection – *"Sir Alex has had 22 years at one football club and he has earned the right to do whatever he wants to do on Sunday. He has got a massive game three days after this game. I would do the same - if I had the option I would play players that won't be playing in the game on Wednesday."*

Adding – *"Unless there was some kind of fear of fitness levels or injury concerns, I would pick the team accordingly. But if Newcastle, Middlesbrough and Sunderland have fears about what is coming out of Manchester United's changing room – I have as well."*

Manchester United are set to rest a clutch of first team stars just three days before their European Cup final match with Barcelona. Only Rio Ferdinand – looking to regain match fitness – and Darren Fletcher who is banned for the Rome final, look candidates to play from the normal first team.

Yet Sir Alex Ferguson claimed – *"No matter which team I play, it will represent Manchester United in the normal way. We will go to win. That is the responsibility we always have. We have a league that has the best integrity in the world and we will play our part in that."*

So there you have it. It will be a contest, of that you can be assured. The Circle now has to recreate the incredible Wembley atmosphere and roar on the black and amber charges to another historic day in this club's history. This is not a time for faint hearts on the touchline, in the stands or on the pitch.

Together we are strong. Between 4pm and 6pm this Sunday, we would all be wise to remember that... Do not fail the shirt, play for the badge and lead from the front. After all, THIS IS THE BEST TRIP WE'VE EVER BEEN ON.

Now why would we all want it to end now?

SUNDAY 24TH MAY 2009 –
HULL CITY 0-1 MANCHESTER UNITED - REPORT

Hull City clinched Premier League survival on the final despite a 0-1 home loss, as results elsewhere fell into place, with other teams failing to wrestle back matters into their own hands. We've done it!

Dawn broke. An unusual trouble-free night of sleep had ensued. Exactly one year ago, I was up with the birds once more. Looking out my hotel window and wondering what fate the giant arc of Wembley would have in store for us. Packing my bag once more a year to the day (this time to go play football) I hoped for similar celebration.

Like Wembley was 12 months ago, it was a baking hot, gloriously sunny day. May 24th, there is something about that date, isn't there? Not the most ideal conditions to play 90 minutes of football in, but duty calls. We ended up losing the match by a hefty 5-1 scoreline, this despite being myself being appointed man of the match at right back. Some consolation...

To be honest, the post match jar had me correlating if similar occurrences would happen to Hull City today. Final day of the season ending in defeat and... then what? A consolation after all? Better to not think about it, I found. Just keep the faith, support the team and what will be, will be. If we survive, we deserve to survive. If we don't, then we never deserved to. We've had 38 games - like everyone else - to sort this out.

I was under no illusions. Despite the pre-match furore and hyperbole of Manchester United's intended line-up, this was still going to be a hard game. They are, after all, Manchester United. Champions of England, Europe, the world. And they're playing in the biggest game in club football three day later when travelling to Rome to meet Barcelona.

Eee... from Hull to Rome to meet Barcelona. That's the Premier League through Manchester United's eyes. Yet the gulf in aspirations in the top flight is massive. Here in Hull we're hankering after a return to the glamour and salubrious locations of Wigan, Bolton and Blackburn. And I kid you not, we want it. We so desperately want it. It's a mad world, eh?

It's not open for ridicule. No jesting is taking place when writing about these north west locations among the other 16 that make up the Premier League - if we survive. To come up from the Championship via the play-offs and then grab 17th is a monumental achievement, groundbreaking, historic and ultimately craved. Our destiny at 4pm was still in our hands.

As roundly expected, Sir Alex Ferguson picked a youthful Manchester United side with only skipper Gary Neville and midfield dynamo Darren Fletcher involved who would be unquestionably recognisable Manchester United players. The rest were an array of hugely talented protégés that undoubtedly will see most grace the first team for many more years to come.

Indeed, the future of Manchester United is in great hands. Sir Alex has done a magnificent job. Who has the right to question what team he selects for Hull City with a title assured, three days before the European Cup final? As the game commenced to a crescendo of noise from the home swathes, it was clear Manchester United were not here for a jolly.

Brown's side roared into their challenge with gusto. Endeavour could not be called into question. The realisation of what was at stake was evident. The fans hollered for the team, the team responded with bravery and commitment. Manchester United meanwhile, relied on craft, guile and skill. All potentially damaging weapons that were met headlong by a City side desperate to fulfil their Premier League aspirations for another year.

Geovanni swung in a couple of testing crosses and Craig Fagan almost released the pressure valve at the Circle when catching Gary Neville out with the offside trap, but a touch a mite too strong afforded Kuszczak to recover - just. We have a chance...

But the kids of Manchester soon settled and the pace of Nani was unsettling, while the cut and thrust of Wellbeck just grew as the game went on - a real thorn in our side.

Manchester United wanted to win and City had their work cut out. Once again, the Tigers were relying on a Geovanni or Dawson free kick, or Turner's head from a corner.

After a quarter of the game, we knew the scale of the task was daunting. The visitors were now in rhythm and pressing. Too much time was given to these whizzkids in key areas and something was brewing. Then, a piercing moment... Darron Gibson was 25 yards out, unchecked and facing goal...

A brute of a shot was unleashed that bent and swerved wickedly on it's trajectory towards goal. Myhill is diving... diving at full tilt... diving in vain. You could almost hear the ball ripple the net. And then, you could definitely hear the sharp intake of breath in the home ranks before the fans behind the opposite goal cheered in delight. Uh-oh... 0-1 Manchester United... It could well be goal of the month, it was that good. DAMN! This is what Manchester United do. They just win. Like a machine, malfunction is not a word in their dictionary. A two yard toe poke, a 25-yard screamer, it doesn't matter. All that matters is winning. The Circle had witnessed one of the greatest goals ever scored here - unfortunately it was against us in the biggest game the Circle had ever seen.

For a few moments, City were rocking. Macheda poked just wide after wriggling free of two defenders. A shot flashed wide of Myhill's upright. The Tigers needed composure, needed to take stock. But Manchester United were relentless, winners that they are. There was to be no respite. Until...

What's this? A text... 'Villa are winning' A moment of disbelief. A second to digest the ramifications. We may well have been 150 miles away, but news speared through the Circle like wild fire and 20-odd thousand Hull City fans were sharing in Villa's delight in unison. If Phil Brown and the players didn't want to know what was going on elsewhere... too late, they clearly knew now!

New urgency was brought to the table by City, the Manchester United storm had been weathered, and Dawson smashed a vicious half volley that Kuszczak beat over the bar. Then, half time was upon us. As it stood, the Tigers were out of the bottom three still, I'll take that. By hook or by crook we were not going down at this moment in time and frankly, unashamedly, we were all desperate for it to stay that way.

It was true the second half lacked the same intensity by the champions. You got the impression if City had somehow snatched a leveller, the retribution would be severe for the remainder of the game. But bravely City tried and tried in the face of such a threat because so much was riding on matters.

Confession time then for me. I began to get twitchy. It was fun to join with the Manchester United fans ribbing Alan Shearer, but the fragility of our situation remained. One goal at Villa Park and the nerves would be replaced by anguish - and the realisation that getting a goal against the champions was looking a near impossibility. Manchester United or the Premier League's integrity couldn't be called into question.

"Andy, are you sure your phone hasn't received another text?" I uttered for the umpteenth time. Stupidly, I'd left my phone in my bag of fanzines that had rather kindly been taken home by the boy - ticketless for the game. I guessed a hatful of texts were coming in and those sending were probably thinking I was the rudest man in Hull. My apologies one and all.

We're not creating chances - the story to the second half of our season - and the clock is now going so slow it's painstaking. Not for events here, it was pretty clear we wouldn't be breaching the champions barring an outrageous stroke of luck despite the effort being deployed. I was watching the clock at the Circle, transposing it into events going on at Villa Park.

Here I am, nerves cut to ribbons, worrying about something I can't even see. Unbearable tension. Nani then goes mightily close to making it 0-2 to the visitors near the end – but not that it matters in the grand scheme of things – everyone was now (wrongly, I accept) praying for the whistle at Villa Park! Bizarre it was; truly surreal scenes.

The whistle goes at the Circle to a stunned and muted crowd. Even Manchester United fans were appreciative of our predicament. It was like Cardiff 0-1 Hull City two seasons ago when the whole of Ninian Park was praying for Leeds' impending relegation. It was all so torturous.

Phil Brown and Sir Alex shook hands and were in conversation then... FINAL SCORE: Aston Villa one, Newcastle United nil! The stadium erupted, all four sides of it, including Manchester United fans. Hull City were staying up! Newcastle were relegated! Fans spilled onto the pitch in celebratory fashion. It was emotionally shattering, but delirious all at the same instant.

I promised myself there would be no blubbing whether we survive or go down. I promised myself. The lump in my throat was ridiculous in size. The eyes were close to welling up and overflowing. Among the soaring emotions, all the discipline I could muster called for a stiff upper lip. No tears appeared, but it was mighty close.

Phil Brown was handed a microphone to call for fans to clear the pitch. In a moment of occasion overtaking the City boss, an impromptu karaoke broke out. Well, as the manager quite rightly pointed out, *"This is the best trip we've ever been on!"* Of course we didn't want to go home...

At the end of the day, many, many pointers and markers could be suggested as to how and why we have preserved our top flight status. In truth, whatever anyone else says, we have been good enough for the toughest and best league in the world. The pontificating, debating and justifying can be left to others.

The fact is; HULL CITY ARE A PREMIER LEAGUE TEAM. Savour it, savour every single second of it. Be proud of this achievement, these are momentous times in the life of our club. Never, ever, take them for granted. Well done, Browny, well done the players - and to each and everyone of you who followed OUR team to glory. We'll be back for a second sitting and I can't tell you how good it feels to pen such words.

THIS IS THE BEST TRIP, WE'VE EVER BEEN ON!

MATCH STATS:
- Hull City: Myhill, Ricketts, Turner, Kilbane, Dawson, Garcia (Cousin 81), Marney, Boateng, Barmby (Mendy 68), Geovanni (Folan 54), Fagan. Subs Not Used: Duke, Hughes, Halmosi, Zayatte.
- Booked: Barmby, Marney.
- Man Utd: Kuszczak, Rafael Da Silva (Eckersley 60), Neville, Brown, De Laet (Possebon 79), Nani, Fletcher, Gibson, Welbeck (Tošić 87), Martin, Macheda. Subs Not Used: Amos, Corry Evans, Drinkwater, James.
- Booked: Gibson.
- Goals: Gibson 24.
- Att: 24,945
- Ref: Alan Wiley (Staffordshire)
- **Final Premier League position: 17th – SURVIVAL! MISSION ACCOMPLISHED.**

SUNDAY 24TH MAY 2009

I've stumbled in from the pub after copious pints to celebrate our survival just in time to witness Match of the Day. Sir Alex Ferguson's face at the final whistle – integrity kept in tact with victory – taps Phil Brown in congratulatory fashion after learning Hull City have survived because Aston Villa have beaten Newcastle and walks away with the broadest grin ever seen in Christendom! Priceless!

EPILOGUE

One of the standout facts of writing this book in chronological fashion has become clear now it is complete. This Premier League journey has seen everyone connected with Hull City scale the highest peaks of the English game on merit, sweeping footballing giants aside with cavalier, attacking aplomb that had the world mesmerised at what this unfashionable northern conurbation was achieving on a football pitch. Yet the fall from grace that followed such breathtaking sequences was equally dramatic and deeply torturous as the story unfolded before our very eyes.

Unquestionably, Hull City's first season in the top flight was firmly the most meteoric rise to stardom the Premier League had ever seen - arguably, in the English game ever. In just ten years, the Tigers had made a perpendicular ascent from 92nd and plum last in the Football League to the very pinnacle of the game. For a very brief moment in October - thanks to victories at Newcastle, Arsenal and Tottenham - Hull City were sitting joint top of the greatest domestic league competition in the world as we know it today. It was some ascent.

The football on show was fearless and engrossing. The team worked harder than I could ever remember them working. Aesthetically speaking it was decent fare to watch. It wasn't 11 behind the ball and winging it; praying you don't concede. No. It was gutsy, brave attack-minded 4-3-3 formations at Arsenal, Manchester United and Liverpool. Indeed, it was unheard of, bordering on insane, at some of the world's finest football stages. But nobody could accuse of Hull City of not going for it. Indeed, we were the breath of fresh air the Premier League so desperately needed. And for a brief moment, the club became everybody's favourite second team.

Yet around November time, something went wrong, very wrong indeed. The Midas touch was disintegrating and the bold attacking tactics were beginning to falter. For me, the home defeat to Bolton was the moment when something snapped inside the club. The proverbial bubble had been burst. We absolutely battered Bolton that day in November at home - but somehow contrived to lose. It was now three defeats in three, two of which had been at home. The confidence within was sapped, the belief was knocked sideways from the players.

It didn't help that loan star Marlon King's bolshie attitude reared its ugly head once again when the club began to wobble. Rather than steady the ship with some wise and valuable Premier League experience for his club, team and manager, King decided to throw his weight - amongst other things - around the place and the cracks began to readily appear at Hull City. It was a real shame

Such a fantastic start – the best start ever by a promoted club in fact – but it was all beginning to unravel before our eyes. The dramatic reversal over Middlesbrough that secured three very welcome points in the last 10 minutes and the stunning 2-2 draw at Anfield a week later, proved nothing more than a false dawn. City simply fell apart thereafter and December was a catastrophic month come the end of it. Wrongly, people point to the alfresco Eastlands half time team talk. The wheels had fallen off well before then, let me tell you, with just one win in nine. I admired the club for landing Jimmy Bullard for £5m during the January transfer window in a brave attempt to remedy City's ailing fortunes. It truly was a statement of intent made by the club to stay in this league. But, when you're down on your luck, what followed was a right royal kick in the proverbials. After just 28 minutes against West Ham, the record signing was ruled out for the season. No, no, no! Manucho, the other winter transfer window signing, clearly needed more support. But the chance for an able foil to come in and help the Tigers cause had simply run out. We had to go with what we had – and by now, I admit it, I was worried for our Premier League status.

Downwards the spiral went, but for some bizarre reason, City held the Indian sign over the London clubs in the Premier League. A monumental point at Stamford Bridge was earned – and that cost World Cup winning manager Luis Felipe Scolari his job. A midweek jaunt to Fulham saw one of those dreamtime away days that we all crave and hope to see so regularly but never do, as your team snatch a dramatic injury time winner to clinch all the points.

Incredibly, it was to be our last top flight victory of the 2008-09 season. Not that we knew it at the time, like. And, had I known that at the time, who in their right mind could foresee we would actually survive? That fact alone appears even more incredible the more you take it in and digest it. It really all adds credence to what can only be described as a truly remarkable tale. And it's about our club, Hull City.

Indeed, as the results failed to recover and the bottom three inched ever nearer to us – from once being joint top of the table way, way back on the cusp of October and November – it was just going to be a matter of time before the relegation places would reel the Tigers in. And it happened. One Monday evening in May, just two games were left, but City had stumbled into the bottom three when Newcastle beat Middlesbrough at St James Park. We're doomed now, surely?

I still believed we'd escape with neither rhyme nor reason to rationalise my faith. The team that had conquered all and sundry at the head of the season was a pale imitation of such now. I kept thinking; we couldn't get relegated, not now, not so close to the finish line. We had to survive. We had to.

The point won at Bolton on the penultimate weekend incredibly dragged us out of the mire and into a final day shoot out with Middlesbrough, Newcastle and Sunderland. That point was one of the happiest points of the season. And it was so, so precious too. We had arrived in 17th... but the champions Manchester United were next in town on the final day...

In typical fashion – and in keeping with current form – all four of the aforementioned clubs demonstrated why they were battling it out to stay in the Premier League by losing their last matches. Of course, it meant Hull City had survived. Survived the mother of all free-fallings to pick themselves up and be handed another go at the top flight.

The objective for the season was always to finish 17th. No Hull City fan of a sound mind will tell you any different since we won at Wembley exactly a year to the day. Yet the passage to achieve such a place in the Premier League was undoubtedly the most inopportune and unorthodox trajectory ever constructed by any club – let alone my club. But then, this is Hull City. We don't do 'normal'. Our season long goal – namely 'TARGET 17th' would be done our way.

However we did it, and nobody can quibble about the fact after we've all played 38 games apiece. The manager, the players, the chairman and the fans, we all pitched in and we did it. We survived, mission accomplished. And I suppose I did it too. I saw the season in its entirety and I wrote a book about it that satisfied my own personal aspirations along the way.

If this book has achieved its own objective of depicting the greatest Hull City story ever told, then it has genuinely been worth all the effort put in to tell the story of the 2008-09 season – Hull City's first season as a Premier League club. I make no bones about the fact it's been an emotional journey, but one I wouldn't swap in the slightest. I can safely say with my hand on my heart...

"This is the best trip, we've ever been on."